THE CULTURE OF FEAR

THE CULTURE OF FEAR

Why Americans Are Afraid of the Wrong Things

BARRY GLASSNER

BASIC
BOOKS

A Member of the
Perseus Books Group
New York

Hardcover first published in the United States by Basic Books,
A Member of the Perseus Books Group
Tenth Anniversary edition published in 2009 by Basic Books.

Books published by Basic Books are available at special discounts for bulk
purchases in the United States by corporations, institutions, and other
organizations. For more information, please contact the Special Markets
Department at the Perseus Books Group, 2300 Chestnut Street, Suite 200,
Philadelphia, PA 19103, or call (800) 810-4145, ext. 5000, or e-mail
special.markets@perseusbooks.com.

Designed by Heather Hutchison

A CIP catalog record for this book is available from the Library of Congress.
Hardcover ISBN: 0-465-01489-5 (cloth); ISBN 0-465-01490-9 (pbk.)
Tenth Anniversary edition ISBN: 978-0-465-00336-5

LSC-C

10 9 8

For
Delaney, Megan, and Samantha Glassner,
Sita Feinberg and Jan Haldipur,
and Ben and Leah Rafferty

CONTENTS

ACKNOWLEDGMENTS

During the many years in which I planned, researched, wrote, rewrote, and expanded this book, my wife, Betsy Amster, endured more than any spouse ought. She had to put up with weekends in which I scarcely left my study, abbreviated vacations, and newspapers and magazines cut up before she had a chance to read them. Yet whenever I completed a draft of a chapter Betsy took time away from her schedule to identify the flaws in my arguments and offer her expert editorial advice.

I am also especially grateful to my agent, Geri Thoma, for her unfaltering friendship and support. Over time, editors and publishers at Basic Books both encouraged and supported me: Tim Bartlett, whose astute queries and suggestions improved the original book greatly, and John Sherer and Tim Sullivan, whose work was invaluable in bringing out this tenth anniversary edition.

Early on, Wendy DeBoer, a doctoral student at the University of Southern California and primary research assistant on the project, helped me find and organize thousands of news stories, television transcripts, and research studies. Special thanks go as well to my friend Morty Schapiro, my faculty colleagues in the Department of Sociology at USC, and Provost C. L. Max Nikias.

Conversations with numerous other friends, colleagues, and editors educated me and helped me sort out my positions on the topics discussed in these pages. In particular I would like to acknowledge Amy Aronson, Cynthia Fuchs Epstein, Howard Epstein, Steve Fraser, Jonathan Glassner, Judith Grant, Martha Harris, Rosanna Hertz, Sue Horton, Darnell Hunt, Michael Kimmel, Julia Loughlin, Tom Lutz,

Morgan Lyons, Mauricio Mazon, Jonathan Moreno, Peter Nardi, Richard Popkin, Hank Rubin, Lillian Rubin, Hilary Schor, David Shaw, Arlene Skolnick, Jerry Skolnick, Gary Taubes, Barrie Thorne, and Alan Wolfe.

INTRODUCTION
TO THE TENTH
ANNIVERSARY EDITION

A decade has passed since the publication of *The Culture of Fear*, during which time the term *culture of fear* has become part of our national lexicon, referenced regularly in academia, the mainstream media, and the blogosphere. Scholarly journals publish papers with titles like "The Culture of Fear and the Politics of Education," while popular magazines like *Newsweek* print essays about "The (Play) Dating Game: Our Culture of Fear Means That We Can No Longer Count on Spontaneity to Bring Children Together." Events such as the terrorist attacks of September 11, 2001, the subsequent "war on terror," school shootings, vaccine scares, and the election of Barack Obama have given new relevance to many of the concepts I introduced in these pages. We saw numerous instances of individuals and organizations using fear to manipulate the population. They succeeded in large part because, as the book explains, after 30 years of nightly news full of dubious threats, we are fertile soil for fear mongers.[1]

Despite landmark events such as the terrorist attacks of 9/11 and the economic downturn that began in 2008, the culture of fear I outlined in this book continues largely as I portrayed it. Pregnant teenagers, monster moms, Internet predators, and suburban thugs still stalk the airwaves. We still shake our heads over the latest mass shooting while failing to limit access to guns to people who shouldn't have them. We fret over the kidnapping of a single toddler while millions of children live in poverty and attend crumbling schools. Atypical tragedies grab our attention while widespread problems go unaddressed.

Politicians, journalists, advocacy groups, and marketers continue to blow dangers out of proportion for votes, ratings, donations, and profits. Fear mongering for personal, political, and corporate gain continues unabated. Indeed, many of the specific scares I addressed have resurfaced, sometimes in the very same form as earlier, sometimes in new clothes. I will discuss these, as well as significant ways in which our culture of fear has changed, in a major new final chapter.

Throughout the opening of this century, Americans have remained inordinately fearful of unlikely dangers. Even so, at least in some regards, there *have* been changes in our culture of fear. Most notably, foreign terrorists replaced domestic bogeymen as the principal figures in fear mongering by politicians and in much of the media. However, the very same scare tactics I discuss in the pages that follow–misdirection, presenting victims as experts, and treating isolated incidents as trends–have been applied with great success in the newer fear narrative. In the months immediately following 9/11, for example, the attacks elevated to newsworthiness minor airline mishaps and phony bomb threats that previously would not have made headlines, and created an exaggerated sense of individual risk.

What Is the Price of Fear—and Who Pays?

Nothing has done a better job of exploiting our anxieties than the phrase *the war on terror*, which the Bush administration used incessantly from late 2001 until they left office in early 2009. As former National Security Advisor Zbigniew Brzezinski noted in the *Washington Post* in 2007, "The little secret here is that the vagueness of the phrase was deliberately (or instinctively) calculated by its sponsors. Constant reference to a 'war on terror' did accomplish one major objective: It stimulated the emergence of a culture of fear. Fear obscures reason, intensifies emotions and makes it easier for demagogic politicians to mobilize the public on behalf of the policies they want to pursue."[2]

The culture of fear predates 9/11 by at least a generation, but Brzezinski accurately described what happens when fear overtakes reason: "The culture of fear is like a genie that has been let out of its bottle. It acquires a life of its own—and can become demoralizing. . . . We are now divided, uncertain, and potentially very susceptible to panic in the event of another terrorist attack on the United States."[3]

Whenever one group uses fear to manipulate another, someone benefits and someone pays, as Brzezinski observed. The war on terror had the effect of making us more paranoid not only about terrorists but also about homegrown crime. After sponsoring a survey in 2003 to gauge just how frightened Americans were, the Chubb Group of Insurance Companies introduced Masterpiece Family Protection. "Home invasion. Child abduction. Carjacking. Stalking threats. Road rage. Air rage. Even hijacking. It's hard to think that these things could happen to you and your family. Yet, these unthinkable crimes punctuate television news coverage and highlight the pages of newspapers, magazines and websites every day," declared the company's website—as if the hyping of these rare events warranted a special insurance policy against them. "Each year, 58,000 children are victims of stranger/non-family abductions," the site continued, referring to a U.S. Department of Justice study. (Never mind that the study itself made clear that of the 58,000 abductions, only about 115 a year were "stereotypical kidnappings" like that of Polly Klaas or Adam Walsh: "Most children's non-family abduction episodes do not involve elements of the extremely alarming kind of crime that parents and reporters have in mind . . . when they think about a kidnapping by a stranger.")[4]

Emotional reactions to rare but disturbing events also lead to expensive and ineffective public policy. Child abductions, for example, inspire passionate advocates (typically grief-stricken families) to push for legislation they hope will solve the problem. Jessica's Law, which was passed in California in 2006, is a case in point. It was drafted in response to the murder of nine-year-old Jessica Lunsford, who was raped and killed by a sex offender who had completed his parole. Jessica's Law stipulates that all sex offenders convicted of a crime in any of thirty-five categories be evaluated by a psychologist before being paroled, even if they had only committed one offense and were juveniles when they committed it. Prior to the legislation, parolees were evaluated if they had committed at least two offenses in any of nine categories. The goal of the parolee evaluations pre– and post–Jessica's Law was to identify people who were most likely to commit a sex crime again, and in some cases, to confine them indefinitely to a state mental-health facility instead of paroling them.[5]

Two years after Jessica's Law was implemented, as California was reeling from a $42 billion budget deficit, investigative reporters at the *Los Angeles Times* looked into its cost. They discovered that more than $24 million had been paid to private psychologists in 2007 to evaluate the sex offenders. The state didn't have enough staff psychologists or psychiatrists to meet the demand, so it had to hire outside evaluators. A few of them made more than a million dollars a year in their part-time gigs for the state. The result? Essentially no change in the number of sex offenders sent to mental hospitals. There were forty-one such cases in the eighteen months prior to Jessica's Law, and forty-two in the eighteen months after it was implemented.[6]

Fear-driven legislation is good for politicians looking to arouse voters, for advocacy groups looking to attract donations, for ratings-hungry media, and for social scientists, attorneys, and other professionals who choose to cash in on them. Taxpayers foot the bill. And there is another, unintended consequence of fear-based legislation for the public: rather than reassure us, these laws further underscore the already-overhyped danger.

Seriously Scary

Before September 11, 2001, the toll taken by the culture of fear was not always obvious. Contrivances such as the "war on drugs" (which I deal with in chapter 6), specious menaces like sociopathic juveniles (chapter 3), and bogus medical scares such as "Vaccine Roulette" (chapter 7) were pricey and delusory, but limited. After the attacks of 9/11, exaggerated and unconfirmed scares had more serious and lasting consequences: invading other nations, relinquishing civil rights, censoring

ourselves, sanctioning the torture of prisoners, and other missteps I out-
line in the book's new final chapter.

As the decade progressed, overblown fears about terrorism and,
later, public unease about the Iraq war distracted us from domestic issues that were growing more urgent by the month. In addition to serious, long-standing dangers to Americans' health and well-being, lax or
nonexistent regulations on financial institutions set the stage for a major
international economic collapse. Threats to the U.S. financial system,
obscured from public view in part by endless attention to the "war on
terror," undermined America's national security more than Osama bin
Laden and his organization ever did. As I note in the first edition's introduction, the serious problems people ignore often give rise to the
very dangers they fear the most.[7]

When I give public talks about the culture of fear, I am frequently
asked, "Well, what *should* I be afraid of?" My answer is not "nothing," as
some of my questioners assume. On the contrary, I point out dangerous
trends that have been around for a while and are thus viewed as old
news and unappealing to the media. Motor vehicle injuries, for example, are the leading cause of death in the U.S. for children ages one to
fifteen. Drowning and fires are second and third. Youngsters' head injuries from bicycle accidents account for nearly 140,000 visits to the
emergency room each year. If a parent is concerned about his or her
children, their money is best spent on car seats, smoke detectors, swimming lessons, and bike helmets as opposed to GPS locators and child
identification kits. They would hardly know that, however, from watching their local TV news or listening to the hype from advocacy groups.[8]

Many of the fear-worthy items I mention in the book are everyday
scares we can deal with sensibly as long as we have the facts. More difficult to grasp is an underlying problem that has worsened in the inter-
vening years: the massive gap between rich and poor. The culture of
fear contributes to this schism by portraying the poor as threatening
and unsympathetic. Yet just as the financial crisis that began in 2008
jeopardized not only people who lost their jobs and homes but also
Americans' strategic foreign interests, the gap between rich and poor
threatens not only poor people but all Americans. "Living in a society

with wide disparities—in health, in wealth, in education—is worse for all the society's members, even the well-off," wrote Elizabeth Gudrais, a journalist and associate editor of *Harvard Magazine*, reporting on a 2008 study about life expectancy in the United States. "Research indicates that high inequality reverberates through societies on multiple levels, correlating with, if not causing, more crime, less happiness, poorer mental and physical health, less racial harmony, and less civic and political participation." Gudrais noted that in 2006 the disparity between rich and poor in the United States was at its highest point since 1928, with the top 1 percent of earners drawing 20.3 percent of the total national income.[9]

Gudrais's article illustrates a positive role that journalists play in the culture of fear. While a major focus of this book is fear mongering by journalists and others, throughout the chapters that follow I take note as well of reporters who bring to light serious dangers about which the public hears little from politicians, corporations, and most of the media. Indeed, again and again I find that it is reporters, rather than government oversight organizations, academics, or other professional truth seekers, who debunk silly or exaggerated scares that other journalists irresponsibly promulgate.

Unfortunately, however, these correctives often occur long after whole sectors of the populace have been scared senseless. Take, for instance, the most public mea culpa I have found in the history of journalistic fear mongering. In 2006, on the twentieth anniversary of its infamous "Marriage Crunch" article, which had declared that a forty-year-old single woman was "more likely to be killed by a terrorist" than to marry, *Newsweek* magazine admitted that "states of unions aren't what we predicted they'd be. . . . Beyond all the research studies and forecasts, the trend-spotting and fear mongering that are too often the stock in trade of both journalists and academics, the real story of this anniversary is the unexpected happily-ever-afters."

So wrote Daniel McGinn, a national correspondent for the magazine. In a lengthy article, he noted that about 90 percent of baby boomers either have married or will marry, and that most single women over forty who want to wed eventually do so. McGinn also tracked down eleven of the fourteen single women *Newsweek* had profiled in the original story. Only three remained single, and none had divorced.[10]

Another gloomy forecast that had been repeated across all media in the 1980s and '90s—the fate of "crack babies"—has been soundly rebuffed by journalists as well. At the time, doctors had warned that the infants, "if they survive, are largely doomed to the underclass because of faulty cognitive and psychological development." Headlines in the nation's leading newspapers foretold a "bleak," "joyless" future for such children, despite, as I discuss in chapter 3, considerable evidence at the time suggesting little cause to single out these children for special worry and stigmatization.

By 2009, journalists began to correct their publications' earlier scare stories. That year, Susan Okie reported in the *New York Times* on the results of studies tracking the lives of these children for nearly fifteen years. "So far, these scientists say, the long-term effects of such [cocaine and opiate] exposure on children's brain development and behavior appear relatively small," wrote Okie. Other media outlets picked up the story or ran their own.[11]

One can only hope that journalists—and public officials, advocates, and academics as well—will not wait so long in the future to question *scares du jour* as they arise.

Better still, one can hope for a future in which fear campaigns fail to sway the public in the first place, a prospect that the Presidential election of 2008 suggested may be more than mere fancy. The entry of Barack Obama early in the campaign provoked many of the racist scare tactics outlined in chapter 5 and added a layer of terrorist and anti-Muslim rhetoric to the mix, with Obama's detractors repeatedly mentioning his middle name (Hussein) and accusing him of "palling around with terrorists." Yet despite this, Obama captured the presidency with 52.4 percent of the popular vote. The final chapter of this new edition discusses the various attempts by both Republican and Democratic opponents to frighten voters away from Obama. That these tactics failed is an encouraging testament to Americans' willingness to vote for—as the Obama campaign put it—hope over fear.

INTRODUCTION:
WHY AMERICANS FEAR
THE WRONG THINGS

Why are so many fears in the air, and so many of them unfounded? Why, as crime rates plunged throughout the 1990s, did two-thirds of Americans believe they were soaring? How did it come about that by mid-decade 62 percent of us described ourselves as "truly desperate" about crime–almost twice as many as in the late 1980s, when crime rates were higher? Why, on a survey in 1997, when the crime rate had already fallen for a half dozen consecutive years, did more than half of us disagree with the statement "This country is finally beginning to make some progress in solving the crime problem"?[1]

In the late 1990s the number of drug users had decreased by half compared to a decade earlier; almost two-thirds of high school seniors had never used any illegal drugs, even marijuana. So why did a majority of adults rank drug abuse as the greatest danger to America's youth? Why did nine out of ten believe the drug problem is out of control, and only one in six believe the country was making progress?[2]

Give us a happy ending and we write a new disaster story. In the late 1990s the unemployment rate was below 5 percent for the first time in a quarter century. People who had been pounding the pavement for years could finally get work. Yet pundits warned of imminent economic disaster. They predicted inflation would take off, just as they had a few years earlier–also erroneously–when the unemployment rate dipped below 6 percent.[3]

We compound our worries beyond all reason. Life expectancy in the United States has doubled during the twentieth century. We are better able to cure and control diseases than any other civilization in history. Yet we hear that phenomenal numbers of us are dreadfully ill. In 1996 Bob Garfield, a magazine writer, reviewed articles about serious diseases published over the course of a year in the *Washington Post*, the *New York Times*, and *USA Today*. He learned that, in addition to 59 million Americans with heart disease, 53 million with migraines, 25 million with osteoporosis, 16 million with obesity, and 3 million with cancer, many Americans suffer from more obscure ailments such as temporomandibular joint disorders (10 million) and brain injuries (2 million). Adding up the estimates, Garfield determined that 543 million Americans are seriously sick—a shocking number in a nation of 266 million inhabitants. "Either as a society we are doomed, or someone is seriously double-dipping," he suggested.[4]

Garfield appears to have underestimated one category of patients: for psychiatric ailments his figure was 53 million. Yet when Jim Windolf, an editor of the *New York Observer*, collated estimates for maladies ranging from borderline personality disorder (10 million) and sex addiction (11 million) to less well-known conditions such as restless leg syndrome (12 million) he came up with a figure of 152 million. "But give the experts a little time," he advised. "With another new quantifiable disorder or two, everybody in the country will be officially nuts."[5]

Indeed, Windolf omitted from his estimates new-fashioned afflictions that have yet to make it into the *Diagnostic and Statistical Manual of Mental Disorders* of the American Psychiatric Association: ailments such as road rage, which afflicts more than half of Americans, according to a psychologist's testimony before a congressional hearing in 1997.[6]

The scope of our health fears seems limitless. Besides worrying disproportionately about legitimate ailments and prematurely about would-be diseases, we continue to fret over already refuted dangers. Some still worry, for instance, about "flesh-eating bacteria," a bug first rammed into our consciousness in 1994 when the U.S. news media picked up on a screamer headline in a British tabloid, "Killer Bug Ate My Face." The bacteria, depicted as more brutal than anything seen in modern times, was said to be spreading faster than the pack of photographers outside the home of its latest victim. In point of fact, however, we were not "terribly vulnerable" to these "superbugs," nor were they "medicine's worst nightmares," as voices in the media warned.

Group A strep, a cyclical strain that has been around for ages, had been dormant for half a century or more before making a comeback. The British pseudoepidemic had resulted in a total of about a dozen deaths in the previous year. Medical experts roundly rebutted the scares by noting that of 20 to 30 million strep infections each year in the United States fewer than 1 in 1,000 involve serious strep A complications, and only 500 to 1,500 people suffer the flesh-eating syndrome, whose proper name is necrotizing fasciitis. Still the fear persisted. Years after the initial scare, horrifying news stories continued to appear, complete with grotesque pictures of victims. A United Press International story in 1998 typical of the genre told of a child in Texas who died of the "deadly strain" of bacteria that the reporter warned "can spread at a rate of up to one inch per hour."[7]

Killer Kids

When we are not worrying about deadly diseases we worry about homicidal strangers. Every few months for the past several years it seems we discover a new category of people to fear: government thugs in Waco, sadistic cops on Los Angeles freeways and in Brooklyn police stations, mass-murdering youths in small towns all over the country. A single anomalous event can provide us with multiple groups of people to fear. After the 1995 explosion at the federal building in Oklahoma City first we panicked about Arabs. "Knowing that the car bomb indicates Middle Eastern terrorists at work, it's safe to assume that their goal is to promote free-floating fear and a measure of anarchy, thereby disrupting American life," a *New York Post* editorial asserted. "Whatever we are doing to destroy Mideast terrorism, the chief terrorist threat against Americans, has not been working," wrote A. M. Rosenthal in the *New York Times*.[8]

When it turned out that the bombers were young white guys from middle America, two more groups instantly became spooky: right-wing radio talk show hosts who criticize the government—depicted by President Bill Clinton as "purveyors of hatred and division"—and members of militias. No group of disgruntled men was too ragtag not to warrant big, prophetic news stories.[9]

We have managed to convince ourselves that just about every young American male is a potential mass murderer—a remarkable achievement, considering the steep downward trend in youth crime throughout the 1990s. Faced year after year with comforting statistics, we either ignore them—adult Americans estimate that people under eighteen commit about half of all violent crimes when the actual number is 13 percent—or recast them as "The Lull Before the Storm" (*Newsweek* headline). "We know we've got about six years to turn this juvenile crime thing around or our country is going to be living with chaos," Bill Clinton asserted in 1997, even while acknowledging that the youth violent crime rate had fallen 9.2 percent the previous year.[10]

The more things improve the more pessimistic we become. Violence-related deaths at the nation's schools dropped to a record low during the 1996–97 academic year (19 deaths out of 54 million children), and only one in ten public schools reported *any* serious crime. Yet *Time* and *U.S. News & World Report* both ran headlines in 1996 referring to "Teenage Time Bombs." In a nation of "Children Without Souls" (another *Time* headline that year), "America's beleaguered cities are about to be victimized by a paradigm shattering wave of ultraviolent, morally vacuous young people some call 'the superpredators,'" William Bennett, the former Secretary of Education, and John DiIulio, a criminologist, forecast in a book published in 1996.[11]

Instead of the arrival of superpredators, violence by urban youths continued to decline. So we went looking elsewhere for proof that heinous behavior by young people was "becoming increasingly more commonplace in America" (CNN). After a sixteen-year-old in Pearl, Mississippi, and a fourteen-year-old in West Paducah, Kentucky, went on shooting sprees in late 1997, killing five of their classmates and wounding twelve others, these isolated incidents were taken as evidence of "an epidemic of seemingly depraved adolescent murderers" (Geraldo Rivera). Three months later in March 1998 all sense of proportion vanished after two boys ages eleven and thirteen killed four students and a teacher in Jonesboro, Arkansas. No longer, we learned in *Time*, was it "unusual for kids to get back at the world with live ammunition." When a child psychologist on NBC's "Today" show advised parents to reassure their children that shootings at schools are rare, reporter Ann Curry corrected him. "But this is the fourth case since October," she said.[12]

Over the next couple of months young people failed to accommodate the trend hawkers. None committed mass murder. Fear of killer kids remained very much in the air nonetheless. In stories on topics such as school safety and childhood trauma, reporters recapitulated the gory details of the killings. And the news media made a point of reporting every incident in which a child was caught at school with a gun or making a death threat. In May, when a fifteen-year-old in Springfield, Oregon, did open fire in a cafeteria filled with students, killing two and wounding twenty-three others, the event felt like a continuation of a "disturbing trend" (*New York Times*). The day after the shooting, on National Public Radio's "All Things Considered," the criminologist Vincent Schiraldi tried to explain that the recent string of incidents did not constitute a trend, that youth homicide rates had declined by 30 percent in recent years, and more than three times as many people were killed by lightning than by violence at schools. But the show's host, Robert Siegel, interrupted him. "You're saying these are just anomalous events?" he asked, audibly peeved. The criminologist reiterated that *anomalous* is precisely the right word to describe the events, and he called it "a grave mistake" to imagine otherwise.

Yet given what had happened in Mississippi, Kentucky, Arkansas, and Oregon, could anyone doubt that today's youths are "more likely to pull a gun than make a fist," as Katie Couric declared on the "Today" show?[13]

Roosevelt Was Wrong

We had better learn to doubt our inflated fears before they destroy us. Valid fears have their place; they cue us to danger. False and overdrawn fears only cause hardship.

Even concerns about real dangers, when blown out of proportion, do demonstrable harm. Take the fear of cancer. Many Americans over- estimate the prevalence of the disease, underestimate the odds of sur- viving it, and put themselves at greater risk as a result. Women in their forties believe they have a 1 in 10 chance of dying from breast cancer, a Dartmouth study found. Their real lifetime odds are more like 1 in 250. Women's heightened perception of risk, rather than motivating them to get checkups or seek treatment, can have the opposite effect. A study of daughters of women with breast cancer found an inverse correlation between fear and prevention: the greater a daughter's fear of the dis- ease the less frequent her breast self-examination. Studies of the gen- eral population—both men and women—find that large numbers of peo- ple who believe they have symptoms of cancer delay going to a doctor, often for several months. When asked why, they report they are terri- fied about the pain and financial ruin cancer can cause as well as poor prospects for a cure. The irony of course is that early treatment can pre- vent precisely those horrors they most fear.[14]

Still more ironic, if harder to measure, are the adverse consequences of public panics. Exaggerated perceptions of the risks of cancer at least produce beneficial by-products, such as bountiful funding for research and treatment of this leading cause of death. When it comes to large- scale panics, however, it is difficult to see how potential victims benefit from the frenzy. Did panics a few years ago over sexual assaults on chil- dren by preschool teachers and priests leave children better off? Or did they prompt teachers and clergy to maintain excessive distance from children in their care, as social scientists and journalists who have stud- ied the panics suggest? How well can care givers do their jobs when reg- ulatory agencies, teachers' unions, and archdioceses explicitly prohibit them from any physical contact with children, even kindhearted hugs?[15]

Was it a good thing for children and parents that male day care providers left the profession for fear of being falsely accused of sex crimes? In an article in the *Journal of American Culture*, sociologist Mary DeYoung has argued that day care was "refeminized" as a result of the panics. "Once again, and in the time-honored and very familiar tradi- tion of the family, the primary responsibility for the care and socialization of young children was placed on the shoulders of low-paid women," she contends.[16]

We all pay one of the costs of panics: huge sums of money go to waste. Hysteria over the ritual abuse of children cost billions of dollars in police investigations, trials, and imprisonments. Men and women went to jail for years "on the basis of some of the most fantastic claims ever presented to an American jury," as Dorothy Rabinowitz of the *Wall Street Journal* demonstrated in a series of investigative articles for which she became a Pulitizer Prize finalist in 1996. Across the nation expensive surveillance programs were implemented to protect children from fiends who reside primarily in the imaginations of adults.[17]

The price tag for our panic about overall crime has grown so monumental that even law-and-order zealots find it hard to defend. The criminal justice system costs Americans close to $100 billion a year, most of which goes to police and prisons. In California we spend more on jails than on higher education. Yet increases in the number of police and prison cells do not correlate consistently with reductions in the number of serious crimes committed. Criminologists who study reductions in homicide rates, for instance, find little difference between cities that substantially expand their police forces and prison capacity and others that do not.[18]

The turnabout in domestic public spending over the past quarter century, from child welfare and antipoverty programs to incarceration, did not even produce reductions in *fear* of crime. Increasing the number of cops and jails arguably has the opposite effect: it suggests that the crime problem is all the more out of control.[19]

Panic-driven public spending generates over the long term a pathology akin to one found in drug addicts. The more money and attention we fritter away on our compulsions, the less we have available for our real needs, which consequently grow larger. While fortunes are being spent to protect children from dangers that few ever encounter, approximately 11 million children lack health insurance, 12 million are malnourished, and rates of illiteracy are increasing.[20]

I do not contend, as did President Roosevelt in 1933, that "the only thing we have to fear is fear itself." My point is that we often fear the wrong things. In the 1990s middle-income and poorer Americans should have worried about unemployment insurance, which covered a smaller share of workers than twenty years earlier. Many of us have had friends or family out of work during economic downturns or as a result of corporate restructuring. Living in a nation with one of the largest income gaps of any industrialized country, where the bottom 40 percent of the population is worse off financially than their counterparts two decades earlier, we might also have worried about income inequality. Or poverty. During the mid- and late 1990s 5 million elderly Americans had no food in their homes, more than 20 million people used emergency food programs each year, and one in five children lived in poverty—more than a quarter million of them homeless. All told, a larger proportion of Americans were poor than three decades earlier.[21]

One of the paradoxes of a culture of fear is that serious problems remain widely ignored even though they give rise to precisely the dangers that the populace most abhors. Poverty, for example, correlates strongly with child abuse, crime, and drug abuse. Income inequality is also associated with adverse outcomes for society as a whole. The larger the gap between rich and poor in a society, the higher its overall death rates from heart disease, cancer, and murder. Some social scientists argue that extreme inequality also threatens political stability in a nation such as the United States, where we think of ourselves not as "haves and have nots" but as "haves and will haves." "Unlike the citizens of most other nations, Americans have always been united less by a shared past than by the shared dreams of a better future. If we lose that common future," the Brandeis University economist Robert Reich has suggested, "we lose the glue that holds our nation together."[22]

The combination of extreme inequality and poverty can prove explosive. In an insightful article in *U.S. News & World Report* in 1997 about militia groups reporters Mike Tharp and William Holstein noted that people's motivations for joining these groups are as much economic as ideological. The journalists argued that the disappearance of military and blue-collar jobs, along with the decline of family farming, created the conditions under which a new breed of protest groups flourished. "What distinguishes these antigovernment groups from, say, traditional conservatives who mistrust government is that their anger is fueled by direct threats to their livelihood, and they carry guns," Tharp and Holstein wrote.[23]

That last phrase alludes to a danger that by any rational calculation deserves top billing on Americans' lists of fears. So gun crazed is this nation that Burger King had to order a Baltimore franchise to stop giving away coupons from a local sporting goods store for free boxes of bullets with the purchase of guns. We have more guns *stolen* from their owners—about 300,000 annually—than many countries have gun owners. In Great Britain, Australia, and Japan, where gun ownership is severely restricted, no more than a few dozen people are killed each year by handguns. In the United States, where private citizens own a quarter-billion guns, around 15,000 people are killed, 18,000 commit suicide, and another 1,500 die accidentally from firearms. American children are twelve times more liked to die from gun injuries than are youngsters in other industrialized nations.[24]

Yet even after tragedies that could not have occurred except for the availability of guns, their significance is either played down or missed altogether. Had the youngsters in the celebrated schoolyard shootings of 1997–98 not had access to guns, some or all of the people they killed would be alive today. Without their firepower those boys lacked the strength, courage, and skill to commit multiple murders. Nevertheless newspapers ran editorials with titles such as "It's Not Guns, It's Killer Kids" (*Fort Worth Star–Telegram*) and "Guns Aren't the Problem" (*New York Post*), and journalists, politicians, and pundits blathered on endlessly about every imaginable cause of youthful rage, from "the psychology of violence in the South" to satanism to fights on "Jerry Springer" and simulated shooting in Nintendo games.[25]

Two Easy Explanations

In the following discussion I will try to answer two questions: Why are Americans so fearful lately, and why are our fears so often misplaced? To both questions the same two-word answer is commonly given by scholars and journalists: premillennial tensions. The final years of a millennium and the early years of a new millennium provoke mass anxiety and ill reasoning, the argument goes. So momentous does the calendric change seem, the populace cannot keep its wits about it.

Premillennial tensions probably do help explain some of our collective irrationality. Living in a scientific era, most of us grant the arbitrariness of reckoning time in base-ten rather than, say, base-twelve, and from the birth of Christ rather than from the day Muhammad moved from Mecca. Yet even the least superstitious among us cannot quite manage to think of the year 2000 as ordinary. Social psychologists have long recognized a human urge to convert vague uneasiness into definable concerns, real or imagined. In a classic study thirty years ago Alan Kerckhoff and Kurt Back pointed out that "the belief in a tangible threat makes it possible to explain and justify one's sense of discomfort."[26]

Some historical evidence also supports the hypothesis that people panic at the brink of centuries and millennia. Witness the "panic terror" in Europe around the year 1000 and the witch hunts in Salem in the 1690s. As a complete or dependable explanation, though, the millennium hypothesis fails. Historians emphasize that panics of equal or greater intensity occur in odd years, as demonstrated by anti-Indian hysteria in the mid 1700s and McCarthyism in the 1950s. Scholars point out too that calendars cannot account for why certain fears occupy people at certain times (witches then, killer kids now).[27]

Another popular explanation blames the news media. We have so many fears, many of them off-base, the argument goes, because the media bombard us with sensationalistic stories designed to increase ratings. This explanation, sometimes called the media-effects theory, is less simplistic than the millennium hypothesis and contains sizable kernels of truth. When researchers from Emory University computed the levels of coverage of various health dangers in popular magazines and newspapers they discovered an inverse relationship: much less space was devoted to several of the major causes of death than to some uncommon causes. The leading cause of death, heart disease, received approximately the same amount of coverage as the eleventh-ranked cause of death, homicide. They found a similar inverse relationship in coverage of risk factors associated with serious illness and death. The lowest-ranking risk factor, drug use, received nearly as much attention as the second-ranked risk factor, diet and exercise.[28]

Disproportionate coverage in the news media plainly has effects on readers and viewers. When Esther Madriz, a professor at Hunter College, interviewed women in New York City about their fears of crime they frequently responded with the phrase "I saw it in the news." The interviewees identified the news media as both the source of their fears and the reason they believed those fears were valid. Asked in a national poll why they believe the country has a serious crime problem, 76 percent of people cited stories they had seen in the media. Only 22 percent cited personal experience.[29]

When professors Robert Blendon and John Young of Harvard analyzed forty-seven surveys about drug abuse conducted between 1978 and 1997, they too discovered that the news media, rather than personal experience, provide Americans with their predominant fears. Eight out of ten adults say that drug abuse has never caused problems in their family, and the vast majority report relatively little direct experience with problems related to drug abuse. Widespread concern about drug problems emanates, Blendon and Young determined, from scares in the news media, television in particular.[30]

Television news programs survive on scares. On local newscasts, where producers live by the dictum "if it bleeds, it leads," drug, crime, and disaster stories make up most of the news portion of the broadcasts. Evening newscasts on the major networks are somewhat less bloody, but between 1990 and 1998, when the nation's murder rate declined by 20 percent, the number of murder stories on network newscasts increased 600 percent (*not* counting stories about O. J. Simpson).[31]

After the dinnertime newscasts the networks broadcast newsmagazines, whose guiding principle seems to be that no danger is too small to magnify into a national nightmare. Some of the risks reported by such programs would be merely laughable were they not hyped with so much fanfare: "Don't miss *Dateline* tonight or YOU could be the next victim!" Competing for ratings with drama programs and movies during prime-time evening hours, newsmagazines feature story lines that would make a writer for "Homicide" or "ER" wince.[32]

"It can happen in a flash. Fire breaks out on the operating table. The patient is surrounded by flames," Barbara Walters exclaimed on ABC's "20/20" in 1998. The problem—oxygen from a face mask ignited by a surgical instrument—occurs "more often than you might think," she cautioned in her introduction, even though reporter Arnold Diaz would note later, during the actual report, that out of 27 million surgeries each year the situation arises only about a hundred times. No matter, Diaz effectively nullified the reassuring numbers as soon as they left his mouth. To those who "may say it's too small a risk to worry about" he presented distraught victims: a woman with permanent scars on her face and a man whose son had died.[33]

The gambit is common. Producers of TV newsmagazines routinely let emotional accounts trump objective information. In 1994 medical authorities attempted to cut short the brouhaha over flesh-eating bacteria by publicizing the fact that an American is fifty-five times more likely to be struck by lightning than die of the suddenly celebrated microbe. Yet TV journalists brushed this fact aside with remarks like, "whatever the statistics, it's devastating to the victims" (Catherine Crier on "20/20"), accompanied by stomach-turning videos of disfigured patients.[34]

Sheryl Stolberg, then a medical writer for the *Los Angeles Times,* put her finger on what makes the TV newsmagazines so cavalier: "Killer germs are perfect for prime time," she wrote. "They are invisible, uncontrollable, and, in the case of Group A strep, can invade the body in an unnervingly simple manner, through a cut or scrape." Whereas print journalists only described in words the actions of "billions of bacteria" spreading "like underground fires" throughout a person's body, TV newsmagazines made use of special effects to depict graphically how these "merciless killers" do their damage.[35]

In Praise of Journalists

Any analysis of the culture of fear that ignored the news media would be patently incomplete, and of the several institutions most culpable for creating and sustaining scares the news media are arguably first among equals. They are also the most promising candidates for positive change. Yet by the same token critiques such as Stolberg's presage a crucial shortcoming in arguments that blame the media. Reporters not only spread fears, they also debunk them and criticize one another for spooking the public. A wide array of groups, including businesses, advocacy organizations, religious sects, and political parties, promote and profit from scares. News organizations are distinguished from other fear-mongering groups because they sometimes bite the scare that feeds them.

A group that raises money for research into a particular disease is not likely to negate concerns about that disease. A company that sells alarm systems is not about to call attention to the fact that crime is down. News organizations, on the other hand, periodically allay the very fears they arouse to lure audiences. Some newspapers that ran stories about child murderers, rather than treat every incident as evidence of a shocking trend, affirmed the opposite. After the schoolyard shooting in Kentucky the *New York Times* ran a sidebar alongside its feature story with the headline "Despite Recent Carnage, School Violence Is Not on Rise." Following the Jonesboro killings they ran a similar piece, this time on a recently released study showing the rarity of violent crimes in schools.[36]

Several major newspapers parted from the pack in other ways. *USA Today* and the *Washington Post*, for instance, made sure their readers knew that what should worry them is the availability of guns. *USA Today* ran news stories explaining that easy access to guns in homes accounted for increases in the number of juvenile arrests for homicide in rural areas during the 1990s. While other news outlets were respectfully quoting the mother of the thirteen-year-old Jonesboro shooter, who said she did not regret having encouraged her son to learn to fire a gun ("it's like anything else, there's some people that can drink a beer and not become an alcoholic"), *USA Today* ran an op-ed piece proposing legal parameters for gun ownership akin to those for the use of alcohol and motor vehicles. And the paper published its own editorial in support of laws that require gun owners to lock their guns or keep them in locked containers. Adopted at that time by only fifteen states, the laws had reduced the number of deaths among children in those states by 23 percent.[37]

The *Washington Post*, meanwhile, published an excellent investigative piece by reporter Sharon Walsh showing that guns increasingly were being marketed to teenagers and children. Quoting advertisements and statistics from gun manufacturers and the National Rifle Association, Walsh revealed that by 1998 the primary market for guns—white males—had been saturated and an effort to market to women had failed. Having come to see children as its future, the gun industry has taken to running ads like the one Walsh found in a Smith & Wesson catalog: "Seems like only yesterday that your father brought you here for the first time," reads the copy beside a photo of a child aiming a handgun, his father by his side. "Those sure were the good times—just you, dad and his Smith & Wesson."[38]

As a social scientist I am impressed and somewhat embarrassed to find that journalists, more often than media scholars, identify the jugglery involved in making small hazards appear huge and huge hazards disappear from sight. Take, for example, the scare several years ago over the Ebola virus. Another *Washington Post* reporter, John Schwartz, identified a key bit of hocus-pocus used to sell that scare. Schwartz called it "the Cuisinart Effect," because it involves the mashing together of images and story lines from fiction and reality. A report by *Dateline NBC* on deaths in Zaire, for instance, interspersed clips from *Outbreak*, a movie whose plot involves a lethal virus that threatens to kill the entire U.S. population. Alternating between Dustin Hoffman's character exclaiming, "We can't stop it!" and real-life science writer Laurie Garrett, author of *The Coming Plague*, proclaiming that "HIV is not an aberration . . . it's part of a trend," *Dateline*'s report gave the impression that swarms of epidemics were on their way.[39]

Another great journalist-debunker, Malcolm Gladwell, noted that the book that had inspired *Outbreak*, Richard Preston's *The Hot Zone*, itself was written "in self-conscious imitation of a sci-fi thriller." In the real-world incident that occasioned *The Hot Zone*, monkeys infected in Zaire with a strain of Ebola virus were quarantined at a government facility in Reston, Virginia. The strain turned out not to be lethal in humans, but neither Preston in his book nor the screenwriters for *Outbreak* nor TV producers who sampled from the movie let that anti-

climax interfere with the scare value of their stories. Preston specu-
lates about an airborne strain of Ebola being carried by travelers from
African airports to European, Asian, and American cities. In *Outbreak*
hundreds of people die from such an airborne strain before a cure is
miraculously discovered in the nick of time to save humanity. In
truth, Gladwell points out in a piece in *The New Republic*, an Ebola
strain that is both virulent to humans and airborne is unlikely to
emerge and would mutate rapidly if it did, becoming far less potent
before it had a chance to infect large numbers of people on a single
continent, much less throughout the globe. "It is one of the ironies of
the analysis of alarmists such as Preston that they are all too willing
to point out the limitations of human beings, but they neglect to point out the limitations of microscopic life forms," Gladwell
notes.[40]

Such disproofs of disease scares appear rather frequently in general-
interest magazines and newspapers, including in publications where
one might not expect to find them. The *Wall Street Journal*, for instance,
while primarily a business publication and itself a retailer of fears about
governmental regulators, labor unions, and other corporate-preferred
hobgoblins, has done much to demolish medical myths. Among my
personal favorites is an article published in 1996 titled "Fright by the
Numbers," in which reporter Cynthia Crossen rebuts a cover story in
Time magazine on prostate cancer. One in five men will get the disease,
Time thundered. "That's scary. But it's also a lifetime risk—the accumulated risk over some 80 years of life," Crossen responds. A forty-year-
old's chance of coming down with (not dying of) prostate cancer in the
next ten years is 1 in 1,000, she goes on to report. His odds rise to 1 in
100 over twenty years. Even by the time he's seventy, he has only a 1 in
20 chance of *any* kind of cancer, including prostate.[41]

In the same article Crossen counters other alarmist claims as well,
such as the much-repeated pronouncement that one in three Americans is obese. The number actually refers to how many are overweight,
a less serious condition. Fewer are *obese* (a term that is less than objective itself), variously defined as 20 to 40 percent above ideal body
weight as determined by current standards.[42]

Morality and Marketing

To blame the media is to oversimplify the complex role that journalists play as both proponents and doubters of popular fears. It is also to beg the same key issue that the millennium hypothesis evades: why particular anxieties take hold when they do. Why do news organizations and their audiences find themselves drawn to one hazard rather than another?

Mary Douglas, the eminent anthropologist who devoted much of her career to studying how people interpret risk, pointed out that every society has an almost infinite quantity of potential dangers from which to choose. Societies differ both in the types of dangers they select and the number. Dangers get selected for special emphasis, Douglas showed, either because they offend the basic moral principles of the society or because they enable criticism of disliked groups and institutions. In *Risk and Culture*, a book she wrote with Aaron Wildavsky, the authors give an example from fourteenth-century Europe. Impure water had been a health danger long before that time, but only after it became convenient to accuse Jews of poisoning the wells did people become preoccupied with it.

Or take a more recent institutional example. In the first half of the 1990s U.S. cities spent at least $10 billion to purge asbestos from public schools, even though removing asbestos from buildings posed a greater health hazard than leaving it in place. At a time when about one-third of the nation's schools were in need of extensive repairs the money might have been spent to renovate dilapidated buildings. But hazards posed by seeping asbestos are morally repugnant. A product that was supposed to protect children from fires might be giving them cancer. By directing our worries and dollars at asbestos we express outrage at technology and industry run afoul.[43]

From a psychological point of view extreme fear and outrage are often projections. Consider, for example, the panic over violence against children. By failing to provide adequate education, nutrition, housing, parenting, medical services, and child care over the past couple of decades we have done the nation's children immense harm. Yet we project our guilt onto a cavalcade of bogeypeople—pedophile preschool teachers, preteen mass murderers, and homicidal au pairs, to name only a few.[44]

When Debbie Nathan, a journalist, and Michael Snedeker, an attorney, researched the evidence behind publicized reports in the 1980s and early 1990s of children being ritually raped and tortured they learned that although seven out of ten Americans believed that satanic cults were committing these atrocities, few of the incidents had actually occurred. At the outset of each ritual-abuse case the children involved claimed they had not been molested. They later changed their tunes at the urging of parents and law enforcement authorities. The ghastly tales of abuse, it turns out, typically came from the parents themselves, usually the mothers, who had convinced themselves they were true. Nathan and Snedeker suggest that some of the mothers had been abused themselves and projected those horrors, which they had trouble facing directly, onto their children. Other mothers, who had not been victimized in those ways, used the figure of ritually abused children as a medium of protest against male dominance more generally. Allegations of children being raped allowed conventional wives and mothers to speak out against men and masculinity without having to fear they would seem unfeminine. "The larger culture," Nathan and Snedeker note, "still required that women's complaints about inequality and sexual violence be communicated through the innocent, mortified voice of the child."

Diverse groups used the ritual-abuse scares to diverse ends. Well-known feminists such as Gloria Steinem and Catharine MacKinnon took up the cause, depicting ritually abused children as living proof of the ravages of patriarchy and the need for fundamental social reform.[45]

This was far from the only time feminist spokeswomen have mongered fears about sinister breeds of men who exist in nowhere near the high numbers they allege. Another example occurred a few years ago when teen pregnancy was much in the news. Feminists helped popularize the frightful but erroneous statistic that two out of three teen mothers had been seduced and abandoned by adult men. The true figure is more like one in ten, but some feminists continued to cultivate the scare well after the bogus stat had been definitively debunked.[46]

Within public discourse fears proliferate through a process of exchange. It is from crosscurrents of scares and counterscares that the culture of fear swells ever larger. Even as feminists disparage large classes of men, they themselves are a staple of fear mongering by conservatives. To hear conservatives tell it, feminists are not only "anti-child and anti-family" (Arianna Huffington) but through women's studies programs on college campuses they have fomented an "anti-science and anti-reason movement" (Christina Hoff Sommers).[47]

Conservatives also like to spread fears about liberals, who respond in kind. Among other pet scares, they accuse liberals of creating "children without consciences" by keeping prayer out of schools–to which liberals rejoin with warnings that right-wing extremists intend to turn youngsters into Christian soldiers.[48]

Samuel Taylor Coleridge was right when he claimed, "In politics, what begins in fear usually ends up in folly." Political activists are more inclined, though, to heed an observation from Richard Nixon: "People react to fear, not love. They don't teach that in Sunday school, but it's true." That principle, which guided the late president's political strategy throughout his career, is the sine qua non of contemporary political campaigning. Marketers of products and services ranging from car alarms to TV news programs have taken it to heart as well.[49]

The short answer to why Americans harbor so many misbegotten fears is that immense power and money await those who tap into our moral insecurities and supply us with symbolic substitutes. This book provides the longer answer by identifying the actual vendors of our fears, their marketing methods, and incentives the rest of us must buy into.

DUBIOUS DANGERS ON ROADWAYS AND CAMPUSES

How Fears Are Sold

Start with silly scares, the kind that would be laughable were they not advanced with utter seriousness by influential organizations, politicians, and news media. Promoted by the same means as other fears—and often to the same ends—they afford a comfortable entry point into the fear mongers' bag of tricks. It becomes easier to recognize how we are bamboozled about serious concerns, having seen the same techniques at work in the promotion of frivolous dangers.

Scenarios Substitute for Facts

"There is no terror in the bang, only in the anticipation of it," said the ultimate master of terror, Alfred Hitchcock. Fear mongers regularly put his wisdom to use by depicting would-be perils as imminent disasters. "They're all around you, everywhere you drive, waiting to explode," exclaimed an announcer at the beginning of ABC's newsmagazine "20/20" in 1996, devoted to what he called "a growing American danger—road rage." Hugh Downs, the program's coanchor, continued the ruse. Eliciting viewers' everyday experiences, he recast them as portentous. "How many times have you been bullied on the road, honked at or tailed, cursed at by another driver? Maybe you've done this yourself. Well, tonight, you will see again where this kind of aggression can lead," said Downs, insinuating that viewers had already anticipated what Tom Jarriel, the reporter whose story he then introduced, was about to detail.[1]

A seemingly innocuous beep of the car horn can lead, Jarriel said, to "anger so explosive it pushes people over the edge: fist fights, even shootings, between perfect strangers." Out in the real world, people honk their horns all the time without getting socked or shot, but in the fluid logic of Jarriel's narrative stark imagery and atypical anecdotes eclipsed reality. "It happens without warning to ordinary people," Jarriel said, and to prove the point, he interviewed a man who was shot in the face after cutting someone off on a highway.

Oprah Winfrey, in a program on road rage in 1997, used the same approach. First she transmuted familiar occurrences into a huge new danger. "We've all been there. It starts out with the tap of the horn, an angry gesture, a dirty look . . . ," she declared. Then she proceeded to recount a few actual incidents in which the outcome was a shooting or fistfight. That expressions of annoyance almost never intensify to a shooting or fight was beside the point. "This is a show that affects so many people," she said, and then cleverly produced an impressive but ultimately meaningless number. "This woman's biggest offense was pulling out of her driveway . . . countless millions of you have done that," she said in the course of introducing someone who had been attacked by another driver.[2]

Journalists in the print media used a slightly different tactic. Call it the foreshadowing anecdote. After relaying the gory details of a particular instance of highway violence, they asserted that the given example "raises the overarching question of road anarchy" (*Time*) or represents "just the latest case of 'road rage' to gain national attention" (*USA Today*). A page-one story in the *Los Angeles Times* in 1998 declared that "road rage has become an exploding phenomenon across the country" and depicted the Pacific Northwest as a region particularly "plagued by a rise in road rage." Only after wading through twenty-two paragraphs of alarming first-person accounts and warnings from authorities did the reader learn that a grand total of five drivers and passengers had died in road rage incidents in the region over the previous five years.[3]

An average of one death a year constitutes a plague? The only other statistical evidence the reporter managed to muster was from a study released in 1997 by the American Automobile Association. Cited habitually in stories about road rage, the AAA study afforded reporters an opportunity to declare that incidents of road rage had "been rising 7% a year" (*Los Angeles Times*), or as *People* magazine put it, "more than 50 percent since 1990." I found only one article that put the AAA's findings in proper perspective: a piece in *U.S. News & World Report* noted that, of approximately 250,000 people killed on roadways between 1990 and 1997, the AAA attributed 218 deaths, or less than one in a thousand, directly to angry drivers. And of the 20 million motorists injured during that period the AAA attributed less than 1 percent of those injuries to aggressive driving.[4]

Big percentages do not necessarily have big numbers behind them. The dramatic "up more than 50%" statistic in the AAA study derived from the difference between two relatively modest figures: the number of traffic incidents that involved major violence in 1990 (1,129) compared to 1996 (1,800). An increase of 671 incidents in fifty states over seven years is hardly "a growing epidemic" (*USA Today*'s description of road rage). Nor does it warrant the thousands of stories about road rage that appeared in print and on radio and television–coverage that helped produce the 671 figure in the first place. The AAA derived their estimates from newspaper, police, and insurance reports, all of which are influenced by hype. The more talk there is about road rage, the more likely are newspaper reporters, police officers, and insurance agents to classify as examples of it incidents that they would have ignored altogether or catalogued differently in the past.[5]

Psychologists refer to this phenomenon as the Pygmalion effect, in deference to George Bernard Shaw. In Shaw's *Pygmalion*, Liza comes to appreciate that, as she puts it to Colonel Pickering, "the difference between a flower girl and a lady is not how she behaves, but how she's treated." Posits Liza, during an exchange with the Colonel, "I shall always be a flower girl to Professor Higgins, because he always treats me as a flower girl, but I know I can be a lady to you, because you always treat me as a lady, and always will."[6]

In the late 1990s police and reporters treated all variety of highway mishaps as road rage. One evening in 1998 the lead image on local news shows in Los Angeles was a car that had been sliced in half by a truck on a freeway. The fatal accident had been caused by the driver going up an exit ramp in the wrong direction, but reporters and highway patrol officers labeled it "another case of road rage." Their justification? Witnesses reported the driver had been tailgating a van just moments earlier. At the time she drove up the exit ramp and into on-coming traffic she was neither a perpetrator nor victim of road rage, but because she may have acted aggressively in the recent past the incident could be counted as road rage.[7]

A few days after that incident, when an off-duty prison guard was shot dead on a freeway ramp, police and reporters described the event as "a random act of violence, like other examples of so-called road rage violence plaguing the nation's motorists" (*Los Angeles Times*). This time too the characterization was unfounded. The victim's husband, who had been driving the car, let police know immediately after the event that it was neither random nor an instance of road rage. According to his account, their assailants had followed them from a shopping mall, forced them to pull off the road, and stolen money. It was when his wife pulled out her state corrections officer badge, the husband re-ported, that they shot her. Police later suspected the husband himself in the murder, but never was road rage a likely hypothesis.[8]

Bad People Substitute for Bad Policies

Stories about road rage left little doubt as to what, or rather who, was responsible—vicious strangers. Over the past decade or so police and reporters had warned of disparate new categories of creeps out to get us—home invasion robbers, carjackers, child nabbers, deranged postal workers. Now they were issuing an even broader warning. Everywhere we go are "strangers in their cars, ready to snap, driven to violence by the wrong move," the announcer on "20/20" cautioned. Indeed, Tom Jarriel went on to suggest, "the most disturbing aspect of the growing trend toward roadway violence is that we can't choose who we drive with on the highways."[9]

In just about every contemporary American scare, rather than con-front disturbing shortcomings in society the public discussion centers on disturbed individuals. Demented drivers rather than insane public policies occupied center stage in the coverage of road rage. Where ref-erence was made at all to serious problems that drivers face, these were promptly shoved behind a curtain of talk about violent motorists.

"Roads are more crowded all the time, which means more delays and more frustration," National Public Radio's Alex Chadwick reported, but rather than pursue the point with insights from, say, experts on mass transit, he quotes someone from the AAA who contends that driving "frees the beast" in people.[10]

In *USA Today* reporter Patrick O'Driscoll notes that 70 percent of urban freeways are clogged at rush hour (up 15 percent over the past fifteen years) and that traffic exceeds road capacity in most U.S. cities. Did he then go on to consider possibilities for relieving the congestion? On the contrary, his next sentence began, "Faced with tempers boiling over like radiators in rush-hour gridlock, police agencies are seeking ways to brand aggressive driving as socially unacceptable . . ."[11]

Rather than traffic experts journalists spotlighted police officials, who understandably took the opportunity to urge the hiring of more officers. Or reporters turned to so-called experts such as Arnold Nerenberg, a psychologist who dubs himself "America's road-rage therapist" and runs a web site (www.roadrage.com) where he brags that he has been featured in dozens of TV programs and magazines. Not a researcher, Nerenberg nonetheless offers authoritative-sounding sound bites that support reporters' portrayal of highway violence as personal pathology. "There's a deep psychological urge," he tells *Newsweek*, "to release aggression against an anonymous other." Road rage is "a mental disorder that is contagious," *USA Today* quotes him. In an interview with the *New York Times*, Nerenberg called on the American Psychiatric Association to add road rage to its *Diagnostic and Statistical Manual of Mental Disorders* (DSM). At some point in their lives, he said, more than half of the U.S. population suffers from the disorder, which Nerenberg described on ABC's "World News Tonight" as "an adjustment reaction disorder."[12]

Such psychoblather only obscures what even Nerenberg himself knows to be the primary instrument of murder on the nation's roadways. Asked directly by *People* magazine whether there is truly any difference between now and twenty years ago, Nerenberg allows, "One thing that makes the problem worse is that we have more Americans arming themselves. Millions of us illegally carry loaded weapons. The more guns in cars, the greater the chance they'll be used."[13]

Most of the coverage of road rage, however, shamelessly disregarded the import of firearms, even though the AAA study found that offenders in road rage incidents often use guns to kill or injure their victims. On Oprah Winfrey's show devoted to road rage the murder of one driver by another was recounted tearfully and in detail by the victim's fiancé as well as by the man who killed him. But at no point in the program did anyone mention that the victim would almost certainly have survived had there not been a gun involved. In fact, when Winfrey brought on the head of the National Highway Traffic Safety Administration, his only mention of weapons was metaphoric. He referred to cars as "three-thousand-pound weapons."[14]

Experts who do try to direct attention to the matter of guns seldom succeed. In a road rage story on CNN occasioned by a fatal shooting, the local district attorney counseled against "too many guns in cars" and made a comparison: "When you go to Canada, they ask you, 'Do you have any guns in your car,' because you have to check them at their border. If you're coming from Canada to this country, they ask you if you have any fruit." Rather than pursue the matter CNN correspondent Dennis O'Hayer promptly shifted the focus. "Even if you don't have a gun, your own driving tactics could be setting you up for a dangerous face-off," he said. Someone identified as a traffic columnist with the *Atlanta Constitution* then proceeded to urge viewers against death-defying acts such as "getting in the left lane and holding up traffic."[15]

One of my initial hypotheses about why pseudodangers receive so much attention was that they provide opportunities to talk about, and perhaps rectify, problems too big to face in their totality. Stupefied by the quantity of guns on the streets, we might focus on doing something about the much smaller number in cars. My hypothesis could not have been farther from the truth. Pseudodangers represent further opportunities to avoid problems we do not want to confront, such as overcrowded roads and the superabundance of guns, as well as those we have grown tired of confronting. An example of the latter is drunk driving, a behavior that causes about eighty-five times as many deaths as road rage (about 17,000 versus 200). Close to half of all fatal traffic crashes involve alcohol, and three in five Americans will be involved in an alcohol-related crash at some point in their lives. Moved by those statistics and by the advocacy group, Mothers Against Drunk Driving, journalists had covered the issue of drunk driving in a sound and sustained way throughout the 1980s and early 1990s. Thanks in part to that coverage, the number of alcohol-related highway deaths plunged by 31 percent between 1982 and 1995. Fatality rates fall twice as rapidly, studies find, in years of high media attention compared to those of relatively little attention. Intensive coverage permits passage of powerful laws, creation of sobriety checkpoints, and new notions such as the "designated driver," all of which save lives.[16]

Yet by the mid-1990s groups like MADD were finding it difficult to be heard in the media over the noise about road rage and other trendy issues. In the years that followed the fatality rate stopped declining. Polls taken on the eastern seaboard during the late 1990s found people more concerned about road rage than drunk driving. Who could blame them when they read in their local paper, "It's not drunken or elderly or inexperienced drivers who are wreaking havoc. Instead, scores of people are severely injured or killed every day by stressed-out drivers who have abandoned civil roadway behavior" (*Philadelphia Daily News*).[17]

The Power of Calling Something "P.C."

If the first of those two sentences by Don Russell of the *Daily News* inverted the truth about dangerous drivers, the second misled more broadly still. Russell is one of several writers on road rage who alluded to the issue of civility. Reporters variously raised the matter themselves or quoted police officers declaring that "people have forgotten how to be civil to each other" (*USA Today*). In so doing they exemplified another unfortunate hallmark of fear mongering: the tendency to trivialize legitimate concerns even while aggrandizing questionable ones.[18]

Worries about Americans acting uncivilly toward one another date back at least to frontier days, and in our present era bad behavior behind the wheel is far from the most significant or pressing form of incivility. At a time when a disabled black man in Texas was beaten by racists then chained to a truck and dragged down a road to his death and a gay college student in Wyoming was tied to a fence, pistol-whipped, and left to die, we would do well to focus our sights on big-time incivilities such as racism and homophobia. Instead we are diverted by willy-nilly references in stories about road rage, or worse, by fear mongers who *intentionally* set out to confuse matters.[19]

One of the most effective scare campaigns of the late twentieth century—political correctness on college campuses—was undertaken for the express purpose of changing the terms of debate about civility. The people who generated the scare did not phrase it in those terms, mind you; they couched their alarmism in First Amendment language. In the late 1980s conservative commentators began warning of what they described as "the greatest threat to the First Amendment in our history" (Rush Limbaugh), "the equivalent of the Nazi brownshirt thought-control movement" (Walter Williams), and "an ideological virus as deadly as AIDS" (David Horowitz).[20]

President George Bush, in a commencement address at the University of Michigan in 1991, put the matter somewhat more soberly when he decried those who would "declare certain topics off-limits, certain expressions off-limits, even certain gestures off-limits." Some professors and students were indeed urging that certain categories of statements and gestures be eradicated from university life. Specifically, they sought to do away with racist, sexist, and homophobic behavior. If anything qualifies as uncivil in a diverse society, they argued, it is precisely these sorts of acts.[21]

People who got chastised as PC were trying to create a more respectful and inclusive environment on campuses for groups that largely had been excluded—a goal that conservatives could not attack head-on lest they lose the already limited support they had in minority communities. Besides, far from being First Amendment absolutists themselves, many conservatives eagerly support restraints on a range of behaviors, from flag burning to the display of homoerotic art. So rather than engage in honest debate with campus liberals and progressives, conservatives labeled them "politically correct." Much the way their forebears had used the epithet "Communist" a few decades earlier, conservatives of the 1990s accused their enemies of being PC. Primarily by means of anecdotes retold time and again in political speeches, in the news media, and in popular books such as Dinesh D'Souza's *Illiberal Education* and Roger Kimball's *Tenured Radical,* they created an impression of armies of PC militants occupying the nation's colleges and universities.[22]

Conservatives told, for instance, of a mob of 200 at the State University of New York at Binghamton who, armed with sticks and canes, invaded a lecture hall and threatened an elderly man who was giving a talk. According to pieces in the *Wall Street Journal* (one of them titled "The Return of the Storm Troopers"), the university's president did nothing about the hooligans because college presidents "live in terror of being politically incorrect."[23]

Then there was the story of a class at Harvard on feminist theory taught by Alice Jardine, a professor of French. According to Dinesh D'Souza, who sat in on the class one day, a student delivered "ribald one-liners about a man who lost his penis . . . and brought loud and unembarrassed laughter from the professor and other students."[24]

Almost invariably, after such stories came out witnesses to the actual events debunked them. Participants at the Binghamton event, as well as a campus police investigator and one of the speakers, reported there had been no violence. The entire incident consisted, they said, of a single student who engaged in disruptive behavior for about four minutes, for which the university placed him on probation. About the class at Harvard, Alice Jardine subsequently explained that the discussion of the missing penis was actually about the myth of Osiris, a deity whose body parts were scattered throughout Egypt. Osiris's wife, Isis, buried each part as she found them. The phallus was never recovered; images of it, which are used in festivals, can be bought at tourist shops in Egypt.[25]

Yet information correcting the faulty reports came out mostly in academic books and journals, not in the mass media. The general public was left with a highly inaccurate image of white men being mercilessly jeered and muzzled at America's public and private universities.

Granted, activists from the political left sometimes behaved with impudence or intolerance. Speakers were shouted down on occasion if they were perceived as racist, sexist, or antigay. The sum of those occurrences did not support, however, a claim that "the delegitimization, even demonization, of the white male has reached extreme lengths," as Paul Craig Roberts of the Cato Institute, a conservative think tank, put it in an op-ed in the *San Francisco Examiner* in 1996. Guilefully trading on the memory of the Holocaust, Roberts went on to assert that affronts to white males on college campuses are "comparable to . . . the denunciation of Jewry by anti-Semites."[26]

Exaggerated assertions of that kind received more public notice than did the true patterns of discrimination and exclusion on U.S. campuses. Perhaps editors despaired of being called PC themselves if they ran the story, but there was an important story to be told. The data were rather shocking: on the eve of the twenty-first century women, blacks, and Hispanics, far from displacing white males in the professorate, mostly hold jobs at lower ranks and with lower pay. At the height of the PC scare, in the early and mid-1990s, women made up less than one-third of full-time faculty at American colleges and universities, a figure just slightly higher than in 1920, when women won the right to vote. Only about one in twenty professors was Hispanic or African American.

Research on students documented additional disturbing trends. Women and students of color often received less attention and encouragement in classrooms than did their white male counterparts, and outside of class they were the targets of tens of thousands of verbal and physical attacks each year. Gay and lesbian students likewise faced assaults, bigotry, and death threats. Even at famously liberal colleges gays and lesbians experienced prejudice. In a survey at Yale almost all gay and lesbian students said they had overheard antigay remarks, and one in four had been threatened. At Oberlin College nearly half of gay, lesbian, and bisexual students said they have to censor themselves when discussing gay issues.

For faculty members in the meantime, to be openly gay or lesbian at many colleges was to risk being denied tenure, promotion, and opportunities to move into administrative positions, research showed.[27]

Smoke Trumps Fire

The PC scare demonstrates how an orchestrated harangue can drown out a chorus of genuine concern. Faculty and students would raise questions about inequities at their schools only to find themselves made into *causes célèbres* of anti-PC fear mongering.

Imagine how surprised people must have been at Chico State University in 1996 and 1997, when just about every prominent conservative commentator took out after them. "Totalitarianism didn't disappear with the collapse of the Soviet Union. It's alive and well on many American college campuses today," wrote Linda Chavez in a column in *USA Today* in reaction to an event at the previously unnoticed California school. Her comment was typical of the commentary by conservative essayists. Reading them, you would have thought that Chico State was under some sort of military occupation. The conservatives in fact were reacting to a one-word alteration in a help-wanted ad. "We are seeking a dynamic classroom teacher . . . ," the draft of an advertisement for a philosophy teacher had read. When a member of the university committee that reviews job ads questioned whether *dynamic* was the best word to describe the kind of teacher the program was actually seeking, the word was replaced by *excellent.* Some highly effective teachers do not have dynamic personal styles, the English professor had observed, and vice versa, some high-spirited teachers do not actually have much worthwhile knowledge. In addition, she suggested, the term *dynamic* may unintentionally discriminate against candidates from certain Asian and Hispanic backgrounds in which personal styles tend to be more unassuming.[28]

Just about everyone involved at Chico State had concurred with the editorial revision, yet in the months that followed the editing of the ad conservatives took every opportunity to assail the modification as PC degeneracy. "This episode typifies the sorry state of higher education today: Academes are so afraid of offending people that they're afraid to ask for strong teachers," Debra Saunders, a columnist for the *San Francisco Chronicle*, blasted without bothering to explain her assumption that excellent teachers are not strong. In San Francisco's other paper, the *Examiner*, Paul Roberts of the Cato Institute suggested that the secret plan at Chico was to exclude white men from faculty positions. "All qualifications are restrictive, which explains their de-emphasis and the plight of overrepresented white males in our brave new world of equal outcomes," Roberts wrote.[29]

By this point in the PC scare sense and sensibility had become optional. Once a pseudodanger becomes so familiar it ends up in the dictionary (not to say the title of a popular TV show hosted by comedian Bill Maher), argument and evidence are dispensable. Indeed, in the late 1990s some of the best-known conservative columnists, no longer feeling obliged to diagnose particular incidents of political correctness in any depth, simply threw out bunches of ostensible examples. George Will, in a piece disparaging what he called "sensitivity-soaked Chico," went on to complain about an entry in a mail-order catalogue for kindling wood "felled by lightning or other natural causes." Even mail-order companies have to act PC, Will bemoaned, "lest the friends of trees have their feelings hurt." John Leo, of *U.S. News & World Report,* likewise included Chico in a laundry list of what he dubbed "p.c. crimes and misdemeanors." His sardonic subhead–"Wanted: Lethargic New Teacher"–was rather mild compared to some others in the same column. Beneath the heading "Tired of Education? Try Gender Courses" Leo warned that "p.c. folk" have been "working to replace useful college courses with dubious ones." He cited as examples "The Politics of Dance Performance" offered at Swarthmore and "Christianity, Violence and Victimization" at Brown.[30]

Both Leo and Will banked on the improbability that anyone would look into their examples. The courses Leo cited did not replace other courses; they were added as electives. Nor did the courses represent dubious additions to the curriculum. A well-educated student of a particular art form ought to know something about its political dimensions, and the serious study of a religion necessarily includes attention to dishonorable as well as glorious moments in its history. As for the mail-order catalogue–the company was merely trying to make an unexceptional product sound special, a common practice in direct marketing.

Success Doesn't Come Cheap

If so many of their examples were untenable, how did conservatives engender such a successful scare? How did it come about that *politically correct*, a phrase hardly used in the media prior to Bush's speech in

1991, appeared in the nation's major newspapers and magazines more than 5,000 times a year in the mid-1900s? In 1997, the last year for which data were available, it appeared 7,200 times.[31]

The short but not incorrect answer is money. Behind the scenes millions of dollars were spent to generate that level of noise. Right-wing foundations such as Coors, Olin, and Bradley, along with corporate and individual contributors, provided funding for a national network of organizations: such think tanks as the Cato Institute and American Enterprise Institute; conservative college newspapers, including the *Dartmouth Review*, where Dinesh D'Souza got his start; magazines such as William F. Buckley's *National Review* and David Horowitz's *Heterodoxy*; and faculty groups, most notably the National Association of Scholars. With an annual budget in the vicinity of $1 million, the NAS had the wherewithal to provide politicians and the press with an unending supply of sound bites, anecdotes, and op-eds.[32]

In an article in *Skeptic* magazine on what he termed "the great p.c. conspiracy hoax" Brian Siano of the University of Pennsylvania compared the strategies of the NAS to a national magazine that asks its readers to send in accounts of psychic experiences or sightings of flying saucers. Such a request would inevitably produce loads of testimonials. "One might be able to debunk one or two accounts, but the rest of this database would remain 'unchallenged,' to be trotted out by the faithful as often as possible," Siano suggests. "Now imagine," he adds, "if you could spend a half dozen years and millions of dollars on such a project."[33]

Siano's comparison is apt. The NAS continually collected reports of political correctness gone amiss, packaged the best, and peddled them to the media. Anyone who dared challenge the reports quickly discovered the power of NAS's home-court advantage. In 1996 after *USA Today* quoted an NAS official's assertion that Georgetown University, as part of a general "dumbing down" of its curriculum, had decided to drop Shakespeare as a requirement for English majors, the dean at Georgetown responded that the school was doing nothing of the sort. Georgetown's curriculum for English majors includes more, not fewer, Shakespeare classes than in the past, he pointed out. Moreover, re-

gardless of their major, all Georgetown students must complete twelve
courses of general-education requirements, including two literature
courses. This factual information from the dean did not appear,
though, in the news story, but only later, in a letter-to-the-editor
column.[34]

When Robert Brustein, artistic director of the American Repertory
Theater, picked up on NAS rhetoric and proclaimed that "most English
departments are now held so completely hostage to fashionable political and theoretical agendas that it is unlikely Shakespeare can qualify
as an appropriate author," journalists found the quote too juicy to resist.
The image appeared widely in the press of PC thugs in ivory towers
forcibly evicting the Bard. But when John Wilson, a graduate student at
the University of Chicago, suspicious of the claim, consulted data from
the Modern Language Association, he discovered that fully 97 percent
of English departments at four-year colleges offered at least one course
on Shakespeare. Almost two-thirds, he learned, required English majors to take a Shakespeare course. In the MLA's on-line bibliography,
Shakespeare received nearly 20,000 entries—more than three times the
next runner-up (James Joyce), and thirty-six times as many as Toni
Morrison, reported Wilson.[35] Wilson's correction to the NAS and
Brustein et al. appeared, however, in the *Chronicle of Higher Education*,
the equivalent of a trade magazine.

To the extent that great literary works were being withheld from
America's youth, PC forces were seldom to blame. The real censors,
though they received scant attention, were people like the school su-
perintendent in Maryland who banned Toni Morrison's *Song of Solomon*
in 1997 after some parents called the classic of African-American literature "trash" and "anti-white." And they were conservatives in the U.S.
Congress and state legislatures. "The real danger to Shakespeare,"
Katha Pollitt accurately noted in *The Nation*, "is not that he will cease to
be compulsory at elite colleges like Georgetown but that he will cease
to be made available and accessible to a broad range of students."
Throughout the 1980s and 1990s conservatives slashed budgets at the
National Endowment for the Humanities, the U.S. Department of Education, and other public programs. Among the unfortunate results of

those reductions in funding, such places as the Shakespeare Theater in Washington, Shakespeare and Company in Massachusetts, and the Folger Shakespeare Library had to curtail programs that train teachers and reach wide audiences.[36]

Conservative politicians had whipped up popular support for such cuts in the first place by—you guessed it—portraying the public agencies as hotbeds of political correctness.

One Scare Supports Another

Once a scare catches on, not only do its advocates have the offensive advantage, as the Shakespeare follies illustrate, but they can also use the scare as a defensive weapon in other disputes. This chapter concludes with an important case in point, in which the PC label was actually used to countermand a scientific fact.

Anyone who commuted by bus or train in the Washington, D.C., area during the mid-1990s or sought an abortion in the South in that period will probably remember this fear campaign. More than one thousand advertisements appeared in buses and subway stations around Washington and Baltimore alluding to a scary statistic: "Women who choose abortion suffer more and deadlier breast cancer." In Louisiana and Mississippi legislators passed laws that require doctors to inform women twenty-four hours before an abortion that the procedure can increase their risk of breast cancer.[37]

Some antiabortion activists had been pushing the point since the early 1980s, when it first became apparent that as the number of abortions rose in the years after 1973, when the procedure became legal, rates of breast cancer also increased. Not until 1994, however, did the news media pay much attention to prolifers' fear mongering. That year, the *Journal of the National Cancer Institute* published an article in which researchers estimated that having an abortion might raise a woman's risk of breast cancer by 50 percent.[38]

To their credit, journalists were circumspect about the study. In contrast to coverage of some other pseudodangers (road rage among them), the news media generally did an excellent job of putting in perspective the 50 percent figure. Reporters noted that other studies had found no increased risk, and that even if future research confirmed the figure, the import would be minimal for most women considering abortion. A 50 percent increased risk may sound large, but in epidemiologic terms it is not. It does not mean that if all women had abortions, half again as many would develop breast cancer; rather, it means that a woman's lifetime risk goes up by 50 percent. If she had a 10 percent probability of developing breast cancer, abortion would raise it to 15 percent. Heavy smoking, by comparison, increases the risk of developing lung cancer by 3,000 percent. Some studies suggest that living in a city or drinking one glass of alcohol a day raises the risk of breast cancer by greater than 50 percent.[39]

Reporters generally did a laudable job the following year as well, when anti-abortion groups heralded two more studies. One estimated a 30 percent increased risk of breast cancer for women who have abortions; the other put the figure at 23 percent. Journalists explained that both studies suffered, as had earlier research, from a potential reporting bias that could substantially skew their results. They quoted the lead researcher on one of the studies, the epidemiologist Polly Newcomb of the Hutchinson Cancer Research Center in Seattle, who noted that women battling breast cancer might be more likely than others to inform researchers that they had had abortions. Cancer patients are more accustomed to giving full and accurate medical histories, Newcomb suggested, and they are searching themselves for an explanation for their illness.[40]

Strikingly, the lead researcher on the other study in 1995, an endocrinologist at Baruch College named Joel Brind, offered no such caveats. On the contrary, he told CNN, "The evidence is quite clear, in fact, it should have been out long ago." Brind advocated that every woman considering abortion be informed of the potential increased risk of breast cancer. When reporters checked into Brind's background, however, they learned that he is an antiabortion activist who contributes frequently to newsletters and web sites published by prolife groups. Richard Knox of the *Boston Globe* reported that Brind told him he had conducted the study specifically to provide legislators with justification for requiring doctors to warn women about a cancer risk.[41]

With Brind as their medical mouthpiece, antiabortion groups intensified their scare drive throughout 1995 and 1996. Some persisted even after a massive study published in 1997 in the *New England Journal of Medicine* showed that the earlier research had been flawed in precisely the ways Polly Newcomb and other experts suspected. Conducted by epidemiologists from the University of Copenhagen, the later study relied not on self-reports but on data produced through the mandatory registration in Denmark of births, cancer cases, and abortions. The scientists were able to compare 281,000 women who had had abortions with 1.2 million others who had not. They determined that neither group was more likely to develop breast cancer.[42]

Joel Brind's rejoinder when a reporter from the *Washington Post* asked him to comment on the study? "This is an apparently large and powerful study with the politically correct result that is not scientifically correct," Brind said. At once reinforcing the PC scare and using it to defend another misbegotten terror, Brind vowed to continue his campaign of fear.[43]

2

CRIME IN THE NEWS

Tall Tales and
Overstated Statistics

If the mystery about baseless scares is how they are sold to a public that has real dangers to worry about, in the case of more defensible fears the question is somewhat different. We *ought* to have concerns about crime, drug addiction, child abuse, and other afflictions to be discussed. The question is, how have we gotten so mixed up about the true nature and extent of these problems?

In no small measure the answer lies in stories like one that broke on March 19, 1991. If you read a newspaper or turned on a TV or radio newscast that day or the several days thereafter you were told that the streets of America were more dangerous than a war zone.

The press had been provoked to make this extreme assertion not by a rise in violent crime but by a dramatic event. The Gulf War had just ended, and a soldier who returned home to Detroit had been shot dead outside his apartment building.

The front-page story in the *Washington Post* portrayed the situation this way:

> Conley Street, on this city's northeast side, is a pleasant-looking row of brick and wood homes with small, neat lawns, a street that for years was the realization of the American dream for middle-income families. But in the past few years, Conley has become a street of crack, crime and occasional bursts of gunfire. And at 2:15 a.m. Monday, the bullets killed Army Spec. Anthony Riggs, something that all of Iraq's Scud missiles could not do during his seven months with a Patriot missile battery in Saudi Arabia.

Described by his mother as a man who deeply loved his family and his country, Riggs had written home from Saudi Arabia, "There's no way I'm going to die in this rotten country. With the Lord's grace and his

23

guidance, I'll walk American soil once again." But before that letter even arrived, while Riggs was moving his wife and three-year-old daughter to a new apartment, five shots rang out and witnesses heard the sound of screeching tires. Some faceless thug had killed him just to get his car. "His wife, Toni, found him dying in a gutter," the *Post* reported.[1]

TV newscasts showed Mrs. Riggs sobbing. She had warned her husband that there had been a shooting on the street earlier in the day, but he wouldn't listen. "He said he'd just got back from having missiles flying over his head, and a few shots weren't going to bother him," according to Toni's aunt, quoted in the *Los Angeles Times*. That of course was the larger point, or as the *Post* put it, "Riggs's death was a tragic reminder of President Bush's words recently when he announced a new crime bill: 'Our veterans deserve to come home to an America where it is safe to walk the streets'."[2]

Oops, Wrong Story

From the point of view of journalists and editors an ideal crime story—that is, the sort that deserves major play and is sure to hold readers' and viewers' attention—has several elements that distinguish it from other acts of violence. The victims are innocent, likable people; the perpetrator is an uncaring brute. Details of the crime, while shocking, are easy to relay. And the events have social significance, bespeaking an underlying societal crisis.

The murder of Anthony Riggs seemed to have it all. The only problem was, very little of this perfect crime story was true. Reporters named the right victim but the wrong perpetrator, motive, and moral.

It was the massive media attention, ironically, that resulted in the real story coming out. Confronted with demands from politicians and citizen groups to catch Riggs's killer, the Detroit police launched an all-out investigation. While digging through garbage cans around the Conley Street neighborhood, an officer came upon a handgun that turned out to belong to Michael Cato, the brother of Riggs's wife, Toni. Nineteen years old at the time and currently serving a life sentence for murder, Michael said in a confession that his sister had promised him a share of $175,000 in life insurance benefits.

Reporters cannot be blamed for failing to possess this information prior to its discovery by the police, but had they been a little skeptical or made a few phone calls they almost certainly would have stumbled on at least some aspects of the truth. They might have learned, for example, that Toni had been making noises about dumping Anthony for some time, or that it was she who arranged a hefty life insurance policy for her husband before he went off to war. Reporters might also have checked into Mrs. Riggs's past and discovered previous irregularities, such as the fact that she had not yet divorced her previous husband when she married Anthony.

Journalists also might have discovered the existence of a letter Riggs wrote to his mother from Saudi Arabia. "Toni has wrecked my car. She is now bouncing checks. . . . She is never home: 2:30 A.M., 4 A.M. . . . I would put my head through the neck of a hot sauce bottle to please her, but now I need happiness in return," *People* magazine, the only major publication that subsequently ran a full-fledged account of the true story, quoted him penning.[3]

Had news writers checked with knowledgeable criminologists or homicide detectives they might have been impressed as well by the improbability of a car thief murdering someone execution-style when a simple shot or two would have done the job. Carjacking victims seldom get shot at all, particularly if they do not resist.[4]

Journalists generally pride themselves on being suspicious about information they are given. Your average journalist "wears his skepticism like a medieval knight wore his armor," Shelby Coffey, head of ABC News and former editor of the *Los Angeles Times*, has said. Yet when it comes to a great crime story, a journalist will behave like the high school nerd who has been approached by the most popular girl in school for help with her science project. Grateful for the opportunity, he doesn't bother to ask a lot of questions.[5]

There are discernible differences, though, between reporters for electronic versus print media. Unlike their colleagues at local television stations, who will go for any story that includes a police chase or a humiliated celebrity, journalists at newspapers and magazines have a particular fondness for crime stories that help them make sense of some other phenomenon they are having trouble covering in its own right. In the Riggs murder the phenomenon in question was the Gulf War. The news media had difficulty reporting accurately on the war because the Pentagon kept the press away from the action and used tightly scripted briefings to spoonfeed only what the generals and the president wanted known. As part of that spin Generals Colin Powell and Norman Schwarzkopf were defined as the war's heroes. Grunts on the battlefield and in the air seemed almost irrelevant to a war fought with smart bombs. Their homecoming consequently had little intrinsic meaning or news value. So when the Riggs murder came along, reporters eagerly used it to mark the end of the war on Iraq and the start of the next phase in the ongoing domestic war on crime.[6]

Oops, Wrong Crisis

If the news media merely got the facts wrong about an occasional homicide, that would be no big deal. But the significance they attach to many of the homicides and other violent crimes they choose to spotlight is another matter. The streets of America are not more dangerous than a war zone, and the media should not convey that they are.

Some places journalists have declared crime ridden are actually quite safe. Consider an article *Time* magazine ran in April 1994 headlined across the top of two pages: "Not a month goes by without an outburst of violence in the workplace—now even in flower nurseries, pizza parlors and law offices." One of literally thousands of stories published and broadcast on what was dubbed "the epidemic of workplace violence," *Time*'s article presented a smorgasbord of grisly photographs and vignettes of unsuspecting workers and managers brutally attacked by their coworkers or employees. "Even Americans who see a potential for violence almost everywhere like to suppose there are a few sanctuaries left. One is a desk, or a spot behind the counter, or a place on the assembly line," the writer sighed.[7]

More than five hundred stories about workplace violence appeared in newspapers alone just during 1994 and 1995, and many included some seriously scary statistics: 2.2 million people attacked on the job each year, murder the leading cause of work-related death for women, the number-three cause for men. "How can you be sure," asked a reporter for the *St. Petersburg Times*, "the person sitting next to you at work won't go over the edge and bring an Uzi to the office tomorrow?" Her answer was, "You can't."[8]

At least one journalist, however, grew leery of his colleagues' fear mongering. Erik Larson, a staff reporter for the *Wall Street Journal*, having come upon the same numbers quoted time and again, decided to take a closer look. The result was an exposé in the *Journal* titled "A False Crisis," in which Larson revealed how the news media had created an epidemic where none existed. Of about 121 million working people, about 1,000 are murdered on the job each year, a rate of just 1 in 114,000. Police, security guards, taxi drivers, and other particularly vulnerable workers account for a large portion of these deaths. Cab drivers, for instance, suffer an occupational homicide rate twenty-one times the national average. On the flip side of that coin, people in certain other occupations face conspicuously low levels of risk. The murder rate for doctors, engineers, and other professionals is about 1 in 457,000, Larson determined.[9]

Another vocational group with relatively low rates, it turns out, is postal workers. The expression "going postal" became part of the American vernacular after some particularly bloody assaults by U.S. Postal Service employees against their supervisors. Yet postal employees are actually about two and a half times *less* likely than the average worker to be killed on the job.[10]

All in all fewer than one in twenty homicides occurs at a workplace. And while most of the media hoopla has been about disgruntled workers killing one another or their bosses—the Uzi-toting fellow at the next desk—few workplace murders are actually carried out by coworkers or ex-workers. About 90 percent of murders at workplaces are committed by outsiders who come to rob. The odds of being killed by someone you work with or employ are less than 1 in 2 million; you are several times more likely to be hit by lightning.[11]

Larson deconstructed as well the survey that produced the relentlessly reproduced statistic of 2.2 million people assaulted at work each year. Most of the reported attacks were fairly minor and did not involve weapons, and once again, the great majority were committed by outsiders, not by coworkers, ex-employees, or bosses. What is more, the survey from which the number comes would not pass muster among social scientists, Larson points out. The response rate is too low. Fewer than half of the people contacted responded to the survey, making it likely that those who participated were not typical of employed Americans as a whole.[12]

Given that workplace violence is far from pandemic, why were journalists so inclined to write about it? Perhaps because workplace violence is a way of talking about the precariousness of employment without directly confronting what primarily put workers at risk—the endless waves of corporate layoffs that began in the early 1980s. Stories about workplace violence routinely made mention of corporate downsizing as one potential cause, but they did not treat mass corporate firing as a social ill in its own right. To have done so would have proven difficult for many journalists. For one thing, whom would they have cast as the villain of the piece? Is the CEO who receives a multimillion dollar raise for firing tens of thousands of employees truly evil? Or is he merely making his company more competitive in the global economy? And how would a journalist's boss—or boss's boss at the media conglomerate that owns the newspaper or network—feel about publishing implicit criticism of something they themselves have done? Pink slips arrived with regularity in newsrooms like everywhere else in corporate America in recent years, and they didn't exactly inspire reporters to do investigative pieces about downsizing.[13]

To its great credit, the *New York Times* did eventually run an excellent series of articles on downsizing in 1996. In one of the articles the authors noted off-handedly and without pursuing the point that about 50 percent more people are laid off each year than are victims of crime. It is an important comparison. From 1980 through 1995 more than 42

million jobs were eliminated in the United States. The number of jobs
lost per year more than doubled over that time, from about 1.5 million
in 1980 to 3.25 million in 1995. By comparison, during that same period most crime rates—including those for violent crimes—declined. A
working person was roughly four to five times more likely to be the victim of a layoff in any given year than to be the victim of a violent crime
committed by a stranger.[14]

For many, job loss is every bit as disabling and demoralizing as being the victim of a crime. You can lose your home, your health insurance, your self-esteem, your sense of security, and your willingness to
report harassment or hazardous working conditions at your next place
of employment. During the economic boom of the late 1990s layoffs
occurred at an even higher rate than in the 1980s. In what former Secretary of Labor Robert Reich dubbed "down-waging" and "down-bene-
fiting," highly profitable companies replaced full-time workers with
part-timers, temps, and lower-paid full-timers, and they subcontracted
work to firms that paid lower wages and provided poorer benefits. Yet
throughout the past two decades the news media printed and broadcast
exponentially more stories about crime. In the early and mid-1990s 20
to 30 percent of news items in city newspapers concerned crime, and
close to half of the news coverage on local television newscasts was
about crime.[15]

Unhappy Halloween

Workplace violence was not the first false crime crisis used by journalists as a roundabout way to talk about other matters they found difficult
to address directly. Even the *New York Times* has been known to engage
in the practice.

"Those Halloween goodies that children collect this weekend on
their rounds of 'trick or treating' may bring them more horror than
happiness," began a story in the *Times* in October 1970 that launched a
long-running crime panic. "Take, for example," the reporter continued,
"that plump red apple that Junior gets from a kindly old woman down
the block. It may have a razor blade hidden inside. The chocolate

'candy' bar may be a laxative, the bubble gum may be sprinkled with lye, the popcorn balls may be coated with camphor, the candy may turn out to be packets containing sleeping pills."[16]

Similar articles followed in the nation's news media every autumn for years to come. In 1975 *Newsweek* reported in its edition that hit newsstands at the end of October, "If this year's Halloween follows form, a few children will return home with something more than an upset tummy: in recent years, several children have died and hundreds have narrowly escaped injury from razor blades, sewing needles and shards of glass purposefully put into their goodies by adults."[17]

In her columns of the mid- and late 1980s even "Dear Abby" was reminding parents around trick-or-treat time that "somebody's child will become violently ill or die after eating poisoned candy or an apple containing a razor blade." An ABC News/*Washington Post* poll in 1985 showed that 60 percent of parents feared their kids could become victims.[18]

This time no journalist stepped forward to correct the media's and public's collective fantasy, even though, as Jan Harold Brunvand, the folklorist and author observed, "it's hard to imagine how someone could shove a blade into a fruit without injuring himself. And wouldn't the damage done to the apple by such a process make it obvious that something was wrong with it?"[19]

The myth of Halloween bogeymen and bogeywomen might never have been exposed had not a sociologist named Joel Best become sufficiently leery that he undertook an examination of every reported incident since 1958. Best, currently a professor at the University of Southern Illinois, established in a scholarly article in 1985 that there has not been a single death or serious injury. He uncovered a few incidents where children received minor cuts from sharp objects in their candy bags, but the vast majority of reports turned out to be old-fashioned hoaxes, sometimes enacted by young pranksters, other times by parents hoping to make money in lawsuits or insurance scams.[20]

Ironically, in the only two known cases where children apparently did die from poisoned Halloween candy, the myth of the anonymous, sadistic stranger was used to cover up the real crime. In the first incident family members sprinkled heroin on a five-year-old's Halloween candy in hopes of fooling the police about the cause of the child's death. Actually, the boy had found and eaten heroin in his uncle's home. In the second incident a boy died after eating cyanide-poisoned candy on Halloween, but police determined that his father had spiked the candy to collect insurance money. Bill Ellis, a professor of English at Penn State University, has commented that both of these incidents, reported in the press at first as stranger murders, "reinforced the moral of having parents examine treats—ironically, because in both cases family members were responsible for the children's deaths!"[21]

Yet if anonymous Halloween sadists were fictitious creatures, they were useful diversions from some truly frightening realities, such as the fact that far more children are seriously injured and killed by family members than by strangers. Halloween sadists also served in news stories as evidence that particular social trends were having ill effects on the populace. A psychiatrist quoted in the *New York Times* article held that Halloween sadism was a by-product of "the permissiveness in today's society." The candy poisoner him- or herself was not directly to blame, the doctor suggested. The real villains were elsewhere. "The people who give harmful treats to children see criminals and students in campus riots getting away with things," the *Times* quoted him, "so they think they can get away with it, too."[22]

In many of these articles the choice of hero also suggests that other social issues are surreptitiously being discussed. At a time when divorce rates were high and rising, and women were leaving home in great numbers to take jobs, news stories heralded women who represented the antithesis of those trends—full-time housewives and employed moms who returned early from work to throw safe trick-or-treat parties for their children and their children's friends in their homes or churches, or simply to escort their kids on their rounds and inspect the treats.[23]

Kiddie Porn and Cyberpredators

The Halloween tales were forerunners of what grew into a media staple of the last quarter of the twentieth century: crime stories in which innocent children fall victim to seemingly innocuous adults who are really perverts. The villains take several familiar forms, two of the more common being the child pornographer and his or her pedophile customers.

A report on NBC News in 1977 let it be known that "as many as two million American youngsters are involved in the fast-growing, multi-million dollar child-pornography business"—a statement that subsequent research by criminologists and law enforcement authorities determined to be wrong on every count. Kiddie porn probably grossed less than $1 million a year (in contrast to the multibillion dollar adult industry), and hundreds, not millions, of American children were involved. Once again, facts were beside the point. The child pornographer represented, as columnist Ellen Goodman observed at the time, an "unequivocal villain" whom reporters and readers found "refreshingly uncomplicated." Unlike other pornographers, whose exploits raise tricky First Amendment issues, child pornographers made for good, simple, attention-grabbing copy.[24]

A conspicuous subtext in coverage during the late 1970s and 1980s was adult guilt and anxiety about the increasing tendency to turn over more of children's care to strangers. Raymond Buckey and Peggy Buckey McMartin, proprietors of the McMartin Preschool in Manhattan Beach, California, were the most famous alleged child pornographers of the era. Their prosecution in the mid-1980s attracted a level of media hoopla unsurpassed until O. J. Simpson's double-murder trial nearly a decade later, and from the start they were depicted as pedophiles and child pornographers. The local TV news reporter who first broke the McMartin story declared in his initial report that children had been "made to appear in pornographic films while in the preschool's care." The media later quoted officials from the district attorney's office, making statements about "millions of child pornography photographs and films" at the school.[25]

Not a single pornographic photograph taken at the McMartin School has ever been produced, despite handsome offers of reward money and vast international police investigations. Yet thanks to the media coverage, when social scientists from Duke University conducted a survey in 1986, four out of five people said they believed that Raymond Buckey was part of a child pornography ring.[26]

In more recent years child pornographers and pedophiles have come in handy for fear mongering about the latest variety of baby-sitter: the Internet. In the 1990s politicians and the news media have made much of the existence of pedophilia in cyberspace. Speaking in 1998 on behalf of legislation he drafted that makes it easier to convict "cyberpredators" and imprison them longer, Representative Bill McCollum of Florida made the customary claim: "Sex offenders who prey on children no longer need to hang out in parks or malls or school yards." Nowadays, warned McCollum, child pornographers and pedophiles are just "a mouse click away" from their young prey.[27]

This time the panic did not rely so much on suspicious statistics as on peculiar logic. With few cases of youngsters having been photographed or attacked by people who located them on-line, fear mongers found it more convenient simply to presume that "as the number of children who use the Internet continues to boom . . . pornography and pedophilia grow along with it" (*New York Times*). Reporters portrayed the inhabitants of cyberspace, children and adults alike, in somewhat contradictory ways. About the kids they said, on the one hand, "Internet-savvy children can also easily access on-line pornography" (*New York Times*). On the other hand, reporters depicted computer-proficient kids as precisely the *opposite* of savvy. They described them as defenseless against pedophiles and child pornographers in cyberspace. "Depraved people are reaching right into your home and touching your child," Hugh Downs told viewers of ABC's "20/20."[28]

To judge from reports by some of the people featured in news reports, cyberspace was largely devoid of other adults who could protect children from these creeps. The Internet is "a city with no cops," the *New York Times* quoted a district attorney from Suffolk County, even though law enforcement officials actually do a great deal of lurking and entrapping. Since 1993 the FBI has conducted an operation code-named "Innocent Images" in which agents assume false identities and post seductive messages on the Internet and on-line services. In one of the more highly publicized busts that resulted from the operation, a thirty-one-year-old Washington, D.C., attorney was arrested when he showed up at a shopping mall to meet a fourteen-year-old girl whom he

had propositioned on-line for sex. In reality he had been correspond-
ing with an adult FBI agent who had assumed a provocative on-line
name—"One4fun4u"—and had sent the man messages stating that she'd
had experience with an older man and "it was a lot of fun." In another
arrest, a fifty-eight-year-old man was snagged by agents who used the
names "Horny15bi" and "Sexcollctr" and described themselves on-line
as "dreaming of kinky sex." One of them gave as her motto, "vice is
nice but incest is best."[29]

Cyberspace has been policed by other adults as well. Reporters for
newspapers and television stations, posing as young teens or preteens,
have responded to solicitations for sex, only to arrive at the agreed-on
meeting place with cameras and cops in tow. Groups with names like
"Cyber Angels" and "Safeguarding Our Children" collect information
on pedophiles via e-mail from children who say they have been approached or molested. Members of adult vigilante groups make it a
practice to disrupt Internet chat rooms where child pornography is
traded and pass along information to police.[30]

While judicial experts continue to debate which of these interven-
tion strategies constitute entrapment or invasion of privacy, there is an
extralegal question as well. David L. Sobel, an attorney with the Electronic Privacy Information Center, framed the question succinctly. "Are
we making the world a better place," he asked rhetorically, "by tempt-
ing some of these people to commit crimes they may not have otherwise committed?"[31]

Subtract from the battery of accounts in news stories all instances
where the "children" lured out of cyberspace were actually undercover
adults, and what remains? Several of the most widely covered incidents
involving real children turn out to be considerably more ambiguous
than they seem on first hearing. Take for instance the murder of eleven-
year-old Eddie Werner in a suburb in New Jersey in 1997. Defined in the
media as the work of a "Cyber Psycho" (*New York Post* headline) and
proof that the Internet is, as an advocacy group put it, "a playground for
pedophiles," the killing actually bore only a tertiary connection to the
Net. Eddie Werner had not been lured on-line. He was killed while selling holiday items door to door for the local PTA. Reporters and activists
made the link to the Internet by way of Werner's killer, Sam Manzie, a

fifteen-year-old who had been having sex in motel rooms throughout the previous year with a middle-aged man he had met in a chat room.

In an essay critical of the reporting about the Werner murder *Newsweek* writer Steven Levy correctly pointed out: "Cyberspace may not be totally benign, but in some respects it has it all over the often overrated real world. After all, one could argue, if young Eddie Werner had been selling his candy and gift-wrapping paper on the Internet, and not door to door, tragedy might not have struck."[32]

In that same vein, consider a suspenseful yarn that took up much of the space in a front-page piece in the *Los Angeles Times* entitled "Youngsters Falling Prey to Seducers in Computer Web Crime." It was about a fifteen-year-old whose parents found him missing. Using the boy's America Online account, they discovered that he had been sent a bus ticket to visit a man with whom he had communicated by e-mail. The parents frantically sent messages of their own to the man. "Daniel is a virgin," one of the parents' outgoing messages said. "Oh, no, he's not," came back the chilling reply. Yet when the reporter gets to the conclusion of Daniel's saga it's something of an anticlimax. The teenager returned home and informed his parents he had not been harmed by his e-mail companion, who was only a little older than Daniel himself. Nonetheless, the moral of Daniel's story was, according to the *Los Angeles Times* reporter: "Such are the frightening new frontiers of cyberspace, a place where the child thought safely tucked away in his or her own room may be in greater danger than anyone could imagine."[33]

Now *there's* a misleading message. For those children most at risk of sexual abuse, to be left alone in their rooms with a computer would be a godsend. It is poor children—few of whom have America Online connections—who are disproportionately abused, and it is in children's own homes and those of close relatives that sexual abuse commonly occurs. In focusing on creeps in cyberspace, reporters neatly skirt these vital facts and the discomforting issues they raise.[34]

Raw Numbers and Pedophile Priests

The news media have misled public consciousness all the more through their voracious coverage of pedophiles in another place that many Americans privately distrust and consider mysterious—the Catholic Church.

John Dreese, a priest of the diocese of Columbus, Ohio, justifiably complained that a generation of Catholic clergy find their "lifetimes of service, fairly faithful for the great majority, are now tarnished and besmirched by the constant drone of the TV reporting." Writing in *Commonweal*, the independently published Catholic magazine, Dreese acknowledged that some of his fellow priests abuse children, and he decried the bishops who let them get away with it. But the media, Dreese argues, "seem more and more ideological. 'Roman Catholic priest' or 'Father' are consistently used in their reporting. Rarely is the generic term of minister or simply, priest, used. Shots of the inside of a Roman Catholic church, of angelic altar boys in cassocks and surplices, and first communicants dressed in pure white dramatically highlight the bold betrayal of this crime."[35]

Asks Dreese, "Is this responsible reporting, is it sensationalism, or is it Catholic bashing?" It is a question that warrants serious consideration by reporters and editors who have been much too accepting of evidence of "epidemics" of priestly pedophilia. The media paid considerable attention, for example, to pronouncements from Andrew M. Greeley, a priest best known as the author of best-selling potboilers, including *Fall from Grace*, a 1993 novel about a priest who rapes preadolescent boys. Although Greeley holds a professorship in the social sciences at the University of Chicago, his statements on pedophiles in the priesthood oddly conflict with one another and with principles of statistical reasoning to which he subscribes in other contexts. "If Catholic clerics feel that charges of pedophilia have created an open season on them," he wrote in an op-ed piece in the *New York Times*, "they have only themselves to blame. By their own inaction and indifference they have created an open season on children for the few sexual predators among them." Yet in a Jesuit magazine Greeley declared that the number of pedophile priests is far more than just a "few". There he estimated that 2,000 to 4,000 Roman Catholic clergy—between 4 and 8 percent of the total—had abused more than 100,000 young people.[36]

These shocking statistics, dutifully publicized in the press, were unreliable to say the least. Greeley extrapolated the number of pedophile priests based on rough estimates from the Catholic Archdiocese of Chicago, which based them on their own internal study, which may or may not have been accurate, and in any event, might not have generalized to clergy nationwide. As for the figure of 100,000 victims, Greeley came up with this estimate on the basis of studies of child molesters outside the priesthood that suggest that active pedophiles victimize dozens if not hundreds of children each. Yet these studies are themselves controversial because they rely on self-reports from men who were apprehended by the police—men who might molest more children than other pedophiles or exaggerate their exploits.[37]

Greeley's critics suggest he exaggerated the number of pedophiles and victims by something like a factor of ten. But whatever the true incidence, the amount of ink and airtime devoted to pedophile priests clearly has created a climate in which, on the one hand, the church has reason to disavow true claims, and on the other, con artists have leverage to bring false claims. Attorneys who specialize in bringing suits against the church and have collected multimillion dollar settlements say they see large numbers of false claims.[38]

The political essayist Walter Russell Mead pointed out a more subtle disservice of the media's focus. In reporting on perverted priests journalists presumably believe they are raising a larger issue about the moral collapse of one of humankind's oldest and most influential spiritual institutions. As Mead points out, however, obsessive attention to pedophile priests obscures more far-reaching problems of the church. He cites in particular corruption in political parties the church has supported in Europe, and a loss of membership in various parts of the world. These trends are considerably more difficult for the press to cover, especially in a manner that audiences will find interesting. Yet they are far more pertinent indicators of the decline and corruption of the church than are pedophile priests. "After all, the church does not teach that its clergy are saints—just the opposite," notes Mead. "Sin is with us every day, says the Catholic Church, and it deliberately teaches that the efficacy of its sacraments and the accuracy of its teachings are

independent of the moral failings of its bishops and priests. From a certain point of view, the sex scandals don't so much disprove the Christian faith as confirm our need for it."[39]

Strange and Sinister Men

In my review of news stories about crimes against children I have been
struck by the frequency with which journalists draw unsubstantiated
conclusions about the pedophilic tendencies of individuals and whole
classes of people.

When a man named Thomas Hamilton gunned down sixteen elementary school children, their teacher, and himself in tiny Dunblane,
Scotland, in March 1996, the event took center stage in the American
news media, much of which portrayed Hamilton as one in a large but
nearly invisible breed of child predators, any of whom might, without
warning, go out and massacre children. "The villain, all too predictably, was an embittered loner and suspected pedophile," wrote
Newsweek. "He was," a columnist for the magazine said in an accompa-
nying piece, "a slightly elderly, crazed version of the social category
that now menaces our societies more than any other: the single male
who has no hope."[40]

The columnist offered up no evidence in support of this slur against
solitary bachelors. He would be hard pressed to do so, in particular
with regard to the danger they pose to women and children. Married
men, having greater access to these groups, commit the lion's share of
violence against them. The pedophile connection is also tenuous. Child
murderers may be *suspected* pedophiles, but only a small number are
confirmed or confessed pedophiles. In the case of Thomas Hamilton,
most major news outlets hinted at his pedophilia or quoted townspeo-
ple who asserted it outright, but on the basis of blatantly weak evidence. As a Reuters news agency story noted, "What really bothered
people were the pictures, often showing boys stripped to the waist for
physical activity—nothing sinister in that, but unsettling, neighbors and
acquaintances said."[41]

Reuters's story on Hamilton was more balanced than many. Other print and broadcast journalists let audiences make what they would of the fact that Hamilton had been kicked out of his post as a scout leader for "inappropriate behavior." Reuters disclosed that, according to the scouting association itself, he had been sacked not for child molesting but for incompetence.[42]

Another interesting fact came out in *People* magazine. Although *People*'s reporters made much of Hamilton's "penchant for photographing boys bare-chested," they let it be known that when town officials shut down a boys' club Hamilton had started, seventy parents and forty-five boys signed a petition saying he had great talent and integrity. "We are all proud to have Mr. Hamilton in charge of our boys," the petition declared. Hamilton himself, in a letter he sent to the news media just before his killing spree, professed he was "not a pervert" and insinuated that it was whispers to the contrary around Dunblane that had driven him to his heinous act.[43]

Still, in their stories about him some journalists were no better than the small-town gossips. They rekindled age-old prejudices linking homosexuality and pedophilia. *Newsweek* ran a sidebar titled "Strange and Sinister," which consisted of a photograph of Hamilton standing beside a boy (fully clothed) and allegations that he was a pedophile who had been caught by police "in a gay red-light district" in Edinburgh "in a compromising position."[44]

Homophobia is a recurring element in journalists' coverage of mass murderers. Research by Philip Jenkins, a professor of history and religious studies at Penn State University, shows that the media routinely emphasize the supposed homosexuality and pedophilia of men who commit multiple murders. News stories over the past quarter century about Randy Kraft, Westley Alan Dodd, John Wayne Gacy, Jeffrey Dahmer, and assorted other killers included phrases like "homosexual homicide horror" and "homosexual sadist." As Jenkins notes, "Emphasizing that such individuals were gay serial killers tended to confound homosexuals with pedophiles and to support contemporary claims that homosexuality represented a physical and moral threat to children."[45]

Studies of pedophiles solidly refute such claims, of course. One recent study published in the medical journal *Pediatrics* indicates that a child is about a hundred times more likely to be molested by the heterosexual partner of a close relative than by a homosexual. Other research finds that many of the men who molest children not only are not gay, they despise gays. In failing to make note of such research in articles where they represent men like Thomas Hamilton as gay pedophiles, journalists do more than misguide those who read or watch their reports; they feed right-wing groups with material that is then used in interviews with the press and in membership solicitations as evidence that gays "seduce our children," as Lou Sheldon put it in a solicitation mailing for his Traditional Values Coalition.[46]

Stealth Weapons

One media commentator did provide an astute assessment of Thomas Hamilton and the search for deeper meaning that his butchery provoked. "We seem to think a monstrous effect must arise from a monstrous cause. But not much evidence turned up to make the eruption possible," suggested Lance Morrow in an essay in *Time* magazine. To depict Hamilton's abominable act as a "pedophiliac-itch-gone-violent" was, Morrow wrote, "inadequate, trivializing . . . almost sacrilegious in its asymmetry." In point of fact no one knows why Thomas Hamilton snapped. The headmaster at the school where the shooting occurred got it right when he said, shortly after the slaughter, "We don't understand it and I don't think we ever will."[47]

Which is not to say that these deaths are inexplicable. Actually, four causes of the bloodbath in Dunblane can readily be identified. That the American news media barely managed to mention them is shameful. They were at once the most proximate and the most verifiable factors in the children's death.

I refer to the two revolvers and two semiautomatic pistols Hamilton used to carry out the carnage. Without his guns Hamilton never would have been able to slay so many people. More rigorous enforcement of Britain's gun licensing laws unquestionably had been warranted in

Hamilton's case. At the local gun clubs Hamilton had a reputation for being unstable, and he was refused membership by one of the clubs five weeks before the killings. And several years before the bloodbath at the school, when a mother accused him of molesting some boys, Hamilton reportedly threatened her with a gun.[48]

Yet many American reporters brushed all this aside. "There were demands for even tougher gun laws in a country where gun homicides are about as common as water buffalo," *Newsweek* brusquely remarked. "In the days after the bloodletting, there were the predictable calls to toughen the country's gun control laws even further," said *People*.[49]

Some of the European press, however, got the point. An editorial in the British newspaper the *Daily Mail* asked the question that by rights should have been at the heart of all of the news media's coverage of the Dunblane massacre: "Why should any private individual be legally allowed to own hand guns that can cause such carnage?" Their answer: "Whatever gun club apologists and sporting enthusiasts may say, there was nothing sporting about the caliber of the weapons which Hamilton was licensed to hoard in his own home. These were not small bore pistols for target practice. They were not suitable for shooting game birds. They are the macho tools of the killer's trade."[50]

Some American reporters and editors have swallowed so much baloney fed to them by the gun lobby they cough up explanations for gun deaths that credit everything *except* guns. They even blame their own industry. A columnist in *Newsweek* wrote of the Dunblane massacre, "Onanistic solitude, lived out in a fantasy world ruled by terror and thrilled by incessant gunfire, poses a lethal combination. Media moguls, enriched by promoting these fantasies, deny any blame for society's degradation. They are only giving society what it demands, they say."[51]

Blame It on the Tube

In other words, it is the guns on TV that cause people to die in real life. Numerous American journalists, including some of the most intelligent among them, have actively endorsed the dizzy proposition that television creates "a reality of its own that may crowd out our real reality," as Daniel Schorr, a network news correspondent for twenty-nine years before he moved to National Public Radio, put it. In an essay in the *Christian Science Monitor* Schorr gave as a case example John Hinckley, who "spent many hours alone in a room with a TV set, retreating into a world of fantasy violence" before his attempted assassination of President Ronald Reagan. Interviewed by the Secret Service after the shooting, his first question was, "Is it on TV?" Schorr also rehearsed familiar statistics about the average eighteen-year-old having witnessed 200,000 acts of violence, including 40,000 murders, on the tube. At these levels of exposure, Schorr contended, young people "no longer know the difference between the bang-bang they grow up with on the television screen and the bang-bang that snuffs out real lives."[52]

He may be right, but some of the historical antecedents of this line of reasoning are worth noting. During the golden age of radio scholars produced studies showing that listening impaired young people's capacity to distinguish reality from fantasy. And centuries earlier Plato cautioned against those who would tell stories to youngsters. "Children cannot distinguish between what is allegory and what isn't," says Socrates in Plato's *Republic*, "and opinions formed at that age are difficult to change."[53]

That society survived both the radio and the scroll should be of some reassurance. So should a recent study from UCLA's Center for Communication Policy, which carefully analyzed 3,000 hours of TV programming on the major networks in the mid-1990s. The study found that a large proportion of the most sinister and decontextualized acts of violence on TV appear in cartoon shows such as "Batman and Robin" and on goofy prime-time programs such as "America's Funniest Home Videos," neither of which is likely to be confused with real life. By contrast, some of the most homicidal shows, such as "NYPD Blue" and "Homicide," portrayed violence as horribly painful and destructive and not to be treated lightly.[54]

In a discerning op-ed piece in the *New York Times* author Patrick Cooke made a parallel observation: If young Americans have seen tens of thousands of murders on TV, surely, he commented, they have seen even more acts of kindness. On sitcoms, romantic comedies, movies of the week, soaps, medical dramas, and even on police shows, people are constantly falling in love and helping each other out. The characters on most prime-time shows "share so much peace, tolerance and understanding that you might even call it gratuitous harmony," Cooke observes. Why not conclude, he asks, that TV encourages niceness at least as much as it encourages violence?[55]

Yet social scientists who study relationships between TV violence and real-world violence, and whose research journalists, politicians, and activists cite in fear mongering about crime on TV, do not make niceness one of their outcome measures. They also neglect to pursue some important cross-cultural comparisons.

Some of the most seemingly persuasive studies relate what people watched as children to how aggressive or violent they are as adults. A heavy diet of TV brutality early in life correlates with violent behavior later on, the researchers demonstrate. Whether these correlations truly prove that TV violence provokes actual violence has been questioned, however, by social scientists who propose as a counterhypothesis that people already predisposed to violence are particularly attracted to violent TV programs. Equally important, when researchers outside the United States try to replicate these studies they come up empty-handed. Researchers in several countries find no relationship between adults' levels of violence and the amount of TV violence they watched as kids.[56]

One widely quoted researcher who has made cross-national comparisons is Brandon Centerwall, a professor of psychiatry at the University of Washington, who has estimated that there would be 10,000 fewer murders each year in the United States and 700,000 fewer assaults had TV never been invented. Centerwall based these numbers on an analysis of crime rates before and after the introduction of television in particular towns in Canada and South Africa. But what about present-time comparisons? David Horowitz, head of the Center for the Study of Popular Culture, a conservative advocacy organization, correctly points out that viewers in Detroit, Michigan, see the same TV shows as viewers in Windsor, Ontario, just across the river. Yet the murder rate in Detroit has been thirty times that in Windsor.[57]

TV shows do not kill or maim people. Guns do. It is the unregulated possession of guns, more than any other factor, that accounts for the disparity in fatality rates from violent crime in the United States compared to most of the world. The inadequate control of guns often accounts for the loss of life in dramatic crime incidents outside the United States as well–the massacre in Dunblane, Scotland, being a case in point. A difference between there and here, however, is that they accept the point and act on it. After the Dunblane tragedy the House of Commons strengthened Britain's already ardent gun laws by outlawing all handguns larger than .22 caliber.[58]

True Causation

This is not to say that there isn't too much violence on the box–both on entertainment programs and on newscasts that precede and follow them, which, as Steven Bochco, creator of "Hill Street Blues," "NYPD Blue," and other police shows has noted, contain more gore than anything the networks air during prime time. A study published in the *Journal of the American Medical Association* in 1997 found that even advertisements feature violence–and not only on programs whose content is violent. A child who watched a game of the World Series in 1996 was almost certain to see commercials that included shootings, stabbings, or other violence, the study documented.[59]

Nor do I imagine that televised violence has no negative impact. I doubt, however, that incitement to commit real-world violence is either the most common or the most significant effect. George Gerbner, Dean-emeritus of the Annenberg School of Communication at the University of Pennsylvania, is closer to the mark with what he calls "the mean-world syndrome." Watch enough brutality on TV and you come to believe you are living in a cruel and gloomy world in which you feel vulnerable and insecure. In his research over three decades Gerbner found that people who watch a lot of TV are more likely than others to believe their neighborhoods are unsafe, to assume that crime rates are rising, and to overestimate their own odds of becoming a victim. They also buy more locks, alarms, and–you guessed it–guns, in hopes of protecting themselves. "They may accept and even welcome," Gerbner reports, "repressive measures such as more jails, capital punishment, harsher sentences—measures that have never reduced crime but never fail to get votes—if that promises to relieve their anxieties. That is the deeper dilemma of violence-laden television."[60]

Questions might be raised about whether Gerbner got the causal order right. (Does watching TV cause fear and conservatism, or is it that people prone to fear and conservatism watch more TV?) Yet it is striking how much resistance Gerbner encountered when he tried to report his research findings to the public. Frequently invited to speak on news programs and at governmental hearings where violence in the media is the topic, he finds himself ignored when he raises broader concerns. Appearing on ABC's "Viewpoint" back in 1983, Gerbner was asked by the host, Ted Koppel, "Is there a direct causal relationship to violence in our society?" A few minutes later, in the course of interviewing another panelist on the program, Koppel summarized Gerbner's response to that question as affirmative, there *is* a straightforward causal relationship between TV violence and real-life violence. Yet Gerbner's actual response had asserted that the true causal relationship is "between exposure to violence and one's feeling of where one belongs in the power structure—one's feeling of vulnerability, one's feeling of insecurity, one's demand for protection."[61]

Ample real-world evidence in support of Gerbner's proposition can be found among the nation's elderly, many of whom are so upset by all the murder and mayhem they see on their television screens that they are terrified to leave their homes. Some become so isolated, studies found, that they do not get enough exercise and their physical and mental health deteriorates. In the worst cases they actually suffer malnutrition as a consequence of media-induced fear of crime. Afraid to go out and buy groceries, they literally waste away in their homes. The pattern becomes self-perpetuating; the more time elderly people spend at home, the more TV they tend to watch, and the more fearful they grow.[62]

All of which is regrettable because in actuality people over sixty-five are less likely than any other age group to become victims of violent crime—about sixteen times less likely than people under twenty-five, according to statistics from the Justice Department. The news media report these statistics on occasion, but more commonly they depict the elderly in the manner a *Boston Globe* article did, as "walking time bombs for crime, easy prey." They speciously tell their older readers, as did the *Los Angeles Times*, "that a violent encounter—one that a younger person could easily survive—may end lethally for them: A purse-snatching becomes a homicide when an old woman falls to the pavement and dies in the hospital; an old man is brutalized and dies when he loses his will to live; an elderly couple are unable to flee their home during an arson fire, dying in the flames."[63]

Journalists further drive home this mistaken message through their coverage of crimes committed against famous older people. After Rosa Parks, the civil rights heroine, was beaten and robbed in her Detroit home in 1994 at the age of eighty-one, the *Washington Post* talked of "weak and elderly citizens living at the mercy of street thugs." Although violent crime against senior citizens had dropped by 60 percent in the previous twenty years, the *Post* went on to declare in an editorial, "What happened to Rosa Parks in Detroit is a common, modern-day outrage that quietly takes place across our land."[64]

Immediately following the attack on Parks her neighbors had expressed concern that media hype would further stigmatize their neighborhood and city, and Parks herself urged reporters not to read too much into the event. Ignoring Parks's own view that she had been assaulted by "a sick-minded person," reporters painted her assailant as "a self-involved brute" who "probably thought that as nice as all that civil rights stuff was, he was kicking the butt of just another now-useless old lady who was holding $50," as another *Washington Post* writer remarked.[65]

To hear the news media tell it, America's youth make a sport of victimizing old folks. *USA Today*, in a roundup article on crime against the elderly, told of Nathaniel Hurt, sixty-one, of Baltimore, who shot and killed a thirteen-year-old boy who had vandalized his property. Hurt said he had had enough of neighborhood teens taunting him. In their article *USA Today* neither depicted Hurt's actions as vigilantism nor provided information about the boy Hurt murdered. Instead, the moral of the story came from Hurt's lawyer: "Police don't want to admit that elderly people in Baltimore can't go out their door without fear."[66]

Crimes Nouveaux: Granny Dumping

The elderly can trust no one, politicians and reporters suggest. Everyone, including those entrusted to care for them, and even their own flesh and blood, may be potential victimizers.

"The American College of Emergency Physicians estimates that 70,000 elderly Americans were abandoned last year by family members unable or unwilling to care for them or pay for their care," the *New York Times* reported in an editorial that followed a front-page story heralding a major new trend. "Granny dumping," as it was called, attracted media attention after an incident in Idaho in 1992. John Kingery, a wheelchair-bound eighty-two-year-old Alzheimer's patient who suffered from incontinence, was abandoned at a dog-racing track by his middle-aged daughter. "John Kingery is no isolated case," said the *Times* editorial, which, along with other accounts in the media, attributed granny dumping to the strains adult children endure in trying to care for their ailing parents.[67]

In point of fact, however, John Kingery *was* a relatively isolated case. When Leslie Bennetts, a freelance writer and former *New York Times* reporter, looked more closely at the Kingery story several weeks later she discovered that Kingery's daughter had not been caring for her father in the first place; moreover, she had been stealing his pension and Social Security money. Bennetts also looked into how the *Times* had arrived at the alarming 70,000 figure and discovered it had not come from the American College of Emergency Physicians but rather from dubious extrapolations made by a *Times* reporter based on a casual, nonscientific survey that ACEP had conducted. Out of 900 emergency room doctors who had been sent a questionnaire only 169 responded, and they reported seeing an average of 8 abandoned elders per week. The *Times* reporter multiplied 8 by 52 weeks and then by 169 to produce the 70,000 statistic.

Even were this a reasonable way to come up with an incidence rate (which it is not), few actual incidents remotely resemble what happened to John Kingery. In the ACEP survey the definition of granny dumping was very broad: a woman who lived by herself and checked into an emergency room for help qualified. "Moreover," writes Bennetts in a debunking piece in the *Columbia Journalism Review*, "even a cursory check of emergency physicians reveals that the most common 'parent-dumping' problem is quite temporary, not the kind of permanent abandonment implied by the *Times*." A typical dumping incident consists of caretakers who put an old person in the hospital over a weekend so they can rest up for a couple of days.[68]

Like Halloween sadism, workplace violence, gay-pedophile mass murder, and so many other *crimes nouveaux*, granny dumping was considerably less common, sensational, or pressing than the media made out. Like other scares about maltreatment of the elderly, the granny dumping scare played off the younger generations' guilt while letting the individual reader or viewer off the hook by focusing on particularly evil people.

Even in coverage of the sorry state of many of the nation's nursing homes the root problems of lack of funding and inadequate oversight disappear amid overdrawn images of evil caretakers. "We found them coast to coast in the best of places. Thugs, rapists, suspected thieves," blares the announcer at the beginning of an edition of ABC's "20/20". "We caught them red-handed rifling through drawers in nursing homes, pocketing valuables and, worst of all, abusing your elderly loved ones." The story, which takes up most of the broadcast, relays incident upon incident of nursing home aides with lengthy criminal records who allegedly robbed and mistreated residents. "Most nursing home owners are not a bit careful about who they hire," someone identified as a former nursing home inspector says, and ABC correspondent Catherine Crier tells of patients being raped and beaten.[69]

Only in passing does Crier note that the pay nursing home aides receive "is notoriously low" for a job that is "difficult and often unpleasant." Nor does the report deal with problems that, unlike rape and other forms of assault, occur on a regular basis in American nursing homes. (According to some reports, 40 percent of nursing home residents suffer from malnutrition, to take one urgent example.)[70]

No, as Crier herself says at the very beginning of her report, "This is not a story about bad conditions in nursing homes, it's about bad people who end up working there." It is, in other words, another in the endless cache of stories about villains and victims, stories in which real people in their real complexity and the real dangers they and the larger society face can be glimpsed only in the shadows.

3

YOUTH AT RISK

Faulty Diagnoses and Callous Cures

America's children face far graver dangers than parents realize. Journalists, politicians, and advocacy organizations reiterate that conclusion incessantly. One way they reiterate it, as we have seen, is through stories about sexual predators in churches, schools, and cyberspace. Another is by asserting that children face huge hazards that the public and policy makers have failed to appreciate.

A front-page article in the sports section of the *New York Times* told the story of young Scott Croteau of Lewiston, Maine, cocaptain of the football team and reportedly the most popular student at his high school. Possessed of good looks and straight-As, Scott was being recruited by Harvard and Princeton at the time he hanged himself from a tree and then shot himself in the head with a revolver. "Suicide," the *Times* reported, "has become one of the major causes of death among American teen-agers, following automobile accidents and homicides." What is particularly disturbing, said a public health expert quoted in the piece, suicide by young people "is a virtually unrecognized national public health problem."[1]

Or consider a page-one headline in the the *Washington Post*: "Prescription Error Claims Dad's 'Angel'–Mistakes on Rise, Pharmacists Say." The story told of little Megan McClave of Hampton, Virginia, who was given medication by her father upon her return home from having her tonsils removed, went to bed for the night, and never woke up. "Pharmacists say their jobs are becoming tougher, and mistakes more common," reports the *Post*, "because of the rapidly increasing number of medications hitting the market every year and the new generic equivalents for older drugs." At some large-chain stores and bulk prescription services pharmacists who fill hundreds of prescriptions a day may be overworked, and as in Megan's case, dispense the wrong pills.[2]

Reading this stuff, most parents undoubtedly think *my child could be next*. But need they? On closer reading, the evidence journalists amass in support of the supposed trends seldom turns out to be overwhelming. "Medical experts say that although a mistake as serious as the one that killed Megan is extremely rare, prescription errors are not as infrequent as commonly believed," was the best the *Post* could muster. The *Times* at least gave some scary-sounding statistics in its story about suicide: the incidence of teen and young adult suicides nearly tripled between 1952 and 1992, to 1,847 in 1992.[3]

Those numbers can be read, however, in a considerably less alarmist way. At the conclusion of a forty-year period during which increases in the divorce and poverty rates, decreases in investment in education and counseling services, and the advent of AIDS put more stress than ever on American adolescents, about 1 in 10,000 saw fit to end his or her life. I do not want to minimize their tragic loss, but the numbers pale beside statistics for other threats faced by teens. One in nine goes hungry for some part of each month, for instance, and the number of hungry young Americans increased by half between the mid-1980s and mid-1990s.[4]

That suicide is the third leading cause of death for teens—a startling fact that the media repeat early and often in stories about kids who take their own lives—also warrants a moment's reflection. Adolescents are unlikely to die of cancer, heart disease, or HIV. Those leading killers of adults generally take years to progress. Fortunately, we live in a period and place where, unlike most cultures throughout history, the vast majority of people survive to adulthood. It is far from surprising that those young people who do lose their lives fall victim to immediate causes, which is to say, accidents, homicide, and suicide.[5]

The trend in youth suicide actually has been moderately encouraging in recent years. Nationwide, an all-time high was recorded in 1988, and since then the rate has stabilized, even decreasing slightly in some years. In the 1990s some locales experienced substantial increases that were widely reported in their local media, while others enjoyed spectacular declines that went almost unacknowledged. In Los Angeles the news media barely took note when the teen suicide rate fell to its lowest level in three decades during the mid-1990s. They focused instead on three adolescents who leapt to their deaths from a cliff in 1996. The deaths, reporters told us, were "a reminder of how astonishingly fraught with danger the teenage years have become in America" (*Time*).[6]

Even more illuminating than speculation about the perilousness of American society or the fluctuations in the numbers of teens who commit suicide is a well-documented change in *how* they end their lives. More kids succeed in suicide attempts these days than in the past because more of them—about 60 percent—use guns. As we have seen, the ready availability of guns also accounts for most teen homicides and many fatal accidents, the other two leading causes of death for this age group. Perhaps politicians, social scientists, journalists, and anyone else who reports on dangers to kids should install on their computers a screen saver that shows a revolver, and beneath it, in big letters: IT'S THE GUNS, STUPID.[7]

Teen Gamblers

As much as the media and politicians would have us believe otherwise, most American children are not in imminent danger from the over-hyped hazards of our age. Researchers have a good idea of what truly puts kids at greater risk. In the case of suicide, for instance, nine out of ten teens who kill themselves are clinically depressed, abusing drugs or alcohol, or coping with severe family traumas.[8]

Scott Croteau, as it turns out, was a case in point. Outwardly he may have appeared to be doing well, but at home Scott was subject to extraordinary levels of stress. The gun he used to kill himself had been purchased by his father, who said he bought it to protect himself from his ex-wife, Scott's mother, a recovering alcoholic who had been arrested several times for theft. The mother, fearful in turn for her own safety, had sought a protective order against Scott's father.[9]

Or consider a less life-threatening but much publicized risk to our youth. To judge by the abundant coverage the press has devoted to it throughout the 1990s, every parent ought to worry about whether her son or daughter has become addicted to gambling. *USA Today* ran a headline—"Teen Gambling: An Epidemic"—and two full pages of stories plus an editorial about what it dubbed "the invisible addiction." According to a story in the *Indianapolis Star*, fully nine out of ten students in Indiana's middle schools and high schools have gambled. Deemed "the latest peril for America's troubled teenagers" (*U.S. News & World Report*), gambling holds "such a fascination for the young a child can get very addicted to it and it becomes his whole life" (ABC News).[10]

"Sociologists are alarmed by studies saying teenagers are four times as likely to gamble as adults," the *Christian Science Monitor* reported. A sociologist myself, I have to confess that I have never experienced that sense of alarm nor heard it expressed by colleagues. The statistic rings untrue, conjuring up as it does images of clandestine casinos in the basements of high schools, with boys whose voices have yet to change serving as croupiers. Actual studies show that the vast majority of kids who gamble engage in nothing more serious than buying Lotto tickets or betting on the Super Bowl with their pals. Kids who do become problem gamblers almost always have other problems, drug and alcohol abuse, delinquency, depression, and relationship troubles being the most common. Among the best predictors is having parents who gamble heavily.[11]

Sue Fisher, a British sociologist, studied teens who gamble obsessively and learned that their compulsion was a response to other problems such as unwanted pregnancy or abusive parents. Often when their troubles eased, so did their gambling. Other heavy-gambling teens, Fisher discovered, are merely going through a routine stage in the transition to adulthood. They may appear "addicted" to gambling, but actually they are rebelling or mimicking their parents, and once their rebellious period ends, they give up or greatly reduce their gambling.[12]

You wouldn't know any of this from stories in the media. Front-page articles in 1998 went on about a nineteen-year-old from Long Island named Moshe Pergament, "a teenager who saw no way out of his gambling debt" (*Seattle Times*) and "decided to end his gambling and his life" (*New York Times*) after going $6,000 in the hole. Reporters told us almost nothing about Pergament's pathway to either gambling or suicide, nor why this young man from an affluent family felt he could not get financial help or counseling. Nor did they question the tall tales of other kids they wrote about—kids such as "Greg from Philadelphia," who told *Time* that a bookie "said he would cut off my mother's legs if I didn't pay."[13]

Reporters do manage to find reputed experts who lend credence to their stories about teen gambling, but the same people get quoted time and again, sometimes saying precisely the same thing. "Public understanding of gambling is where our understanding of alcoholism was some 40 or 50 years ago," said psychologist Durand Jacobs of Loma Linda University in both *Time* and the *Los Angeles Times.* He has been a favorite as well with the *Christian Science Monitor,* which has run a story almost every year since 1989 proclaiming that teen gambling is "growing."[14]

Read apart from the fear mongering coverage in which they are embedded, studies of gambling by teens suggest little cause for rampant parental panic. Psychologist Howard Shaffer of Harvard made headlines with his assertion that the rate of problem gambling among adolescents is more than twice that of adults. Depending on which report of Shaffer's you read and which level of severity he is describing, the number of teens with gambling problems is between 4 percent and 22 percent. But Shaffer concedes that, as with other risky behaviors young people try, most will lose interest in gambling as they get older and settle into work and family roles.[15]

No one knows whether teen gambling is more extensive or injurious today than in previous eras. Many of us adults recall losing our lunch money in betting pools for sports events, poker games with our buddies, and "Casino Nights" the high school threw to raise money for the marching band. Some of us also remember our uncles' or grandfathers' stories about sneaking into racetracks and pool halls and wagering everything they made as newspaper delivery boys. Look beyond the scary headlines about today's teen bettors and you discover they are probably no worse. Although they are coming of age in an era of explosive growth for the casino industry, most have resisted temptation and stuck to rather benign wagering. A survey of sixth- through twelfth-graders in Louisiana, conducted after riverboat and Indian casinos opened there, provoked alarmist reactions from politicians and journalists for its finding that about nine out of ten of the state's adolescents had gambled. Yet unpack that shocking statistic and you discover that two thirds of the students had bought scratch-off lottery tickets, about half had wagered on cards and sports teams, and just 3 percent had been to a riverboat casino and 4 percent to a land-based casino.[16]

Cybersmut

About the only researcher willing to paint a picture of teens as casino aficionados was a young man whose studies made headlines in the early 1980s. He captured journalists' attention with a survey he claimed showed that 64 percent of students at Atlantic City High School bet in local casinos. The researcher, Marty Rimm, also conducted an experiment in which, clad as an Arab sheik, he entered the Playboy Hotel and Casino and was offered instant credit and given royal treatment even though he was only sixteen years of age.

Vigorously criticized by the gaming industry as inaccurate, Rimm's studies nonetheless garnered tremendous attention and motivated the New Jersey legislature to raise the gambling age in casinos from eighteen to twenty-one. It took another fourteen years, however, before Marty Rimm established himself as what he really is: a media manipulator *par excellence*. He secured this distinction upon the appearance of *Time* magazine's July 3, 1995, issue, the cover of which was filled from border to border with the face of a little boy sitting in front a computer keyboard, illuminated in an ominous blue-gray glow from a monitor, his mouth open and eyes aghast at what he saw. "CYBERPORN," read the huge headline below the child's chin, and below that, "EXCLUSIVE: A new study shows how pervasive and wild it really is. Can we protect our kids—and free speech?"[17]

The story's main point—that cyberspace so overflows with smut, some is sure to leak out of your child's computer screen—was anchored to seemingly solid scientific evidence. "A research team at Carnegie

Mellon University in Pittsburgh, Pennsylvania, has conducted an exhaustive study of online porn," *Time* reported. They found "917,410 sexually explicit pictures, descriptions, short stories and film clips." The *Time* article identified Marty Rimm as "the study's principal investigator," a rather reverential way of referring to him, considering that Rimm conducted the research as an undergraduate student and some of the people he listed as members of his research "team" renounced the study. Rimm's resumé didn't exactly qualify him as a research scientist, either. He had spent much of his time in the years since his previous research project working in Atlantic City casinos (where he was the subject of investigations by the New Jersey Division of Gaming Enforcement) and writing and self-publishing a lewd novel and a nonfiction work entitled *The Pornographer's Handbook: How to Exploit Women, Dupe Men & Make Lots of Money.*[18]

Rimm's exclusivity agreement with *Time* ensured that true experts on computer networks could neither see nor comment on his study until the magazine hit the stands. As soon as these folks did get their hands on his paper, however, they pulverized it. Donna Hoffman and Thomas Novak, professors at Vanderbilt University, pointed out that by his own admission in his paper, of the 917,410 files Rimm says he found, only 3 percent actually contained potentially pornographic images. The images were not readily available to children in any event, because they were on bulletin boards that required membership fees. Of 11,576 World Wide Web sites Rimm examined—cyberplaces children *might* actually visit—only nine (.08 percent) contained material that Rimm considered R- or X-rated.[19]

Another of Rimm's statistics included in the *Time* article had an impact beyond the pages of the magazine. "On those Usenet newsgroups where digitized images are stored, 83.5% of the pictures were pornographic," *Time* reported. Within days that figure got repeated throughout the media and by members of Congress who were pushing a piece of legislation to censor the content of the Internet. Conservative groups such as Pat Robertson's Christian Coalition and Gary Bauer's Family Research also had a field day. The 83.5 percent figure became a mainstay in their solicitation mailings and speeches.[20]

When critics got a look at Rimm's paper, however, they discovered that the 83.5 percent referred to the proportion of porn postings at just seventeen Usenet news groups. At the time of Rimm's study there were thousands of Usenet groups in existence. Only a tiny percentage of these contained any dirty pictures, and you needed special software to view them.[21]

What Rimm's study suggested, if anything, was that adult, middle-class, computer-literate men no longer had to frequent seedy store-fronts to view smut. But a cover story on that topic wouldn't boost circulation, so *Time* opted instead for the kids-at-risk hook. "The great fear of parents and teachers" is that "this stuff" will fall into the hands of children "who are not emotionally prepared to make sense of what they see," the article asserted. To back up the claim, they quoted a mother in Skokie, Illinois, who refused her sons' request for Internet access. "They could get bombarded with X-rated porn," the mom exclaimed, and *Time* provided a quote from a U.S. senator confirming as much. "We face a unique, disturbing and urgent circumstance, because it is children who are the computer experts in our nation's families," Republican Dan Coats of Indiana remarked, tapping into a perennial parental paranoia about adult obsolescence–a paranoia that fear mongers continued to mine in subsequent years when thousands of porn-selling sites appeared on the Internet, many of them offering free samples. By then, however, parents had a bounty of smut-blocking software available for their home computers, as well as Internet services that vetted out questionable content. Yet claiming that parents could not protect their kids from web filth, politicians and pundits pushed through the Communications Decency Act in 1996. The Supreme Court overturned the act the next year on the same grounds that courts had rejected other censorial legislation: it could have had the effect, as Justice Felix Frankfurter once put it, of "reducing the adult population to reading only what is fit for children."[22]

Missing Children

The cyberporn episode demonstrates, on the one hand, that a deficient study–even one that experts easily identify as bunk–can precipitate a panic that continues well after the study is discredited. The episode also points up another way in which the culture of fear grows and persists: while giving birth to new scares, fear mongers resuscitate old ones.

Inundated with criticism following its cyberporn cover, *Time* came as close as it could to recanting. In a full-page article three weeks after the cyberporn edition the magazine took note of some of the flaws in Rimm's research and acknowledged that Rimm has "his own credibility problems." In light of those admissions, and the undeniable seductiveness of Rimm's offer to *Time* (great sex in the safe environment of a respected university, enhanced by the latest in technology), I am not sure that I blame the editors for having succumbed. I do fault them, however, for a sleazy connection they made between cyberporn and another overstated menace: in the context of reporting that as many as a dozen children had been lured on-line by child molesters, the magazine informed us that "more than 800,000 children are reported missing every year in the U.S."[23]

By including this statistic, which has nothing to do with cyberporn, *Time* helped to perpetuate one of America's most enduring but fallacious panics. In national surveys conducted in recent years three out of four parents say they fear that their child will be kidnapped by a stranger. They harbor this anxiety, no doubt, because they keep hearing frightening statistics and stories about perverts snatching children off the street. What the public doesn't hear often or clearly enough is that the majority of missing children are runaways fleeing from physically or emotionally abusive parents. Most of the remaining number of missing children are "throw aways" rejected by their parents, or kids abducted by estranged parents. According to criminal justice experts, a total of 200 to 300 children a year are abducted by nonfamily members and kept for long periods of time or murdered. Another 4,600 of America's 64 million children (.001 percent) are seized by nonfamily members and later returned.[24]

Without question every such incident is a horrible tragedy, but once again, kids are not equally at risk. Child molesters, both inside and outside families, tend to target vulnerable children: youngsters with disabilities and poor communications skills, troubled kids whose reports adults distrust, and children whose parents are absent or inattentive.[25]

Most of these facts and figures have been known since 1985, when Diana Griego and Louis Kilzer published a series of Pulitzer Prize–winning articles in the *Denver Post* and revealed that then-current estimates of missing children were largely fantasies of politicians who had seized on what one congressional aide called "the perfect apple pie issue." Congressman Paul Simon, in one of several governmental hearings on the problem, had put forward 50,000 as a "conservative estimate." Other public figures had thrown out numbers as high as 400,000. John Walsh, father of Adam Walsh, whose abduction and murder in 1981 at a shopping mall in Hollywood, Florida, got the country focused on missing children in the first place, proclaimed the country "littered with mutilated, decapitated, raped, strangled children."[26]

Following the *Denver Post*'s revelations, for several magnificent months the media actually set about to correct the record and calm people down. CBS News ran a story in which they showed an excerpt from a commercial for one of the many products being marketed to worried parents at the time—a warning buzzer that attached to a child's clothes—and quoted an expert suggesting that people not waste their money. "Exact figures are in dispute, but child abduction by strangers appears relatively rare," CBS correspondent Steve Young noted at the end of his report.[27]

The *Washington Post*, in a page-one article in late 1985 entitled "Abduction Publicity Could Scare Children," told of an elementary school counselor in Silver Spring, Maryland, who spent much of her time consoling children who worried that someone would follow them home. "They're scared, and I feel like they're not having fun anymore," the *Post* quoted her. On milk cartons, television programs, billboards, posters, and at mass fingerprinting sessions in shopping malls, the article went on to catalogue, kids were being bombarded with the message that "today's world is a dangerous place." The article said that famous pediatricians such as Benjamin Spock and T. Berry Brazelton regard this onslaught as unhealthy for children. "I don't think it's really appropriate to make them afraid of everybody," Brazelton was quoted.[28]

The trend toward corrective reporting was short-lived, however, and easily offset by aggressive campaigns from advocacy groups such as the

Adam Walsh Center, Vanished Children's Alliance, and others whose spokespersons are parents of abducted children. Soon after Missing Children's Day in 1995, NBC's "Today Show" ran a segment with John Walsh, whose more recent claim to fame is as host for nearly a decade of "America's Most Wanted," a popular "reality" television show whose stock in trade is stories about psychopathic killers who ambush innocent, unsuspecting women and children. The police have "new information about the case," Katie Couric reported in voice-over at the top of the segment, while a snapshot of little Adam filled the screen. When she introduced Walsh, however, he did not actually discuss any new information, and the interview quickly deteriorated into fanciful speculation. "I truly believe that if Adam's murderer isn't found in this life," Walsh said, "he will get justice in the next life." The segment ended with Walsh wondering whether "Adam's murderer has gone on to kill other children or might try to hurt our family again."[29]

Walsh is an exemplar of a particularly influential category of person in the culture of fear: the grieving parent-cum-celebrity. Politicians respond to these people by passing legislation memorializing their dead child. Dale Russakoff, a reporter at the *Washington Post*, documented that in just an eighteen-month period ending in mid-1998 more than fifty laws had been passed by state legislatures with names like Jenna's Law (New York), Amber's Law (Texas), and Stephanie's Law (Kansas). Commenting on the trend, Stephen Schulhofer, a law professor at the University of Chicago, suggested to Russakoff, "Policy issues are reduced to poster children and you have an up-and-down emotional vote as if you're choosing between the killer and a particular child."[30]

In the media too policy issues around child abduction get framed by parents-cum-celebrities. During the time period that Schulhofer studied, for instance, John Walsh was almost omnipresent in television and print coverage about child abductions and murders. Following the murder of six-year-old JonBenet Ramsey in Boulder, Colorado, on Christmas night 1996 and the publication of Walsh's memoir, *Tears of Rage*, in 1997, the media couldn't get enough of Walsh. And his advice to parents could not have been more chilling. "Don't let your guard down for a minute," the *Buffalo News* quoted him. "It can happen anywhere.

These creeps are all over the place. They're mobile. They're so violent and remorseless, they think nothing of killing someone for twenty-five dollars or a car stereo."[31]

On Geraldo Rivera's show a few weeks after the Ramsey murder Walsh reproached the mayor of Boulder for presuming to suggest to residents of his city that they have little to fear. Branding the mayor's plea for calm "a Chamber of Commerce type of move," Walsh said, "I don't agree with that philosophy that says, 'we don't have a problem here in beautiful little Boulder, Colorado.' They have a big problem." The view accorded well with Geraldo's own position. In another program in 1997 devoted to child abductions Rivera effused to the camera, "This isn't a commentary, this is reality: they will come for your kid over the Internet; they will come in a truck; they will come in a pickup in the dark of night; they will come in the Hollywood Mall in Florida. There are sickos out there. You have to keep your children this close to you [he gestures with his fingers]—this close to you."[32]

Even in media accounts where more complete and realistic information is provided about stranger danger, the overall impression often reinforces parental anxieties. For example, although the author of an article in *USA Today* in 1994 took pains midway through the piece to deemphasize stranger abductions, by that point readers had already been given another impression. The headline read, "MISSING CHILDREN: A Fearful Epidemic," and the story opened with tales of kids who had disappeared and been murdered. Tragedies like theirs "have awakened Americans to the vulnerability of children everywhere," the article stated. And the piece was illustrated (as stories about missing kids often are) with snapshots of adorable boys and girls who are identified by name and the dates on which they were abducted or discovered dead.[33]

Book publishers also help perpetuate undeserved anxieties about child nabbing, and not just by bringing out memoirs by grieving parents. A paperback from HarperCollins titled *On the Safe Side* at first appears to be a collection of general safety tips for youngsters. Yet most of the 245 pages are devoted to providing parents with ploys they can teach their children to use in scaring off potential molesters and abductors, as well as surveillance methods parents themselves can use to check up on baby-sitters and day care providers.[34]

The publication of another book, *Child Lures*, resulted in a mini-explosion of media fear mongering about child snatching when the author, Kenneth Wooden, helped producers at TV newsmagazines and talk shows set up mock abductions. CBS's "48 Hours" placed hidden cameras in a toy store and had parents watch behind one-way mirrors as a middle-aged man lured their children out of the store with come-ons about needing help finding his dog. "It's scary. It can bring tears to your eyes," said one of the moms, as her eleven-year-old son walked out of the store with the stranger. "My worst fears were confirmed," confessed the store owner.

CBS didn't cite any real-life examples of kidnappings at toy stores, mind you, such occurrences being, if not nonexistent, certainly rare. Still, author Wooden promised that there are perverts for whom "the challenge is getting a kid out of a Sunday school, getting a kid out of your home, getting a kid out of a toy store." Neither CBS nor other shows that featured Wooden during this period in the mid-1990s took note of the fact that in the 1970s and 1980s he had been a leading advocate for questionable scares about "devil worshipers" and serial murderers abducting children. Appearing on programs like ABC's "20/20" and before congressional hearings, Wooden claimed that children were being brutally raped and murdered, their bodies left to rot in trash trucks and garbage dumps.[35]

Making Money

Groups such as the National Safe Kids Campaign, whose objective is to educate parents about the true leading causes of death and disability among children, find they cannot compete in this media environment. How do you interest TV producers in stories about preventable accidents? Thousands of young lives could be saved each year, and hundreds of thousands of emergency room visits averted, if parents and elected officials paid more attention to simple safety measures in homes and public spaces. Yet when Safe Kids Campaign conducts its own surveys of parents' concerns the results confirm what other researchers find: kidnapping remains at the top of the list.[36]

Responsibility for perpetuating the confusion rests not only with journalists, celebrity advocates, and politicians but also with marketers who have devised a whole range of strategies for profiting from missing children. Among the more creative companies is Advo Inc., which mails out an estimated 57 million postcards each week to American households. Each card features on one side the smiling face, birth date, eye color, hair color, and other vital information for a missing child, and on the reverse side an advertisement for a local business. The question "Have you seen me?" printed above the child's picture has multiple meanings: it asks if we've seen the child and, at time same time, if we've seen the advertisement and the product or service it advertises. As Marilyn Ivy, an anthropologist at the University of Washington, notes in an essay about this marketing device, "That a child is missing—not at home—also brings up fears that perhaps we as residents at home are missing something, too."[37]

To produce results any advertisement must do two things: It has to grab the audience's attention, and it has to persuade the audience that they have a problem whose solution is the item being advertised. Advo's mailers cleverly and quickly accomplish both tasks. The photo of the missing child immediately elicits feelings of guilt, fear, and fascination, which compel a person to look at the card rather than toss it into the wastebasket along with the rest of the day's junk mail. And the mailer creates a problem-solution situation for the reader at a subconscious level. "Since we probably can't find the missing child," Ivy observes, "the packet of ads is there to tell us what else we might be missing and where to find it: Domino's Pizza, Sterling Optical, Tireman, Hydroflo, Twining's Upholstery and Carpet Cleaning, Jiffy Lube."[38]

Other entrepreneurs of the 1990s have marketed products that respond more directly to fears about missing kids. Ident-A-Kid, a Florida firm, sold more than 3 million child-identification cards a year at $5 each through a nationwide network of salespeople who visit schools. Saf-T-Child, a Texas company, marketed a more elaborate package for $25 that included two ID cards and an instructional cassette for parents about how to prevent child nabbing. Then there's the Blockbuster Video chain, which lures movie-renting parents into its stores by offering free videotaping of children—the tapes to be used by police should the kids ever go missing.[39]

By far the most ambitious and well-financed effort to capitalize on parents' fears of losing their children came from the Ideon Group, whose stock trades on the New York Stock Exchange. The nation's leading provider of registration services for credit cards, Ideon marketed an analogous service for children. In full-page advertisements that ran in major newspapers and newsmagazines throughout the country in 1995 the company professed: "If Your Child Were Missing You'd Think About It Every Minute. Same With Us." For $50 a year Ideon's "Family Protection Network" service would register a child's picture and other identifying information in a national data bank. For $250 a year the company would provide investigative services as well. "We have a network of over 1,000 highly qualified, licensed, independent agents, including former agents from the FBI, CIA, and Departments of Treasury and Justice," the ads proclaimed.[40]

Through market research Ideon learned that parents were worried about the amount of help the police and FBI can provide if a child vanishes. For only $250 a year, the ads suggested, parents could lessen that worry. Or as Georgia Hilgeman, mother of a formerly missing daughter and founder of Vanished Children's Alliance and a supporter of Ideon's new service put it when I interviewed her in 1995, "We have insurance on our homes and our cars, why not to insure our children's safety?"

Ideon's CEO said he got the idea for the new business after the 1993 kidnapping and murder of twelve-year-old Polly Klaas in Petaluma, California. Once again reporters were claiming that the public ought to be, as *Newsweek* put it, "more aware of how vulnerable children are." The media blaze ignited by the Klaas murder continued for years, refueled periodically by Marc Klaas, the girl's father, and by drawn-out legal proceedings against Polly's accused killer, Richard Allen Davis. The Ideon service raised fears of its own, however, for some missing-children crusaders. "What perfect information for a pedophile to have access to. They'll know your mom and dad's name—the perfect way to trick your child," Kim Swartz, who runs a foundation in honor of her seven-year-old daughter, Amber, missing since 1988, commented to a reporter from the *San Francisco Chronicle* about Ideon's information. "I think everybody ought to be very cautious about this group," Swartz advised. "Who knows if they're going to be around in a year?"[41]

As it turned out, they were not. After spending close to $21 million in the first half of 1995 on marketing and operational costs Ideon had too few subscribers to justify further investment. It closed the business and refunded money to parents. In explaining what went wrong, company officials pointed to gaps in their market research. Fears about child abduction and police preparedness did not translate into parents' willingness to forward substantial amounts of money and personal information to a company they had never heard of.

It would not be surprising were a similar service to appear sometime in the future. Officers at Ideon have considered experimenting with a more modest operation that would operate through their credit card registration service. And at the time the company decided to bail out it had spent an estimated $17 million defending itself against a suit from another firm, LifeFax, whose owner claimed he originated the idea and planned to market his own child-registration and recovery service.[42]

Making Scary Kids

The misbelief that every child is in imminent risk of becoming a victim has as its corollary a still darker delusion: *Any kid might become a victimizer.* Beneath such headlines as "Life Means Nothing," "Wild in the Streets," and "'Superpredators' Arrive," the nation's news media have relayed tale upon blood-soaked tale of twelve- and fourteen-year-olds pumping bullets into toddlers, retirees, parents, and one another. Armed with quotes from experts who assert, often in so many words, "everyone's kids are at risk," journalists stress that violent kids live not just in the South Bronx or South Central L.A. but in safe-seeming suburbs and small towns.[43]

The news media seldom pay heed to the fact that in eight out of ten counties in the United States entire years go by without a single juvenile homicide. As has been discussed, journalists and politicians were able to take a string of schoolyard shootings in 1997 and 1998 and present them as proof that kids in small towns were becoming maniacal; when it comes to the suburbs, incidents need not even come in clumps. Pasadena, California, is a suburb of 125,000 located at the foot of the San Gabriel Mountains, about a dozen freeway miles from South Central Los Angeles. Best known as home to the annual Tournament of Roses parade and football game, it garnered national media attention for another reason not long ago. The inciting event occurred on Halloween night in 1993. In what reporters accurately described as "a quiet neighborhood of neatly tended bungalows," three teenage boys were gunned down while trick-or-treating. The shooters, gang members from a neighborhood nearby, apparently had set out after some of their rivals and mistakenly hit the trick-or-treaters.[44]

This awful but isolated incident got retold in the media repeatedly over the coming months as evidence of the unbridled spread of youthful violence into previously safe areas. The coverage culminated in a *New York Times* story a full year after the event. Headlined "Mistaken Killing of Three Teen-Agers Erodes a California City's Confidence," the piece was hard to take seriously if you knew much about what actually had transpired in Pasadena over the twelve months following the shootings. There had been no epidemic of violence by the city's youth and no mass exodus of homeowners or merchants, many of whom depend heavily on the tourist trade. On the contrary, Pasadena's "Old Town" section was booming with new restaurants and clothing boutiques, and violent crime in Pasadena actually dropped by 20 percent in 1994. On Halloween night that year community groups sponsored an outdoor carnival on the steps of City Hall that went off without incident.[45]

Stories commemorating the anniversary of violent events further add to what has become an extraordinary volume of coverage about kids and crime. When a professor of communications at the University of California at Santa Barbara monitored the media for a month in the early 1990s he discovered that stories about health and economic issues together accounted for a measly 4 percent of newspapers' and television newscasts' coverage of children. By contrast, 40 percent of all news reports about children in the nation's leading newspapers concerned crime and violence. The figure for evening newscasts on ABC, CBS, and NBC was 48 percent.[46]

Local newscasts are worse still. In a paper published in 1997 in the *American Journal of Public Health* researchers from the University of California at Berkeley reported the results of an analysis they conducted of all news stories broadcast on local television stations in California over a twelve-day period. Fifty-five percent of stories about young people concerned violence committed by or against them.[47]

Reports about violence by youths customarily contain two elements that together guarantee the audience will sit up and shudder: vivid depictions of the young criminals and their crimes, and numbers showing dramatic increases on some dimension or other. A *New York Times* story typical of the genre began with a kid and a crime: "It was a wave of the hand from a 10-year-old boy with a Botticelli face and Dennis the Menace bangs that brought Elizabeth Alvarez to her death on a humid afternoon last August." Then the story related the kid and the crime to a statistical trend: "As overall violent crimes leveled off, those committed by people under 18 rose 47 percent."[48]

If instead of percentages reporters concentrated either on the actual numbers of such crimes committed by kids in these age groups or on historical comparisons, they wouldn't have much of a story. "The number of homicides committed by children age 12 and under grew by 125%," *USA Today* let its readers know, at a time when fewer than forty kids under the age of thirteen were convicted of murder each year. In the mid-1990s homicide by children under thirteen occurred less often than in 1965. A report from the Justice Department stated unambiguously, "Today's serious and violent juvenile offenders are not significantly younger than those of 10 or 15 years ago."[49]

Particularly rare are kid criminals whose behaviors, given the rest of their lives, are very surprising. You have to dig deep into the media accounts, though, to glimpse that reality. It was the angelic face of Jacob Gonzales, in a large photograph just beneath the masthead at the top of the front page of the *New York Times* in 1994, that most readers undoubtedly remembered for weeks to come. Headlined "2 Boys, a Debt, a Gun, a Victim: The Face of Violence," the story tells how Jacob helped his buddy, a fourteen-year-old drug dealer, murder a pregnant mother of three who refused to hand over $80. "Jacob's take was $20. He bought a chili dog and some Batman toys," says the article, second in a four-part series on kids who kill. The installment about young Jacob occupies close to two pages of the *Times*. Fully one-quarter of a page is taken up with a second photo in which Jacob, photographed in his cell at the children's home where he was being held, is the epitome of an average American boy. Clad in a University of Michigan sweatshirt, he has a sweet smile on his face and a cute little hand puppet in one hand. Beside him is a collection of football trading cards.[50]

Only a patient reader learns how far from normal was Jacob's larger reality. Well into the article, the reporter lets us know that Jacob lived in a crack house and that his father, who used to beat his mother, was murdered when Jacob was four or five, about the same time that Jacob witnessed one of his seven siblings get shot in the face. Jacob's mother, raped when she was in seventh grade, had once sold her children's clothes for drug money, according to court documents. When she testified in court on Jacob's behalf, she was drunk.

Perhaps if journalists talked more with children, as Margaret Tinsley of the *Daily Telegraph* in London did, they would come to see the folly in purveying an impression that every kid is at risk of becoming a killer. When Tinsley spoke with her ten-year-old son about the widely publicized story of two boys his age who abducted a toddler from a shopping mall and brutally murdered him, the child was totally baffled. "What's the point? Why would they want to?" Tinsley's son asked her. When Tinsley drew a parallel to bullies at his school, he balked. "That's different. They're your own age. Hurting a baby is just stupid. Like pushing over an old lady," the boy avowed.[51]

The *Telegraph*, along with the rest of the British media, had gotten swept up in speculation about what this murder meant about the decline of civilization. A more reasonable response, Tinsley recommends, is to see young murderers for the exceptions that they are. "A child who has grown up with any love at all, who has had a reasonable amount of self-respect left intact, may succumb to greed or mischief or anger or panic. But he or she will not see 'the point' of gratuitous cruelty, any more than my son did," she notes. "Our growing fear of children is itself a great social evil," Tinsley correctly concludes.[52]

Stupid Policy Tricks

Our fear grows, I suggest, proportionate to our unacknowledged guilt. By slashing spending on educational, medical, and antipoverty programs for youths we adults have committed great violence against them. Yet rather than face up to our collective responsibility we project our violence onto young people themselves, and onto strangers we imagine will attack them.

For young people who go astray the consequences of our projections are dire. The more fearful people are of crime, the more punitive their attitudes toward juvenile criminals, studies show, and politicians capitalize on this correlation to build more and meaner prisons. "We must shift the focus of the juvenile justice system from rehabilitation to punishment," Bob Dole proposed during the 1996 presidential campaign, ignoring the fact that many juveniles serve longer sentences than adults for the same crimes, and that many juvenile facilities, grossly overcrowded and understaffed, provide rehabilitation services in name only. At $30,000-plus per youth per year and with 100,000 youths behind bars on any given day it is the prison–industrial complex, not American society, that comes out the big winner from laws mandating longer and stiffer sentences for juveniles. In a page-one investigative piece in 1998 on a privately operated juvenile prison in Louisiana that he described as "rife with brutality, cronyism and neglect," *New York Times* reporter Fox Butterfield noted that some of the worst conditions in juvenile facilities nationally are found among privately operated prisons.[53]

Other research on private prison companies documents that these firms, which include Corrections Corporation of America, among the half dozen largest gainers on the New York Stock Exchange in the mid-1990s, achieve their high profitability in large part by economizing, particularly on personnel and rehabilitation programs. Criminologists have expressed concern about the lengths to which prison companies will go to lobby for harsher sentences and other criminal-justice policies that guarantee high occupancy when crime rates are down.[54]

But why would the public care about such matters when for every news story about private prisons many more relay tale upon melodramatic tale of killer kids getting off lightly? In a piece typical of the genre, ABC correspondent Jackie Judd, reporting from Warwick, Rhode Island, on "ABC World News Tonight," informed viewers: "The horror of the community turned to anger when they saw a killer, someone who had taken four lives, committed to only five years in this juvenile detention center." Once released, Judd said, the fifteen-year-old offender "could buy a gun or apply for a job as a day care worker without anyone knowing his history as a murderer. All of this, because legally Craig Price was a child when he killed." Judd's report illustrates how our fear of children has made us unwilling to grant that violently disturbed kids are still kids. "He's not a child," a captain with the Warwick police department declares on camera. "When you kill somebody when you're fifteen years old and you wipe out an entire family and kill in the manner in which he killed, you're not a child anymore."[55]

The commander in chief concurred. Although studies find that young people incarcerated with adults are five times more likely to be sexually assaulted and fifty times more likely to be attacked by a weapon than youth in juvenile facilities, Bill Clinton, in his State of the Union address in 1996, vowed "to seek authority to prosecute, as adults, teenagers who maim and kill like adults."

Surely the flaw in this line of reasoning is obvious: acting like an adult doesn't make someone an adult. Otherwise, teens eager to grow up would be well advised to smoke cigarettes and have babies. Yet the zeal with which politicians and those who vote for them go after the criminal young seems to know no bounds. In nearly half of the states ten-year-olds can be tried as adults, and in a Gallup poll in 1994 60 percent of people said they favor the death penalty for teenage killers—more than five times as many as in the 1960s.[56]

On the same "World News Tonight" broadcast with Jackie Judd's story about Rhode Island was a report about the Colorado legislature having passed ten new laws in five days in response to media hoopla over a series of shootings. The legislation included provisions to send violent kids to boot camps and adult prisons. "It's an iron fist," the Denver district attorney said proudly, apparently unaware or unconcerned about a preponderance of evidence that such harsh penalties fail to deter other kids from committing crimes. In states such as New York, Illinois, Florida, and California, which enacted similar legislation earlier, juvenile crime rates increased. Nor do longer or more severe sentences appear to deter those kids who receive them. On the contrary, attorneys, criminologists, and the youths themselves point out that in adult prisons kids learn to survive by intimidating others. They tend to lose whatever respect they had for authorities and for themselves. Once released, they engage in more or worse crimes.[57]

As for boot camps, thirty states built them between the late 1980s and mid-1990s, for a total of about 7,000 beds. Money that would have been better spent on education, housing, job development, or nutrition for young people at risk got diverted into hiring former drill sergeants, busing in convicts, shaving their heads, subjecting them to predawn marches and endless rounds of push-ups, and teaching them to say "Sir" and "Ma'am" to everybody. The result? Great photo opportunities for tough-on-crime politicians. Studies show that graduates of boot camps were just as likely to commit future crimes as parolees from regular detention facilities.[58]

Is Society Sick?

We adults have developed a pair of theories to justify both our fear of children and our maltreatment of them. One holds that the world is worse than it ever was. The other holds that some kids are just born defective.

According to the first of these theories, a unique set of social realities has conspired to turn today's children into monsters. "The world has changed in the nearly 20 years Judge Lacey has been on the bench," the *Times* asserted, referring to the judge in the juvenile court where little Jacob Gonzales awaited trial. "There was a time when men could look forward to a job on the automobile assembly line, when the majority of inner-city children were born to married women, not single mothers, when people fought with fists, not guns, and crack did not exist."[59]

This sort of statement validates an observation attributed to Harry Truman: "There is nothing new in the world except the history you do not know." In actuality, violent youth have always been with us. "A new army of six million men are being mobilized against us, an army of delinquents. Juvenile delinquency has increased at an alarming rate and is eating at the heart of America," a juvenile court judge warned in 1946. Earlier, in nineteenth-century America, hordes of teens and pre-teens, labeled "predatory beasts" by police and the press, ran wild in city streets, dodging authorities, "gnawing away at the foundations of society," as a commentator put it at the time. In 1850 alone New York City recorded more than 200 gang wars fought largely by adolescent boys. In 1868 in San Francisco a gang of teenagers robbed a Chinese man and then beat him, sliced up his face, and branded parts of his body with hot irons. Violence by teens against Chinese immigrants was common during this period in U.S. history.[60]

Earlier still, in 1786, a Connecticut girl murdered a baby in her care. Twelve years old, she holds the distinction of being the youngest American ever to receive the death penalty.[61]

In support of the idea that the world is worse today than ever before much bogus evidence has been put forward. An example was a pair of lists, reprinted in the *Wall Street Journal* in 1992, comparing "top problems in the public schools as identified by teachers" in 1940 and 1990. The contrast was shocking. The main problems in 1940 were talking, chewing gum, making noise, running in the halls, getting out of turn in line, wearing improper clothing, and not putting paper in wastebaskets. By 1990 the leading problems had become pregnancy, suicide, drug and alcohol abuse, rape, robbery, and assault.

Barry O'Neill, a professor at Yale, revealed in 1994 in an exposé published by the *New York Times* that by the time the *Journal* printed the two lists they had already been in wide circulation. Passed around in fundamentalist Christian circles since the early 1980s, they first appeared in a national magazine in 1985, when *Harper's* published them as a curiosity piece. Two years later in his *Newsweek* column George Will printed the lists as factual, and they were quickly picked up by CBS News. In the late 1980s and early 1990s the lists appeared in literally hundreds of news outlets, books, and political speeches authored by luminaries as disparate as Anna Quindlen, Ann Landers, Joycelyn Elders, and William Bennett.[62]

"They have become the most quoted 'results' of educational research, and possibly the most influential," O'Neill reported in the *Times* (a paper that had cited the bogus lists six times itself and did so yet again, without comment, two years later when it quoted them in full from a speech by presidential candidate Ross Perot). The best O'Neill could determine, the original source for the later list of problems was a survey conducted in 1975 by the National Center for Education Statistics. That survey, which was of principals rather than teachers, asked about crimes, not general problems. When teachers *have* been asked about the biggest problems in their schools, they responded with items such as parent apathy, lack of financial support, absenteeism, fighting, and too few textbooks–not rape and robbery. In a nationwide survey in 1996 almost half of teachers said that textbook shortages prevented them from assigning homework; one in five reported that classroom disruptions had resulted from students being forced to share text books.[63]

Public schools are safer, studies show, than other locations where kids hang out, such as cars and homes. Attacks of all types against kids occur far more often away from schools than inside them. So do the bulk of non–crime-related injuries and accidents, the exception being sports injuries, a majority of which are sustained at school.[64]

Municipalities do not raise taxes, however, to buy state-of-the-art safety equipment for student athletes. They raise them to buy more surveillance cameras and metal detectors, and to station more police officers in schools. A few years ago the city of Dallas built a $41 million school that includes a high-tech command center where officers scan thirty-seven cameras that monitor nearly every inch of the building. Some of the school's 2,100 students complained that the five full-time security officers and numerous teacher-monitors invade their privacy. Teachers and parents raised questions about diverting so much money from educational programs into policing and about what one Dallas newspaper referred to as the "authoritarian style" of the school's leadership. But Dallas officials defend the facility as a haven from the ills of the larger community.[65]

Are Children Sick?

Another way we adults justify our excessive fears and brutal policies toward the nation's children is by shifting the blame to nature. We convince ourselves that millions of children are born defective. Children whom adults find frightening and difficult to control are said to suffer from various psychological or biomedical disorders.

Melvin Konner, a physician and anthropologist at Emory University, has suggested that, were Tom Sawyer and Huckleberry Finn alive today, they'd be diagnosed with attention-deficit hyperactivity disorder (ADHD) and put on Ritalin (methylphenidate). The drug of choice for kids who talk back, can't sit still, get in trouble, and are easily bored, Ritalin is taken daily by more than 1 million children in the United States. The number of kids on Ritalin quadrupled between the mid-1980s and the late 1990s. With more than 11 million prescriptions written each year—up from 4.5 million in the early 1990s—this country uses five times as much Ritalin as the rest of the world.[66]

The upsurge may have resulted from greater recognition and treatment of ADHD symptoms among parents, teachers, and doctors in recent years, as a report from the American Medical Association's Council on Scientific Affairs concluded, or from overdiagnosis and overmedication, as other research suggests. Either way, crucial questions remain, central among them: At what cost do we choose to view hyperactive children as neurologically and chemically damaged? The point at issue was put well by the psychologist Kenneth Gergen of Swarthmore College. "As we have so painfully learned in recent years, whether homosexuality is or is not a disorder is essentially a matter of cultural politics. Similarly, children may vary biologically in their activity levels, but whether we view a high level of activity as Attention Deficit Disorder depends on our conception of the ideal classroom," Gergen wrote in a journal article in 1997.[67]

Our view depends as well on conceptions of the ideal medical practice, as other social scientists and medical ethicists suggest. From the point of view of managed care companies in the 1990s this ideal sometimes boils down to spending as little as possible to remove a patient's symptoms. Why provide expensive individual or family therapy to address a child's emotional, developmental, or family problems when with a simple prescription you can dispose of the behaviors that distress the child's parents and teachers? Medical ethicist Lawrence Diller points out in an article in the *Hastings Center Report* that reliance on Ritalin relieves all sorts of adults—doctors, parents, teachers, and policy makers alike—from having to pay attention to children's social environments, which may worsen as a consequence. "Should dysfunctional family patterns and overcrowded classrooms be tolerated just because Ritalin improves the child's behavior?" Diller asks.[68]

But Ciba-Geigy, the company that made Ritalin and doubled its profits in the first half of the 1990s, was hardly the first to cash in on adults' eagerness for medical solutions to child-rearing problems. Numerous psychiatric hospitals did so, for example, in the 1980s. Over the course of that decade adolescent admissions to private psychiatric hospitals quadrupled, and the number of units catering to children and adolescents increased at least twofold. Fear advertising—lots of it—produced much of the growth. One TV commercial that ran in New York City showed a teenage girl holding a gun to her head. As the screen cut to the hospital's name and phone number, the sound of a gunshot rang out and parents were urged to call if they worried about their own children. In the Reno, Nevada, newspaper an ad that ran on the day local schools issued grades displayed a report card studded with Fs, beneath which read the foreboding question Is Your Child Failing Life? along with the name and number of a psychiatric facility.[69]

The ads offered parents relief from their feelings of guilt and impotence by assuring them that there was little they themselves could do apart from hauling their kid to the hospital. Indeed, some ads explicitly ruled out any parental culpability. "Studies indicate that anti-social behaviors in adolescents usually are not 'reactions' to home, school or community involvements. They, more often than not, are disorders of neurological development," read the copy for a psychiatric center in Cerritos, California.[70]

Parents who responded to these pitches frequently were informed by psychiatrists that their children suffered from illnesses specific to adolescence that go by names like oppositional deficit disorder, conduct disorder, and adjustment reaction. Parents who took the time to look up these ailments in the American Psychiatric Association's *Diagnostic and Statistical Manual* discovered that they are little more than fancy pseudonyms for adolescent rebellion—or as the director of a patients' rights organization put it, "pain-in-the-ass kid." Based on the DSM, a child qualifies for the label "oppositional deficit disorder" and is a prime candidate for hospitalization if he or she often does any five of the following: argues with adults, defies adults' requests, does things that annoy others, loses his or her temper, becomes easily annoyed, acts spiteful, blames others for his or her own mistakes, gets angry and resentful, or swears.[71]

How many of us made it out of adolescence without going through periods in which we acted like that?

Girls had an especially easy time qualifying for hospital admission; they didn't have to be mean and nasty, just sexually active. The National Association of Private Psychiatric Hospitals published guidelines in 1984 that urged "immediate acute-care hospitalization" for girls guilty of "sexual promiscuity."[72]

All told, at least 40 percent of adolescent admissions to private psychiatric hospitals during the 1980s were inappropriate, the Children's Defense Fund estimated. The hospitals' advertising campaigns were one reason. When researchers from the University of North Carolina questioned mothers of high school students about their reactions to a dozen fear-based newspaper ads for psychiatric facilities they came up with a paradoxical discovery. The ads had the greatest impact on parents of children who least needed mental health services.[73]

"Jails for middle-class kids" is how Ira Schwartz, dean of the School of Social Work at the University of Pennsylvania, described private psychiatric hospitals of that period. His studies in the mid-1980s showed that the length of time kids stayed in these places depended primarily on how long their insurance would pay. Adolescents frequently came home more estranged from their parents and society than when they went in, Schwartz and others learned, and felt powerless for having been institutionalized against their will.[74]

The ads and hospitalizations eventually were curtailed by a competing economic force—the very one that boosted Ritalin sales. With the 1990s came managed care and an emphasis on short-term, out-patient mental health care. Insurance companies were no longer willing to pay out the $30 billion a year it was costing them for child and adolescent psychiatric hospitalization.[75]

The price for the promiscuous institutionalization of teenagers was not borne, however, only by insurance companies, their customers, or the kids who got locked up. As is so often true when middle- and upper-income Americans purchase escape hatches from their anxieties, the poor also paid. During the period of reckless expansion of private psychiatric hospitals uninsured children with severe psychiatric problems had trouble obtaining care. Between the mid-1970s and late 1980s the number of children and adolescents in *public* psychiatric facilities actually decreased.[76]

Bad to the Bone: Crack Babies

The idea that some children are born bad gets applied to poor and minority children with a vengeance. Many of them get written off as irredeemable.

"Crack babies," the focus of cover stories in *Newsweek*, *Time*, and other major news outlets in the late 1980s and early 1990s, are a revealing case in point. The *New York Times* declared in a page-one story that these children have "brain damage that cuts into their ability to make friends, know right from wrong, understand cause and effect, control their impulses, gain insight, concentrate on tasks, and feel and return love." What, a front-page story in the *Washington Post* asked, will become of our schools when "teachers become preoccupied with the crack-affected youngsters' overwhelming problems"? The expense alone was said to be staggering. "Just to get one crack baby ready for school costs more than $40,000 a year," the *Los Angeles Times* exclaimed in an editorial. "For all 8,974 babies [identified nationally] that could add up to $1.5 billion before they are 5 years old!" (exclamation in the original).[77]

This is only the beginning. An essayist in *Newsweek* wondered what would become of "the very fabric of society" by the year 2000, when thousands of crack babies enter adulthood. A "CBS Evening News" report concluded with the foster mother of a crack baby speculating, "She may in fact be[come] a twenty-one-year-old with an IQ of perhaps fifty, barely able to dress herself and probably unable to live alone."[78]

No group of people deserves to be demonized from birth, but the stigmatization of children of crack users was particularly undeserved. Reporters and their editors had good reason to question the term *crack baby* itself. For one thing, the typical crack-abusing mother uses a spectrum of other drugs, from alcohol and marijuana to amphetamines and heroin. Some journalists alluded to this pattern of polydrug use in their stories but promptly negated its relevance by baptizing crack the "most frequent ingredient in the mix" (*Time*) or declaring that the "crack epidemic has created a generation of youngsters who can sap even the most tenacious parent's strength" (*Washington Post*), as if crack per se were the culprit.[79]

Journalists depicted crack babies as a breed apart, even though they had information to the contrary. "Trying to identify crack-affected children through behavior alone is tricky," as one *Washington Post* reporter put it. "Many of these children look and act like other kids," *Time* noted, hastening to add, "but their early exposure to cocaine makes them less able to overcome negative influences like a disruptive family life."[80]

In the first several years after birth cocaine-exposed kids develop normally, studies show, if they are given basic nutrition, education, and nurturance. Evidence from child health experts and medical researchers indicates that the behavioral and physical symptoms of children exposed to crack stem largely from poor prenatal care, malnutrition, low birth weight, and other deprivations common among youngsters born to poor parents. To the extent that research has documented any direct effects of prenatal cocaine exposure, they are subtle and not entirely adverse for success in life: cocaine-exposed kids appear to be somewhat more impulsive, aggressive, and easily distracted than their peers, and less easily startled.[81]

In time the media was forced to backpeddle. By the mid-1990s crack babies were in school, functioning much like their peers, and reporters and editors changed their spin. The less candid among them reframed the crack baby story as a war that had been won. "City Government Officials and Kind-Hearted People Actually Solved the Crack-Baby Crisis," read the headline on a *Washington Post* story in 1994. Other journalists simply fessed up: their apocalyptic predictions had been unfounded. "Not a Lost Generation" stated a subhead in a *New York Times* piece in 1993. "Tell me, what does a crack baby look like? Nobody who talks about them ever comes in to see them," an Associated Press story quoted the director of a children's center asking angrily. "They'll come in here and look at our kids and they look normal. So they say, 'Where are the drug babies?' I tell them, 'They're right here.'"[82]

A story in the *Cleveland Plain Dealer* went so far as to quote educators with the Cleveland public schools about the detrimental effect of the label *crack baby*. Used by health officials and teachers to catalogue kids as developmentally handicapped, the term gets "tossed around on school playgrounds by children to taunt each other," the newspaper reported.[83]

Part of the credit for the demise of the crack baby panic goes to Ira Chasnoff, a Chicago pediatrician who had been the media's expert of choice and the source of an oft-quoted estimate that 387,000 babies had been born to crack-addicted women. (The figure was more like 100,000, according to government estimates, a number some experts say is still inflated.) Chasnoff's research, published in medical journals from 1985 through 1988, suggested that crack-exposed infants experienced a daunting list of physical and emotional problems. Within a few years, however, Chasnoff was publishing papers showing that crack-exposed kids suffer little permanent damage. He began to complain to reporters that their coverage of crack babies was perpetuating what he termed an "us-versus-them idea" about poor children. And when a journalist asked him to comment on studies suggesting that prenatal co-caine exposure has a slight impact on IQ, he replied, "The greatest im-pediment to cognitive development in young children is poverty."[84]

Crack babies in fact served as screens on which the American public could displace its worries about the youngest generation as a whole—fears that the young, having been cheated and neglected, would be-come "an unmanageable multitude" or "a lost generation," as a *Time* cover story on crack babies aptly titled "Innocent Victims" put it. We focused on the crack baby crisis because, unlike our deeper fears, the crack baby crisis was contained. It existed only in other people's neigh-borhoods, and it could be solved if only pregnant women would keep away from crack.[85]

Throughout the 1980s and 1990s Americans welcomed every per-missible excuse to avoid facing up to our collective lack of responsibil-ity toward our nation's children. When Hillary Rodham Clinton's book *It Takes a Village* came out in 1996, she toured the country to urge better health care, day care, and nutrition for America's youth. What did me-dia interviewers and audiences concentrate on? A dubious real-estate investment she was involved in years earlier, whether she fired mem-bers of the White House travel office, and if her feminism made her a lousy First Lady. In an interview with Clinton on ABC's "20/20" Bar-bara Walters began with a statement and question: "Instead of your new book being the issue, you have become the issue. How did you get into this mess, where your whole credibility is being questioned?" Later, when Walters finally got to the book, she framed her question not in terms of children but in terms of the great Republican fear—Big Government. "You want universal health care for children. You want federally funded early education, HeadStart. You want funding for proper day care. You seem to be swimming against the tide, you know? All we hear about is less government, less money. You're saying just the opposite," Walters asserted.[86]

On "CBS This Morning" Hillary appeared for a full hour, but it wasn't until three-quarters of the way through that the host, Harry

Smith, realized he hadn't asked about her book. He too framed his question in terms of Big Government. "Let's talk about those disadvantaged children for a couple of seconds, because we live in an age now where there's these trends to take government out of a lot of different kinds of businesses," said Smith. "Distill your philosophy for me, for a second, about what government role you think should be played in the lives of disadvantaged children."[87]

A second indeed. With a commercial break looming Hillary had just enough time to raise what should have been a focal point for the entire hour's discussion. "Government has become the whipping boy, and it takes the rest of us off the hook. More families will be affected by the downsizing of American corporations that is going on right now and the insecurity that feeds in families than any government programs. So I think that we need to say, 'Each one of us has a responsibility,'" she asserted.[88]

In the final portion of the program, after the commercials, the hosts never returned to those topics.

4

MONSTER MOMS

On the Art of Misdirection

Another frightening thing about America's children: they have children of their own. Or so politicians and the media would have us believe.

The most talked about pregnant person in the world in early 1996 was a ten-year-old runaway. "With heavy makeup framing her exotic almond-shaped eyes and her long, dark hair piled high, Cindy Garcia looked at least 14," began an Associated Press story. "It wasn't until two weeks ago that the shocking truth came out. Cindy—8 ½ months pregnant—had innocently handed welfare workers her birth certificate to qualify for food stamps and child support. Cindy, her belly bulging, was only 10."[1]

Throughout a four-day period during which the Texas police hunted for her the media ran stories about how, as Britain's *Daily Telegraph* put it, "police and doctors are in a race against time," knowing that "with a 10-year-old body, she is going to require a Caesarean section and a lot of medical attention." Talk radio show hosts had a field day with the story as listeners and legislators discoursed on how sick our society has become.[2]

Only grudgingly did the news media eventually take note of the fact, revealed after the girl's capture, that she was actually fourteen and had said as much from the start. Never mind that neighbors had told reporters that Cindy was a pregnant teenager, or that social workers said her reading and math skills were those of a ninth or tenth grader. In the story's brief heyday reporters casually dismissed these observations. "The truth is, she's a 4th-grade dropout. She hasn't been to school for more than a year," the Associated Press had avowed.[3]

As it turns out the girl's name wasn't even Cindy Garcia, it was Adella Quintana. Her mother, Francesca Quintana, had gotten a phony birth certificate for her daughter when she moved from Mexico to Houston to enroll the girl in American schools.[4]

Now You See It, Now You Don't

The real story here is not about "babies having babies," as commentators put it, but the plight of a mother and her teenage daughter who, like millions of families before them, fled their homeland for what they hoped would be a better life in the United States only to experience a sea of new troubles. In the latter part of the twentieth century, however, this story was scarcely being told. It had been nearly obliterated from American public discourse, partly by intense fear mongering about Spanish-speaking immigrants and partly by what magicians call the art of *misdirection.*

To make an object seem to vanish, a magician directs the audience's attention away from where he hides it. Stories such as the one about Cindy-Adella likewise misdirected, focusing public attention away from real and enduring struggles of women trying to care for their children in an uncaring world.

During the early and mid-1990s teen mothers were portrayed as much more ominous and plentiful than they actually were. Although only about one-third of teen mothers were younger than eighteen, and fewer than one in fifty was fourteen or younger, you would not have known it from the media. An edition of the *Ricki Lake* Show in 1996 titled "I'm Only 13 But I'm Gonna Make a Baby" began with the popular TV talk show personality asking her studio audience, "Is it possible for a thirteen-year-old to be ready to be a mother?" The audience yelled "No-o-o!" as Lake introduced Kassie and Angela, thirteen-year-olds who looked even younger than their age. For close to an hour the two girls had insults and allegations hurled at them by members of the audience, by their own mothers, by Ricki Lake, and by a regretful sixteen-year-old mother of two.[5]

Kassie and Angela proved themselves remarkably composed and articulate. Accused of having no experience raising children, they pointed to skills they had gained from bringing up their younger siblings. Asked who would take care of their babies when they were at school, the girls nominated relatives who could help out and said they knew of schools that provided day care. Told by a member of the audience that her boyfriend would abandon her once the baby arrived, one of the girls calmly replied, "I know he's not going to be around."[6]

All in all they came off as more thoughtful potential parents than some I have known who are twice or three times their age, but no matter. Neither of these girls was actually "gonna make a baby" anytime soon. Kassie's mother let it be known that she had had her daughter injected with a birth control drug that would make her infertile for several months, and Kassie herself blurted out at one point that she knew she wasn't ready yet. Angela, meanwhile, made it clear that she had no intention of getting pregnant, though she did hope to convince her mother to adopt a child whom she would help raise. In other words, Ricki Lake's producers had come up with a pregnant topic but no pregnant thirteen-year-olds.

More high-minded programs also promulgated the fiction of an epidemic of pregnancy among very young teens. In an interview on National Public Radio's "Morning Edition" in 1995 Gary Bauer of the conservative Family Research Council intoned: "It was not many years ago in this country when it was not common for thirteen-year-olds and fourteen-year-olds to be having children out of wedlock. I'm enough of an optimist to believe that we can re-create that kind of a culture." The interviewer, NPR's Bob Edwards, failed to correct this patently misleading statement. Nowhere in the segment did he indicate that it remains extremely uncommon for thirteen- and fourteen-year-olds to have children.[7]

Nor did Edwards note that, until relatively recently, most thirteen- and fourteen-year-olds were *unable* to bear children. Considering the tendency of American journalists to overemphasize studies that show biochemical causes for a range of other social problems, such as hyperactivity in children, depression in adults, and crime in the streets, they have done little to call the public's attention to a fundamental statistic about teen pregnancy. As recently as a century ago the average age for menarche was sixteen or older, whereas today girls typically have their first menstrual period by age thirteen, and some as early as age nine. Some scientists blame high-calorie diets and sedentary lifestyles for the early biological maturity of contemporary girls, but whatever the reason, the implications of early menarche are plain. Only lately have girls been called on by society to wait so long from the onset of sexual maturity before having children.[8]

Reporters, politicians, and social scientists all give intricate explanations for why adolescents get pregnant. But why not account for teen pregnancies the same way we do other pregnancies? As the British sociologists Sally Macintyre and Sarah Cunningham-Burley noted in an essay, "Ignorance about contraception, psychopathology, desire to prove adulthood, lack of family restraint, cultural patterns, desire to obtain welfare benefits, immorality, getting out of school—a host of reasons are given for childbirth in women under 20, while 'maternal instinct' is thought to suffice for those over 20."[9]

America's Worst Social Problem

The causes of teen motherhood *must* be treated as distinct and powerful. Otherwise, it would make no sense to treat teen moms themselves as distinct and powerful—America's "most serious social problem," as Bill Clinton called them in his 1995 State of the Union address. Nor would it have seemed rational when legislators included in the 1996 Federal Welfare Law $250 million for states to use to persuade young people to practice premarital abstinence.

In what may well qualify as the most sweeping, bipartisan, multimedia, multidisciplinary scapegoating operation of the late twentieth century, at various times over the past decade prominent liberals including Jesse Jackson, Joycelyn Elders, and Daniel Patrick Moynihan and conservatives such as Dan Quayle and Bill Bennett all accused teen moms of destroying civilization. Journalists, joining the chorus, referred to adolescent motherhood as a "cancer," warned that they "breed criminals faster than society can jail them," and estimated their cost to taxpayers at $21 billion a year. Members of my own profession, social science, had alarming things to say as well. "The lower education levels of mothers who began childbearing as teenagers translates into lower work force productivity and diminished wages, resulting in a weaker, less competitive economy," Stephen Caldas, a policy analyst, wrote in an educational research journal. (Translation: You can thank teen moms for America's declining position in the world economy.)[10]

These claims are absurd on their face. An agglomeration of impoverished young women, whose collective wealth and influence would not add up to that of a single Fortune 100 company, do not have the capacity to destroy America. What these pundits did was to reverse the causal order. Teen pregnancy was largely a response to the nation's educational and economic decline, not the other way around. Girls who attend rotten schools and face rotten job prospects have little incentive to delay sex or practice contraception. In 1994 at least 80 percent of teenage moms were already poor before they became pregnant.[11]

Early motherhood in itself does not condemn a girl to failure and dependency. Journalists put up astounding statistics such as "on average, only 5 percent of teen mothers get college degrees, compared with 47 percent of those who have children at twenty-five or older" (*People*, in an article bleakly titled "The Baby Trap"). Yet the difference is attributable almost entirely to preexisting circumstances—particularly poverty and poor educational opportunities and abilities. Studies that compare teen moms with other girls from similar economic and educational backgrounds find only modest differences in education and income between the two populations over the long term. Some experts report that young women tend to become *more* motivated to finish school and find jobs once they have offspring to support. Data indicate too that teen moms are less likely than their peers to engage in other self-destructive behaviors, such as drug abuse, participation in gangs, and suicide. Motherhood can bring about what sociologist Joan Moore of the University of Wisconsin, an expert on delinquent girls, calls "a conversion to conventionality."[12]

The failure of greater public awareness of conventional teenage mothers results in part because studies about them receive relatively little media attention and in part because adults in positions of power actively strive to make their achievements invisible. In 1998 two seventeen-year-old mothers in Kentucky filed suit against their school board after they were denied membership in the National Honor Society. Exemplary students with grade-point averages of 3.9 and 3.7 on a scale of 4.0, the girls were told they did not meet the "character" requirement. The admissions committee announced they did not want the girls to be seen as role models for other students.[13]

Another stereotype of adolescent mothers envisions them as invariably incapable of rearing healthy children. This one too has been conclusively refuted. Researchers document that teenagers having recently cared for younger siblings are sometimes more realistic in their expectations about parenthood than older parents, and more devoted to parenting as a primary endeavor. They tend to have more help than most of the public realizes because as a rule they live with parents or other relatives. At the height of the teen motherhood scare fewer than 22,000 teen moms throughout the entire United States lived without supervision, according to a report from the Congressional Budget Office.[14]

Evidence of adolescent mothers' own competence turns up in a variety of studies but usually goes unnoticed. An ironic case in point is a famous set of experiments conducted by the psychologist René Spitz in the 1940s. Spitz compared two groups of babies, the first housed in a nursery where their mothers cared for them, the other in a foundling home where they were cared for by nurses. The babies tended by their mothers flourished, while those cared for by strangers cried and screamed excessively, became depressed, and lost weight. Within two years more than a third of the second group died, and much has been made of their sad fate by those who advocate the importance of early bonding between mothers and their children. Largely neglected in the debates over Spitz's studies is the fact that the nursery where he observed mothers taking care of their babies was a penal institution for delinquent girls. The mothers of the children who developed normally in Spitz's experiments were adolescent moms.[15]

Over the longer haul and out in the real world children of teenage mothers do appear to fare poorly compared with other children, thereby providing politicians and reporters with the oft-cited finding that 70 percent of men in prison were born to teenage mothers. The implication, however, that their mothers' age when they were born was the single or most important variable that caused them to end up in jail is iffy at best. When the children of teenage mothers are compared to the children of older mothers from similar socioeconomic circumstances there is little difference between the two groups in outcomes such as criminality, substance abuse, or dropping out of school. The age at which a woman gives birth appears to be far less consequential for how her child turns out than are factors such as her level of income and education, and whether she suffered physical and emotional abuse in her own youth.[16]

Bearers of Illegitimate Children

In addition to all the contemporary evidence contradicting their position, those who would blame teen moms for the nation's social ills confront an awkward historical reality. The teenage birth rate reached its highest level in the 1950s, not the current era. Indeed, between 1991 and 1996 the rate declined by nearly 12 percent.[17]

Demonizers of today's young mothers either ignore such facts, or when they cannot, direct the audience's attention away from them. Jean Bethke Elshtain, a professor of ethics at the University of Chicago and contributing editor of *The New Republic*, began a book review in that magazine with the words "I was a teenage mother." Considering that she would go on to condemn the book under consideration (Kristin Luker's *Dubious Conceptions*) for being too accepting of teen moms, this was a provocative confession on Elshtain's part. Yet Elshtain quickly clarified that she, like most other teen mothers of the 1950s, was *married* when she had her child. The "prevalent concern" of the American public today, Elshtain declared, is "the growing rate of out-of-wedlock births, with all their attendant difficulties." The real problem, Elshtain argued, is "illegitimacy."[18]

It is a measure of how clouded our public discourse has become that *illegitimacy*, having largely disappeared from the lexicon, would make a comeback in an era when nearly one in three children was born to an unwed mother. But what a powerful comeback. The U.S. Senate, following the election of large numbers of conservative Republicans in 1994, seriously considered applying an "illegitimacy ratio" to determine how much money states were eligible to receive in federal block grants. States with high rates of unwed motherhood or abortion would have lost funds. Although the proposal lacked sufficient support from Democrats to succeed, a couple of years later a bonus system did pass Congress. States with the lowest out-of-wedlock birth rates were eligible for $20 million each in 1998. Even liberals joined in the panic mongering about illegitimacy. "I don't think anyone in public life today ought to condone children born out of wedlock . . . even if the family is financially able," Health and Human Services Secretary Donna Shalala told reporters.[19]

Newspaper and magazine columnists called illegitimacy "the smoking gun in a sickening array of pathologies—crime, drug abuse, mental and physical illness, welfare dependency" (Joe Klein in *Newsweek*) and "an unprecedented national catastrophe" (David Broder in the *Washington Post*). Richard Cohen, also of the *Post,* asserted that "before we can have crime control, we need to have birth control" and deemed illegitimacy "a national security issue."[20]

A national security issue? Images come to mind of children of single moms selling state secrets to Saddam Hussein. Again, when pondering the effects of single motherhood it is important to compare apples to apples. Studies that compare single-parent households and two-parent households with similar levels of income, education, and family harmony find few differences in how the children turn out. The great majority of children of single mothers don't become criminals, drug addicts, mentally ill, or security threats. A study that looked at 23,000 adult men found that those raised by single mothers had income and education levels roughly equal to those raised by two parents. Research shows that as a group, children of single moms tend to fare better emotionally and socially than do offspring from high-conflict marriages or from those in which the father is emotionally absent or abusive.[21]

Scare campaigns can become self-fulfilling, producing precisely the negative outcomes that the doomsayers warn about. Exaggerations about the effects of unwed motherhood on children stigmatize those children and provoke teachers and police, among others, to treat them with suspicion. Why do so many children from single-parent families end up behind bars? Partly, studies find, because they are more likely to be arrested than are children from two-parent households who commit similar offenses. Why do children from single-parent families do less well in school? One factor came out in experiments where teachers were shown videotapes and told that particular children came from one-parent families and others from two-parent families. The teachers tended to rate the "illegitimate" children less favorably.[22]

Pay No Attention to the Man Behind the Curtain

Fear mongering about mothers directs attention away from fully half of America's parent population—the fathers. Warnings parallel to those about mothers are nowhere to be found. Rarely do politicians and journalists warn about unwed dads, and seldom does the National Honor Society refuse admission to them. On the contrary, wifeless fathers are practically revered. A headline in *USA Today* in 1997 proclaimed, "Unwed fathers, increasingly unencumbered by social stigma, are raising kids in greater numbers than ever before."[23]

There *was* one noteworthy scare about dads, and political leaders and social scientists issued warnings seemingly as dire as those about monster moms. "The single biggest social problem in our society may be the growing absence of fathers from their children's homes, because it contributes to so many other social problems," President Clinton declared in a speech at the University of Texas in 1995. "Father absence is the engine driving our biggest social problems," echoed David Blankenhorn, author of *Fatherless America*, in an "Eye on America" segment on CBS's "Evening News." "Our national crime problem," he said, "is not driven by young black males. It is driven by boys who are growing up with no fathers." Blankenhorn went so far as to suggest that violence against women is attributable to boys who grow up without dads and become resentful.[24]

A front-page story in the *New York Times* posed the fatherlessness menace no less sweepingly: "Over all, children in homes without fathers are more likely to be poor, to drop out of high school and to end up in foster care or juvenile-justice programs than are those living with their fathers."[25]

But notice the logic here. Unlike mothers, who are deemed deficient on account of what they do or what they believe, dads are judged on whether or not they're around. Men's mere *presence* is apparently adequate to save their children and the nation from ruin.

In truth, the crusade against fatherlessness is but another surreptitious attack on single mothers. Most advocates are too sophisticated to offer sound bites such as that given by Wade Horn, president of the National Fatherhood Initiative, to the *Washington Post*: "Growing up without a father is like being in a car with a drunk driver." However one phrases it, to insist that children are intrinsically better off with fathers regardless of who the fathers are or how they behave is to suggest that no single mother can adequately raise a child. About boys Blakenhorn made this claim explicitly. A mother cannot raise a healthy son on her own, Blankenhorn decreed, because "the best mother in the world can't tell her son what it means to be a man."[26]

Scares about missing dads also impugned lesbian mothers, whose children Blankenhorn disparaged as "radically fatherless," though in fact studies find that kids reared by lesbians have no greater academic, emotional, or behavioral difficulties than other children—aside from those caused by discrimination against homosexuals.[27]

Several bodies of research—mostly missing from media accounts about the fatherlessness menace—reveal the spuriousness of the evidence behind the scare. Literature on divorce shows that the main negative impacts on children are conflicts between the parents before the divorce and loss of the father's income afterward, rather than absence of the father per se. Research on how children fare following divorce also disputes the alleged power of poppa's presence. Studies of children who live with their divorced or separated mothers find, for instance, no improvement in school performance or delinquency when the children's fathers visit more often.[28]

A large national study was conducted by Kaiser Permanente and Children Now of troubled children in *two-parent* families. Asked to whom they turn for help, only 10 percent selected their fathers, while 45 percent chose their mothers, and 26 percent chose their friends.[29]

One category of children, invisible in the brouhaha over fatherless-ness, clearly benefits by *not* having their fathers around. Studies of child abuse often focus on mothers, but in fact fathers commit about half of all parental child abuse. In some surveys more than half of divorced women say that their former husbands struck them or their children. Blanket statements about the dangers of fathers' absence conveniently ignore the existence of such men. They overlook the unfortunate fact that, apart from the extra money and "respectability" fathers might provide, many have little they are willing or able to contribute to their children's well-being, and some do considerable harm. If as a group kids from fatherless homes fare less well, this is partly because women have difficulty supporting themselves and their children on what they are paid, and more than half of divorced dads get away with underpay-ment of child support. Such a result is also attributable to the factor mentioned earlier: the continuing stigma of growing up in a single-par-ent household, a stigma further reinforced through fear mongering about fatherlessness.[30]

Wicked Witches

Of the innumerable myths told about single mothers the most elemen-tal is single status itself. In reality, many are single only temporarily or only in the legal sense. Two out of five women who are unmarried when their first child is born marry before the child's fifth birthday. One in four unwed mothers lives with a man, often with the child's fa-ther.[31]

On occasion mothers portrayed as single do not qualify even on temporary or legal grounds. In its coverage of Awilda Lopez, the New York woman who brutally murdered her young daughter, Elisa Izquierdo, the *New York Post* spoke of the man in Lopez's life as her "boyfriend." In fact, Lopez was married. As Richard Goldstein of the *Village Voice* suggested in a critique of the coverage, an intact family might have confused the issue of who was to blame for the horrific treatment of Elisa, especially since the husband apparently participated in the little girl's abuse, and neighbors said he beat and stabbed Lopez, sometimes in front of her children. Yet the *Post* depicted him as a man who would "cook, clean, and take the children out to a nearby playground."[32]

Much of the media framed the Elisa Izquierdo tragedy literally as a fairy tale. *Time*, in a five-page cover story, reported that Elisa, like the princesses in fairy tales, was "born humble" but "had a special enchanted aura" and liked to dance. "And," the article went on, "unlikely as it may seem, there was even a prince in Elisa's life: a real scion of Greece's old royalty named Prince Michael, who was a patron of the little girl's preschool." But in this real-life fairy tale, the story went, neither the prince nor any government agency could rescue the princess from the wicked witch, Elisa's "single" mother. "Some Mothers Are Simply Evil," read a headline in the *New York Post*. "A monster like this should have stopped living long ago," proclaimed a writer for the *New York Daily News*.[33]

Time, in its cover article, relayed police reports from neighbors, of little Elisa pleading, "Mommy, Mommy, please stop! No more! No more!" as Lopez sexually molested her with a toothbrush and a hairbrush. When her screams grew too loud, *Time* said, Lopez turned up the radio.[34]

That these sordid details made their way into the pages of a family newsmagazine that repeatedly decries graphic depictions of depravity in print, on television, and in cyberspace is telling in itself. There must be something terribly compelling about gruesome tales of sadistic moms. Katha Pollitt of *The Nation* captured part of their appeal when she commented that "lurid replays of Awilda Lopez's many acts of sadism, while officially intended to spur outrage, also pander to the readers' sadomasochism." An observation by Bruno Bettelheim in an essay on children's fairy tales also helps to explain the allure of what are essentially fairy tales for adult readers. "The fairy tale suggests how the child may manage the contradictory feelings which would otherwise overwhelm him," Bettelheim wrote. "The fantasy of the wicked stepmother not only preserves the good mother intact, it also prevents having to feel guilty about one's angry thoughts and wishes about her."[35]

Media tales about monster moms serve a parallel purpose for adults. They say that we—or our wives, sisters, daughters, or friends—are good mothers by comparison. They invite us to redirect (more accurately, misdirect) our self-doubts. When we lose our temper or strike out at our children we may secretly worry about our potential for child abuse. But at least we know we could never do the things Awilda Lopez did.

How can we be so certain? Reporters spelled out for us precisely how Lopez differed from us. "Drugs, drugs, drugs—that's all she was interested in," *Time* quoted a neighbor saying of Lopez, and not just any drugs, not the sort that subscribers to *Time* might use. Lopez was "dominated by crack," a drug that, according to the *New York Times*, "can overwhelm one of the strongest forces in nature, the parental instinct." Crack "chemically impairs" mothers, the *Times* quoted one psychologist as saying, to the point where they "can't take responsibility for paying the rent or seeing that there is food on the table for their children."[36]

Infanticidal mothers are routinely depicted by the media as depraved beyond what any of us can imagine about ourselves or our friends and relatives. The year before Awilda Lopez, the media-anointed monster mother was a South Carolinian named Susan Smith, who drowned her two little boys in a lake. She too was portrayed as severely degenerate. She had been having an affair with her boss's son and planned to dump her husband and marry the boyfriend. After her lover wrote her a note saying he wasn't ready for the responsibilities of fatherhood, the story went, she decided to kill her kids. As if all of this weren't perverse enough, she had been having consensual sex with her stepfather, reporters revealed.

It took some doing, though, for the news media to portray Smith as the personification of depravity. They had to invalidate everything they themselves had been saying about her. Throughout the first week after the death of her children the press depicted her as a loving, heroic, small-town mom. They even bought in to Smith's weepy tale about a black man carjacking her kids, a story that should have made reporters wary, considering their embarrassment five years earlier after Charles Stewart, a Boston man, hoodwinked them with exactly the same racist ruse following the murder of his pregnant wife in an insurance scam.[37]

When the truth came out that Susan Smith had strapped her kids in car seats and let the car roll into the lake, reporters recast her faster than you can say "baby-killing bitch" (a neighbor's description quoted the following week in *Newsweek*). All of the glowing descriptions that journalists had been printing about Smith suddenly evaporated. There was no more discussion of her classmates having voted her "friendliest senior" of the class of 1989, or her teachers describing her as "a good kid," or the neighbor who said of Smith and her husband, "I saw the love that they had for these children."[38]

Reporters also had to ignore reports that Smith's stepfather, a six-foot-four, 300-pound man, admitted to sexually abusing Smith ever since she was fifteen, when he allegedly began fondling her breasts and forcing her to rub his genitals. Presumably journalists felt justified in referring to this man's sexual assaults as an "affair" because Smith herself had called them that. Most failed to point out that she had done so when she was neither legally nor psychologically capable of giving consent: Smith had made the statement at age seventeen, during an interview with therapists at a hospital after she had swallowed thirty aspirin in a suicide attempt.[39]

As much as we might like to settle on some fatal character or behavior flaw to explain why a woman killed her children, the truth is seldom so clear-cut. The women's own pathologies are invariably more complex, and other parties usually are involved. Even extreme cases like Awilda Lopez are not as simple as they may seem. To attribute her actions to her crack addiction is to disregard the obvious fact that most crack abusers do *not* kill their kids. Nor do they lose their maternal instincts, as the article in the *Times* suggested. "These women are not monsters. They do not hate their kids, they do not hit their kids any more than their counterparts who do not use crack," Sheigla Murphy and Marsha Rosenbaum of the Institute for Scientific Analysis in San Francisco, who have studied crack-using mothers extensively, report. No one denies that a mother's use of crack injures her children, or that children are ignored or abused when their mothers go on crack binges. But many of the crack users Murphy and Rosenbaum followed took great pride in their children's achievements and worked to steer them away from drugs. During periods when their own drug use got out of hand they placed their children with relatives.[40]

It may have provided a handy way for the American public to differentiate themselves from her, but Awilda Lopez's use of crack defines neither what kind of mother she is nor the cause of Elisa's death. Numerous other parties besides Elisa's mother and her crack dealer–from Lopez's husband to the entire New York City child welfare administration–also were at fault.[41]

The Woman Next Door

Like the elephant that vanishes behind clouds of smoke on the magician's stage, the larger cast of characters that give rise to child mistreatment are obscured amid melodramatic reporting about evil mothers. The coverage can leave the impression that it is not so much social policies or collective irresponsibility that endanger many children in this country but rather an overabundance of infanticidal women.

Making a fairly small number of women appear massive is an impressive feat of legerdemain, and several features of the media's coverage of child abuse intersect to create the illusion. Coupled with the relentless attention paid to notorious baby killers such as Smith and Lopez, there is an *underplaying* of stories about a much larger and more important group of deficient parents. Michael Shapiro, a professor of journalism at Columbia University, calls these parents "the screwups."

> There have always been parents who kill their children, and there always will be psychotic and evil parents who do. The true story of child welfare–the more than half a million children in the care of the state, the twenty state child welfare agencies across the nation in such disarray that they are under court-ordered supervision, the seeming inability of the state to help the children it feels it must take from their homes–is about "the screwups."

Screwup parents, Shapiro goes on to explain, love their children and neither torture nor murder them. They simply have trouble providing for them in a consistent and competent manner. Critical of journalists' infatuation with infanticidal parents, Shapiro observes, "When the death of a child becomes the context in which all subsequent child welfare stories get reported and written, then all the failing parents become the homicidal parent and all their children are in grave peril."[42]

Local newspapers and TV news programs pick up where the national media leave off in creating the false impression that a large proportion of failing parents are homicidal. Local media run story upon story about deadly mothers who never make it to national infamy. Around the time of the Smith and Lopez chronicles, for example, the New York City media ran hundreds of news stories about a woman named Sherain Bryant, who tortured and beat her four-year-old daughter to death in 1994. A focus of media attention for the following two years, Bryant was finally sentenced to twenty-five years to life in prison.

Following her conviction in 1996 the *New York Daily News* ran an editorial that concluded with a leading question: "She has now been removed. But how many more Bryants are out there?" As if to answer the question, around this same time the *Daily News*—along with most of the rest of the New York City media—relayed hideous particulars about several other local moms as well. Two notable examples are the Brooklyn woman who scratched and burned her seven-year-old daughter while smoking crack cocaine in front of her, and the Queens mother who, despondent after an argument with her husband, shot her two-year-old and six-year-old in the head, killing them both.[43]

The *New York Times* article about the Queens woman includes another common journalistic gambit: implying that behind any door may reside a would-be murderous mom. A neighbor is quoted, saying what neighbors are so often quoted as saying after a woman has killed her child. "She seemed like such a nice lady. She was a friendly person, and she had nice little kids. I'm shocked," the manager of a nearby laundromat says, suggesting ipso facto that other nice, friendly moms might someday slaughter their children too.[44]

Stories that blithely pass along frightening statistics on child abuse likewise promote the mythic impression of a nation teeming with potentially lethal women. Donna Shalala announced in 1996 that the number of children abused and neglected by their parents had doubled during a recent seven-year period, from 1.4 million to 2.8 million, and the number of seriously abused children had quadrupled from about 143,000 to nearly 570,000. She did not specify how much of the abuse was committed by mothers, but since the vast majority of single parents are women (and Shalala emphasized that children of single parents are almost twice as likely to be harmed), she implicitly singled out mothers.[45]

By and large reporters took the numbers at face value and labeled them "alarming," and crusaders for various causes used them to argue for everything from greater spending on welfare programs to a ban on abortion—the latter from the author of an op-ed piece in the *Minneapolis Star Tribune*, who argued that "abortion on demand has had a polluting effect, which is at least partially responsible for the dramatic rise in child abuse and neglect."[46]

Absent from almost all of the coverage was readily available evidence suggesting that rates of child abuse had not increased as drastically as Shalala indicated. For instance, statistics from the National Committee to Prevent Child Abuse showed that the annual number of fatalities resulting from child abuse had increased by only about 200 during the period in question, from 1,014 in 1986 to 1,216 in 1993. If the number of kids seriously abused and neglected quadrupled, as Shalala avows, should not then the number of deaths have increased by a large number as well?[47]

A closer look at Shalala's study reveals that much of what is described as a "skyrocketing" increase in child abuse is really a growth in *expectations* of abuse. According to Douglas Besharov, a former director of the National Center on Child Abuse and Neglect who helped design the study and lately has been on the staff of the American Enterprise Institute, more than half of the additional 1.4 million children were not actually said to be abused or neglected but rather "endangered." That is to say, these children were deemed by social services professionals to be at risk of future harm.[48]

She Beats Her Old Man Too

Another ill-reported set of statistics further buttresses the illusion of an epidemic of savage mothers. Their interest sparked initially by Lorena Bobbitt, who severed her husband's penis in 1993, and by O. J. Simpson, who claimed in 1994 that his murdered wife had battered him, journalists set out to inform the public about the prevalence of "husband abuse."

"It's Far More Widespread Than People Think" read a headline in the *Washington Post* in 1993 in a lengthy story revealing the existence of battered husbands, about whom the mental health community and general public "have been in deep denial," according to the reporter. How common is husband battering? According to a headline in *USA Today* in 1994, "Husbands Are Battered as Often as Wives." In an article the following year a writer for the *National Review* cited a study showing that "54 per cent of all severe domestic violence is committed by women." In 1996, in one of several columns he has published on this issue, John Leo of *U.S. News & World Report* revealed that "children are now more likely to see mommy hit daddy" than the other way around. Not only that, the whole thing has been covered up by "feminist scholars," according to Dennis Byrne of the *Chicago Sun-Times.* "Researchers have known for years that women are as, if not more, likely to report violently abusing their husbands or partners," Byrne revealed in 1998.[49]

A major source of statistical information behind these stories is research conducted by a colleague of mine, the sociologist Richard Gelles, director of the Family Violence Research Program at the University of Rhode Island. The writers accurately identified Gelles's research as the best available studies, but they wrongly reported the findings. Gelles does not hold that millions of men get beaten by their wives, as a casual reader of newspapers and magazines might be led to believe. On the contrary, he maintains that 100,000 to 200,000 men are battered in the United States—a number that pales in comparison to the 2 million battered women. Supporting Gelles's findings, FBI data show that one in four female murder victims is killed by a husband or boyfriend, compared to just 3 percent of murdered men slain by wives or girlfriends.[50]

By overlooking or downplaying what Gelles considers vital, writers make his assertions seem like evidence of an epidemic of moms beating up dads. "The statement that men and women hit one another in roughly equal numbers is true," Gelles admits. "But it cannot be made in a vacuum without the qualifiers I always include in my writing: number one, women are seriously injured at seven times the rate of men; and number two, women are killed by partners at more than two times the rate of men." When women do kill their husbands, he adds, they are often reacting to years of brutal assaults or to a current attack. In reality, when mommies hit daddies most of the time they don't hurt them very much, but unfortunately the same cannot be said the other way around. As Gelles puts it, "The most brutal, terrorizing, and continuing pattern of harmful intimate violence is carried out primarily by men."[51]

Husband abuse never became a predominant scare on a par with, say, teenage motherhood. Yet the fact that several respectable publications helped to promote it evinces how intense the moral panic over motherhood became in the 1990s. That conservative columnists and talk show hosts continue to promote the scare in the late 1990s—half a decade after Gelles began publicly condemning it as misogynistic—also demonstrates something. Fear mongers do not have to stop performing their hocus-pocus just because their secrets have been revealed.[52]

5

BLACK MEN

How to Perpetuate Prejudice
Without Really Trying

Journalists, politicians, and other opinion leaders foster fears about particular groups of people both by what they play up and what they play down. Consider Americans' fears of black men. These are perpetuated by the excessive attention paid to dangers that a small percentage of African-American men create for other people, and by a relative *lack* of attention to dangers that a majority of black men face themselves.

The dangers to black men recede from public view whenever people paint color-blind pictures of hazards that particularly threaten African-American men: discussions of disease trends that fail to mention that black men are four times more likely to be infected with the AIDS virus and twice as likely to suffer from prostate cancer and heart disease than are white men; reports about upturns in teen suicide rates that neglect to note evidence that the rate for white males crept up only 22 percent between 1980 and 1995 while the rate for black males jumped 146 percent; or explorations of the gap between what middle-class Americans earn and the expenses of maintaining a middle-class lifestyle that fail to point out that the problem is more acute for black men. (College-educated black men earn only as much as white men with high school diplomas.)[1]

The most egregious omissions occur in the coverage of crime. Many more black men are casualties of crime than are perpetrators, but their victimization does not attract the media spotlight the way their crimes do. Thanks to profuse coverage of violent crime on local TV news programs, "night after night, black men rob, rape, loot, and pillage in the living room," Caryl Rivers, a journalism instructor at Boston University, has remarked. Scores of studies document that when it comes to *victims* of crime, however, the media pay disproportionately more attention to whites and women.[2]

On occasion the degree of attention becomes so skewed that reporters start seeing patterns where none exist—the massively publicized "wave" of tourist murders in Florida in the early 1990s being a memorable example. By chance alone every decade or two there should be an unusually high number of tourists murdered in Florida, the statistician Arnold Barnett of MIT demonstrated in a journal article. The media uproar was an "overreaction to statistical noise," he wrote. The upturn that so caught reporters' fancy—ten tourists killed in a year—was labeled a crime wave because the media chose to label it as such. Objectively speaking, ten murders out of 41 million visitors did not even constitute a ripple, much less a wave, especially considering that at least 97 percent of all victims of crime in Florida are Floridians. Although the Miami area had the highest crime rate in the nation during this period, it was not tourists who had most cause for worry. One study showed that British, German, and Canadian tourists who flock to Florida each year to avoid winter weather were more than 70 times more likely to be victimized at home. The typical victim of crime in Florida, though largely invisible in the news, was young, local, and black or Hispanic.[3]

So was the typical victim of drug violence in New York City in the late 1980s and early 1990s, when some reporters and social scientists avidly implied otherwise. "The killing of innocent bystanders, particularly in the cross fires of this nation's drug wars, has suddenly become a phenomenon that greatly troubles experts on crime," began a front-page story in the *New York Times*. It is "the sense that it could happen to anybody, anywhere, like a plane crash" that makes these attacks so scary, the reporter quoted Peter Reuter from the RAND Corporation. According to the *New York Daily News*, "spillover" crime from the drug wars even affected people in "silk-stocking areas." In fact, a *New York* magazine article revealed, thanks to a crack cocaine epidemic, "most neighborhoods in the city by now have been forced to deal with either crack or its foul by-products: if not crack houses and street dealers or users, then crackhead crimes such as purse snatchings, car break-ins, burglaries, knife-point robberies, muggings, and murders." TV newscasts, needless to say, breathlessly reported much the same, with pictures at eleven.[4]

One expert eventually became skeptical of the reporting and set out to examine whether New Yorkers were truly at equal and random risk of falling victim to drug-related violence. What Henry Brownstein, a researcher with the New York State Division of Criminal Justice Services, found when he looked at data available from the police was almost exactly the opposite. About two out of one hundred homicides in New York City involved innocent bystanders, and most drug-related violence occurred between people connected to the drug trade itself. When innocent people did get hurt, Brownstein discovered, often they were roughed up or shot at not by drug users but by police officers in the course of ill-conceived raids and street busts.[5]

Drug violence, like almost every other category of violence, is not an equal opportunity danger. It principally afflicts young people from poor minority communities, and above all, young black men. But reporters and politicos never seem to lack for opportunities to perpetuate the myth of indiscriminate victimization. "Random Killings Hit a High—All Have 'Realistic' Chance of Being Victim, Says FBI," read the headline in *USA Today*'s story in 1994 about a government report that received big play that year. Had the academics and elected officials who supplied reporters with brooding comments about the report looked more closely at its contents, however, they would have learned that it was misleading. As Richard Moran, a sociology professor at Mount Holyoke College, subsequently pointed out in a commentary on National Public Radio, the FBI report made random killings seem more prevalent than they are by lumping together two distinct categories of murders: those that remained unsolved, and those committed by strangers. Many an unsolved murder later turns out to have been committed by a relative or other acquaintance of the victim.[6]

To suggest that all Americans have a realistic chance of being a victim of homicide is to heighten already elevated anxieties among people who face little risk. In spite of the impression given by stories like the one in *Time* titled "Danger in the Safety Zone: As Violence Spreads into Small Towns, Many Americans Barricade Themselves," which focused on random murders in several hamlets throughout the country, tens of millions of Americans live in places where there hasn't been a murder in years, and most of the rest of us live in towns and neighbor-hoods where murder is a rare occurrence.[7]

Who *does* stand a realistic chance of being murdered? You guessed it: minority males. A black man is about eighteen times more likely to be murdered than is a white woman. All told, the murder rate for black men is double that of American soldiers in World War II. And for black men between the ages of fifteen and thirty, violence is the single lead-ing cause of death.[8]

Of Dogs and Men

David Krajicek, a journalism instructor at Columbia University, re-calls a term that he and his editor used when he worked as a crime re-porter for the *New York Daily News* in the 1980s. The term was *unblees*—unidentified black males. "Unblees," Krajicek notes, "rarely rated a story unless three or four turned up at the same location. We paid little attention to these routine murders because the police paid little atten-tion."[9]

Police inattention is one of several factors that journalists accurately cite to account for why white crime victims receive more media atten-tion than black victims. Journalists also cite complaints from African-American leaders about the press paying too much attention to prob-lems and pathologies in black communities. But are crime victims the best candidates to overlook in the service of more positive coverage? A host of studies indicate that by downplaying the suffering of victims and their families the media do a disservice to minority neighborhoods where those victims live. Criminologists have documented that the amount of coverage a crime victim receives affects how much attention police devote to the case and the willingness of prosecutors to accept plea bargains. As a rule, the more coverage, the more likely that an as-sailant will be kept behind bars, unable to do further harm to the victim or community. In addition, when a neighborhood's crime victims are portrayed *as* victims—sympathetically and without blame, as humans rather than as statistics—people living in other parts of the city are more inclined to support improved social services for the area, which in turn can reduce the crime rate.[10]

Underreporting of black victims also has the effect of making white victims appear more ubiquitous than they are, thereby fueling whites' fears of black criminals, something that benefits neither race. Helen Benedict, a professor of journalism at Columbia University, has documented that rapes of white women by black men—which constitute a tiny proportion of all rapes—receive considerable media attention. In a separate study of women's concerns about crime Esther Madriz, a sociology professor at Hunter College, discovered that stories in the news media "reinforce a vision of society in which black men are foremost among women's fears."[11]

Another explanation journalists and editors give for their relative neglect of black victims might be called the Journalism 101 defense. Those of us who took an introductory journalism course in college remember the teacher pounding into our cerebrums the famous dictate attributed to John Bogart, city editor of the *New York Sun* in the 1880s: "When a dog bites a man that is not news, when a man bites a dog, that is news." Everyone *expects* black crime victims, the argument goes, so their plight isn't newsworthy. Here is how a writer for the *Los Angeles Times*, Scott Harris, characterized the thoughts that go through reporters' and editors' minds as they ponder how much attention, if any, to accord to a city's latest homicide: "Another 15-year-old shot to death? Ho hum. Was he an innocent bystander? What part of town? Any white people involved?"[12]

As heartless and bigoted as this reasoning may sound, actually there would be nothing objectionable about it if news organizations applied the man-bites-dog principle universally. Obviously they do not; otherwise, there would never be stories about crimes committed by black men, since no one considers black perpetrators novel or unexpected.[13]

My friend David Shaw, media critic at the *Los Angeles Times*, offers a simpler explanation for the scant attention to black victims. To stay in business newspapers must cater to the interests of their subscribers, few of whom live in inner-city minority neighborhoods. The same market forces result in paltry coverage of foreign news in most American newspapers, Shaw suggests.[14]

Now *there's* a study someone should do: compare the amount of attention and empathy accorded by the U.S. press during the 1990s to black men shot down in American cities to, say, Bosnians killed in that country's civil war. I wouldn't be surprised if the Bosnians fared better. The tendency to slight black victims extends even to coverage of undeniably newsworthy crimes such as shootings of police by fellow officers. In 1996, after a white New York City police officer, Peter Del-Debbio, was convicted of shooting Desmond Robinson, a black plainclothes transit officer in the back, wounding his kidneys, liver, lungs, and heart, reporters and columnists evidenced great sympathy for Del-Debbio. They characterized him as having made an innocent mistake and suffering overwhelming remorse. The agony of Robinson and his family, by contrast, received more modest attention. Few reporters seriously questioned—and some overtly endorsed—the official spin from the district attorney, mayor, and defense attorneys that the shooting had nothing to do with race and was largely the victim's fault—even though in testimony Del-Debbio recalled having reacted not to seeing just any man with a gun but "a male black with a gun."[15]

While some writers made note of the fact that black officers say their white colleagues are quick to fire at African Americans working undercover because they view them as suspects, no reporter, the best I can determine, investigated the issue. When Richard Goldstein, a media critic for the *Village Voice*, reviewed the coverage of the shooting he found that only the *Daily News*—not the *Times* or *Post*—made note of the fact that, since 1941, twenty black police officers in New York had been shot by white colleagues. During that time not a single white officer had been shot by a black cop. "Imagine," wrote Goldstein, "the shock-horror if 20 female officers had been shot by male cops. But when it comes to race, the more obvious the pattern the more obscure it seems."[16]

The Nation's Foremost Anti-Semites

The reverse is true as well. When it comes to race, obscure patterns become accepted as obvious and are put to use in perpetuating racial fears. Consider a scare about black men that has been directed at people like me. As a Jew, I am susceptible to fear mongering about anti-

Semitism. I am not as paranoid as the Woody Allen character in *Annie Hall* who hears the word *Jew* when someone says "did you"; but neither am I among those Jews who, never having experienced anti-Semitism personally, imagine that it vanished from the globe when Germany surrendered in 1945.

In my own life anti-Semitism has been an almost constant presence. Growing up in a small town in the South in the 1950s and 1960s, I was attacked—verbally on numerous occasions, physically a few times—and members of my family were barred from joining particular clubs and living in certain neighborhoods on account of our religion. Throughout my career as a professor as well I have endured anti-Semitic remarks from students, staff, and fellow faculty, and Jewish students have come to me for advice about how to handle bigoted teachers and classmates. My writing also brings me into contact with anti-Semites. Because I have a Jewish-sounding name, when I publish controversial articles in newspapers and magazines I can count on receiving letters that go beyond criticizing my views and accuse me of being part of an international Jewish conspiracy.[17]

So far as I can determine, on none of these occasions was the anti-Semite black. To judge by stories in the news media and reports from advocacy groups, apparently I have a phenomenally skewed sample. Blacks, we have been led to believe, are America's preeminent anti-Semites. When I conducted a search of databases for major U.S. newspapers, magazines, and network news programs for the eight-year period beginning in 1990 the vast majority of stories about anti-Semitism were on two topics: attacks on Jews in Eastern Europe following the demise of communism and anti-Semitism by African Americans. The sorts of anti-Semites I and my students most often encounter—bitter white people—received relatively little attention.

Even their most fanatical cousins went largely unnoticed. In 1993 white supremacists terrorized Jews, blacks, and other minorities in Billings, Montana, for months on end. A swastika appeared on the door of a synagogue, bottles and bricks were tossed at homes of Jewish families, racist and anti-Semitic literature appeared on windshields and in mailboxes. Yet according to a study by the sociologists Joe Feagin and

Hernán Vera of the University of Florida, only four stories on the violence appeared in the nation's news media. "In contrast," Feagin and Vera report, "during the same period more than one hundred national media stories focused on anti-Semitic remarks made by Khalid Muhammad, until then a little-known minister of the small religious group, the Nation of Islam."[18]

Indeed, the coverage of Khalid Muhammad provides a textbook illustration of how a small story, when placed in a heated media environment, can explode into a towering concern. Initially, Muhammad's description of Jews as "hook-nosed, bagel-eatin'" frauds was heard only by the few dozen students who bothered to turn out one night in November of 1993 for his speech at Kean College in Union, New Jersey. During that address Muhammad lashed out at gays, black leaders he disliked, and the "old no-good Pope," about whom he suggested, "somebody needs to raise that dress up and see what's really under there." The intense coverage and commentary that followed focused, however, on his anti-Semitism. For months it went on, with *New York Times* columnist A. M. Rosenthal and *Washington Post* columnist Richard Cohen enjoining black leaders to renounce Muhammad.[19]

By February 1994 the commotion had begun to die down when Christopher Farley of *Time* magazine kicked it up again by running a report on the resentment of some African Americans at white journalists and politicians who, as Farley put it, "feel a need to make all black leaders speak out whenever one black says something stupid." A month earlier, when Senator Ernest Hollings, a white man, joked about African cannibalism, there had been no pressure put on white leaders to repudiate him, Farley observed, much to the annoyance of A. M. Rosenthal. "Politicization, distortion, ethical junk," he labeled the Farley article in a convulsive column in which he went on to compare the Nation of Islam—a minority movement within a minority community— to Stalinism and Nazism.[20]

A segment on the CBS newsmagazine "Eye to Eye with Connie Chung" several weeks later propelled Muhammad's star still higher. At a speech at Howard University the producers had filmed not only the minister's anti-Semitic tirade and the audience enthusiastically cheering him and another anti-Semitic speaker but also individual students declaring that Jews spied on Martin Luther King and arranged for his assassination. One of America's premier African-American universities is ablaze with anti-Semitism, the segment suggested, though the crowds at Muhammad's speeches at Howard reportedly consisted largely of people with no affiliation with the campus. As Otesa Middleton and Larry Brown, editors of the student newspaper, subsequently pointed out in an op-ed piece in the *Los Angeles Times*, the producers of the CBS segment included comments from only two Howard students but made it appear that the two represented the views of everyone at Howard. Not only was the impression false, the student editors argued, planting it was journalistically irresponsible. "The media would do better to devote its resources to exposing the real causes of racial and social injustice," they wrote.[21]

But the infatuation with Muhammad continued. He garnered major attention for a speech in 1997 at San Francisco State University in which he denied that 6 million Jews died in the Holocaust and spoke of Zionists with "hairy hands" whom he said were "pimping the world." When he announced that he would lead a youth march in Harlem in 1998, Mayor Rudolph Guiliani provided reporters with anti-Semitic statements Muhammad had made over the years and urged them to reprint the slurs. Bob Herbert of the *New York Times* was among those who took the bait. In one of his columns, Herbert made it sound as if Jews had great cause for worry about Muhammad, and about black anti-Semitism more generally. Quoting several of Muhammad's most loathsome anti-Jewish slurs from the past few years, Herbert issued a challenge to black leaders: "It would be helpful if some prominent African-American leaders, faced with the grotesque reality of a virulent anti-Semite playing Pied Pier to the nation's black children, would stand up and say enough is enough."[22]

Various black leaders, having been chastised several years earlier, had already done so, but others shared the view of Representative Don Edwards, who observed that "this scoundrel would become a national and international hero" by being stigmatized. Indeed, the main beneficiaries of the lavish attention directed at demagogues like Khalid

Muhammad are the demagogues themselves. Nation of Islam leaders use Jew-bashing to attract the media and pull crowds. Even Louis Farrakhan has been a fixture in the press largely on account of his anti-Semitic remarks, which distinguish him from other, more mainstream black leaders. Jonathan Kaufman, a reporter for the *Wall Street Journal*, goes so far as to suggest that Farrakhan's black political rivals are his true targets when he speaks of Jews as "bloodsuckers" or slave traders. In making such statements he establishes himself, notes Kaufman, as the lone black man who will stand up to whites and openly condemn a powerful group of them. In Kaufman's view, when Farrakhan slanders Jews what he's really saying is, "All those other black leaders are too timid to speak out and tell the truth."[23]

Farrakhan says much the same about African-American journalists. "A scared-to-death Negro is a slave, you slave writers, slave media people," he bellowed in a speech in 1996 to a convention of the National Association of Black Journalists. Perhaps what angered Farrakhan about black journalists in the mainstream media is their neglect of him. It has been a group of white columnists, after all, who have built Farrakhan up as more momentous than he is. In addition to Rosenthal, Cohen, and Herbert, there's the *Village Voice* columnist Nat Hentoff, who has written about him and Muhammad in at least a dozen pieces, and Fred Barnes, the magazine editor and former White House correspondent, who on a network TV talk show dubbed Farrakhan the "leading anti-Semite and separatist in this country," thereby ignoring thousands of skinheads, klansmen, neo-Nazis and militiamen, and several well-known leaders of the Christian right, all of whom have equal claim to that title. Randall Terry of Operation Rescue, for instance, holds "Jewish doctors" responsible for one-quarter of the nation's "baby killings," and Rev. Donald Wildmon of the American Family Association sees Jewish entertainment executives as promoting "anti-Christian" television programming and movie making. Pundit and presidential candidate Pat Buchanan has spouted enough anti-Semitic remarks over the years that even right-wingers like David Frum of the *Evening Standard* have commented on it. Yet the cumulative coverage in the major media of these white guys' anti-Semitism barely qualifies as a mole hill beside the mountain of reporting on black anti-Semitism.[24]

Even the Best and Brightest Are Bigots

Some surveys do find larger proportions of blacks than whites endorsing anti-Semitic sentiments. Questions beg to be asked, however, about how best to interpret these numbers. Are blacks more negative toward Jews than they are toward other whites, or was James Baldwin correct in an essay he published thirty years ago titled "Negroes Are Anti-Semitic Because They're Anti-White"? Anti-Semitism may be a subspecies of antiwhitism, and it may be largely limited to particular segments of the African-American community. Hubert Locke, former dean of the School of Public Affairs at the University of Washington, has argued that only at the fringes of African-American communities does serious anti-Semitism exist. In reanalyzing a series of questions from a survey of African Americans Locke found blacks as a group less hostile toward Jews than some researchers have suggested.[25]

One thing is certain. Black anti-Semitism is not concentrated on college campuses, as much media coverage has implied. "The number of anti-Semitic incidents reported annually on the nation's college campuses has more than doubled since 1988, the Anti-Defamation League said today," began an Associated Press story a few years ago that was picked up by the *New York Times*, among other publications. The ADL "attributed that increase in part to messages of 'racial hate' that it said were spread by Louis W. Farrakhan, head of the Nation of Islam, and other speakers popular with some black students," the story said without so much as a rejoinder from an African-American leader or social scientist who might have put the ADL's findings in perspective.[26]

As suggested earlier in the discussion about road rage, teen suicide, and preteen murderers, when a problem is said to have multiplied it is a good idea to ask, From what size to what size? When advocacy groups use surveys to draw attention to their causes the reported change—however extreme the organization may make it sound—is often from small to slightly less small. Read the entire article about anti-Semitism on campuses and you discover that "more than doubled" equals 60 incidents. Between them, the nation's 3,600 colleges and universities reported 60 more anti-Semitic incidents than four years earlier, for a total of 114 incidents. By my calculation, with about 14 million students enrolled in U.S. colleges that comes out to a rate of less than 1 reported anti-Semitic act per 100,000 college students. The story fails to mention how many of these acts were related to Farrakhan and other black speakers, or how the ADL could possibly measure their influence. Even in the unlikely event that black students committed a majority of the anti-Semitic acts, however, only a tiny proportion of black college students were involved.[27]

Fear mongers did not need many incidents to give the impression that black anti-Semitism flows as freely as beer on college campuses. Subsequent to the speeches at Kean College and Howard came an event in fall 1995 at Columbia University that reporters and commentators made into a bigger deal than it was. The student newspaper *The Spectator* published a column by an African-American senior who wrote of "evilness under the skirts and costumes of the Rabbi." He wagered, "If you look at the resources leaving Africa, you will find them in the bellies of Jewish merchants."[28]

Judging by the quantity and length of stories in the press about this student's comments and the dissections of his personal and educational biography, you would have thought there was something special about his column. Maybe he had ushered in an ingenious new set of lies about Jews, or maybe, as some writers asserted, he was living proof that in an age of political correctness the only prejudice that can be spoken openly on college campuses is by blacks against Jews.

Wrong. The student's remarks are ignorant and offensive yet familiar, and no worse than what I have read in college newspapers in recent years about a range of groups—immigrants, gays, feminists, conservatives, and (alas) blacks. The main difference between the Columbia student's column and other bigoted commentaries in college newspapers is the amount of attention they receive. Around the same time as the Columbia *Spectator* incident a student newspaper at the University of Wisconsin ran a column that said of the verdict in the O. J. Simpson murder trial, "to believe that one cop led a multi-million dollar plot to execute or lock up one nigger (oops did I say nigger? . . .) is completely ludicrous." After student groups protested and called on the university administration to end support for the paper the newspaper's editors responded, as adolescents will, by publishing an even more objectionable column, this one full of obscenities and epithets about "fags" and "bitches." The news media paid no attention to the controversy.[29]

Also around this time, at Pennsylvania State University, swastikas appeared in two dormitories, and on the door of a black student's room appeared the letters "K.K.K." Close to two thousand students and professors attended a rally to protest the hatred. There were rallies as well, likewise neglected in the media, at Dartmouth College after anti-Asian and antigay slurs had been scrawled on students' doors and on literature from student organizations.[30]

Nationwide, 20 to 30 percent of students from racial and ethnic minority groups report being physically or verbally attacked during their college careers, according to surveys. That is, tens of thousands of attacks per school year—only a small portion of which could conceivably be the doing of black anti-Semites. For every anti-Semitic African American enrolled in America's colleges and universities there are dozens, if not hundreds, of white anti-Semites, racists, and homophobes.[31]

Makers of the Nation's Most Hazardous Music

Fear mongers project onto black men precisely what slavery, poverty, educational deprivation, and discrimination have ensured that they do not have—great power and influence.

After two white boys opened fire on students and teachers at a schoolyard in Jonesboro, Arkansas, in 1998 politicians, teachers, and assorted self-designated experts suggested—with utter seriousness—that black rap musicians had inspired one of them to commit the crime. A fan of rappers such as the late Tupac Shakur, the thirteen-year-old emulated massacrelike killings described in some of their songs, we were told. Never mind that, according to a minister who knew him, the Jonesboro lad also loved religious music and sang for elderly residents at local nursing homes. By the late 1990s the ruinous power of rap was so taken for granted, people could blame rappers for almost any violent or misogynistic act anywhere.[32]

So dangerous were so-called gangsta rappers taken to be, they could be imprisoned for the lyrics on their albums. Free speech and the First Amendment be damned—when Shawn Thomas, a rapper known to his fans as C-Bo, released his sixth album in 1998 he was promptly arrested and put behind bars for violating the terms of his parole for an earlier conviction. The parole condition Thomas had violated required him not to make recordings that "promote the gang lifestyle or are anti-law enforcement."

Thomas's new album, "Til My Casket Drops," contained powerful protest lyrics against California governor Pete Wilson. "Look how he did Polly Klaas/Used her death and her family name/So he can gain more votes and political fame/It's a shame that I'm the one they say is a monster." The album also contained misogynistic and antipolice lyrics. Thomas refers to women as whores and bitches, and he recommends if the police "try to pull you over, shoot 'em in the face."[33]

Lyrics like these have been the raw material for campaigns against rappers for more than a decade—campaigns that have resulted not only in the incarceration of individual rappers but also in commitments from leading entertainment conglomerates such as Time Warner and Disney, as well as the state of Texas, not to invest in companies that produce gangsta albums. William Bennett and C. Delores Tucker, leaders of the antirap campaigns, have had no trouble finding antipolice and antiwomen lyrics to quote in support of their claim that "nothing less is at stake than civilization" if rappers are not rendered silent. So odious are the lyrics, that rarely do politicians or journalists stop to ask what qualifies Bennett to lead a moralistic crusade on behalf of America's minority youth. Not only has he opposed funding for the nation's leader in quality children's programming (the Public Broadcasting Corporation), he has urged that "illegitimate" babies be taken from their mothers and put in orphanages.[34]

What was Delores Tucker, a longtime Democratic party activist, doing lending her name as coauthor to antirap articles that Bennett used to raise money for his right-wing advocacy group, Empower America? Tucker would have us believe, as she exclaimed in an interview in *Ebony*, that "as a direct result" of dirty rap lyrics, we have "little boys raping little girls." But more reliable critics have rather a different take. For years they have been trying to call attention to the satiric and self-caricaturing side of rap's salacious verses, what Nelson George, the music critic, calls "cartoon machismo."[35]

Back in 1990, following the release of *Nasty As They Wanna Be*, an album by 2 Live Crew, and the band's prosecution in Florida on obscenity charges, Henry Louis Gates confided in an op-ed in the *New York Times* that when he first heard the album he "bust out laughing." Unlike *Newsweek* columnist George Will, who described the album as "extreme infantilism and menace . . . [a] slide into the sewer," Gates viewed 2 Live Crew as "acting out, to lively dance music, a parodic exaggeration of the age-old stereotypes of the oversexed black female and male." Gates noted that the album included some hilarious spoofs of blues songs, the black power movement, and familiar advertising slogans of the period ("Tastes great!" "Less filling!"). The rap group's lewd nursery rhymes were best understood, Gates argued, as continuing an age-old Western tradition of bawdy satire.[36]

Not every informed and open-minded follower of rap has been as upbeat as Gates, of course. Some have strongly criticized him, in fact, for seeming to vindicate performers who refer to women as "cunts," "bitches," and "hos," or worse, who appear to justify their rape and murder, as did a track on the 2 Live Crew album that contained the boast, "I'll . . . bust your pussy then break your backbone."

Kimberlé Williams Crenshaw, a professor of law at UCLA, wrote in an essay that she was shocked rather than amused by *Nasty As They Wanna Be*. Black women should not have to tolerate misogyny, Crenshaw argued, whether or not the music is meant to be laughed at or has artistic value—both of which she granted about *Nasty*. But something else also concerned Crenshaw: the singling out of black male performers for vilification. Attacks on rap artists at once reflect and reinforce deep and enduring fears about the sexuality and physical strength of black men, she suggests. How else, Crenshaw asks, can one explain why 2 Live Crew were the first group in the history of the nation to be prosecuted on obscenity charges for a musical recording, and one of only a few ever tried for a live performance? Around this same time, she observes, Madonna acted out simulated group sex and the seduction of a priest on stage and in her music videos, and on Home Box Office programs the comic Andrew Dice Clay was making comments every bit as obscene and misogynistic as any rapper.[37]

The hypocrisy of those who single out rap singers as especially sexist or violent was starkly—and comically—demonstrated in 1995, when presidential candidate Bob Dole denounced various rap albums and movies that he considered obscene and then recommended certain films as wholesome, "friendly to the family" fare. Included among the latter was Arnold Schwarzenegger's *True Lies*, in which every major female character is called a "bitch." While in real life Arnold may be a virtuous Republican, in the movie his wife strips, and he puts her through hell when he thinks she might be cheating on him. In one gratuitous scene she is humiliated and tortured for twenty minutes of screen time. Schwarzenegger's character also kills dozens of people in sequences more graphically violent than a rapper could describe with mere words.[38]

Even within the confines of American popular music, rappers are far from the first violently sexist fictional heroes. Historians have pointed out that in country music there is a long tradition of men doing awful things to women. Johnny Cash, in an adaptation of the frontier ballad "Banks of the Ohio" declares, "I murdered the only woman I loved/Because she would not marry me." In "Attitude Adjustment" Hank Williams Jr. gives a girlfriend "adjustment on the top of her head." Bobby Bare, in "If That Ain't Love," tells a woman, "I called you a name and I gave you a whack/Spit in your eye and gave your wrist a twist/And if that ain't love what is."

Rock music too has had its share of men attacking women, and not only in heavy metal songs. In "Down By the River" amiable Neil Young sings of shooting his "baby." And the song "Run for Your Life," in which a woman is stalked and threatened with death if she is caught with another man, was a Beatles hit.[39]

Just a Thug

After Tupac Shakur was gunned down in Las Vegas in 1996 at the age of twenty-five much of the coverage suggested he had been a victim of his own raps—even a deserving victim. "Rap Performer Who Personified Violence, Dies," read a headline in the *New York Times*. " 'What Goes 'Round . . .': Superstar Rapper Tupac Shakur Is Gunned Down in an Ugly Scene Straight Out of His Lyrics," the headline in *Time* declared. In their stories reporters recalled that Shakur's lyrics, which had come under fire intermittently throughout his brief career by the likes of William Bennett, Delores Tucker, and Bob Dole, had been directly implicated in two previous killings. In 1992 Vice President Dan Quayle cited an antipolice song by Shakur as a motivating force behind the shooting of a Texas state trooper. And in 1994 prosecutors in Milwaukee made the same claim after a police officer was murdered.[40]

Why, when white men kill, doesn't anyone do a *J'accuse* of Tennessee Ernie Ford or Johnny Cash, whose oddly violent classics are still played on country music stations? In "Sixteen Tons" Ford croons, "If you see me comin'/Better step aside/A lotta men didn't/A lotta men died," and in "Folsom Prison Blues" Cash crows, "I shot a man in Reno just to watch him die." Yet no one has suggested, as journalists and politicians did about Shakur's and 2 Live Crew's lyrics, that these lines overpower all the others in Ford's and Cash's songbooks.[41]

Any young rap fan who heard one of Shakur's antipolice songs almost certainly also heard one or more of his antiviolence raps, in which he recounts the horrors of gangster life and calls for black men to stop killing. "And they say/It's the white man I should fear/But it's my own kind/Doin' all the killin' here," Shakur laments on one of his songs.[42]

Many of Shakur's raps seemed designed to inspire responsibility rather than violence. One of his most popular, "Dear Mama," was part thank-you letter to his mother for raising him on her own, and part explanation of bad choices he had made as an adolescent. "All along I was looking for a father—he was gone/I hung around with the thugs/And even though they sold drugs/They showed a young brother love," Shakur rapped. In another of his hits, "Papa'z Song," he recalled, all the more poignantly, having "had to play catch by myself/what a sorry sight."[43]

Shakur's songs, taken collectively, reveal "a complex and sometimes contradictory figure," as Jon Pereles, a music critic for the *New York Times*, wrote in an obituary. It was a key point missed by much of the media, which ran photos of the huge tattoo across Shakur's belly— "THUG LIFE"—but failed to pass along what he said it stood for: "The Hate You Give Little Infants Fucks Everyone." And while many mentioned that he had attended the High School of Performing Arts in Baltimore, few acknowledged the lasting impact of that education. "It influences all my work. I really like stuff like 'Les Miserables' and 'Gospel at Colonus,'" Shakur told a *Los Angeles Times* interviewer in 1995. He described himself as "the kind of guy who is moved by a song like Don McLean's 'Vincent,' that one about Van Gogh. The lyric on that song is so touching. That's how I want to make my songs feel."[44]

After Tupac Shakur's death a writer in the *Washington Post* characterized him as "stupid" and "misguided" and accused him of having "committed the unpardonable sin of using his immense poetic talents to degrade and debase the very people who needed his positive words most—his fans." To judge by their loving tributes to him in calls to radio stations, prayer vigils, and murals that appeared on walls in inner cities following his death, many of those fans apparently held a different view. Ernest Hardy of the *L.A. Weekly*, an alternative paper, was probably closer to the mark when he wrote of Shakur: "What made him important and forged a bond with so many of his young black (especially black male) fans was that he was a signifier trying to figure out what he signified. He knew he lived in a society that still didn't view him as human, that projected its worst fears onto him; he had to decide whether to battle that or to embrace it."[45]

Readers of the music magazine *Vibe* had seen Shakur himself describe this conflict in an interview not long before his death. "What are you at war with?" the interviewer asked. "Different things at different times," Shakur replied. "My own heart sometimes. There's two niggas inside me. One wants to live in peace, and the other won't die unless he's free."[46]

It seems to me at once sad, inexcusable, and entirely symptomatic of the culture of fear that the only version of Tupac Shakur many Americans knew was a frightening and unidimensional caricature. The opening lines from Ralph Ellison's novel, *Invisible Man*, still ring true nearly half a century after its publication. "I am an invisible man," Ellison wrote. "No, I am not a spook like those who haunted Edgar Allan Poe; nor am I one of your Hollywood-movie ectoplasms. I am a man of substance, of flesh and bone, fiber and liquids—and I might even be said to possess a mind. I am invisible, understand, simply because people refuse to see me."[47]

6

"SMACK IS BACK"

When Presidents and
the Press Collude,
the Scares Never Stop

Many scares, like Hollywood stars, have their heyday and then fade from sight, more or less permanently. Witness panics over razor blades in Halloween apples, abortion as a cause of cancer, or children dumping their elderly parents at racetracks. Other fears have more staying power, as the discussion of scares about black men suggests.

Another perennial scare owes its long run to powerful sponsorship. For three decades U.S. presidents and media organizations have worked in unison to promote fears of drug abuse. Unlike almost every other hazard, illicit drugs have no interest group to defend them. So they are safe fodder for winning elections and ratings.[1]

Drug abuse is a serious problem that deserves serious public attention. But sensationalism rather than rationality has guided the national conversation. Misinformed about who uses drugs, which drugs people abuse, and with what results, we waste enormous sums of money and fail to address other social and personal problems effectively. Federal drug enforcement, a $6 million expense in the 1960s, passed the $1 billion mark in the mid-1980s during Ronald Reagan's presidency and more than $17 billion during Bill Clinton's. Throughout the 1980s and 1990s, an era of budget cutting and distaste for Big Government, agencies involved in drug control were about the only places within the federal government to grow.[2]

The money has been spent almost exclusively on curbing illegal drugs, a curious policy given that abuse of legal drugs is a huge problem. More Americans use legal drugs for nonmedical reasons than use cocaine or heroin; hundreds of millions of prescription pills are used illicitly each year. More than half of those who die of drug-related medical problems or seek treatment for those problems are abusing prescription drugs. By the American Medical Association's own estimates one in twenty doctors is grossly negligent in prescribing drugs, and according to the Drug Enforcement Agency, at least 15,000 doctors sell prescriptions to addicts and pushers. Yet less than 1 percent of the nation's antidrug budget goes to stopping prescription drug abuse.[3]

The gargantuan disparity in spending reflects—and is perpetuated by—what the nation's media and political leaders have chosen to focus on. Scares about heroin, cocaine, and marijuana issue forth continually from politicians and journalists. But except for burps when a celebrity overdoses, they have been largely silent about the abuse of legal drugs.

A White House Tradition

It all started on April 9, 1970. An event at 1600 Pennsylvania Avenue inaugurated a new and lasting collaboration between presidents and the media. At Richard Nixon's request, White House officials held a day-long meeting with producers and executives from the major television networks, production companies, and advertising agencies to enlist their support in curtailing illegal drug use. Many of the most influential decision makers in the TV industry participated.

Prior to the event, Jeb Magruder, a press secretary, described the approach he and his colleagues would take. "The individuals being invited think in dramatic terms. We have therefore tailored the program to appeal to their dramatic instincts," Magruder wrote in a memorandum. And indeed, throughout the day undercover agents, pot-sniffing dogs, recovering addicts, and the president himself paraded before the forty attendees. Nixon gave a passionate speech about the need to "warn our youth constantly against the dangers of drugs." Touted as "off-the-cuff," it had actually been written by Patrick Buchanan, Nixon's chief speech writer on social issues and himself a candidate for the presidency a couple of decades later. "If this nation is going to survive," Nixon intoned, "it will have to depend to a great extent on how you gentlemen help raise our children." The TV guys ate it up. At times "there was hardly a dry eye in the whole hard-boiled crowd," according to a producer who attended. So successful was the White House event, not only did network news stories about drug abuse increase, many of TV's top dramatic series–"Marcus Welby, M.D.," "Hawaii Five-O," "The Mod Squad"–had episodes with antidrug themes during the next season.[4]

Presidents prior to Nixon had not made drug abuse a prime focus of concern for themselves or the media. But every subsequent commander-in-chief has actively solicited the media to the cause. "In the newsrooms and production rooms of our media centers, you have a special opportunity with your enormous influence to send alarm signals across the nation," Ronald Reagan urged, and he has been proven right. After Reagan's successor, George Bush, declared in his first televised address as president that "the gravest domestic threat facing our nation today is drugs," the number of stories on network newscasts tripled over the coming few weeks, and public opinion changed significantly. In a nationwide survey conducted by the *New York Times* and CBS two months into the media upsurge, 64 percent of those polled selected drugs as the country's greatest problem, up from 20 percent five months earlier.[5]

David Fan, a professor at the University of Minnesota, conducted a study in which he correlated the number of stories in major print media that included the phrase "drug crisis" with variations in public opinion from 1985 through 1994. At times during that period only one in twenty Americans ranked drugs as the nation's most important problem; at other times nearly two out of three did. The immense variations could be explained, Fan showed, by changes in the press coverage.[6]

Psychologists call this the *availability heuristic*. We judge how common or important a phenomenon is by how readily it comes to mind. Presented with a survey that asks about the relative importance of issues, we are likely to give top billing to whatever the media emphasizes at the moment, because that issue instantly comes to mind. Were there a reasonable correspondence between emphases in the media and the true severity of social problems, the availability heuristic would not be problematic. When it comes to drug crises, however, the correspondence has been lousy, owing in no small measure to bad information from the nation's top political leader. President Bush's speech in 1989 remains the most notorious example. While addressing the nation live from the Oval Office via all three TV networks, he held up a sealed plastic bag marked "EVIDENCE." "This is crack cocaine seized a few days ago by Drug Enforcement agents in a park across the street from the White House," Bush said. "It's as innocent looking as candy, but it's murdering our children."[7]

The *Washington Post* subsequently corrected the president's report. At Bush's request DEA agents tried to find crack in Lafayette Park but failed, *Post* reporters learned. There was little drug dealing of any sort in that park, and no one selling crack. With Bush's speech already drafted to include the baggie prop, the agents improvised. In another part of town they recruited a young crack dealer to make a delivery across from the White House (a building he needed directions to find). When he delivered the crack the DEA agents, rather than "seizing" it, as Bush would report, purchased it for $2,400.

In the aftermath of this sham one might have expected reporters and news editors to become leery of presidentially promoted drug scares; by and large they did not. Although irate about the phony anecdote, journalists generally endorsed the conclusion it had been marshalled to prove. "With the country and the nation's capital ensnared in a drug problem of dramatic proportions, there did not seem to be a need to confect a dramatic situation to suit the needs of a speech," wrote Maureen Dowd in a front-page article in the *New York Times* that summed up a predominant sentiment within the press.[8]

But maybe confection *had* been required. Over the previous decade drug use in the United States had declined considerably. And theatrics may have seemed particularly necessary when it came to crack cocaine. For the previous few years politicians and journalists had been presenting crack as "the most addictive drug known to man . . . an epidemic . . ." (*Newsweek*, 1986), though neither characterization was true. A year before Bush's speech the Surgeon General had released studies showing that cigarettes addict 80 percent of people who try them for a length of time, while fewer than 33 percent of those who try crack become addicted. Never among the more popular drugs of abuse, at the height of its popularity crack was smoked heavily by only a small proportion of cocaine users.[9]

Drugs to Ease Collective Guilt

As a sociologist I see the crack panic of the 1980s as a variation on an American tradition. At different times in our history drug scares have served to displace a class of brutalized citizens from the nation's moral conscience.

Flash back for a moment to the early 1870s in San Francisco. Chinese laborers, indispensable in building the transcontinental railroad during the previous decade, had become a superfluous population in the eyes of many whites. With an economic depression under way and 20,000 Chinese immigrants out of work, politicians, newspaper reporters, and union leaders all pointed to opium dens as evidence of the debauchery of Chinese men, whom they proposed to exclude from jobs and further immigration.

In actuality, opium dens, like British pubs, were genial gathering places where men shared stories and few participants were addicts. But as popularly portrayed, opium dens were squalid places in which wasted men fought with one another and defiled white women and children. "What other crimes were committed in those dark fetid places when these little innocent victims of the Chinamen's wiles were under the influence of the drug, are almost too horrible to imagine," Samuel Gompers, president of American Federated Labor (the AFL), wrote in a pamphlet titled *Some Reasons for Chinese Exclusion.*[10]

Out of that line of reasoning came the nation's very first drug prohibition law, a San Francisco ordinance of 1875 that outlawed opium dens. Other antiopium and anti-Chinese laws followed in the coming decades, justified in part by the simple, chimerical precept: "If the Chinaman cannot get along without his 'dope,' we can get along without him," as a committee of the American Pharmaceutical Association put it.[11]

Similarly, in the 1980s as poverty, homelessness, and associated urban ills increased noticeably, Presidents Reagan and Bush, along with much of the electorate, sidestepped the suffering of millions of their fellow citizens who had been harmed by policies favoring the wealthy.

Rather than face up to their own culpability, they blamed a drug. "Crack is responsible for the fact that vast patches of the American urban landscape are rapidly deteriorating," Bush's drug czar, William Bennett, decreed.[12]

A by-product of social and economic distress, crack became the *explanation* for that distress. American society still suffers repercussions of this perverse reasoning. In the late 1980s Congress mandated prison sentences one hundred times as severe for possession of crack, the form of cocaine for which African Americans are disproportionately arrested, as compared to cocaine powder, the type commonly used by whites. Partly as a consequence of that legislation, by the mid-1990s three out of four people serving prison sentences for drug offenses were African American, even though several times as many whites as blacks use cocaine. In federal courts 94 percent of those tried for crack offenses were African American. In 1995 the U.S. Sentencing Commission, whose recommendations had never previously been refused, urged greater parity and noted that there was no rational basis for the inconsistency in sentencing. The White House and Congress, rather than risk being called "soft on drugs," aggressively opposed their recommendations, and by a vote of 332 to 83 they were struck down in the House of Representatives. That vote, along with the disparities in the justice system, prompted rioting by inmates in federal prisons, suspicions among African Americans of government conspiracies against them, and increased tensions between the races.[13]

Busting Boomers' Chops

It wasn't supposed to be that way. When Bush's successor, Bill Clinton, won the White House in 1992, pundits predicted that ill-conceived drug policies and excessive fear mongering would die down. For a while it looked as if they were right. But then, in his bid for reelection in 1996, Clinton faced an opponent who tried to capitalize on his quiet. "Bill Clinton isn't protecting our children from drugs," the announcer on a Bob Dole-for-President TV ad exclaimed. "Clinton's liberal drug policies have failed." To which the president responded by upping the ante, thereby positioning himself as more antidrug than his opponent. In the near future, Clinton warned, the "drug problem . . . will be almost unbearable, unmanageable and painful" unless the Republican party, which controlled Congress, where Dole served as Senate Majority Leader, approved an additional $700 million to fight the problem.[14]

Clinton won reelection and got the money. But his continued occupancy of the White House afforded his political opponents and the media another hook on which to hang a drug scare. During Clinton's second term his daughter, Chelsea, finished high school and began her college career—a peak developmental period for drug experimentation. Though there was no hint that Chelsea used drugs, the fact that Clinton and others of his generation had done so was taken as grounds for asserting that "Baby Boomers Tolerate Teen Drug Use" (*St. Louis Post-Dispatch*, 1996).[15]

In tracing the history of scares several times I found that they stay around and reproduce themselves the way mosquitoes do, by attaching to whomever is available. By the mid-1980s, in line with the anti-1960s sentiment of the era, TV news programs had already started running reports that recycled footage of hippies in Haight Ashbury and characterized boomers as "dropping out and getting high" in the 1960s, only to drop back in as parents, "still getting high . . . teaching the next generation to self-destruct, one line, one drink, one toke at a time" (CBS, 1986). That the negative image of "flower children . . . educating their own teen-aged children about drugs" (as an article in the *Detroit News* put it in 1996) had little basis in reality mattered not at all. Only a minuscule portion of the baby boom generation ever qualified as "flower children" in the first place, and far fewer were potheads than myth would have it. But such facts did not stop news correspondents from rewriting boomers' drug history and current attitudes toward drug use.[16]

"The children of the sixties have kids of their own and a new conflict with the generation gap. This time, it's about their own drug use and what to tell their children about their past," Deborah Roberts proclaimed on ABC's "20/20" in 1997 as a Jefferson Airplane song played in the background and stock footage of hippies filled the screen.

Boomer parents who had gotten high in their youth are in a no-win situation, Roberts suggested. They can take a "do as I say, not as I did" approach and risk being branded hypocrites by their children, or they can lie about their drug use and sacrifice any right to demand honesty from their kids in return.[17]

Roberts and her producers apparently paid no mind to evidence showing that few parents actually experienced that dilemma. A year before the "20/20" broadcast a nationwide survey found that 40 percent of parents had never tried marijuana, and more than three-quarters believed that a parent should never allow a child to take drugs. Fewer than one in ten said they felt hypocritical in forbidding their own children from using drugs. Most seemed to feel the way Bill Clinton did when ABC's Peter Jennings suggested on another ABC program that "a lot of people at home," knowing he's "a baby boomer president," consider it hypocritical of him to tell Chelsea to avoid drugs. "I think this business about how the baby boomers all feel too guilt-ridden to talk to their kids," a slightly exasperated Clinton replied, "is the biggest load of hooey I ever heard."[18]

Although scares about boomer parents have popped up frequently, they boil down to a non sequitur: "Many baby-boomer parents of teen drug users probably used drugs themselves, and therefore have not offered stern enough warnings about the dangers" (*New York Times*, 1996). The first part of the statement is true, but the second doesn't follow; most boomers who have used drugs say they *have* cautioned their kids about the dangers. Should they have been more stern in their warnings? Not if adolescent drug use is a form of rebellion, as some experts believe. Parents who make a big deal about drugs might provoke more of the behavior they are attempting to prevent.[19]

This Is the Media on Drugs

Hectoring is exactly what parents have been told they should do. "Every time that a parent is with their child, it's an opportunity for them to discuss drugs," a physician from the American Academy of Pediatrics urged with a straight face on ABC's "Good Morning America" in 1997. Parents who took his prescription literally must have had some curious interchanges with their offspring: *"That's great news about your straight A's, let's talk about LSD."*[20]

Presumably the doctor himself would acknowledge the absurdity of his dictum, at least in retrospect. He'd gotten caught up in the fervor of the times, or more accurately, of the network on which was appearing. He made his comment during what ABC called its "March Against Drugs"—an unprecedented overdosing of antidrug propaganda throughout an entire month in 1997. Every news show and almost every other program as well, including sitcoms, soaps, and sports events, contained at least one advertisement, plot line, feature story, or interview segment cautioning against teen drug abuse. The onslaught concluded on March 31 with an interview with President Clinton in which he goaded parents to lecture their children about drugs and thanked ABC for providing "a great service to the country."[21]

Some groups of parents came in for particularly harsh criticism during the network's MAD month. Boomers got bashed repeatedly, as did single mothers. News stories and entire episodes of entertainment programs focused on unmarried, addicted moms and on single women who abstain from drug use themselves but failed to pay attention to the early signs of abuse in their offspring. An episode of the sitcom "Grace Under Fire" brought a whole stew of such themes together when Grace, a casualty of the 1960s, finds drugs in her son's room and has trouble taking a hard line with him.[22]

ABC's harangue elicited criticism from media critics as well as from authorities on drug abuse. Pointing out that intensive scare campaigns usually fail to dissuade young people from taking drugs and may even backfire, they also criticized the network for biased news reporting. Instead of providing a variety of points of view about drug use, news programs stuck closely to the same story lines that ran in soaps and public service advertisements throughout the month. News correspondents and anchors, rather than provide level-headed examinations of America's drug problems and plausible remedies, rambled on about how schoolchildren "can get marijuana faster than a Popsicle," and how "more and more teens are falling for heroin's fatal allure."[23]

The Return of Heroin

Critics understandably accused ABC, which had fallen from first to last place among the big three networks over the previous two years, of engaging in a ratings grab: "cause-related marketing," they call it in the trade. In my view, however, the charge is not entirely fair. All of the scares the network put out that month had been promoted by the rest of the media as well over the past decade. In touting a resurgence in heroin use, for example, ABC was merely singing one of the media's favorite tunes. Year after year, even though Americans reportedly accounted for only about 5 percent of the world's heroin market and usage levels remained fairly stable, headlines proclaimed, "The Return of a Deadly Drug Called Horse" (*U.S. News & World Report*, 1989), "Heroin Is Making a Comeback," (*New York Times*, 1990) or "Smack's Back" (*USA Today*, 1994).[24]

Most heroin users are neither middle class nor young, but those groups regularly serve as the pegs for stories about heroin's resurgence. As far back as 1981 *Newsweek* was reporting that heroin had migrated from the ghetto and created "middle-class junkies," a muddled assertion repeated periodically ever since. As evidence of a "middle-class romance with heroin" (*New York Times*, 1997), reporters and politicians concentrate on various high-profile groups: Wall Street stockbrokers, fashion models, professional athletes. And perpetually they proclaim that "heroin has its deadly hooks in teens across the nation" (*USA Today*, 1996).[25]

Smack has become "the pot of the '90s . . . as common as beer," *USA Today* declared; "The New High School High," ABC titled a special edition of its newsmagazine, "Turning Point." According to Peter Jennings on ABC's "World News Tonight," the "disturbing comeback" of heroin among the young is "almost impossible to exaggerate . . . a cautionary tale for all parents and all children." Yet in support of these drastic contentions reporters offered only vague, emotion-laden evidence. On "Turning Point," Diane Sawyer effused: "The statistics are heartbreaking. In the last few years, hundreds and hundreds of young people have died from heroin. Some were among the best and the brightest—star athletes, honor students, kids with promise."[26]

To come up with their few examples of such fatalities, her producers must have had to search far and wide. With less than 1 percent of high school students trying heroin in a given year and the bulk of heroin use concentrated among inner-city adults, heroin is one of the least common causes of death among teens.[27]

Michael Massing, an author who writes frequently about drug abuse, recounted in an essay in the *New York Review of Books*: "Not long ago, I had a telephone call from an ABC producer who was working on a program about the resurgence of heroin. 'We're trying to get some middle-class users—people who are sniffing, rather than injecting,' she said, asking for some leads. I said that while middle-class use somewhat increased, most of the new consumption was occurring among inner-city minorities. 'Oh, they've been around for years,' she said. 'The fact that heroin is spreading into other sectors is what people will sit up and listen to.'"[28]

Good Numbers Gone Bad

Some journalists do make a point, of course, of combating exaggerations with facts. Christopher Wren, who covers drug issues for the *New York Times*, is particularly conscientious in this regard. When President Clinton joined in the teen heroin scare by telling a group of mayors in 1997, "We now see in college campuses and neighborhoods, heroin becoming increasingly the drug of choice," Wren included the quote in his article about the speech, but immediately put the president's comment in its proper context. Although there had been reports of heroin experimentation at certain colleges, Wren noted, alcohol still retained its title as the drug of choice among the nation's high school and college students, with marijuana a distant second.[29]

As a rule, though, reporters maximize claims about youthful drug abuse rather than contextualizing them. Most of the major media ran stories about a survey released in 1997 by a research center at Columbia University headed by Joseph Califano, the former Secretary of

Health, Education and Welfare. There had been a huge increase in the use of hard drugs by young kids, several of the stories reported. Specifically, 23.5 percent of twelve-year-olds (more than twice as many as the previous year) reported use of cocaine, heroin, or LSD. In reality, the 23.5 percent figure represented the percentage of twelve-year-olds who said they *knew* someone who used those drugs, not *their own* drug use. While most reporters did not conceal that the question had been asked this way, they called the survey "an urgent new alarm to address what many label a growing crisis" (CNN), and their stories appeared beneath headlines such as, "Poll Finds Sharp Rise in Drug Use Among Youngsters" (*Los Angeles Times*). When I first read the alarmist statistic red lights went off in my head. General readers and viewers, however, would have to be uncommonly attentive to how the question is worded to register that the true finding isn't as "alarming" (NBC) as the media made it seem.[30]

The Califano poll showed only that about one in four twelve-year-olds was willing to speculate about a friend or classmate having used hard drugs. Just a week earlier the results of a far larger and more trusted poll had come out, the National Household Survey on Drug Abuse. That survey asked people about their own drug taking and found teen drug use *down* almost 17 percent, with the steepest decline among twelve- to fifteen-year-olds.[31]

Indeed, when Califano subsequently released more detailed results from his survey a month after his press blitz, it turned out that an overwhelming number of twelve-year-olds—71 percent—said their schools were entirely drug free. And as for use by friends, only 4 percent said that half or more of their friends even used marijuana, never mind hard drugs. Three out of four said that if someone were using illegal drugs at school, they would report them.[32]

In drug abuse surveys America's adolescents report increases in consumption of particular drugs sometimes and decreases other times. More important in the long run is the most consistent finding in these surveys, one that the news media seldom mention: The great majority of adolescents never or hardly ever use drugs. Fully three-quarters of twelve- to seventeen-year-olds report, year after year, that in the past twelve months they have not used drugs at all—not so much as a puff of pot. For hard drugs, only about ten to fifteen out of a thousand report using them as frequently as once a month. Even among college students drug use is less pervasive than the hype would have it. Half of America's college students make it to graduation without having smoked marijuana; better than eight out of ten have not tried cocaine in any form.[33]

The vast majority of teens who do use drugs in high school or college give them up by their early thirties. A study that tracked more than 33,000 young Americans over an eighteen-year period found that drug use decreases dramatically when people marry. The only substance most users do not give up in early adulthood, the study found, is cigarettes. Of those who smoked half a pack or more a day as seniors in high school, seven out of ten were still smoking at age thirty-two.[34]

Poster Girl for the Drug Crisis

Drug scares are promoted primarily by three means: presidential proclamations, selective statistics, and poster children. The first two posit a terrifying new trend, the last gives it a human face.

The scare about adolescent drug use had several poster children, most of them teens whose sad stories were told only in their hometown newspapers and local newscasts, or in passing on TV newsmagazines. One notable exception, a young woman named Miki Koontz, attracted attention from the national media, where her story was told repeatedly for a couple of years. The *way* in which much of the media told Miki's story—as a heart-pounding true-crime story (even with a chase scene) but with important details omitted—further illustrates something we have seen before. People's stories seldom make the simple or singular point that journalists profess they do.[35]

A "homecoming queen, cheerleader, and above-average student whose bags were packed for college" (Associated Press), Miki inexplicably became a crackhead and lost her life as a result, the media reported. America has fallen far, the articles said or implied, when such a thing can happen to a "very, very nice" (*Pittsburgh Post–Gazette*) girl from Williamson, West Virginia, a town of 4,300 straight out of a Jimmy Stewart movie (the drugstore still has a soda fountain).

The villain of these pieces, Jerry Warren, a black man in his mid-forties, sold crack out of his home to the tune of $30,000 a month and enticed local white kids to get hooked. Miki and the chump of the piece, Chris Pennington, were among Warren's customers.

Miki and Chris made for an unexpected but endearing duo, the story went. Homely, learning disabled, the son of a coal miner, Chris seemed an unlikely friend for a "petite brunette with hazel eyes" (Associated Press) whose father was a millionaire coal executive. But Miki and Chris had been buddies since sixth grade. "Miki never put me down when friends of hers did," Chris recalled to a reporter. He had not wanted to put Miki in harm's way, but he found himself in a tough bind. Unemployed and struggling to support a little boy he had fathered with a woman he picked up in a bar, Chris owed Jerry Warren $2,000—a debt that Warren offered to erase if Chris delivered Miki to him at a predetermined time and place.

So on August 25, 1995, Chris asked Miki to pick him up and drive him to go get some pot. Outside of town Chris reached into his pants, pulled out a knife, pressed it against Miki's side, and told her where to drive. What followed was like a scene out of some rustic remake of *Pulp Fiction*. For more than an hour they drove around, Miki thinking Chris was joking with her, Chris growing increasingly anxious and insistent, until finally he instructed her to park the car near a sewer plant. There, Jerry Warren was waiting. Believing that Miki had been snitching on him to the police, he ordered her out of the car and commanded Chris to shoot her with a rifle. Chris tried to refuse, but Warren threatened to shoot them both if he did not comply.

"Miki knelt on the ground and asked to pray. Saying nothing, Chris pointed the rifle at Miki's head, closed his eyes, turned his head and fired," an article in *Rolling Stone* recounted. The next thing he heard, Chris said, was "a gargling sound of blood running from her head. Like when you're pouring water out of a bottle: gloop, gloop, gloop."

The *Rolling Stone* piece, in line with other coverage of middle-class American kids undone by drugs, put much of the blame on the dealer.

Jerry Warren had "enormous power over . . . previously untouchable middle-class white girls," the magazine quoted an assistant U.S. attorney. But unlike other stories about Miki Koontz in the news media and on tabloid TV shows, the article in *Rolling Stone* provided some telling details: Miki was not, in fact, a Tipper Gore-in-training debutante living the ideal life in a bucolic hamlet. Nor did she suddenly become a crack addict, thereby proving that the same could happen to any mother's child before she realizes that something has gone awry. Way back when Miki was still in kindergarten her parents had formally divorced but agreed to live together for the sake of appearances and to raise Miki and her sister. Not until Miki's senior year in high school did her father finally move out of the house. By then he had long since lost his fortune and twice filed for bankruptcy in this gloomy Appalachian town where unemployment stood at nearly 14 percent and half of the population had left since the 1950s.

Miki fought frequently with her mother and had two friends in jail. Upon being named Homecoming Queen, she wrote a friend: "I really wish fucking some other prep bitch would have got it so it would be them and I could be myself . . . I'm not growing up, I'm just burning out."

Well before her death Miki was using drugs and alcohol, sometimes heavily, but, significantly, crack was not her drug of choice. Casting her as a crackhead allowed for well-turned headlines such as "A Crack in the All-American Dream" (*Post-Gazette*) and for pseudosociological subplots about the migration of a big-city drug to the countryside. But Miki's sister and others close to her said she had used crack only a couple of times. By and large she stuck to marijuana, alcohol, and Somas, a prescription muscle relaxant.

The Roofie Myth

If Miki Koontz's story illustrates anything, it is reporters' penchant for chalking up drug deaths to whatever substance they're on about at the moment. The deaths of Kurt Cobain in 1994 and Smashing Pumpkins' keyboardist Jonathan Melvoin in 1996 were catalogued as part of "a resurgence in heroin use in the '90s," though both musicians used a variety of legal and illicit substances, and Cobain died not from a heroin overdose but suicide. News reports asserted, without evidence, that Cobain "killed himself because he couldn't kick his heroin habit." But a month before his suicide, when he had come close to death from an overdose, the drug in question was not heroin. Cobain had fallen into a coma after overdosing on champagne and Rohypnol, a prescription sleeping aid.[36]

Why has there been no national hysteria over the mixing of alcohol and prescription medication, a commonplace in overdose fatalities—or, for that matter, simply over the abuse of prescription drugs, the category that sends adolescents to emergency rooms more often than cocaine, heroin, marijuana, and LSD combined?[37]

Exponentially more stories about drug abuse focus on illegal drugs than on legal drugs. The reason cannot be that there is little to report about prescription drug abuse. My examination of the relatively small number of investigative reports that *have* appeared in the major news media demonstrates this fact. An article in the *Washington Post* made reference to studies suggesting that one in six physicians regularly uses opiates and one in nine regularly uses tranquilizers and sleeping pills. The article pointed out that long hours, coupled with stressful changes in the medical profession over the last several years and easy access to drugs make doctors vulnerable to addiction. A report on National Public Radio, meanwhile, noted that a significant number of doctors with addiction problems pretend otherwise and receive no treatment.[38]

Then there's the elderly. Thanks in part to careless prescribing and pressures put on doctors by insurers and HMOs to spend little or no time with patients, millions of elderly Americans are at risk of becoming dependent on tranquilizers. According to one recent study, 2.8 million women sixty years and older abuse psychiatric medications. Yet as an article in the *Los Angeles Times* observed, no one actually knows how many older Americans misuse drugs. In stark contrast to the torrent of statistics about teenage drug use, we know little about drug use in old age. Our relative lack of information speaks volumes about our national inattention both to the elderly and to prescription drug abuse.[39]

There is also the vital question of why women in the United States are twice as likely as men to be prescribed psychotropic drugs. Apart from coverage in feminist publications such as *Ms.*, stories about sexism in the prescribing of drugs almost never appear. Moreover, how many of the 50 million Americans who take Prozac and similar antidepressants either do not need or do not benefit from the pills they pop each day? How many suffer side effects that exceed the benefits they receive from the drugs?[40]

Politicians' dependence on the pharmaceutical industry for campaign contributions and the news media's dependence on them for advertising revenues probably has something to do with which forms of drug abuse they most bemoan. In the 1996 election cycle alone drug company PACs dispersed $1.6 million to federal campaigns. And pharmaceutical companies, America's most profitable industry, are among the nation's biggest spenders on television, magazine, and newspaper advertising.[41]

For the abuse of a pharmaceutical to get star billing it has be recast as something exotic. The drug that helped put Kurt Cobain in a coma, for instance, received little attention in the media in the late 1980s and early 1990s, when it was a popular choice in parts of this country and Africa among people looking to get high. A single pill makes you feel as drunk and uninhibited as a six-pack of beer, Rohypnol enthusiasts said. "You don't hear anything bad about it, like heroin or crack, where people die or anything," the *New York Times* quoted a high school senior in Miami in 1995, in one of the few stories about Rohypnol that appeared in the national news media prior to 1996, and among a small number that ever took note of the most common reasons why women and men take the drug.[42]

In 1996 through 1998 stories about Rohypnol appeared by the hundreds, but use of the pill to get high was scarcely mentioned. Christened the "date-rape drug" and referred to as "roofie," Rohypnol was presented to the American public as "a loaded gun . . . a weapon used to facilitate sexual assault" (then senator Joseph Biden). "Rape Is Only Thing That This Drug Is For," read a headline in the *St. Louis Post-Dispatch.* Dubbed by reporters "the mightiest Mickey Finn ever concocted," Rohypnol represented, according to a story in the *Dallas*

Morning News, "all the fears of parents whose daughters have hit dating age packed into one white pill the size of a dime."[43]

Every so often a journalist would do a follow-up report on a much-hyped "roofies rape" from the recent past and let it be known that Rohypnol had not actually been involved. Mostly, though, journalists heedlessly repeated vague assertions from the police ("lots of girls have been coming in . . ."), and they proffered unfounded generalizations of their own. "Rohypnol has become a favorite tool of predators," *USA Today* asserted in 1996, though almost any authority on rape could have told them that the percentage of all rapes committed with Rohypnol was a tiny number.[44]

There is good reason to suspect that in fact the *total* number of assaults accomplished with the aid of Rohypnol was small. I searched widely for sound studies of the true prevalence and found only one, but it was telling. From mid-1996 through mid-1998, while the roofie scare was in full bloom, Hoffmann–La Roche, the Swiss company that makes the drug, provided test kits to rape-crisis centers, hospital emergency rooms, and police throughout the country. Rape victims who believed they had been drugged were asked to provide a sample of their urine, which was sent to an independent laboratory for analysis. Of the 1,033 tests returned, only six contained Rohypnol. About one-third of the samples contained no drugs; the remainder contained a variety of legal and illegal substances, alcohol being far and away the most common.[45]

That other countries were not reporting outbreaks also says something. Hoffmann–La Roche takes in about $100 million annually from sales of Rohypnol, which has been on the market since 1975. Two million people in eighty countries worldwide swallow one to two pills a day by prescription. But in the United States the drug is illegal. Does it truly seem likely that the only place experiencing an "epidemic" (*Los Angeles Times*) of roofie rapes would be where molesters have to rely on a black market rather than simply reach into a medicine cabinet?[46]

Mickey Finn to the Rescue

Roofie stories did not contain great truth, but they did help redirect controversies in convenient ways. Rohypnol may have been utilized by only a small proportion of rapists, and few abusers may have used it for sexual assaults. But for a range of people, from the President of the United States to jaded readers of local newspapers, roofies provided a tidy way of talking about matters that had become messy.

In his bid for reelection in 1996 Bill Clinton staged an event three weeks before voters went to the polls. Fighting a lawsuit brought against him by Paula Jones, who said he summoned her to a hotel room, opened his pants, and asked her to kiss his penis, Clinton held a highly publicized ceremony at which he signed an antidrug bill. The drug in question was not marijuana, which Clinton had already confessed on MTV he wished he had inhaled. Standing on the tarmac at the Denver airport, a line of police officers as his backdrop, Clinton signed a bill providing a twenty-year prison sentence for anyone who used roofies or similar drugs to commit sexual assault, symbolically demonstrating his opposition both to drug abuse and to acquaintance rape.[47]

For journalists and their audiences of the mid- and late 1990s the roofie narrative served a somewhat different purpose. It afforded a clear and uncontroversial explanation for a phenomenon that had been hotly but unsatisfyingly debated for more than a decade. When studies came out in the 1980s indicating that one in three female college students is forced to have sex against her will, feminist groups played up the findings. Before long a backlash developed. Conservative columnists and politicians disputed the statistics, and in 1993 Katie Roiphe, a recent Harvard grad, launched her writing career with a polemic titled *The Morning After.* Condemning women she called "rape-crisis feminists," Roiphe spoke of a "grey area in which someone's rape may be another person's bad night."[48]

Compared to debates about how to define rape or whether radical feminists or rabid conservatives are more dangerous to women, stories about roofies were interesting and easy to follow. Graphic and mildly prurient, they focused on entirely blameless women, such as the freshman at Clemson University who was given a drink at a fraternity party and taken to three different locations where she was raped by at least thirteen men.[49]

In the media women like her supplanted typical victims of acquaintance rape, who are very much awake when they find themselves being attacked by men they know. More recent research on date rape—research that defines rape more narrowly—still finds an appalling problem. One in five college women reports she has been forced to have sexual intercourse. Usually the attacker is a friend or a man she was dating, a fact obscured in the furor over date-rape drugs.[50]

Once the roofie scare began to die down media attention shifted to gamma hydroxybutyric acid (GHB), promptly dubbed the "new" date-rape drug. Used for almost two decades by partygoers for a high and by bodybuilders as an alternative to steroids, GHB suddenly got depicted as "the Mickey Finn of the '90s" (*Chicago Sun–Times*), more dangerous than roofies.[51]

And so the cycle continued.

7

METAPHORIC ILLNESSES

How Not to Criticize
the Establishment

In an essay on cancer and another on AIDS Susan Sontag documented the perils of thinking metaphorically about illnesses. Imagining viruses as invading armies instead of microscopic matter, or scientists as warriors instead of researchers, does little good and can cause considerable harm, Sontag urged. "My purpose was, above all, practical," she has said of her book, *Illness as Metaphor*. "For it was my doleful observation, repeated again and again, that the metaphoric trappings that deform the experience of having cancer have very real consequences: they inhibit people from seeking treatment early enough, or from making a greater effort to get competent treatment." Sontag cited as examples people who waive chemotherapy in favor of quackery that promises to change so-called cancer-causing personality traits.[1]

Continuing the line of argument I have been advancing, I propose a corollary to Sontag's observations. Not only do we use metaphors to help us understand fatal illnesses that most of us are poorly equipped to comprehend scientifically, we also create certain illnesses, what I call "metaphoric illnesses," to help us come to terms with features of our society that we are unprepared to confront directly. Historically, the most famous such illness was neurasthenia. Diagnosed in the United States mostly during the nineteenth century and disproportionately in women, the symptoms of neurasthenia were said to include extreme fatigue, muscle aches, mental confusion, chills, and fever. Like the people diagnosed with the ailments examined in this chapter, neurasthenics were not, by and large, hypochondriacs. They were verifiably sick, sometimes seriously so.[2]

But what caused their symptoms? Later research suggests a variety of familiar causes ranging from viruses to food poisoning to bad marriages. Back in 1881, however, George Beard, the physician known as the "father of neurasthenia," attributed the illness to modern technology and the education of women. Then as now, people believed in metaphoric illnesses partly owing to graphic stories about ordinary women and men being struck down, and partly because the illnesses helped them justify fears, prejudices, and political ideologies they held. The disease of neurasthenia provided living, breathing proof that newly developed technologies and women's emancipation truly *were* pernicious. Similarly, metaphoric illnesses of the 1990s such as Gulf War Syndrome (GWS), multiple chemical sensitivity, and breast implant disorders have served to confirm present-day doubts.[3]

Battle Fatigue

Americans have yet to engage in a serious or sustained public discussion of the Persian Gulf War of 1991, which was an unprecedented event in world history, a "deceptive war," as the French sociologist Jean Baudrillard put it, in which "the enemy only appear[ed] as a computerized target," never face to face. Depicted by the U.S. military and media as a swift, clean, nearly bloodless war won by "surgical air strikes" of buildings and munitions, in fact it was a brutally lopsided affair. One hundred forty-six Americans died, while allied troops killed upward of 100,000 Iraqis, many during the ground war inside Kuwait, but including about 10,000 Iraqi soldiers and 2,500 civilians who died directly from less-than-precise bombing operations. After the $61 billion bloodbath, tens of thousands of Iraqi children died as well, from poor public health conditions, food shortages, and Kurdish revolts that the war left in its wake.[4]

All for What?

One might have thought that the American people, in the years that followed the war, would have debated that question. Saddam Hussein, whom President George Bush dubbed "Hitler revisited," remained in power. Much of the moral rationale for liberating Kuwait from the Iraqis also proved bogus. A high-profile story and set of photographs about Iraqi soldiers destroying incubators in Kuwait hospitals and leaving babies to die, for instance, turned out to have been planted by the daughter of the Kuwaiti ambassador to the United States. Later determined to have been greatly exaggerated if not completely false, that and other horror stories were key factors in gaining public support for the war. They were fed to the media by an American public relations firm, Hill and Knowlton (headed by Bush's former chief of staff), which the Kuwaitis paid $11.5 million.[5]

To this day there has been little national discussion of the possibility that the American people were duped by publicists who recognized that we "would be more likely to fight because of atrocity stories than because one feudal fiefdom was invaded by another," as Arthur Rowse, a former editor of *U.S. News & World Report*, put it. (Among other brutalities following the war, hundreds of Palestinians in Kuwait disappeared and many were tortured in retaliation for Yasir Arafat's support of Iraq. Kuwaiti authorities eventually drove 400,000 Palestinians out of the country.)[6]

Many Americans probably still retain a falsely sunny picture of the war experience for American troops as well. In fact, as the Department of Defense noted in a report released four years after the war:

> U.S. troops entered a bleak, physically demanding desert environment, where they were crowded into warehouses, storage buildings and tents with little personal privacy and few amenities. No one knew that coalition forces eventually would win a quick war with relatively few battle casualties. Consequently, most troops did not fight a "four-day war" but spent months isolated in the desert, under constant stress, concerned about their survival and their family's well-being at home, and uncertain about when they would return home.

They also had to deal with propaganda from Iraq about its willingness to use biological warfare, as well as gossip among the troops about medications given to them by their own superiors to protect them from desert conditions and possible chemical warfare.[7]

If the realities of the Gulf War itself were not major topics for public discussion, however, Gulf War Syndrome—which surely resulted in part from those wartime conditions—was abundantly debated. Legions of presidential commissions, committees of Congress, Pentagon officials, panels of scientists, and veterans groups held hearings, conducted studies, released reports, and set up web sites. Thousands of news stories and commentaries appeared in the media, relaying a seemingly endless supply of anecdotes about sick veterans, illustrated with photos of them in wheelchairs or beside their deformed children.[8]

Some of the widely quoted anecdotes were subsequently discredited, including those from Michael Adcock, the first vet whose death was widely attributed to GWS. He said he came down with lymphoma in the Gulf—a medical improbability, since Adcock died within months of his return home, and lymphomas take years to develop. Yet throughout the 1990s activists and their supporters in Congress and the media continually disseminated tales about infirmities caused by service in the Gulf.[9]

Some of these people seemed to catch a bug of their own that disabled their crap detectors. Consider, for example, J. R. Moehringer of the *Los Angeles Times*. A journalist who has won awards for excellent reporting on other topics, he waxed melodramatic in a piece in 1995. "He has a Purple Heart. It lies beneath a ragged line in the middle of his chest," Moehringer's article began. It continued, unexpectedly: "His nanny coos at him as she unbuttons his cotton jumpsuit, exposing the vivid incision made last month by a surgeon's knife." Illustrated with heartbreaking photos of little Christian Coats, whose misshapen heart purportedly resulted from his father's service in the Gulf War, the story tells of "a mini-plague" of physical ailments that veterans contend are "seeping into the next generation."[10]

Moehringer notes briefly, for the sake of balance, a Pentagon study that concluded that soldiers were not exposed to lethal chemicals and have no unique illnesses, much less diseases inherited by their children. The bulk of the article, however, endorses the theory that Christian's troubles began when his father inhaled "black, cottony smoke of burning oil wells, stood beside sky-high stockpiles of radioactive ammunition, and ingested fistfuls of experimental medicine." The future father had a funny feeling about those medicines at the time, but when he told his lieutenant, he was instructed "to shut the hell up" and swallow, Moehringer reported.[11]

A study published in the *New England Journal of Medicine* in 1997 strongly refuted the birth defect scare. Comparing 33,998 infants born to Gulf War veterans and 41,463 babies of other military personnel, the researchers found no evidence of an increase in the risk of birth defects for children of Gulf War vets. Their study was reported by Moehringer's newspaper in a story written by another reporter. For his part, however, Moehringer was still writing scare stories. A few months before the *New England Journal* study came out he published a piece– "Gulf War Syndrome Feared to Be Contagious"–that made an impact well beyond California. Newspapers throughout the country reprinted it, and TV networks and international wire services ran their own reports.[12]

The basic premise–that medical professionals contracted GWS from vets they treated–had already been rebutted by the Centers for Disease Control, the Presidential Advisory Committee on Gulf War Veterans' Illnesses, and various independent medical scientists. Scientists also had rebutted an alarming possibility Moehringer raised about dangers to the nation's blood supply from donations to the Red Cross by Gulf veterans. Moehringer instead chose to give prominence to the views of a biochemist in Irvine, California, named Garth Nicolson, who had conducted investigations of members of his own family and others he believed caught GWS from veterans. Nicolson told Moehringer that he himself "lost four teeth and had part of my lower jaw removed."[13]

Other news outlets, in covering Moehringer's story, essentially repeated what he had reported. Of those I located, only CNN managed to add that, although Nicolson had been pushing his theory for two years, he remained the only researcher to claim evidence that Gulf War Syndrome is contagious.[14]

Circuitous Critique

Why would major news media disseminate the speculations of a wannabe expert many months after he had been refuted by certified experts?[15]

The answer to this question is to be found, I believe, in some telling language early in Moehringer's article: "Despite failing to find favor with official Washington and colleagues, many remain convinced that the cause of Gulf War illness is an infectious microbe . . ." Gulf War Syndrome provided an occasion for criticizing the Pentagon—something that none of the main participants in the war had much motivation to do about the war itself. Veterans of the war, having been heralded for ending America's post–World War losing streak and curing what had come to be known as the "Vietnam Syndrome," certainly were not inclined to find fault with how the war was waged. Nor were politicians, who shared, Republicans and Democrats alike, in the glory of America's victory. Nor were journalists who had engaged in what CBS News anchor Dan Rather described as "suck-up coverage" of the military and exhibited "a lack of guts to speak up, to speak out, to speak our minds" during the war.[16]

Throughout the mid- and late 1990s GWS became *the* vehicle for criticizing the Pentagon; but was it a good one? Susan Sontag addressed the dangers of employing metaphors such as warfare to make sense of serious diseases. Correlatively, I am concerned about the use of a syndrome to come to terms with shortcomings of the military. To use disease to talk of war is as problematic as the other way around.

To begin with it is problematic for ailing veterans themselves. Elaine Showalter, a professor of humanities at Princeton, observes in a discussion of GWS in her book *Hystories: Hysterical Epidemics and Modern Media* that thousands of Gulf War vets have undergone countless medical exams rather than getting the psychological counseling they needed. Convinced they have a unique organic illness, veterans "tend not to see psychotherapists even when their stories make clear that anxiety, fear, and anger are among their symptoms," Showalter writes.[17]

Using GWS to critique the military is problematic on logical grounds as well. Any pronouncements the Pentagon made about veterans' health became fair game for more fear mongering about GWS and further criticism of the military. When the Pentagon released studies showing that Gulf veterans were no more ill than would be expected by chance and that their ailments were similar to those that afflicted veterans of previous wars, the news media quoted "leading critics" saying "no one's going to accept these studies," and veterans claiming the Pentagon "lied . . . every step of the way." Yet when the Pentagon admitted that, contrary to its own earlier claims, more than 20,000 American soldiers may have been exposed to chemical agents and given experimental drugs, such admissions were greeted with ever greater condemnation and suspicion. Some in Congress, extending the analogy Bush had used against Saddam Hussein during the war, made comparisons to gas chamber experiments on U.S. troops in the 1940s. Senator Jay Rockefeller accused the Pentagon of "reckless disregard for the health and well-being of U.S. servicemembers."[18]

Some studies do suggest that some veterans' ailments resulted partly from the numerous inoculations they received against a half dozen diseases ranging from cholera to anthrax, as well as insect repellents they wore. These studies too have been discredited by prominent medical authorities, and in any event, the Pentagon administered the drugs out of *regard* for the soldiers, in hopes of safeguarding them, not to harm them.[19]

Not until well into the twenty-first century are medical scientists likely to have sufficient long-term studies to reach a definitive conclusion about the causes of Gulf War Syndrome. Yet the nation's journalists, happy to recast the Gulf War Syndrome story as "a good old-fashioned cover-up" rather than a "complicated . . . medical mystery," as an analysis in the *American Journalism Review* put it, poured forth with non sequiturs of their own. "Whether or not there is a coverup, the case represents the Pentagon's self-protective culture at its worst," declared a *Washington Post* story in 1996 on possible causes of GWS. Wrote *New York Times* reporter Philip Shenon around the same time: "Although there is no convincing evidence that American troops were made ill from exposure to Iraqi chemical or biological weapons during the war, the silence of major government figures from the war has added to the suspicion of ailing veterans that the Pentagon is withholding evidence that might explain their health problems."[20]

It fell to seasoned skeptics at these same newspapers to question their colleagues' innuendos of a governmental conspiracy against our troops. Gina Kolata of the *New York Times* consulted prominent scientists at medical schools, who suggested that, whether or not veterans were exposed to chemical weapons, such exposure could not explain GWS. For one thing, if toxic exposure had been great, large numbers of veterans should have been hospitalized. Instead, their hospitalization and death rates were about the same as those of their peers who did not serve in the war. The range of symptoms veterans reported were also too diverse, Kolata pointed out, to be explained by chemical exposure.[21]

David Brown of the *Washington Post*, in a detailed story in 1997, put the matter even more baldly. "The theory that many veterans of the Persian Gulf War are ill because they were unwittingly exposed to nerve gas more than five years ago contradicts most of what's known about the health effects of chemical weapons," he wrote. People exposed to nerve gases almost invariably exhibit symptoms immediately, and three decades of research contradict the likelihood of permanent or delayed damage as a result of exposure.[22]

Yet in 1997 and 1998 a predominant impression conveyed by much of the media was that nerve gas had caused the ailments that nearly 100,000 Gulf War vets were reporting. Several lengthy articles in the *New York Times* by Philip Shenon and a book by Seymour Hersh gave prominent play to scientists who argued that exposure to nerve gas had caused cognitive and other health problems for Gulf War vets. The impression was bolstered by a TV movie in May 1998 advertised as "the movie the Government doesn't want you to see." Utilizing the Cuisinart effect discussed earlier, the film intercut scenes with stars Ted Danson and Jennifer Jason Leigh and interviews with real-life vets and politicians. "The lines between fact and fiction are collapsing," John Sacret Young, the writer and executive producer of the movie, declared in a piece about the making of the film. Young referred to Gulf War Syndrome as "a neurological holocaust."[23]

Three days before Young's much-hyped film aired, a short piece by Gina Kolata, buried deep inside the *Times*, reported on a study suggesting that stress played a crucial role in Gulf War maladies. By then there had been many studies indicating the same, and four months had passed since a report on "Frontline," the investigative program on National Public Television, criticized editors at the *Times* for having assigned Shenon, its Pentagon reporter, to cover Gulf War Syndrome rather than a medical reporter. The program pointed out what most of the media had not: thousands of veterans who were ill had not been exposed to nerve gas, and, vice versa, most of the troops who may have been exposed were not ill.[24]

Multiple Chemical Sensitivity

Fears feed off of one another. Speculation that Gulf War Syndrome resulted from veterans' exposure to assorted chemicals helped those who monger scares about multiple chemical sensitivity (MCS), a metaphoric illness that has received plenty of favorable, anecdote-dependent coverage in its own right. A half-page article in the *Los Angeles Times* in 1996, for instance, presented a man named Alan Bell, another victim-cum-expert who founded his own foundation "directed to research and raising public awareness." A mild-mannered attorney and loving father in excellent health before his "life as he knew it came to a crashing halt," Bell succumbed to exposure to sprays and pesticides when his home was being remodeled, according to the reporter, Michael Haederle. For the past several years, Haederle reported, Bell followed a macrobiotic diet, seldom left his home, and wore only cotton clothing that has been washed in baking soda, vinegar, and powdered milk.[25]

The article about Bell, eulogistically headlined "He Fights So Your Next Breath Won't Make You Sick," was one of several unquestioning pieces in the major media about MCS. An Associated Press story in 1995 spotlighted Peggy Magidson, an MCS sufferer who abandoned her career and friends to live out in the woods. "I used to be a fashionable executive lady with designer dresses and high heels," the story quoted Magidson saying, whose faded flannel shirt and dungarees were stained, the reporter said, from having been washed in a brew of baking soda, vinegar, and bleach. The writer went on to present the scary (if absurd) statistic that MCS afflicts anywhere from 15 to 33 percent of the population: people who, like Magidson, become violently ill at the smell of perfumes, pesticides, household cleansers, and innumerable other common chemicals.[26]

Some of the coverage of MCS was generated by alliances between activists and businesses trying to make a buck off the metaphorical ailment. When Debra Lynn Dadd, an MCS activist, published a book of recommendations on how to stay clear of dangerous household products, the maker of Bon Ami, a "chemical free" cleanser, contacted her. They sent Dadd on a media tour in which she promoted her booklet as well as Bon Ami. Dadd's and Bon Ami's efforts were reported on favorably, in turn, in *Sierra*, a publication of the environmental organization.[27]

Taking victims' accounts almost at face value, few of the feature stories I located about MCS bothered to mention the many medical studies documenting that people said to have MCS actually suffer from common conditions such as eczema, asthma, and depression, and that some are merely possessed of an unusually sensitive sense of smell. Articles that *did* take note of medical knowledge about MCS often treated medical scientists as just another group with an opinion or perspective. "It's an allergy-like condition generally regarded by the mainstream medical establishment with skepticism, though more people are reporting MCS symptoms all the time," wrote a *Washington Post* reporter in an article in 1994 about a ban on perfumes and colognes at the University of Minnesota.[28]

Journalists were not alone in downplaying evidence from medical science in favor of anecdotes from MCS sufferers. Some of my colleagues in the social sciences adopted the same position. People such as Magidson and Bell are harbingers of "society's next national health problem," predicted Steve Kroll-Smith and Anthony Ladd in the academic journal *Sociological Spectrum*. The reports of MCS sufferers should be taken very seriously, these sociologists argued, irrespective of the conclusions of medical authorities.[29]

And *why* should we embrace the reports of the metaphorically ill? Because, as Linda and Bill Bovie, advocates for both MCS and Gulf War Syndrome, put it in an op-ed in the *Cleveland Plain Dealer*: "The accounts these individuals give of how their illnesses developed all seem to have a remarkable consistency. Most of them sound as though they were perfectly normal, average people who had never given a thought to the possibility of chemicals jeopardizing their health before becoming acutely ill from a close encounter with some toxic substance."[30]

Much the same can be said, of course, about many religious fundamentalists and smokers' rights enthusiasts—or, for that matter, people who claim they were abducted by space aliens. They are usually sincere and ordinary folks, and their accounts often have a great deal of consistency. Yet when have fundamentalist Christians been taken seriously by journalists or sociologists in their contention that AIDS is God's punishment for homosexuality, or anecdotes from smokers' rights groups about chain-smoking octogenarians accepted over scientific evidence about tobacco and lung cancer?

Parallel reports from large numbers of ordinary people do not necessarily add up to truth. People often tell similar stories that are not accurate depictions of reality, as any anthropologist or police officer can testify. Like novelists and playwrights, regular folks adopt common images, plot lines, and themes—elements of what literary critics call *intertextuality*—in telling stories about themselves. "We need not assume that patients are either describing an organic disorder or else lying when they present similar narratives of symptoms," notes Elaine Showalter. "Instead, patients learn about diseases from the media, unconsciously develop the symptoms, and then attract media attention in an endless cycle."[31]

What keeps the cycle going—what tantalizes journalists, academics, and others about stories from the metaphorically ill and distinguishes them from others with improbable theories—is the critiques they afford of major social institutions. We have begun to see that each metaphoric illness serves as evidence of deficiencies in a particular institution: Gulf War Syndrome and the military, MCS and the consumer products industry. In an article about MCS in the journal *Feminism and Psychology*, Pamela Reed Gibson of James Madison University posits that we live in "a chemical culture" that seeks "to neutralize the message of the person with MCS . . . i.e., that the environment is unsafe." According to Steve Kroll-Smith of the University of New Orleans and H. Hugh Floyd of Samford University in their book, *Bodies in Protest*, MCS patients are "people whose bodies rebel in the presence of extremely low levels of putatively benign consumer products and environments."[32]

Gulf War Syndrome and MCS raise questions as well about a common institution: medicine. Kroll-Smith and Ladd proclaim in their journal article that by "not responding to biomedicine's use of invasive treatments," MCS patients represent "a serious challenge to the legitimacy of institutionalized medicine." Internists and allergists are not equipped to understand an illness caused by chemicals in the environment rather than by traditional pathogens such as bacteria or viruses, the sociologists go on to assert. Patients and advocates of Gulf War Syndrome make similar claims, even though for both GWS and MCS, much knowledge has been gained by researchers from the medical disciplines most intensely criticized.[33]

Hearing Voices

The most sustained and influential critique of medical science has come, however, from sufferers of another variety of metaphoric illness: breast implant disorders. "We are the evidence. The study is us sitting here," a woman in the audience yelled out during an Oprah Winfrey Show in 1995, upbraiding the CEO of Dow Corning, the leading manufacturer of silicone breast implants, for daring to suggest that studies from the Mayo Clinic, Harvard, University of Michigan, and elsewhere should be taken seriously. These studies found no evidence that implants had caused diseases in women who used them, but in many quarters scientific evidence could scarcely get a hearing amid the cries of implant victims.[34]

Emotional accounts being the stuff of TV talk shows, it is probably unreasonable to expect medical expertise to prevail in these forums. The clamor over breast implants raises profound questions, however, about whose voices, and which kinds of knowledge, are heard in fear-driven public policy debates. One of the greatest triumphs of anecdotes over science occurred at a federal regulatory agency whose express mission is to enact policies on the basis of scientific data. In 1992, when the U.S. Food and Drug Administration banned the use of silicone implants except for breast cancer patients willing to participate in research studies, the agency's leaders made their decision not primarily in response to findings from medical science (the American Medical Association denounced the ban). Rather, the FDA banned implants in the wake of congressional hearings and TV talk shows where implanted women spoke poignantly of a variety of ailments from chronic fatigue to rheumatoid arthritis to cancer, all attributed to their implants.[35]

Although at the time of the ban the FDA issued alarmist projections that 75,000 women would develop major health problems as a result of their implants, epidemiological studies have documented quite the opposite: women with implants have come down with illnesses at about the same rates as women without implants. The issue, like many in science, is not entirely resolved. Another major epidemiological study—this time focused on atypical diseases—is due out in 1999. It is important to bear in mind that with a million women with silicone implants, hundreds of thousands will become ill by chance alone. The general public can be excused for failing to appreciate this fact. Whenever another major scientific study came out refuting the claim that implants made women ill, anti-implant activists made sure we knew that "many women with implants don't find the new study reassuring," as reporter Joanne Silberner indicated on National Public Radio in 1996, following the release of a Harvard study of 23,000 women.[36]

Regardless of how large the study or how impressive the findings, reporters consistently offset the numbers with anecdotal statistics. In the words of ABC News correspondent Cokie Roberts on "Nightline" in 1995, "There are the thousands upon thousands of women who have breast implants and complain of terrible pain. Can they all be wrong?" Some social scientists also elevated first-person reports over scientific expertise. The sociologist Susan Zimmermann, author of *Silicone Survivors*, a book published in 1998, complains that "the medical community relies on research such as the Mayo Clinic study instead of trusting their patients' accounts of their symptoms."[37]

For Zimmermann and other feminists who have spoken out against them, implants represent the literal embodiment of male oppression.

After all, the critics point out, prior to the FDA ban four out of five implant operations were for cosmetic purposes. (Read: in the service of male fantasies.) And when implanted women became ill, physicians–almost always males–dismissed them. "We have been down this road before," wrote Jennifer Washburn in *Ms*. "Women in real pain going to doctors and being told that it is all in their heads. Women being encouraged to use medical devices that don't function properly and being told these devices are perfectly safe when they aren't."[38]

But lurking behind debatable analogies to the Dalkon Shield and legitimate concerns about taking women's reports seriously lay more than a little inconsistency. If listening to women about breast implants is important, why not listen to informed women such as Marcia Angell, a feminist physician and executive editor of the *New England Journal of Medicine*? Alternately ignored and denounced by implant activists, Angell eventually acknowledged how much it hurt her personally to be told, "this is a women's issue and if you don't believe that breast implants cause connective tissue disease you are therefore anti-feminist or anti-women."[39]

Rather than condemning Angell, feminists might reasonably have been expected to praise her for standing up for women. In 1992 after the FDA ban Angell accused the agency's director of "treating women like little girls." Echoing the position taken by the National Council of Breast Cancer Organizations and by Y-ME, the leading support group for breast cancer patients, Angell argued that by removing implants from the market the FDA had declared, in effect, that women are unable to weigh the costs and benefits and make a rational decision.[40]

Nor was Angell the only knowledgeable feminist shunned for her skepticism about implant illnesses. Elinor Brecher, a feature writer with the *Miami Herald*, took both a professional and personal interest in the controversy, having received implants herself following a double mastectomy in 1985. Not trusting her own experiences as representative (Brecher reported that her implants did not cause her problems), she surveyed friends, none of whom said they had had more than minor problems with their implants, and she called officials at cancer clinics around the country, from whom she learned that follow-up studies of implant patients had recorded few problems.

Brecher readily acknowledges, as does Angell, that breast implants can produce considerable pain and disfigurement by causing capsular contracture (hardening of the breast tissue), but no matter where she checked—Brecher also interviewed physicians from an assortment of specialities—could she find support for the claim that implants cause serious or systemic disease. In a series of articles in the *Herald* in the early 1990s she reported the encouraging findings of her investigative journalism, but her well-researched and persuasive pieces were neither picked up by the national press nor did reporters at other publications follow her lead and conduct their own investigations. The reason, Brecher suspects, is simple. "The better story, the sexier story, was the one about women being disfigured by horrible diseases caused by greedy plastic surgeons," she told me. That story created, though, considerable fear and suffering in women with implants. "Women called me up scared to death. It broke my heart. 'These things are ticking time bombs in my chest. Please give me the name of a doctor to get them ripped out'," Brecher paraphrased a panicked caller.[41]

The ban on implants and the scares about them may have created a greater cancer risk than the implants themselves, some doctors told Brecher, because some women who would have come forward for early diagnosis and treatment delayed doing so—because they feared, wrongly, that there would be no possibility of reconstruction. Marcia Angell goes even further: the implant scare harmed Americans seeking treatment for a variety of illnesses, she contends. Manufacturers of silicone-containing devices such as artificial joints, heart valves, and jaw implants, and companies such as Dow and DuPont that supply raw materials for such devices, scaled back production or got out of the business entirely rather than fight lawsuits.[42]

Cashing In

While some industries were cashing out of the implant business, others were cashing in—most notably, TV talk shows and law firms.

Never in the wretched history of talk TV was there a juicier story, from the ratings-ravenous perspective of producers, than that of Laura

Thorpe, the woman who took a razor and cut out her own breast implants. After an article about her appeared in a newspaper in 1992 producers of talk shows scrambled to book the unemployed woman on their programs. So eager were staffers at the "Sally Jesse Raphael" show when they discovered that Thorpe had no telephone, they rushed to the trailer park in New Mexico where she lived and flew her, her husband, and three of her five children to New York. Producers of "Maury Povich," not to be outdone, smoked out where Thorpe was staying and convinced her to appear on their show. They whisked her away to a studio and taped a program before Sally's people even knew she had been nabbed.

"The audience is breathless, and so am I. I mean, we just want to clutch ourselves," Povich gushed as he introduced Thorpe, a woman he portrayed as burdened with awful ailments caused by her implants but unable to afford surgery to have the implants removed. Her extreme action seemed almost rational in light of the maladies caused by the implants, including gangrene in her fingers and autoimmune diseases. "If you're going to die if you don't do something, you've got to do something," Thorpe exclaimed.[43]

Neither Thorpe nor Povich offered proof that those physical ailments actually existed, of course, or that implants had caused them. Nor did they entertain the possibility that Thorpe was suffering from a psychotic break or severe depression, as psychologists Jeanne Heaton and Nona Wilson later concluded after they researched Thorpe for their book, *Tuning in Trouble: Talk TV's Destructive Impact on Mental Health*. It took all of Povich's interviewing skills, Heaton and Wilson show, to keep Thorpe from sounding deranged during the broadcast. In answer to questions about the implants, she rambled on about having grown up in orphanages and foster homes, her unemployed husband, and feeling sorry for men because they have to shave. Povich managed to redirect Thorpe back to the matter of the implants before she wandered too far afield, and his producers kept the TV audience focused by flashing across the screen, "BREAST IMPLANT HORROR," the program's title.[44]

The horrors of implants became commonplace topics throughout talk television during the early and mid-1990s. Ultimately, though, it was not people with names we recognize, such as Povich and Winfrey, who most benefited from translating women's aches and pains into implant illnesses. That distinction belongs to attorneys whose names are not household words, but who persuaded juries to award women anywhere from a couple of thousand to $25 million each for illnesses purportedly caused by their implants. The lawyers took as much as 40 percent of these awards.[45]

If the FDA ban on implants had been a grand victory of anecdote over science, grander still were the victories in court. In 1994 a federal court granted $4.25 billion—that's billion with a *b*, the largest product liability settlement to that date—in a global settlement to compensate women nationwide for maladies allegedly resulting from leaking implants. Because the main manufacturer, Dow Corning, subsequently declared bankruptcy, the money was not paid out and legal wrangling continued. By 1998, when Dow Corning reached an agreement to pay $3.2 billion to settle claims and emerge from bankruptcy, a rigorous review of more than one hundred studies, published in the *Journal of the National Cancer Institute*, had concluded that implants do not cause breast cancer—the most serious disease the lawsuits alleged. Little or no scientific evidence existed to connect implants to any other disease either. Large studies had found no association, for instance, between implants and connective tissue diseases, and research published in the *Journal of the American Medical Association* suggested that lifestyle choices, rather than implants, might be factors in some of the women's ailments. Comparing women with implants to other women, the scientists discovered that those with implants tended to be heavier drinkers, have more sex partners, use hair dyes, and take birth control pills.[46]

Marcia Angell accurately observed in a commentary in the *New England Journal of Medicine*, "Despite the lack of published epidemiologic studies, the accumulated weight of anecdotes was taken by judges and juries as tantamount to proof of causation." But anecdotes do not accumulate on their own. Enterprising attorneys aggressively solicited them. A television commercial urging women to call a particular law firm at a toll-free number declared, "Joint pain, fatigue and autoimmune diseases are associated with breast implants." A headline in a newspaper ad asked, "ARE DREAM BREASTS TO DIE FOR?"[47]

Some firms became litigation factories. One pair of attorneys in Houston, John O'Quinn and Rick Laminack, mass-produced suits on behalf of more than 2,500 women. Described as "the lawyers from hell" in a cover story in *Fortune* magazine, O'Quinn and Laminack grossed around $100 million in implant settlements. In addition to hordes of paralegals and file clerks who worked exclusively on implant cases, they employed a full-time nurse and set up their own courtroom where they rehearsed witnesses.[48]

Recognizing the need to make their carefully molded anecdotes sound to judges and juries like medical facts, lawyers worked also with highly paid physicians. Some of these docs ran what Gina Kolata and Barry Meier of the *New York Times* described in an investigative story as "assembly-line practices" for certifying plaintiffs as legitimately ill. One physician in Houston, whose income in 1994 was $2 million, told the *Times* he had seen 4,700 women with implants, at least 90 percent of whom came from referrals from lawyers. Law firms typically paid the lion's share of his fee, and in turn, he authenticated 93 percent of the women as ill, thus qualifying them to collect part of the multibillion-dollar settlement or to sue on their own.[49]

Not all medical professionals were treated so hospitably, however, by the implant-milking attorneys. Prominent medical researchers whose findings might hamper the litigation caught hell from plaintiffs' firms. Following publication of the Mayo Clinic study, O'Quinn and Laminack subpoenaed huge numbers of documents from Marcia Angell and the *New England Journal of Medicine*, which published the study, while another Houston law firm, representing 3,000 women in implant suits, went directly after the scientists at Mayo. Sherine Gabriel, one of those researchers, told Kolata that responding to demands for thousands of research manuscripts, data bases, and the medical records of women in their studies was exceedingly stressful and compromised her ability to do research.[50]

The assaults had a chilling effect. Scientists at other research centers, concerned for their careers and the costs of lawsuits, vowed not to do implant studies.

Bizarre Bedfellows

To an observer not caught up in them, the breast implant debates have a *Through the Looking Glass* air. Consider the response from a feminist media commentator at Fairness and Accuracy in Reporting (FAIR), the liberal watchdog group, to Gina Kolata's reports. For exposing the activities of a gang of doctors and lawyers who exploit women's suffering, Kolata and her editors at the *New York Times* might reasonably have expected praise from Laura Flanders, who covers women's issues for FAIR. Instead Flanders accused Kolata of practicing "junk journalism" by allowing herself to be "spoon-fed . . . fake facts" by implant manufacturers. The Mayo Clinic study and others might be biased, Flanders suggested, because they were published in the *New England Journal,* a publication "cram-packed with advertisements by medical suppliers including Dow Corning," which also provided partial funding for some of the research on implants.[51]

I am a fan of much of Flanders's work—earlier I cited her perceptive analyses of how the media demonize impoverished mothers—but I was dumbfounded by her harangue against Kolata. *Does Flanders take prescription drugs when she's ill?* I began to wonder as I read her critique. Presumably she does not—since drug advertisements provide much of the revenue for the medical journals that publish studies about drugs, and drug makers help pay for much of the research done on the safety and effectiveness of medications.[52]

Personally, these facts don't particularly trouble me, for the same reason they fail to disturb most doctors and medical researchers. We know that the results of corporate-supported medical research can generally be trusted, particularly when it is conducted at academic research centers and published in eminent scientific journals. The scientific method itself, as well as the peer review process at the journals, have many safeguards built in. Besides, were biased or fraudulent studies to find their way into print, subsequent studies would likely refute them.[53]

To be sure, corporate sponsors sometimes try to deter scientific research that might hurt their profits. But do they succeed in preventing truth from getting out? In one celebrated recent case a pharmaceutical company blocked publication for seven years of a study it paid for that found its brand-name thyroid drug no better than cheaper, generic versions. Yet the study ultimately did come out in the prestigious *Journal of the American Medical Association*, accompanied by an apology from the president of the drug company.[54]

Or consider an episode that anti-implant advocates have publicized to great advantage. While serving as a $300-an-hour consultant to lawyers defending Dow Corning, Peter Schur of Harvard served as an editor of the journal *Arthritis and Rheumatism*. In his role as gatekeeper he rejected several papers that implicate implants in autoimmune diseases such as rheumatoid arthritis, yet published a paper he himself co-authored that denies any connection between implants and the diseases.

Lawyers for implanted women painted Schur's actions as a clear instance of the partisan suppression of research findings. When a panel of medical experts subsequently reviewed the rejected papers, however, they ruled that Schur's decisions had been scientifically sound. Moreover, in light of the controversy, Schur resigned from another Harvard study of breast implants to protect the research from accusations of bias.[55]

By comparison, advocates for metaphoric illnesses seldom apologize or back off, and they are proven effective at something more menacing than trying to suppress scientific results. Through intimidation they *prevent* research. Implant researchers are not the only scientists who have been hassled into submission. Just ask physicians Gregory Simon and Edward Wagner of the University of Washington, whose research showed that blood tests used to support liability and disability claims for people with multiple chemical sensitivities might be meaningless. Following publication of Simon's and Wagner's study an advocacy group for MCS patients tried to get the doctors' medical licenses revoked and filed complaints about them with the university and medical groups where they worked, as well as with a federal agency. All of the complaints were eventually dismissed, but only after much time, embarrassment, and stress on the part of Simon and Wagner, who swore never to study MCS again.[56]

In the breast implant melee, lawyers, by frightening off respected researchers, most likely did more to forestall the truth about implants than chemical companies did by placing advertisements in medical journals or helping to pay for studies. How, then, to explain why Flanders and others on the political left chose to side with a bunch of rapacious good-old-boys from Texas, over and against accomplished women journalists and scientists?[57]

At least part of the explanation lies in the age-old adage, *thy enemy's enemy is thy friend.* Those old boys from Texas functioned as mercenaries in a war that liberals and progressives were waging with conservatives over a separate but related issue called tort reform. In the mid-1990s a Republican Congress set out to enact legislation that would place caps on the damages plaintiffs can receive in product liability cases and medical malpractice lawsuits. To seduce public support they supplied the media with horror stories of what presidential candidate Bob Dole dubbed "lawsuit abuse." Reporters and commentators took the bait and told again and again anecdotes about a woman who spilled McDonald's coffee in her lap and got $3 million, and a tricycle manufacturer ordered to pay $7.5 million in a suit over the color of its bikes, which the plaintiffs said concealed a dangerous flaw in a wire handbasket on the handlebars.[58]

News organizations that bothered to check out the McDonald's case discovered that a judge reduced the $3 million coffee award to $480,000, not an ungodly amount considering that the elderly woman had endured two hospitalizations and painful skin grafts, and McDonald's had kept its coffee at a blistering 180°F to 190°F. And those that looked into the tricycle tale learned that color was a peripheral issue in a case brought by the family of a child who suffered permanent brain damage from riding a bike with numerous design flaws, only one of which had to do with the paint job. The family actually ended up receiving only a fraction of what the jury had initially recommended.[59]

In short, breast implant settlements proved to be among the few genuine examples of what the Republicans' "Contract With America" referred to as "outlandish damage awards [that] make a mockery of our civil justice system." In the entire period between 1965 and 1990 juries had handed down awards of more than $10 million in only thirty-five product liability cases. The multimillion- and multibillion-dollar judgments in implant cases in the early 1990s provided some of the best evidence for the conservatives' argument, and liberals and progressives could ill afford to concede the point. Instead they turned the tables. They claimed that journalists who criticized the implant settlements were out to "vindicate 'victim' corporations," as Flanders put it. And they suggested that corporations such as Dow, with the help of unwitting reporters, were propagandizing about the implant issue in order to weaken laws that protect the public from unsafe products. The tort reform movement was just "another case of corporations using their political clout to escape potential liability," according to the author of a *Ms.* article about implants.[60]

A Shot at Sanity

Following Bill Clinton's reelection in 1996 the firestorm over tort reform died down, leaving behind little actual reform but lots of silly warning labels. Starbucks Coffee, hoping to avoid lawsuits like the one against McDonald's, put on the side of its cups, "Careful, the beverage you are about to enjoy is extremely hot." A Batman costume carried the following notice: "FOR PLAY ONLY: Mask and chest plate are not protective; cape does not enable user to fly."[61]

Yet while shoppers were being told the obvious about consumer products, the most important question in the tort reform debate never did get answered: *Is it possible to put the brakes on runaway lawsuits while at the same time ensuring product safety and restitution for victims?*

The question is answerable, and may even be yes. In my research into yet another metaphoric illness I discovered an example of legislation that curtailed lawsuits, generously compensated victims, and at the same time protected manufacturers, who ended up producing a safer product. The legislation, which created something called the Vaccine Injury Compensation Program, was instituted by Congress in 1986 as a kind of antidote to a countrywide hysteria that had begun four years earlier—on the evening of April 19, 1982, to be precise.

That night, during an hour-long news program titled "DPT: Vaccine Roulette," broadcast on WRC-TV, the NBC affiliate in Washington, D.C., a new medical entity was given birth: the vaccine-damaged child. The program, illustrated with footage of severely handicapped children and heartbreaking testimonials from their parents, revealed that the pertussis (or "whooping cough") part of the diphtheria-pertussis-tetanus (DPT) vaccine could cause horrible neurological disorders and even death. Over the coming weeks excerpts from "Vaccine Roulette" appeared on NBC's "Today" show and in newspapers, effecting a media-generated panic. Pediatricians throughout the country were deluged with calls from panicked parents asking if their kids were going to die from the shots they had been given.[62]

Medical and governmental organizations promptly responded to the flawed exposé. Physicians at the FDA issued a forty-five-page, sentence-by-sentence refutation, copiously footnoted with studies from top medical journals, showing that deaths and serious complications result from the DPT vaccine either never or extraordinarily rarely. Other health officials and individual pediatricians also went to the media with evidence of their own about the safety of vaccines and the dangers from whooping cough itself. They reminded parents too young to remember that prior to 1949, when the vaccine was introduced, 7,500 children died from whooping cough and another 265,000 came down with various of its symptoms, which persist for five to twelve weeks and commonly include vomiting, seizures, and pneumonia on top of the violent coughing fits that gave the disease its name.[63]

Injections of truth stand little chance of stopping the spread of a metaphoric illness, particularly early on. Much of the media downplayed the reasoned responses from physicians. And within weeks of the broadcast an organization called Dissatisfied Parents Together was formed by a victim-cum-expert, Barbara Loe Fisher, who recruited members and financial support with anecdotes about her son, whom she "watched convulse, collapse and go into a state of unconsciousness within hours of his fourth DPT shot at age two."[64]

By 1984, following media appearances, protest marches, and congressional testimony by Fisher and other parents, and mammoth lawsuits, two of the three manufacturers of the DPT vaccine had gotten out of the market, creating a dangerous shortage of the vaccine. Fewer children were being vaccinated, and health officials forecast an epidemic of whooping cough. They pointed to Japan, where a decade earlier panic over the vaccine had resulted in a ban on the drug, a tenfold increase in cases of whooping cough, and a tripling of the number of whooping-cough-related deaths. In England as well, although vaccines were available, immunization rates fell by 40 percent during a scare, and over an eight-year period 100,000 Britons came down with the illness.[65]

It was against such a backdrop that the U.S. Congress, in a rare show of clear-headedness, enacted the legislation in 1986 designed to do four things at once: prevent a public health crisis, shield major drug companies from inevitable litigation, assuage parents who believe their children have been damaged by vaccines, and free the courts of interminable and highly adversarial trials. Financed initially by an $80-million-a-year federal appropriation, and since 1988 through taxes paid by vaccine manufacturers, the no-fault Vaccine Injury Compensation Program has largely met all four goals.[66]

Public concern over vaccine dangers subsided after the program went into effect, due also to a couple of massive studies published in prominent medical journals and reported in the media. With a combined sample of nearly 1 million children, the studies demonstrated ever more definitively the relative safety of the vaccine. A child's odds of brain damage or death from the disease of whooping cough, these studies showed, clearly exceed risks from the vaccine.[67]

Keeping Doubt Alive

I wish that were the bottom line on the great vaccine scare. I wish I could close this chapter with the encouraging news that strong action by government, coupled with strong findings from medical science, put an end to superstition.

Instead, the vaccine scare underscores a fundamental if regrettable reality about metaphoric illnesses, and more generally, about the persistence of fear in American society. A scare can continue long after its rightful expiration date so long as it has two things going for it: it has to tap into current cultural anxieties, and it has to have media-savvy advocates behind it.

The vaccine scare had both. In the late 1980s and throughout the 1990s it resonated with growing concerns over the impact of government and medicine on people's private lives. As Emily Martin, an anthropologist at Princeton, noted in a book on Americans' views of the human body, "Accepting vaccination means accepting the state's power to impose a particular view about the body and its immune system—the view developed by medical science." And the vaccine scare had a tireless champion, Barbara Loe Fisher, who continually strove to tap into public prejudices. At the end of the 1980s and in the early 1990s, when concern over vaccines ebbed, she continued to publish a newsletter in which she inveighed against the "medical elite" and recast vaccination—a social responsibility if ever there was one—as an individual choice.[68]

Reporters seldom took Fisher's bait during those dry years, but by the mid-1990s she made it back onto their Rolodexes. In 1994 NBC's prime-time magazine show "Now" ran a sensationalistic report introduced by anchor Katie Couric and inspired by Fisher. "What if," she asked, "we told you that one of the shots designed to protect your children might actually hurt or cripple them? It's frightening." Taking precisely the same approach as NBC's exposé of 1982, the program featured affecting tales from parents about their vaccine-damaged kids, shown drooling, stumbling, or being pushed in wheelchairs. This time, though, Fisher provided parents and children featured in the story, and her organization, which had changed its name to the official-sounding National Vaccine Information Center (NVIC), greatly profited. By their own count they received more than 65,000 phone calls to their 800 number as a result of the broadcast.[69]

A few weeks later NVIC enjoyed another bonanza, this time courtesy of the Miss America Pageant. When Heather Whitestone of Alabama, who is deaf, won the contest, news organizations reported, based on what her mother told them, that the cause of her disability was a DPT shot she received when she was eighteen months old. The vaccination "wiped out all but a tiny sliver of her hearing," went the story in the *Atlanta Journal and Constitution* and other media, and reporters included comments from NVIC to the effect that this sort of tragedy occurs regularly.[70]

One can hardly imagine a clearer example of the ignorance that results when journalists eschew real experts in favor of advocates and intimates. A couple of days after the initial stories came out and doctors had reviewed her medical records, the American Academy of Pediatrics announced that Whitestone's hearing loss had actually been caused by an infection. Ironically, the Heather Whitestone story, rather than being an occasion for frightening parents about vaccines, was an opportunity to educate them about the *benefits* of vaccination. The infection that left Whitestone deaf (haemophilus influenzae bacteria) can be prevented by means of a vaccine that became available in the late 1980s.

Some journalists did make a point of correcting the earlier reports, but tellingly, even during this subsequent phase of the coverage, NVIC spokespeople were given space to push their paranoias. An article in the *Washington Post*, for instance, included a comment from Fisher suggesting that medical records may be inaccurate because physicians discount parents' reports.[71]

In the years that followed as well Fisher and her group garnered respectful coverage for dubious contentions that vaccinations were responsible for everything from Gulf War Syndrome to increased incidence of asthma and diabetes to exorbitant profits by pharmaceutical companies. A long piece in *Money* magazine in 1996 provocatively titled "The Lethal Dangers of the Billion-Dollar Vaccine Business" referred to Fisher as an "expert." And after a new DPT vaccine was approved by the FDA that same year articles in the *Los Angeles Times* and *Washington Post* went so far as to claim that "the doggedness of Fisher's group . . . paid off." Less likely to cause side effects such as swelling, fever, and irritability, which sometimes accompanied the old shot, the new vaccine is "a happy culmination of 15 years of effort" by NVIC, the media quoted Fisher saying.[72]

In fact the new vaccine was in development before the public panic began. Research and testing on the vaccine came to successful fruition thanks less to campaigns by Fisher and her compatriots than to the availability of new technology. Moreover, agitation over the old DPT vaccine may well have delayed introduction of the new one, at least in the United States. Drug companies and the FDA, fearful of lawsuits, took an especially cautious approach in testing and approval of the new product, which is not, in any event, as exemplary as its champions make it sound. Compared to the old vaccine, it is less effective and more expensive.[73]

Whatever else advocacy groups may achieve through fear campaigns about metaphoric illnesses, they rarely facilitate the advance of medical science.

8

PLANE WRECKS

Small Danger, Big Scare

Upon landing at the Baltimore airport, as he taxied to the terminal, the pilot of my flight from Los Angeles announced: "The safest part of your journey is over. Drive home safely."

He was right. We stood a greater chance of being killed driving the few miles into Washington from the airport than in the 2,500-mile trip across the continent. In the entire history of commercial aviation, dating back to 1914, fewer than 13,000 people have died in airplane crashes. Three times that many Americans lose their lives in automobile accidents in a single year. The average person's probability of dying in an air crash is about 1 in 4 million, or roughly the same as winning the jackpot in a state lottery.[1]

The news media do make reference to these sorts of numbers. They may dish out exaggerated statistics about multiple chemical sensitivity, heroin use among the middle class, road rage, and innumerable other superfluous scares, but not about plane wrecks. They let their readers and viewers know that the likelihood of dying in an airplane crash is roughly on a par with "the risk of being brained by a meteorite," as one editorial in *USA Today* put it. "U.S. airlines are so safe now that accidents are largely random events. The average passenger would have to take a flight every day for thousands of years before he would be in a plane crash," Adam Bryant of the *New York Times* has noted.[2]

The media's record isn't perfect, of course. Occasionally a set of numbers gets misreported. In 1988 the *Washington Post* ran the headline "Airline Accident Rate Is Highest in 13 Years," even though the accident rate in fact had been declining for several years. The writers and editors had mistaken *incidences* for *rates*. While the total number of accidents had increased, the rate—or number of accidents per 100,000 departures—had declined. Put another way, more flights were taking off, so there were more accidents, but the likelihood of being in one of those accidents had decreased. Indeed, since the 1960s the volume of flights had more than doubled, yet the accident rate had gone down by 85 percent.[3]

Another error journalists sometimes make is to report a statistic out of context. *U.S. News & World Report*, in a cover story in June 1995, reported that "last year alone . . . 269 people lost their lives," thereby implying that the nation's skies were becoming more dangerous. Yet just three years earlier, in 1992, only thirty-three people had died in air crashes, and three years later, in 1998, no one would die.[4]

Foul-ups like these are exceptions, however. By and large the news media, the *Post* and *U.S. News* included, make sure their readers know that, overall, the safety statistics for America's airlines are impressive. Yet amazingly enough, the media promote fears of flying nonetheless. They acknowledge that a person is ten times more likely to die in his or her bathtub than in an airplane accident and yet run stories titled "Air Safety–Under a Cloud" (*Time*) and "High Anxiety in the Skies" (*USA Today*). Many times, in the very same article or TV news segment a reporter will note the minuscule risk of injury or death in air travel *and* proclaim there is serious reason to worry should we dare to step aboard an airplane.[5]

This chapter is about how journalists and the people they quote accomplish this extraordinary feat of illogic. I reviewed the coverage of airline safety in the nation's major newspapers, magazines, and television networks over a recent three-year period–1994 through 1996–and found journalists grouping together isolated incidents, depicting them as dangerous trends, and allowing those pseudotrends to overshadow the larger reality of the safety of air travel.

1994: BEWARE USAir!
STAY CLEAR OF SMALL PLANES!

Air travel may be safe in general, but journalists would like you to believe that particular categories of airlines, or individual carriers, are hazardous to your health. Unfortunately, that message casts doubt over *all* air travel.

Prior to fall 1994 few fretted over the airworthiness of USAir, a leading carrier that had flown several million flights with only a handful of crashes. Yet after one of its jets went down near Pittsburgh, killing all 132 people onboard, numerous reporters depicted the accident as "the airline's fifth crash in as many years" and observed that all three of the most recent fatal air crashes of regularly scheduled airlines were USAir flights.[6]

To regain consumer confidence USAir eventually had to appoint a former Air Force general as "Vice President for Safety" and spend more than $1 million in advertising. Yet the succession of accidents was probably a chance occurrence, as Gina Kolata wrote in the *New York Times.* Kolata used as a main source for her article a professor of statistics at MIT named Arnold Barnett. By comparing the safety records of major airlines during three ten-year periods (1973–1983, 1978–1988, and 1983–1993), Barnett had determined that differences in safety records between airlines are statistically insignificant. "The first-ranked airline was different in all three periods and, strikingly, the airline that was best in one period always fell in the bottom half of the rankings in the other two," Barnett had written in an article in the journal *Technology Review.*[7]

Barnett scolded the International Airline Passengers Association (IAPA), an advocacy organization that frequently received favorable attention from the media, when it issued alerts about the hazards of air travel. (Never mind that the IAPA sold flight insurance to passengers and had a stake in fostering their unease.) A rating system the IAPA devised in 1993, which divided up the airlines according to their accident records, was practically worthless, Barnett suggested. The data the association used "provide a pitifully tenuous basis for putting airlines into two distinct categories—a point that was overlooked both by IAPA's analysts and by the newspapers that publicized their results," wrote Barnett.[8]

Yet criticism from Barnett and other aviation safety experts failed to dissuade the news media from taking IAPA pronouncements seriously. When the association spread another scare in late 1994 it received even greater attention. Here's how *USA Today* began its front-page story: "Steer clear of commuter planes with fewer than 30 seats and 'don't even consider flying them at night or in bad weather,' warns a consumer group." The IAPA's alarmist recommendation, coming on the heels of several commuter airline crashes, made its way into other major newspapers as well and was the lead story on the CBS evening news.[9]

No sooner had the unmerited uproar over USAir died down than this new panic began. Now, not just one airline, but an entire sector of the nation's air transport system was deemed unsafe—and, again, for no good reason. As Federal Aviation Administration officials quickly pointed out, accident rates for commuter airlines were almost identical to those of the major carriers once you remove Alaskan bush flights, air taxis, and helicopters from the IAPA's analysis.

Some news organizations in the coming days and weeks did report this fact and include comments from critics of the IAPA. They did so, however, while continuing to monger fears about commuter air travel. "It's not against [IAPA's] financial interests to make people worried," *Time* quoted a transportation expert at Northwestern University saying. "But," the article went on to say, "government officials were also becoming increasingly concerned" about commuter air safety—this in spite of unambiguous statements from FAA officials to the contrary. Accident rates for commuter aircraft, FAA data showed, had remained steady in the past three years; a praiseworthy accomplishment considering that the number of passengers traveling on small planes had increased by about 40 percent during that time.[10]

To come up with evidence of unsafety at commuter airlines reporters had to dig deep. Richard Newman of *U.S. News & World Report,* for instance, in a cover article titled "How Safe Are Small Planes?" warned of something he dubbed "pay-your-way piloting." "More than a dozen regional airlines require would-be pilots to pay for their own training, which can cost up to about $9,000," Newman revealed. According to the head of a pilots' union quoted in the article, "Little Lord Fauntleroy can get a job as a pilot, while more skilled candidates may not have $9,000 for training."[11]

Many surgeons of course pay for their own training too, and no one questions them on that account or opts to be operated on only by those who received scholarships. But 'pay-your-way piloting' was just one in an unending barrage of pseudoshocking realities about commuter airlines the news media tossed out in late 1994. During the final three months of that year exposés by the dozens came out in newspapers and magazines, and network TV newsmagazines ran sixteen segments on the presumed perils of commuter air travel. "From the news coverage of recent aviation accidents," Stephen Chapman, a columnist for the *Chicago Tribune* suggested in December, "most Americans presumably now believe that traveling by commuter airliner is roughly as hazardous as jumping out of a 25th floor window into a toxic waste tank full of crocodiles while smoking an unfiltered cigarette."[12]

1995: CAUTION! UNSAFE SAFETY AGENCY

At least in 1994 reporters were responding to actual domestic air disasters. In the following year the only fatal crash of a U.S. airliner occurred late in December, when an American Airlines jet smashed into a mountain in Colombia. Yet the media managed to find a pretense for keeping the fear of flying alive in 1995. They wrote exposés about the government agency charged with safeguarding air travel. The FAA, journalists repeatedly asserted, operates with a "tombstone mentality." Its officials agree to tighten safety standards only when forced to do so by the publicity surrounding fatal accidents.[13]

In reality the FAA had mandated scores of safety requirements over the years, only a small proportion of which were in response to pressures following particular accidents. True enough, before putting a new rule in place the FAA conducted a cost-benefit analysis to assess whether enough lives and property would be saved to justify the cost of the regulation. Described in a certain way such reasoning can sound almost immoral. Instead of immediately mandating a reform they know will prevent fatalities, officials look at ten or twenty years' worth of accident data and extrapolate the number of lives likely to be lost in the future. They then multiply that number by the government's estimated value of a life ($2.6 million last I checked), add the expected dollar figure for property loss, and compare the result to the price tag for the new regulation. If the safety rule costs more than the value of the lives and property it will save, the agency may opt to let some people die.

Reporters could not avoid the temptation to juxtapose this impersonal process with poignant comments from actual women and men who had lost loved ones in crashes that could have been averted had the FAA not engaged in cost-benefit analysis. Not surprisingly, the agency did not come out looking good. But it makes no sense to impose every regulation that might save a life, regardless of cost. For one thing, each time the FAA institutes a new requirement the money has to come from somewhere. Mostly it comes from higher airline ticket prices, which in turn may prevent some people from traveling at all and push others to take to the highways, where they face greater risk of death or injury.[14]

Consider child safety seats, one of the media's poster children for the evils of cost-benefit analysis. "When it comes to federal regulation of the airlines, safety experts have known for years that child safety seats could help save lives. Yet even today the airlines have more safety rules about your luggage than about your child. How could this be?" demanded Connie Chung on CBS's "Evening News." "You can't hold your laptop computer on your lap, but we've seen in accidents, a 33-pound child allowed to be loose in the cabin," someone from the National Transportation Safety Board declared in the report that followed, which included no rejoinder from FAA officials. "Requiring safety seats is too costly, says the FAA" is all that CBS presented of the other side of what is actually a legitimate dispute. Regulations to require safety seats would have cost about $1 billion to implement—an amount that almost certainly would save more lives if spent on other airline safety measures.[15]

Reports on CBS and elsewhere in the media centered on the tragic deaths of two babies—one in an airplane accident in 1990, the other in 1994—and gave the impression that these deaths were merely two among many. In fact, as near as I can determine, they were about the only fatalities in the past several years that experts believe would have been prevented had safety seats been required. Indeed, a rule mandating child seats might well have resulted in a *greater* number of deaths.

Were passengers forced to buy separate tickets for their children rather than carry them on their laps, some parents, unable or unwilling to bear the additional cost, would have driven rather than flown. And while proponents of safety seats are correct to point out that people who have children in their cars tend to drive more safely than the average motorist, even for careful drivers the risk of death is greater in a car than in a plane.[16]

1995–1996: WARNING! BOGUS PARTS

A second major scare the media promoted in 1995 likewise lacked a sense of proportion and got pinned on the FAA. Each year 26 million airplane parts are replaced, and every part must, by law, carry paperwork certifying that it has been manufactured in accordance with strict FAA standards. With such volume of activity it would be extraordinary if no corruption entered into the production and certification process, particularly given the fact that fakes of many of the simpler parts, such as bolts and blades, can be produced for a few bucks and sold for ten to one hundred times as much. And sure enough, reporters got great copy from self-described "aircraft parts consultants" who regaled them with accounts of machinists who shine up old parts and sell them back to airlines. Strip-and-dip operations, as they are colorfully called.

Mary Schiavo, the inspector general of the Department of Transportation (of which the FAA is a part), also served up some choice quotes. "We shouldn't have to wait for another plane to drop out of the sky for the FAA to take action," she is fond of saying. Having made something of a professional fetish out of spare airline parts since her arrival in 1990–sometimes devoting more than half of her staff of investigators to the matter–Schiavo brought scads of shocking stories and bogus parts with her when she testified before Congress or the news media.[17]

Only one major crash had been attributed to a counterfeit part. In 1989 a Norwegian charter flight with fifty-five people aboard ended up in the North Sea after bolts in its tail section broke apart. Pictures of that airplane, which had been recovered in pieces and painstakingly re-assembled in a hanger, served as the principal illustrations for several scare stories, including ABC's newsmagazine, "Primetime." Brian Ross, identified on screen as "ABC News Chief Investigative Correspon-dent," flew to Norway and had himself filmed beside the plane. There were, said Ross, many more defective parts in the aviation pipeline, "parts that could be putting thousands of lives at risk, raising serious questions about just how good a job the FAA is doing on a critical safety issue."[18]

Ross's report was enough to make you reach for a life jacket, but the operative word is *could*. Thousands of lives *might* have been put at risk. The FAA *may* have been doing a lousy job. But apparently, neither is the case. Were the problem as serious as Ross and Schiavo suggest, how come more than a half million flights are completed every week with-out incident?[19]

The level of illogic was high in news coverage of the bogus parts is-sue, but the story had legs. In June 1996, a year and a half after the "Primetime" segment aired, the reconstructed Norwegian plane ap-peared in the U.S. press again. A photo of it filled nearly half a page in a *Business Week* cover story titled, "Warning! Bogus parts have turned up in commercial jets. Where's the FAA?" Largely a rehash of material contained in earlier TV and print reports, the article did have a new hook. A ValuJet airliner had crashed a few weeks earlier in Florida, killing 110 people. By means of some fancy word work, *Business Week*'s reporter, Willy Stern, connected the bogus parts issue to that crash.

There is no reason to believe that bad parts played a role in the Valu-Jet crash. Stern forged the connection circuitously by relating the crash to an accident a year earlier. On that previous occasion, the engine in another ValuJet aircraft had exploded prior to takeoff, possibly as the result of a mismanufactured part. "The accident," Stern wrote, "caused no fatalities—unlike last month's crash of ValuJet Flight 592 into the Everglades. But in some ways, it was more ominous, because it high-lights a safety issue that affects every carrier in the air: the growing stream of substandard or bogus parts that are finding their way into commercial aircraft."[20]

If this seems like a weird claim—an accident in which no one died is more ominous than a crash that killed everyone onboard?—Stern's pronouncement that the airline industry is "underregulated" is weirder still. Had he been writing in *The Nation, Mother Jones*, or some other liberal or progressive publication, such a statement might be expected. But *Business Week* isn't exactly noted for endorsing greater government regulation of big business. In fact, when I ran a Nexis search of the contents of *Business Week* for the previous five years to see if I could turn up other occurrences of the word *underregulate*, I could not. When I ran a search for the word *watchdog*, on the other hand, I discovered that it had appeared 115 times.

1996: UH-OH! DISCOUNT TICKETS

When it comes to aviation safety, some editors and reporters seem to suppress no speculation, however disparate from their publication's larger outlook or from the facts. An article in *Time* during this same period announced, "The fatal crash of a ValuJet plane with 109 people aboard raises questions about no-frills flying," even though the ValuJet accident represented the first-ever fatal crash of a low-cost airline. In the eighteen years since deregulation several dozen discount airlines had come into existence and flown billions of miles without a fatality. Far from raising safety concerns, by stimulating people to fly instead of drive, cut-rate airlines *saved* lives—approximately 190 to 275 per year, according to a study in the journal *Accident Analysis and Prevention*.[21]

Still, *Time* was far from alone in implying that price reductions and reduced safety may go hand in hand. Scores of newspapers and every major TV network ran stories proffering this theory. Prominent among them was a story in the *Chicago Tribune*, widely referenced by other news outlets, which leaked a draft of a forthcoming report from the FAA. Low-cost carriers have significantly higher accident rates than full-fare airlines, the report seemed to suggest. In point of fact, however, as FAA officials promptly demonstrated by releasing the final version of the report and the data on which it was based, no such trend exists. On the contrary, ten of the fourteen discount carriers had *no* serious accidents in a recent five-year period, and the largest of them, Southwest, had not had a fatality in its entire twenty-four years of operation. A couple of the carriers, ValuJet being one, had higher-than-average accident rates, but as a group, the safety record for the discounters was about the same as that of the major airlines.[22]

FAA administrators, besides releasing the report, stated decisively that there is no relationship between ticket prices and safety standards. But reporters had already left a different impression. A poll conducted during this period found that while most Americans had confidence in the safety of the major airlines, 57 percent had concerns about the discounters. The results of the poll, conducted by CNN and *Time*, were widely publicized, further legitimating fears about budget carriers by giving the impression that such fears are normal and provoking significant decreases in business at many small and low-priced airlines for months.[23]

Even while she still worked as inspector general, Mary Schiavo bolstered those fears in an alarmist article she wrote for *Newsweek*. Pumping up her own celebrity and in the same breath public concern, Schiavo boasted of taking her first flight at age ten and getting her pilot's license at eighteen, then declared that of late, she was afraid to fly. In particular, she wrote, she stayed away from commuter planes, "marginal airlines," and particular carriers she considered problematic, including ValuJet. There's "reason enough to worry" about the safety of commercial air travel, Schiavo cautioned.[24]

Two months later, following criticism from FAA officials, other aviation safety experts, and both Democrats and Republicans in Congress, each of whom objected to Schiavo's tendency to make incendiary comments in the press that undermined confidence in air safety, she resigned. But reporters continued to seek her out for comments in the months and years that followed. After TWA Flight 800, bound for Paris, went down shortly after takeoff from JFK in July, Schiavo became something of a fixture in TV and print news coverage. There, as well as in *Flying Blind, Flying Safe*, a best-selling book she published the next year, Schiavo tossed out a range of reasons to worry about air travel. She could no longer monger precisely the same scares she had been pushing—TWA was a long-established, full-price airline—but she suggested nonetheless that Flight 800 might have gone down owing to "a bogus part sold to the airline by shady dealers" or "an incompetent mechanic [who] missed something." And Schiavo joined a cacophony of voices that speculated a bomb had caused the TWA disaster.[25]

According to Graham Boynton in a page-one story in the *New York Observer*, "On Thursday, July 18, New Yorkers woke up to find that they were living in a different city. When a bomb—and it was surely a bomb—blew up TWA Flight 800 . . . it also obliterated our sense of invulnerability." The *New York Post* concurred. "IT WAS NO ACCIDENT," their full-cover headline declared. Even the *New York Times*, while more cautious, tossed out heavy hints that the plane had been bombed. One story noted that "TWA's connection to one of the world's most turbulent regions, the Mideast, has been long and prominent." Another spoke of "the lax scrutiny of air cargo loaded on passenger planes." And a column by Clyde Haberman opened with, "This may seem to be jumping the gun, since so much is still not known about what brought down TWA Flight 800. But it is probably time for Americans to accept terrorism as a fact of life requiring certain impositions, like personal searches in public places, to preserve communal safety."[26]

In the two years following the crash hundreds of thousands of person-hours and millions of dollars were spent searching for a cause, but federal investigators reached only two firm conclusions: a spark ignited the plane's center fuel tank; and there had been no terrorist attack. These findings hardly put an end, needless to say, to hairy headlines that "A Missile Destroyed TWA Flight 800" (*Village Voice*).[27]

The lack of a simple, certain explanation itself provided fuel for fear mongering. "If TWA 800 was an accident—even a million-to-one freak accident—it could theoretically happen again," a *Newsweek* article vacuously observed.[28]

Selling the Latest Air Scare

Absent statistical or scientific causes for concern about whatever air scare they are advancing at the moment, journalists rely on provocative statements of their own or from fear mongering officials and former officials such as Mary Schiavo. Or, at least as common, they quote people who possess no technical expertise whatsoever. They go to airports and corner people they describe as "seasoned travelers," who provide quotes like, "I fly constantly, but after this recent crash, even *I* have white knuckles."[29]

Or a journalist will seek out someone who saved her own life or the lives of loved ones by canceling a trip. "When Dawn O'Day, a New York homemaker, saw a TV report last week on commuter-airline safety, she got worried—and then she got on the phone," began an article in *Time*. It went on to explain that O'Day's daughter, Misty, a college student in North Carolina, was booked on an American Eagle commuter flight for part of her trip home for the holidays. Fortunately, though, Misty's mom had been following the news coverage about the dangers of commuter air travel and had her daughter take ground transportation instead of the American Eagle flight, which subsequently crashed and killed fifteen of its twenty passengers.[30]

By playing Misty's story for us, *Time* effected two illusions. The magazine gave the impression that the scare mongering they and most of the rest of the media were doing about commuter air travel was in the service of saving lives. And they turned a tiny probability into a huge one. The average reader's odds of dying on his or her next commuter flight are one in several million, but Misty's appears to have been three out of four.

To dramatize the odds, journalists also use actual victims of airline accidents. Following every major crash reporters single out a small number of sympathetic victims for profile pieces. After the ValuJet crash, for instance, a single family and one of the pilots got most of the attention. The photograph of the Neal and Judy McNitt family—Mom and Dad with the three kids on their laps, everyone smiling and happy—that went out from the Associated Press practically commands the copy that would accompany it. "They were one of those All-American families that we're all going to miss," a neighbor quoted in *USA Today* put it. "My God," the children's aunt exclaimed in the same heartrending article, "they'll never experience prom, or marriage, or babies. Their whole future has been taken away."[31]

Stories about the pilot were affecting on other grounds. One of the nation's few female airline captains, Candi Kubeck, age thirty-five, had already logged almost 9,000 hours of flying and maintained a nearly flawless safety record. "Flying," the *New York Times* wrote, "was not really work to her. It was a lifelong labor of love." Her husband, a pilot for America West, told reporters that Candi was meticulous about safety. She checked out everything, he said, and saw to it that flights were delayed or canceled if necessary. Both the *Times* and *USA Today* ended their stories with him saying, "We planned on growing old together."[32]

There was a rather pathetic irony, though, in the tender treatment accorded Candi Kubeck after her death. For the previous few years the media had been critical of airline pilots, and especially of pilots at commuter and discount airlines. Anecdotes and adverbs ruled the day in those earlier accounts. "Pilots routinely report falling asleep in the cockpit and making mistakes while landing, taking off and navigating their planes," *U.S. News & World Report* had written, neither bothering to define *routinely* nor to cite any evidence apart from tales told to their reporters by some unnamed pilots. "Alcohol and drug abuse is a real problem," Gareth Cook claimed in an article in the *Washington Monthly*. His sole evidence? "One pilot who was found dead at the controls of a plane that crashed had a blood alcohol level of .16 percent, the rough equivalent of downing seven drinks in an hour." Candi Kubeck made a different kind of good copy, and for that she was lionized.[33]

Say Something Often Enough . . .

How do the news media minimize the excellent safety record of America's airlines? The same way discount appliance stores bring down prices on VCRs. It is a commonplace that retailers need not make a large profit per sale if they make a lot of sales. Likewise, reporters need not scare the daylights out of us in individual stories if they run lots of stories.

In the ValuJet crash 110 people died. Yet *USA Today* alone ran more than 110 stories about the crash. Just in the first two weeks after the plane went down *USA Today* published seventy-one pieces. The *New York Times, Chicago Tribune, Washington Post*, and CBS and NBC evening newscasts each ran about fifty articles during that fortnight. By the one-month anniversary of the accident coverage of the crash had faded to an average of less than one story per day in most of the major media, but the reprieve was short-lived. When the results came out from an FAA investigation launched just after the crash, a whole new frenzy ensued. Over a thirty-day period the FAA had brought in sixty inspectors and carried out two thousand inspections of ValuJet's fifty-one planes. That they turned up enough irregularities to shut down ValuJet is hardly surprising; the company's president was probably right when he said that almost any airline would come up short under that unprecedented level of scrutiny.[34]

Whether reporters were justified in dubbing as "serious" the half dozen accidents that the FAA uncovered in ValuJet's history is arguable. One of the accidents consisted of a flight attendant breaking her ankle when a plane hit turbulence; another resulted from a tow bar breaking while a plane was being pushed back from a gate. In total, the FAA listed thirty-four safety violations, nearly all of them minor, and investigators later determined that the probable cause of the Valujet crash, a cargo fire, was the result of an error not by ValuJet but by SabreTech, a subcontractor whose employees mistakenly labeled 144 oxygen generators as empty.[35]

Arguably more newsworthy than what the FAA found were the human consequences of the action they took. In grounding ValuJet the FAA put 4,000 people out of work, stranded scores of travelers, and made low-cost seats difficult to impossible to obtain between several East Coast cities during the summer vacation period. Few journalists were inclined to highlight the downsides of the grounding. After all, they had been haranguing FAA officials to get tough. In the days just after the crash whenever agency spokespeople dared to reassure the public about ValuJet, journalists thrashed them. On ABC's "Nightline," Secretary of Transportation Federico Pena noted that the carrier had been responsive to FAA concerns and that he personally would have no hesitation about flying ValuJet. To which Ted Koppel responded by lecturing Pena that he "owed a little more candor to the American people" and would do well to change his tune and fess up that ValuJet wasn't airworthy.[36]

Transportation officials couldn't win. Once they capitulated by shutting down the airline, the story became "ValuJet Shutdown Exposes Flaws of the FAA" (*Wall Street Journal*). "Nightline," on the day the grounding was announced, devoted its entire half hour to attacks on Pena and the FAA. Early on, correspondent Brian Ross spoke of "a massive failure on the part of the agency in charge of enforcing airline safety . . . another example of the FAA's so-called tombstone mentality." Then the anchor for the evening, Forrest Sawyer, gave FAA chief David Hinson a grilling. "What in the world took you so long," Sawyer demanded. When Hinson responded that ValuJet had been taking steps to correct deficiencies inspectors brought to its attention, and that a shutdown earlier would not have stood up in court, Sawyer would have none of it. "The airplane did go down, there were 110 people killed," Sawyer said, pointedly accusing Hinson of having ignored complaints from ValuJet's own employees.[37]

A separate interview with the president of the flight attendants' union seemed to back up Sawyer's claim. "I hear a lot of concerns from the flight attendants about the safety of the airline," she said. Asked for specifics, however, her answer suggested she was promoting a broader agenda. "I think safety comes in different forms. The way that ValuJet treats its employees is one of the safety concerns, because it's a direct reflection on how it maintains the aircraft," she replied.[38]

While her reasoning may be specious (an airline certainly may treat its workers poorly and at the same time fly its customers safely), who can fault her for capitalizing on the crash to draw attention to the plight of her members? ValuJet flight attendants were paid far less than their counterparts at major airlines, and their duties also included cleaning the cabin between flights. Yet what were the odds of "Nightline" devoting a program to the working conditions of low-level airline employees?[39]

Neglect Something Long Enough . . .

The same questions I have raised about other scares beg to be answered about the colossal attention the media devote to airline safety:

Are other hazards receiving less attention than they deserve, and if so, how do journalists justify, in their own minds, the disproportionate coverage?

The answer to the first question is a resounding yes. Hazards that kill and injure many more people receive much less attention. In the mid-1990s, while the press obsessed over airline accidents—which resulted in fewer than a dozen deaths in the best years and a few hundred in the worst—more than 5,000 Americans died in work-related fatalities each year. Almost 7 million suffered injuries. An unconscionable number of these victims were under the age of eighteen; well in excess of 5,000 children and adolescents showed up in emergency rooms with work-related injuries each year. Reporters spewed out hundreds of stories about hypothetical gaps in oversight by the FAA at a time when profound gaps existed at the Occupational Health and Safety Administration (OSHA), an agency created by an Act of Congress in 1970 "to assure so far as possible every working man and woman in the nation safe and healthful working conditions."[40]

Studies find that, on average, when a company is inspected by OSHA and slapped with a penalty, the injury rate at the firm declines by 20 percent over the following three years. But with only 2,000 inspectors to oversee 6 million workplaces, OSHA was in a position to inspect the average American work site once a century.[41]

Unsurprisingly, the rate of occupational injuries in the United States was rising. Making matters worse, a group of openly anti-OSHA Republicans had been elected to Congress in 1994 partly with money from corporations that wanted to weaken the agency still further. Yet among the leading major news organizations only the *Washington Post* ran major investigative pieces about OSHA. As a rule, media coverage of workplace health and safety issues was, as journalist Frank Swoboda described it in *Nieman Reports* (a journalism review published by Harvard), "sporadic and most often nonexistent." News organizations do not have reporters whose "beat" is worker safety. There is no one like the *New York Times*'s Adam Bryant and his colleague Matthew Wald, who between them published an average of one story on airline safety every week from 1994 through 1996.[42]

During that period, when news stories mentioned OSHA or work site safety they were seldom about dangerous equipment or illnesses caused by unhealthy working conditions. Instead the focus was on a couple of red herrings. One of these, workplace violence, I addressed earlier. The other, allegations of excessive regulation by OSHA, consisted of little more than Republican-planted anecdotes. Particularly popular were tales of dentists who wouldn't let kids take their baby teeth home because OSHA forbade it. (There was no such OSHA ruling, of course. The regulations in question were designed to protect the public against the spread of AIDS, hepatitis, and other serious illnesses and did not prohibit dentists from abetting the tooth fairy.)[43]

Had reporters chosen to look they would have found plenty of genuine stories waiting to be written about OSHA. On the one hand, the agency had pulled off some amazing feats in the recent past that had gone largely unreported. For instance, from the late 1970s through the mid-1980s they brought about a 95 percent reduction in brown lung disease among textile workers by instituting rules limiting exposure to cotton dust. On the other hand, some workplace hazards that should have been remedied long ago continue to kill and injure substantial numbers of workers. An example that OSHA officials themselves tried for years to get the press to write about: at least three hundred Americans die each year from silicosis, a lung disease caused by inhalation of dust. Largely preventable through controls on exposure at work sites, the disorder was recognized as far back as the first century A.D., when Pliny the Elder, the Roman naturalist, warned about it.[44]

"Enterprising editors and reporters might find a refreshing change of pace and a wealth of stories, if they ventured out to worksites in their area and took a look at the problems firsthand," Swoboda recommended in his *Nieman Reports* article.[45]

Why Aviation?

Journalists tend to offer a couple of explanations for their preoccupation with airline safety. Some say that plane crashes are naturally newsworthy. "When a plane falls from the sky, the story is compelling, albeit morbidly so: the pictures of twisted metal, luggage hanging from trees, the screaming mother at the airport where the flight never arrives," wrote Gareth Cook in the *Washington Monthly*–and he's right, as far as he goes. Unquestionably, plane wrecks make compelling news stories, which explains the immediate eruption of coverage. Yet why do wrecks remain in the news for months–sometimes years–on end, well after the luggage has left the trees and the mothers have buried their children? How come, during periods in which there have been *no* crashes for long stretches of time, do the media continue to run scads of frightening stories about air safety? And if it is the availability of affecting photographs and screaming mothers that makes plane wrecks compelling, why don't reporters flock to other sites where those elements are present? (Understaffed emergency rooms in public hospitals come to mind, as do encampments of homeless women and children, and hazardous worksites.)[46]

The way some journalists see it, air safety objectively deserves a high level of coverage, not just on account of the drama surrounding plane crashes but because plane wrecks produce lasting effects on people's psyches and on the U.S. economy. "Why does the prospect of a plane crash frighten us so much–when the risk of drowning in the bathtub is 10 times higher?" Melinda Beck asked in a cover article on aviation safety in *Newsweek* in 1995. Her reply: "Because the statistics don't reflect the powerful emotional impact that an air disaster has or the ripples it sends through the economy. The crash of Flight 427 in Pittsburgh not only killed all 132 people on board and disrupted their families forever, it also cost USAir $40 million in canceled bookings and half of its stock price. The company, which employs 44,328, may yet go bankrupt, its accounting firm warned last week. Each plane crash also vividly reminds us of how vulnerable we are, hurtling at 500 miles per hour, 7 miles above the earth, sealed in a pressurized metal can."[47]

Once again, the argument is accurate but conspicuously incomplete. Beck might as well explain an arson fire without mentioning the arsonist. A plane wreck does not, in itself, cause canceled bookings or "vividly remind" people of anything. Both of these are effects of how the media cover a crash. It is reporters who implant images of "hurtling . . . in a pressurized metal can" and who, erroneously taking a string of accidents as indicative of bad safety management, draw dubious ties between the carnage of a crash and an airline's balance sheets. USAir would have lost far fewer bookings after the Pittsburgh crash had there not been articles like the one that came out in *Time*, which began with lurid descriptions of rescue workers pulling charred body parts out of trees and then told readers what to make of the spectacle. "Such ghastly scenes," the author instructed, "raise again questions the U.S. had almost forgotten: Can air travel maintain its recent glowing safety record? Or are financially troubled airlines–USAir in particular– skimping dangerously on maintenance and crew training to cut losses?"[48]

In news coverage of aviation hazards, as of other dangers the media blow out of proportion, a self-justifying, perpetual-motion machinery operates. Incessant reporting and pronouncements by reporters generate financial crises and crises in public confidence, which in turn justify more hysterical coverage. Perhaps the real question here is why no one interrupts the cycle–why editors, producers, and management fail to put on brakes. Why, in many news organizations, doesn't anyone step in when the quantity or irrationality of the reporting starts getting out of hand?

A veteran reporter at the *Los Angeles Times* (who prefers I not use her name) provided me with at least part of the answer to this question when I asked her, over lunch a couple of weeks after the ValuJet crash, why her paper had been devoting so much space to this event. I had anticipated one or both of the replies I'd been getting elsewhere– "crashes make for compelling copy" or "crashes are profound psychoeconomic events"–but she had a different take. "There's an expression around the newsroom," she responded. "News is what happens to your editors."

She did not mean, of course, that her editors had been on the ValuJet flight that went down. She meant that her editors–and their bosses, the executive editors and senior management at Times Mirror Corporation–fly a lot. So do their families, friends, and business associates.

They are more likely than many people to know someone who has been in a plane crash or narrowly avoided one. They can imagine as well that unless greater attention is paid to airline safety, they will know victims in the future or could end up on a fatality list themselves.

It would be wrong to imply that the interests and experiences of those who oversee news organizations determine the content of the media. It would be equally wrong, however, to pretend that those interests and experiences have nothing to do with which hazards and categories of victims are favored by the news media. As media consumers, we are well advised to take note of those interests and apply a correction factor. K. C. Cole, a science writer for the *Los Angeles Times*, made the crucial point. When President Clinton gave $1 billion to improve airport security following the TWA Flight 800 crash, Cole found herself cheering. "As a fearful flier myself, I figure I can use all the help I can get," she wrote. "But I also know that dozens of 747s worth of children throughout the world die every day due to easily preventable causes like hunger and disease. The price of lives lost on airlines is clearly higher—according to the powers that be—than lives lost to simple hunger."[49]

9

FINAL THOUGHTS

The Martians *Aren't* Coming

In the course of my research, as I read frightening stories in newspapers and magazines or watched them on TV, periodically I thought to myself, *it's 1938 all over again.*

To be sure, there are major differences between the instances of fear mongering I have discussed and the CBS radio broadcast on Halloween night that year. Orson Welles's adaptation of *War of the Worlds,* the H. G. Wells novel about an invasion from Mars, was entirely fictional, and although it generated what newspapers later described as a "tidal wave of terror that swept the nation," the scare was short-lived. Within hours anyone who had been taken in by the performance learned the truth from friends or from announcements on the radio.[1]

Still, resemblances to latter-day scares are striking. The invaders in "War of the Worlds" were barely more alien, fictitious, or threatening than the "bio-underclass" of crack babies we were told would decimate the nation's schools and urban neighborhoods. Or the legions of "illegitimate" children said to represent "a national security issue" (*Washington Post*). Or teen "superpredators" for whom "life means nothing" (*Newsweek*) and against whom our president warned we had better act promptly "or our country is going to be living with chaos." Or for that matter, young black men, the very thought of whom terrifies many Americans and motivates them to support the building of more and bigger prisons.[2]

The pressing question is the same now as it was in 1938: Why do people embrace improbable pronouncements? How did listeners to "War of the Worlds" manage to disregard four announcements during the broadcast that identified the program as a radio play? Why do people today believe in the existence of mysterious new illnesses even when medical scientists say they do not exist? Why do we entertain preposterous claims about husband abuse, granny dumping, or the middle-class romance with heroin?

Soon after the broadcast of "War of the Worlds," Hadley Cantril, a social psychologist at Princeton, set out to determine why more than a million Americans had been frightened and thousands found themselves "praying, crying, fleeing frantically to escape death from the Martians." In a book that resulted from his research—*The Invasion from Mars,* first published in 1940—Cantril refuted social scientists of his day who presumed, as one put it, that "as good an explanation as any for the panic is that all the intelligent people were listening to Charlie McCarthy" on the rival network. Based on his analysis of the broadcast itself and interviews with people who heard it, Cantril showed that the explanation lay not in a lack of intelligence on the part of listeners but in the acumen of the program's producers and in social conditions at the time.

The program had a credible feel, Cantril suggested, largely because it featured credible-sounding people professing to report scientific or firsthand information. The character played by Orson Welles, Professor Richard Pierson of the Princeton Observatory, was only one of several with distinguished titles and affiliations. Other professors and scientists spoke as well, and at various points in the drama people identified as secretary of the interior, vice-president of the Red Cross, and commander of a state militia chimed in.

In nearly every episode of fear mongering I discussed in the previous chapters as well, people with fancy titles appeared. Hardly ever were they among the leading figures in their field. Often they were more akin to the authorities in "War of the Worlds": gifted orators with elevated titles. Arnold Nerenberg and Marty Rimm come immediately to mind. Nerenberg (a.k.a. "America's road-rage therapist") is a psychologist quoted uncritically in scores of stories even though his alarming statistics and clinical descriptions have little scientific evidence behind them. Rimm, the college student whom *Time* glorified in its notorious "cyberporn" issue as the "Principal Investigator" of "a research team," is almost totally devoid of legitimate credentials.

I have found that for some species of scares—Internet paranoia among them—secondary scholars are standard fixtures. Bona fide experts easily refute these characters' contentions, yet they continue to appear nonetheless. Take scares about so-called Internet addiction, a malady ludicrously alleged to afflict millions of people and sometimes cause death. Far and away the most frequently quoted "expert" has been psychologist Kimberly Young, whom journalists dubbed "the world's first global shrink" (*Los Angeles Times*). Her "major study" (*Psychology Today*) turns out to have been based on unverifiable reports from a nonscientific sample of people who responded to her postings online. Young's research was rebutted on basic methodological grounds by scholars within and outside her field. Yet she managed to give Internet addiction a clinical air and tie it to serious afflictions by talking of "a newfound link between Net addiction and depression" (*USA Today*) and offering ill-suited similes. "It's like when a smoker thinks they can quit anytime they want, but when they try they can't," Young told a reporter.[3]

Fear mongers make their scares all the more credible by backing up would-be experts' assertions with testimonials from people the audience will find sympathetic. In "War of the Worlds" those people were actors playing ordinary citizens who said they had seen the Martians, experienced the destruction they wrought, or had a plan for how to survive the attack. In the stories I studied comparable characters appear: victims of Gulf War Syndrome, multiple chemical sensitivity, and breast implant disorders who testify before congressional panels, juries, and talk show audiences; "seasoned travelers" who express their concerns to reporters at airports after plane crashes; former friends and neighbors of women who have murdered their children.

Professional narrators play an important role too in transforming something implausible into something believable. Cantril observed of "War of the Worlds" that "as the less credible bits of the story begin to enter, the clever dramatist also indicates that he, too, has difficulty in believing what he sees." When we are informed that a mysterious object is not a meteorite but a spaceship, the reporter declares, "this is the most terrifying thing I have ever witnessed." Anchors on TV newsmagazines utter similar statements at the beginning or end of scare stories. "It's frightening," NBC's Katie Couric says as she introduces a report suggesting that "shots designed to protect your children might actually hurt or cripple them." ABC's Barbara Walters opines at the conclusion of a report about a woman who falsely accused her father of sexual abuse, "What a terrifying story."[4]

Statements of alarm by newscasters and glorification of wannabe experts are two telltale tricks of the fear mongers' trade. In the preceding chapters I pointed out others as well: the use of poignant anecdotes in place of scientific evidence, the christening of isolated incidents as trends, depictions of entire categories of people as innately dangerous.

If journalists would curtail such practices, there would be fewer anxious and misinformed Americans. Ultimately, though, neither the ploys that narrators use nor what Cantril termed "the sheer dramatic excellence" of their presentations fully accounts for why people in 1938 swallowed a tall tale about martians taking over New Jersey or why people today buy into tales about perverts taking over cyberspace, Uzi-toting employees taking over workplaces, heroin dealers taking over middle-class suburbs, and so forth.[5]

The success of a scare depends not only on how well it is expressed but also, as I have tried to suggest, on how well it expresses deeper cultural anxieties. In excerpts Cantril presents from his interviews it is clear what the primary anxiety was in his day. Another year would pass before Britain went to war with Germany, and more than three years before the United States finally joined the Allies in World War II. But by late 1939 Hitler and Mussolini were already well on their way to conquering Europe, and less than two weeks after the "War of the Worlds" broadcast Nazi mobs would destroy Jewish synagogues, homes, and shops in what came to be known as *Kristallnacht*.

Many Americans were having trouble suppressing their fears of war and at the same time their sense of culpability as their nation declined to intervene while millions of innocent people fell prey to the barbarous Nazi and fascist regimes. For a substantial number of listeners "War of the Worlds" gave expression to those bridled feelings. Some actually rewrote the script in their minds as they listened to the broadcast. In place of martians they substituted human enemies. "I knew it was some Germans trying to gas us all. When the announcer kept calling them people from Mars I just thought he was ignorant and didn't know that Hitler had sent them all," one person recalled in an interview in Cantril's study. Said another, "I felt it might be the Japanese—they are so crafty."[6]

Such responses were not the norm, of course. Most listeners envisioned the invaders pretty much as Welles and company described them. Yet this didn't stop some of them from making revealing connections to real dangers. "I worry terribly about the future of the Jews. Nothing else bothers me as much. I thought this might be another attempt to harm them," one person said. Reported another: "I was looking forward with some pleasure to the destruction of the entire human race and the end of the world. If we have fascist domination of the world, there is no purpose in living anyway."[7]

Flash forward to the 1980s and 1990s and it is not foreign fascists we have to put out of our minds in order to fall asleep at night, even if we do fantasize about hostile forces doing us great harm. (Witness the immediate presumption after the Oklahoma City bombing and the crash of TWA Flight 800 that Middle Eastern terrorists were to blame.) Mostly our fears are domestic, and so are the eerie invaders who populate them—killer kids, men of color, monster moms. The stories told about them are, like "War of the Worlds," oblique expressions of concern about problems that Americans know to be pernicious but have not taken decisive action to quash—problems such as hunger, dilapidated schools, gun proliferation, and deficient health care for much of the U.S. population.

Will it take an event comparable to the Japanese attack on Pearl Harbor to convince us that we must join together as a nation and tackle these problems? At the start of the new century it ought to be considerably easier for us to muster our collective will and take decisive action than it was for our own parents and grandparents six decades earlier. This time we do not have to put our own lives or those of our children at risk on battlefields halfway around the globe.

We *do* have to finance and organize a collective effort, which is never a simple matter, but compared with the wholesale reorientation of the

U.S. economy and government during World War II, the challenge is not overwhelming. Fear mongers have knocked the optimism out of us by stuffing us full of negative presumptions about our fellow citizens and social institutions. But the United States is a wealthy nation. We have the resources to feed, house, educate, insure, and disarm our communities if we resolve to do so.

There should be no mystery about where much of the money and labor can be found—in the culture of fear itself. We waste tens of billions of dollars and person-hours every year on largely mythical hazards like road rage, on prison cells occupied by people who pose little or no danger to others, on programs designed to protect young people from dangers that few of them ever face, on compensation for victims of metaphorical illnesses, and on technology to make airline travel—which is already safer than other means of transportation—safer still.

We can choose to redirect some of those funds to combat serious dangers that threaten large numbers of people. At election time we can choose candidates that proffer programs rather than scares.[8]

Or we can go on believing in martian invaders.

10

NEW FEARS FOR A NEW CENTURY

And Some Old Ones Updated

In the final chapter of this book's first edition, I asked whether it would take an event comparable to the Japanese attack on Pearl Harbor to shift Americans' attention away from puffed-up dangers and onto very serious ones we have largely ignored. Not long after the book was published such an event occurred: the terrorist attacks on the World Trade Center and Pentagon on September 11, 2001. In the aftermath of those attacks, what became of the dubious and overblown fears I discussed? How have they fared since 9/11?

In the short term, the response was heartening. In the weeks following the far-too-real horrors of that event, the counterfeit horrors that had occupied much of the popular media almost completely disappeared from public discourse. No longer were TV news programs and newsweeklies obsessed, as they had been just prior to the attacks, with dangers to swimmers from shark attacks and to Washington interns from philandering politicians. Gone were warnings about roller-coaster accidents and coyotes prowling suburban neighborhoods.

Nor did the latest incident of violence in a workplace or school make headlines and provoke pundits to decry the sorry state of America's youth. Part of the reason for that change was clear: the loss of thousands of lives and the threat of more terrorism utterly overshadowed any such stories. Even producers at local TV news programs and cable news shows could not fail to understand that for some time, stories about bioterrorism, airport security, and hate crimes against Arab-Americans would hold more interest and importance for viewers than the usual fare.

But there was a more important and longer-lived reason that some of the old scare stories did not occupy the news media post-9/11: a powerful and pernicious narrative of the past few decades largely lost its usefulness for fear mongers in the news industry and for the politicians and pundits they quote–what I dubbed the "sick-society" narrative. In that narrative, the villains are domestic, heroes are hard to find, and the storyline is about the decline of American civilization. That narrative is incompatible with another that came to the fore after the terrorist attacks. The new narrative was about national unity, villains from foreign lands, and the greatness of American society. One result of this new narrative was a shift in the putative dangerousness of certain categories of people and behaviors.

The demise of the sick-society narrative augured especially well for one sector of the U.S. population. Young Americans in their late teens and twenties were portrayed in the media throughout the first decade of this century as heroes in the New York City Fire Department and in the military, or alternatively, as campaigners for world peace. It's a striking departure from how this age group was characterized in the 1990s–as "seemingly depraved adolescent murderers," "superpredators," and teenaged single moms who "breed criminals faster than society can jail them." Plainly, that old story didn't fit the celebration of American society and its citizens, or the appeals to young Americans to make wartime sacrifices.

Nor do some of the supposed causes of youth violence fit into the new narrative. Consider, for example, the public discussion of the shootings at Columbine High School in Littleton, Colorado, in April 1999, a gruesome incident that occurred between the time I sent the manuscript of this book to the publisher and when it arrived in bookstores. In the national response to Columbine, there was misdirection away from real trends and dangers that confront children and adolescents, like the fact that millions do not have health insurance, are malnourished, and attend deteriorating schools. There was misdirection as well away from the most proximate and verifiable factor in the deaths at Columbine and elsewhere–namely, the ready availability of guns to people who shouldn't have access to them. A study published in the *Journal of the American Medical Association* the same year as the Columbine shootings documented that, even though the number of youth homicides had been declining, guns were responsible for an increasing proportion of the killings.[1]

Yet instead of a clear, focused discussion on keeping guns out of kids' hands, in the wake of Columbine, the public was treated to scares about all sorts of peripheral things like the Internet, video games, movies, rap music, trench coats, and Marilyn Manson (who observed in *Rolling Stone*: "I think that the National Rifle Association is far too powerful to take on, so most people choose Doom, *The Basketball Diaries* or yours truly").[2]

But post-9/11, it was no longer fashionable to disparage our popular culture. In stories about America's war on terrorism, the culture was referenced not as an infectious agent that turns kids into killers but as a feature of our society that is wrongly reviled by our enemy. "We are battling a bunch of atavistic ascetics who hate TV, music, movies, the Internet (except when they're planning atrocities), women, and Jews," *New York Times* columnist Maureen Dowd put it.[3]

Plane Wrecks and Road Rage

In the second half of this chapter, I'll explore in some detail how responses to the attacks of 9/11 played out in—and further precipitated—the culture of fear. But first, let's return to questionable scares I investigated from the 1990s that still live on. Given their shadiness, one might have expected them to vanish in an age of terror and economic turmoil, yet they persistently reappeared.

About the only dubious dangers that faded out for long periods of time were those for which fear mongers could find no incidents whatever from which to project a trend. In 2007 and 2008, for instance, there was hardly any talk about the topic of chapter 8 since not a single passenger died in an airline crash of a U.S. carrier during those two years.

It took but one fatal crash, however, for the hysteria to start up again. After a commuter plane went down in February 2009, the *New York Times* began its online story—"50 Killed as Plane Hits House Near Buffalo"—with a sentence that managed at once to suggest a trend of airline disasters in the region, and connect the incident to the planes that flew into the World Trade Center seven and a half years earlier. "All the people aboard the Continental flight, including the widow of a 9/11 victim and one person in the house, were killed on Thursday, officials said, in the second major crash in a month in New York State," the article began, even though no lives were lost in the previous crash. In the print edition two days after the crash, the *Times* devoted much of the front page to photos and profiles of victims, and two full inside pages of the first section to the accident.[4]

Other reporters magnified the Continental crash by quoting doomsayers who claimed that airlines had become lax about safety, and by digging deep in their files for alarming accounts and frightening photos of planes that had veered off runways or had engine trouble over the previous several years. Of the major print and TV media, I could find only one that made plain the real and reassuring trend in airline safety over the previous years. The second paragraph of the lead story on *USA Today*'s website soon after the crash read: "The crash was the first fatal accident on a U.S. passenger flight since Aug. 27, 2006, ending the longest period on record without a death." And in the print edition four days after the crash—when the cable networks were running scare stories about airline safety—*USA Today*'s lead, front page story appropriately began by reiterating that point, "Before Thursday, airlines had made more than 25 million flights in the United States during the past 2 1/2 years without a passenger being killed."[5]

Little evidence has been necessary to keep alive a whole array of specious scares I discussed in the previous chapters. Take road rage. In chapter 1, I selected road rage as a textbook example of an uncommon danger that was grossly overblown and that misdirected attention from more structural problems. Its appeal to fear-mongering journalists lay in its presumed randomness: anytime, anywhere, anyone could be a victim. Throughout the first decade of the new century, an average of about 100 magazine, newspaper, and television stories a month still featured the scare. To judge by those news stories, the definition of road rage expanded to include everything from honking to running someone over.[6]

And road rage became a medical malady. "They're the victims of a newly defined psychiatric disorder," announced Richard Schlesinger on *CBS Morning News* in June 2006. "Intermittent Explosive Disorder is caused by improper functioning of a brain chemical." Sixteen million Americans may be affected, he warned. "[They] each have an average of 43 attacks in their lifetime. Something to think about when you're in heavy traffic."[7]

Call this the *neurologizing of social problems*, a common feature of popular discourse in the early twenty-first century. Ignoring societal conditions, this approach looks inward. At the time of the CBS story, nearly 10 million Americans had a round-trip commute of more than two hours, and soaring housing prices had driven people far from city centers to achieve the American dream of owning a home. Slower, more crowded roads, coupled with deficient investments in roads and public transportation, and high gas prices—and later in the decade, collapsing home values and record numbers of foreclosures in outlying areas—predictably produced overheated drivers.

But the news media tended to focus on the besieged individual's brain rather than the larger society. Rather than talking to experts on, say, telecommuting or transportation infrastructure, journalists quoted those who advise drivers to treat their road rage with Prozac, therapy, or by learning karate so they can be prepared when raging drivers leap from their vehicles and attack.[8]

E-Fear Redux

Coverage of supposed dangers of the Internet suffered from tunnel vision as well. In a decade when the United States had the highest rates of childhood poverty in the developed world and the lowest rates of spending on social services, American journalists and politicians portrayed cyberspace as the scariest place a child can be, more menacing by far than anything young people face in a non-virtual world. "I've covered murders, grisly accidents, airplanes falling out of the sky and, occasionally, dirty politics. But in nearly two decades of journalism, nothing has made my insides churn like seeing what my 13-year-old daughter and her friends are up to on MySpace.com," reporter Catherine Saillant warned in the *Los Angeles Times* in 2006. After nosing around on daughter Taylor's MySpace page and finding a bulletin from another girl urging Taylor to add a certain "hott guy" [*sic*] to her friends list, Saillant hyperventilated, "Loosely translated, the teenage girl was 'pimping' a teenage boy . . . If Taylor added him to her MySpace 'friends' list, the tousled-hair teen would be able to look at her website and send messages to her."[9]

If in the 1990s parents were spooked by predators who lurked on on-line chat rooms, as we saw in chapter 2, in the 2000s that scare matured along with the Internet. Now parents learned that legions of adults drool over their children's photos on MySpace, the social networking website dating to 2003, and gawk at the videos teens post on YouTube, which launched in 2005.

Not that patterns of abuse had changed what I reported a decade ago. The vast majority of crimes against children and adolescents—sexual and otherwise—continued to be perpetrated by parents, relatives, and other adults the child or teen knows. More than four out of five victims are abused by a parent, and another 10 percent by a caregiver, accord-ing to the U.S. Department of Health and Human Services. The inci-dence of actual abuse as a result of an online connection is "vanishingly small," as a sociologist who has studied the data put it.[10]

A group of researchers at the University of New Hampshire put it bluntly: "The publicity about online 'predators' who prey on naive children using trickery and violence is largely inaccurate. Internet sex crimes involving adults and juveniles more often fit a model of statu-tory rape—adult offenders who meet, develop relationships with, and openly seduce underage teenagers—than a model of forcible sexual as-sault or pedophilic child molesting." That declaration, atop an article they published in 2008 in *American Psychologist*, a journal of the Ameri-can Psychological Association, is noteworthy not only for its clarity but for the occasion of its writing. Fed up with frightening and misleading statements by reporters, advocacy groups, and public officials, many of whom are cited in the paper, the authors wrote the piece in part to cor-rect the record about their own research.[11]

Indeed, it was a report of theirs, published two years earlier by an advocacy group, that gave rise to a favorite statistic of the fear mongers: "One in seven young people has been sexually solicited online." Hearing or reading that sentence, almost anyone would imagine that an astounding number of American youngsters had been solicited online by the sort of dirty older men featured in NBC's *To Catch a Predator* series that aired from 2004 through 2008–and later in reruns on MSNBC–and involved hidden cameras and sting operations. Actually, though, in the UNH study, nearly half of the solicitations reported were teens hitting on other teens; just 9 percent were adults. (In other cases, the age was unknown.)[12]

When adults do solicit minors online, the UNH researchers find, the young person almost invariably knows that the person at the other computer is an adult. Trickery about the perpetrator's age or intentions is rare. Moreover, as an exhaustive study in 2009 from Harvard University pointed out, youths who are approached and respond are typically teens already at risk because of their own drug abuse or troubled home environments. Many engage willingly with the adult who solicits them.[13]

Fear mongers make online social networking scary by pretending away those sorts of findings. "Children are solicited every day online. Some fall prey, and the results are tragic. That harsh reality defies the statistical academic research underlying the report," an attorney general from Connecticut who campaigns against Internet dangers vacuously told the *New York Times* when the Harvard study came out.[14]

While adults were being told their kids were endangering their lives online–or at best, wasting them away–studies were finding that the online activities of youths are not only nontoxic, they're productive. A report in 2008 from the John D. and Catherine T. MacArthur Foundation got little attention, but the extensive three-year study showed that youth use online media primarily for self-directed learning and to gain and extend friendships. "The digital world is creating new opportunities for youth to grapple with social norms, explore interests, develop technical skills, and experiment with new forms of self-expression," the researchers wrote.[15]

Even entertainment sites like YouTube are used in those ways, as I learned firsthand. When a student at the university where I work mentioned in passing that she relies on YouTube for help in understanding her math and science classes, I did a little checking and found a wealth of material. Upon typing "calculus" in the search box at youtube.com, I was sent to "Calculus in 20 Minutes," a series of instructive, fast-paced mini-lectures by a professor of mathematics at Williams College. The one I watched had received nearly 150,000 views. A search for "physics" brought a lecture by a University of California, Berkeley, professor on atoms and heat that had received a quarter of a million hits. To be sure, those numbers don't compare to the twelve million hits the video "Best Break Dance Ever" received, but they aren't shabby.[16]

Missing Children, Missing Dollars

Scares about children being abducted *off*-line continued as well. Even in the wake of the terrorist attacks of 9/11, when one might plausibly have expected pressing concerns to eclipse pseudoterrors, the media were preoccupied with missing kids. In the summer of 2002, just months after the attacks, I wrote an article for the *Wall Street Journal* about a little experiment I did. Over the course of a couple of weeks, whenever I had the chance, I turned on the TV and flipped between MSNBC, Fox News Channel, and CNN to see what they were covering. Rarely did I have to wait more than twenty minutes to get a report about one or more child abductions. Most of the time, I didn't have to wait at all.

How did editors and journalists defend spending so much airtime on child abductions? They used words like "trend" or "epidemic" even as child abductions remained extremely rare, and they threw out bogus numbers. On his Fox News Channel show, Bill O'Reilly talked of "100,000 abductions of children by strangers every year in the United States," though an exhaustive study from the U.S. Office of Juvenile Justice and Delinquency Prevention (OJJDP) that year found only 115 cases a year of "stereotypical kidnappings" (children abducted by non-family members and kept for long periods of time or murdered). "The majority of victims of stereotypical and other nonfamily abductions were teens—not younger children—and most were kidnapped by someone they knew somewhat—not by strangers or slight acquaintances," a subsequent report in 2006 from the OJJDP noted.[17]

Yet the obsession with kidnapped kids has shown no signs of slackening. In the late 2000s, the high-profile missing children were Caylee Anthony and Madeleine McCann. Madeleine, just shy of her fourth birthday, went missing in May 2007 from a resort in Portugal, and the story continued to get media attention for a couple of years, well after the Portuguese police had closed the case. Caylee Anthony disappeared in June 2008; her mother was eventually arrested for her murder. Caylee's tragedy combined two high-voltage scares I have discussed in the book: the missing child and the monster mom.

Such sensational stories provided heart-wrenching material for all news outlets, but special credit in recent years would have to go to Nancy Grace, a former prosecutor who relentlessly covered missing children on her nightly HLN (CNN's Headline News Network) program. CNN might as well rename HLN "CAN, as in Caylee Anthony Network, because HLN has been riding the toddler's demise for hours each day," *Los Angeles Times* media critic James Rainey noted after watching her program for a few days in 2009.[18]

And the TV show wasn't the half of it. Television and the Internet have become more symbiotic since this book was first published; nervous viewers can now access the details twenty-four hours a day. Around the time of Rainey's column, I scanned the "Nancy Grace" home page and was greeted with: "Nancy Grace reports on George Anthony telling police about the smell of death in his daughter's car trunk. Click here to watch!"[19]

In public lectures and media interviews, when I mention examples like those, and the actual statistics about kidnapped kids, I am often asked: Other than appealing to our baser appetites, what harm is there in the news media obsessing over missing children? My answer is, a lot of harm, ranging from expensive and ill-conceived legislation to needless restrictions on children's ability to play and get exercise.

The nationwide AMBER Alert system, named for a child murdered in Texas in 1996, costs the federal government $5 million annually and the states many times that amount, and produces frequent notices in

the media about kidnapped children. But "the system does not typically work as designed (i.e., to save children who are in life-threatening
danger) and might be generally incidental to the safe return of most of
the hundreds of children for whom the alert system is said to have been
'successful,'" a team of criminologists at the University of Nevada concluded from their extensive study of AMBER Alerts over a three-year
period beginning in 2003.[20]

Even were that system and others like it to become more successful
than the research suggests thus far, crucial questions would remain. As
criminologist James Alan Fox of Northeastern University noted in an
op-ed in the *New York Times,* "More important than the risk of ineffec-
tiveness is the danger of misuse. What should the criteria be for deter-
mining reliable information? Who might get hurt in the process of hur-
riedly chasing down inaccurate leads and wrong suspects? What might
happen, for example, if an incorrect license plate of a suspected abduc-
tor is displayed on electronic highway signs? Might some poor motorist
be pulled over by authorities or, worse, chased down by a group of vig-
ilantes? These concerns are especially salient in the climate of fear and
hysteria that surrounds what many have accurately called a parent's
worst nightmare."[21]

For children, too, fear and hysteria about stranger danger are harmful. While they should certainly be taught commonsense rules about
interacting with strangers, too many warnings can lead to the "mean-
world syndrome" I mentioned at the beginning of this book. Children
raised to view every adult with distrust might have little desire to become engaged in civic life when they are adults.

Missing children coverage is also bad for citizens who would like to
get some actual news with their news. The hours and column-inches
wasted on these stories could be put to better use. Focusing on bizarre
and uncommon cases distracts us from the *common* dangers millions of
children face every day like malnourishment, poverty, lack of health
insurance, and crowded and crumbling public schools. In a UNICEF
study in 2007 that looked at factors like poverty, health, safety, and education, children in the United States were found to be at much greater
danger than anywhere else in the developed world.[22]

More Risky Business: Teens Gone Wild

The other major fright about America's youth—teen pregnancy—broadened in scope in the mid-'00s. No longer focused primarily on low-income girls of color, the scare got expanded to include young women from other ethnic and income groups, and to non-pregnant girls, even girls who had yet to have intercourse. In 2005, Katie Couric reported "horror stories of kids growing up way too fast, having oral sex at ridiculously young ages." To find out "what's really going on," she gathered a group of teenage girls from across the nation for an NBC news special, "The 411: Teens and Sex."[23]

"I was in a journalism classroom and we could hear through the bathroom vent and so every time anybody was having sex, we like run in there and say, 'Caught,'" said Natalia.

"Supposedly during gym class a bunch of guys were in the bathroom for a long time and they were in a line and the girl was in the bathroom," said Kameron.

"I'm 16 . . . I don't think oral sex should be expected in a relationship, but unfortunately, I think it is," said Kierstin.

To their credit, Couric and her colleagues recognized that a roomful of gossiping teenage girls does not an epidemic make, and in conjunction with *People* magazine, NBC News commissioned a national survey of 1,000 teens between the ages of thirteen and sixteen. Among the results: just 12 percent said they had had oral sex, and 13 percent said they'd had intercourse. "In fact there is good news," Couric properly reported. "Our survey shows that seven out of ten teens between the ages of thirteen and sixteen are not sexually active and haven't really gone beyond kissing."

But no good news shall go unchallenged. In the coming years, scary teen sex stories continued to surface, and in 2008 much was made of the findings from a survey commissioned by Liz Claiborne Inc. "'Horrors' Found in Tween, Teen Dating," blared a CBS *Early Show* story. "Forty percent of the youngest tweens, those between the ages of eleven and twelve, report that their friends are victims of verbal abuse in relationships," the network alerted. "Nearly three-in-four tweens (72 percent) say boyfriend/girlfriend relationships usually begin at age fourteen or younger."

Had newswriters taken a moment to examine the survey results, as sociologist Mike Males did, they could have learned that this survey also contained reassuring news for nervous parents. Only 1 percent of eleven- and twelve-year-olds, and 7 percent of thirteen- and fourteen-year-olds, said they had done more than kiss. Just 2 percent had ever felt their safety was threatened by a partner or had experienced violence. "How did Claiborne turn 2 percent into 37 percent or even 72 percent?" Males asked in a commentary. "By rigging the survey with crude statistical shenanigans, including: (a) asking young teens if they imagined 'persons your age' might be having sex or being abused by partners, and (b) defining terms ludicrously broadly. Note that what 'friends' (undefined) are doing could result from one case known to many other students, or gossip, or rumors, or speculations from media reports like the ones Claiborne pushed."[24]

What was the purpose, as Males put it, of making "America's fifth graders sound like a mob of brutal sluts?" Perhaps it was to inflate the relevance of Claiborne's loveisrespect.org, their National Teen Dating Abuse Helpline website, the latest addition to the company's Love Is Not Abuse campaign, a PR effort launched in 1991 to revitalize the aging brand.[25]

In 2008, the year Claiborne's survey grabbed headlines, the media went wilder still over a fable about a supposed "pregnancy pact" at Gloucester High School in Massachusetts. The episode further illustrates a strategy I described in chapter 6 for keeping a scare alive when low-income youths fail to accommodate fear hawkers by decreasing their rates of involvement: claim the problem has moved beyond the inner cities and is tainting middle and upper class teens. In chapter 6 my focus was on drug use, but in the mid- and late-'00s, when teen pregnancy rates had been declining since 1990 and were at their lowest rates since the 1970s, the strategy got put to use to keep fear alive about pregnant teens.[26]

The Gloucester fairy tale was told first by *Time* magazine, which reported that "nearly half" of a group of seventeen girls at Gloucester High School in Massachusetts, none older than sixteen, "confessed to making a pact to get pregnant and raise their babies together. Then the story got worse: 'We found out one of the fathers is a twenty-four-year-old homeless guy,' the principal says, shaking his head." Numerous media outlets quickly repeated the story, calling it "shocking" (CBS) and "disturbing" (CNN), wondering "shall we go to the mall—or get pregnant" (Salon.com headline) and "what happened to shame" (Fox News), and denouncing Gloucester High for its "proteen birth" agenda (Fox News).

"The pact is so secretive," CNN said, "we couldn't even find out the girls' names," a difficulty that may have resulted from there being no such pact, as reporters who dug an inch deeper learned from other officials at the school and in the town, as well as from one of the pregnant students. The notion of a pact arose from stories about a group of girls who had promised to help one another care for their children, she suggested. It was only *after* they'd learned they were pregnant, the student explained, that they made the promise.[27]

In an op-ed in the *Los Angeles Times* after the pregnancy pact story had been roundly debunked, Mike Males proposed that politicians, reporters, and social scientists abandon the term "teenage pregnancy" altogether. Contrary to the misimpression that phrase conveys, in the majority of cases the mother is not "a child herself," she's in her late teens, and the father isn't a teen at all. He is in his twenties.[28]

Too, panics over "teen pregnancy" invariably disparage low-income girls of color—even when the story is ostensibly about well-to-do white girls. As Veronica Cassidy of Fairness and Accuracy in Media noted, "a racial subtext ran through most coverage" of the pregnancy pact story. "The *Time* article pointed out that Gloucester is a 'mostly white' town, and subsequent coverage consistently mentioned that these girls were white—a point that seemed to imply that teen pregnancy is only expected of young women of color," Cassidy wrote.[29]

Still Iffy After All These Years

Another of the youth-related scares I discussed got updated as well. The panic I reported in chapter 7 over chilling reports that the DPT (diptheria-pertussis-tetanus) vaccine caused serious impairment in children resulted in substantial numbers of parents refusing to immunize their children. The upshot, as subsequent studies documented, has been significant increases in the number of cases of whooping cough. (The risk of pertussis is about six times higher for unvaccinated children.)[30]

Indeed, health officials have become concerned in recent years that the number of parents who buy into panics over vaccines and refuse to vaccinate their babies may be endangering the population broadly. Their concerns have been raised by incidents of diseases that had largely disappeared in the United States, such as whooping cough, measles, and *Haemophilus influenzae* type b (known as Hib), as well as a more sweeping danger. When vaccination rates fall sufficiently, a population loses what's known as "herd immunity," where the number of immunized people is so large, even those who have not been vaccinated are safe because they never come in contact with an infected person.[31]

Yet, apparently having learned nothing from the adverse effects on children of their crusade against DPT shots, the same array of forces—advocacy groups and ratings- and vote-hungry media and politicians—coalesced more recently to fill parents with fear about a preservative in the MMR (measles, mumps, and rubella) vaccine that supposedly causes autism. Well after it was definitively debunked by the medical community, the MMR vaccine–autism link continued to pop up in the media—even making its way into primetime programming. In the 2008 premiere episode of *Eli Stone*, an ABC courtroom drama, attorney Stone represents the parents of an autistic child in their lawsuit against a vaccine manufacturer. In his closing argument, Stone declares, "Is there proof mercuritol causes autism? Yes. Is that proof direct or incontrovertible proof? No. But ask yourself if you've ever believed in anything, in anyone, without absolute proof."[32]

Or, in this case, any proof. Back in the real world, the preservative that allegedly caused problems in the MMR vaccine was no longer in use by 2007, and Andrew Wakefield, the physician who had first raised the issue in a 1998 study published in *The Lancet*, had been brought up on medical misconduct charges in Great Britain and retracted that study.[33]

Yet the victim-cum-expert I cited as a driving force behind the DPT vaccine scare of the 1990s, Barbara Loe Fisher, was still actively advocating for "vaccine safety and informed consent" via the National Vaccine Information Center (NVIC), an organization she founded in 1982. A quote from Fisher on NVIC's home page makes their position clear: "If the State can tag, track down and force citizens against their will [to] be injected with biologicals of unknown toxicity today, there will be no limit on what individual freedoms the State can take away in the name of the greater good tomorrow."

Fisher has been joined in the past decade by a slew of new antivaccine crusaders and advocacy groups whose websites garner millions of hits, and whose spokespeople have come to include a category that scarcely existed when I wrote the earlier edition but has become commonplace—the *celebrity victim-cum-expert.*

In the vaccine scare, former *Playboy* model Jenny McCarthy was arguably among the most physically attractive celeb victims. The parent of an autistic child ("vaccine injured," she likes to say), McCarthy asked on CNN, with nothing to suggest the question had merit, "With billions of pharmaceutical dollars, could it be possible that the vaccine program is becoming more of a profit engine than a means of prevention?" Even as scores of scientists and physicians were urging that the antivaccine advocates be granted no more respect than Holocaust deniers and AIDS deniers, producers at cable news stations and shows like "Oprah" and "Imus in the Morning," gave McCarthy and fellow zealots lots of airtime to implant ill-informed anxieties in anxious parents' minds.[34]

Auspiciously, by late in the decade, knowledgeable science journalists were actively countering the twaddle on those shows. In particular, Sharon Begley, *Newsweek*'s science reporter, published a lengthy rebuttal of the MMR–autism scare in 2009. "It is bad enough that the vaccine-autism scare has undermined one of the greatest successes of preventive medicine and terrified many new parents," Begley avowed at the conclusion of the article. "Most tragic of all, it has diverted attention and millions of dollars away from finding the true causes and treatments of a cruel disease."[35]

No effort to shine the light of science on a metaphorical illness, regardless how sizeable or decisive the evidence, seems to be enough, however, to settle down the media and politicians for long if the ailment has sympathetic victims, motivated attorneys, energetic advocacy groups, and heartbreaking anecdotes buoying it. Consider another metaphorical illness I highlighted. Headlines in major newspapers and on radio and television in 2008 blared "Gulf War Syndrome Is Real," and the stories said the causes were a drug given to soldiers and pesticides to which troops were exposed in the 1991 Persian Gulf War. But in point of fact, my conclusion in chapter 7 was probably closer to the mark: "Not until well into the twenty-first century are medical scientists likely to have sufficient long-term studies to reach a definitive conclusion about the causes of Gulf War Syndrome" (p. 159).

Reporters and advocates variously ignored or played down the fact that the 2008 report from a Congressional advisory committee of scientists and veterans was just one of at least a dozen expert summaries of the matter, and far from the most persuasive, comprehensive, or prestigious. Two years earlier, for instance, a panel assembled by the National Academy of Science's Institute of Medicine reviewed nearly all the scientific literature—850 studies—and concluded that while Gulf War veterans suffer awful symptoms and deserve better care than they've received, GWS has no clear diagnosis, cause, or recommended treatment.[36]

It is, therefore, an apt metaphor for America's involvement in the Gulf, where we have now gone to war twice: briefly in the '90s, lengthily in the '00s, each time without clear provocation, diagnosis of conditions, or realistic battle plans, and with scarce attention to protecting and caring for our soldiers.

An iffy illness of more recent origin likewise resonates as a metaphor for other collective failings and anxieties. Said to cause a mountain of miseries, from infections, bleeding gums, and pulmonary hemorrhages to brain lesions, memory loss, seizures, and even dementia, household mold spawned an industry that encompasses everything from fumigators to home mold-detection kits to mold-sniffing dogs.

The panic took off in 2001, after a Texas family was awarded $32.1 million for a mold problem in their twenty-two-room mansion. That case, which was widely publicized, had the effect of a starting gun at the Indy 500. At the time, there were about 227 lawsuits over toxic mold. At the time of this writing there are tens of thousands.

It fell to Daniel Heimpel, a writer for the *L.A. Weekly,* to bring to light the victim-cum-advocate who started it all, Sharon Kramer, a former realtor whose daughter Erin is among a small group of people suscepti-ble to mold allergies because of previously compromised immune sys-tems (Erin has cystic fibrosis). In 1998 Erin was diagnosed with allergic bronchopulmonary aspergillosis, which she contracted from mold dur-ing a hospital stay. With her daughter's case as proof of the syndrome, Sharon Kramer made toxic mold her life's work. A decade later she was still fighting. "She saw a conspiracy funded by businesses out to end mold claims while risking the public's health. She believed that the well-being of thousands depended on her exposing that deceit," writes Heimpel. "Kramer's belief has consumed her."[37]

When I checked the scientific literature, it wasn't hard to learn that "the term 'toxic mold' is not accurate. While certain molds are toxi-genic, meaning they can produce toxins (specifically mycotoxins), the molds themselves are not toxic, or poisonous," as the Centers for Dis-ease Control (CDC) notes. "Certain individuals with chronic respira-tory disease (chronic obstructive pulmonary disorder, asthma) may ex-perience difficulty breathing. Individuals with immune suppression may be at increased risk for infection from molds."[38]

When a blue-ribbon panel of scientists conducted an exhaustive ap-praisal of the scientific evidence well into the panic, they reported that while mold can worsen a person's asthma condition and produce com-mon if annoying upper respiratory tract symptoms in most anyone, "the available evidence does not support an association between either indoor dampness or mold and the wide range of other health com-plaints that have been ascribed to them."[39]

As with other metaphoric illnesses, most of the alleged symptoms of toxic mold syndrome are vague and far-flung. And like other impas-sioned advocates, Sharon Kramer pits herself against the medical estab-lishment, which she believes is in league with business—in this case, housing developers and contractors. For Kramer and other advocates, anecdotal evidence trumps scientific study, and those anecdotes can go far in making for good news stories and tearful testimony in court cases, before legislatures, and on advocates' websites and blogs.

A metaphor for anxieties shared by a great many Americans—that our health is at the mercy of powerful, mysterious forces that do not care about us—toxic mold syndrome, unlike mold itself, is unlikely to fade away under the light of day.

The March of Crimes

Neither is another illogicality I discussed in earlier chapters: an overemphasis of uncommon crimes and deemphasis of the common instrument of death and serious injury in those and other crimes.

In TV newsrooms, *if it bleeds it leads* remains the watchword. A study of 559 newscasts in twenty television markets across the United States compared the crimes covered by local news to the number and types of crimes actually committed. Although crime had fallen for eight years prior to the 2004 study, in all twenty markets "audiences were told essentially the same story—that random, violent crime was a persistent and structural feature of American society," the researchers found. All the more misleading, the newscasts consistently gave the impression that murder and other serious crimes are rampant in places where they are rare.

In the nation's largest cities, murder accounted for only .2 percent of all crimes, and in the suburbs of those cities, murder accounted for just .01 percent. Yet not only are murder stories a staple of the coverage in those cities, accounting for 36 percent of the crimes reported on the TV news, the newscasts warned suburban viewers that crime was moving to their areas.[40]

Why scare the suburban audiences? They tend to have the buying power advertisers like, the study suggested: "The notion that the newscast is the product and that the audience is the customer is exactly backwards." The advertisers are the customers and access to the audience is the product. Crime stories are a cost-effective way to capture an audience. The more vulnerable the viewing public is made to feel, the more essential the role of the local newscaster as a neighbor who "sounds the alarm for collective defense."

Thus the pattern I noted in the 1980s and '90s continues. And as then, the most immediate and confirmable factor in most of the deadly crimes—access to firearms by people who should not have them—continues to be largely ignored in the coverage. Having been on the receiving end of vitriolic attacks by gun lovers for daring to make that point in this book and elsewhere, I confess to being somewhat wary of returning to an issue that so many politicians, journalists, and scholars have decided to brush aside rather than endanger their careers or their families' peace of mind.

But the dearth of attention to gun violence ought not to go entirely unremarked. Shortly after the bloodbath at Columbine, Jeffrey Fagen, director for the Center for Violence Research and Prevention at Columbia University, pointed out that three common themes apply to school shootings: the perpetrator has a long-standing grievance, a mental illness, and access to firearms. None of these alone produces a massacre, he noted; their convergence does.[41]

Eight years later, that point was driven home again for those who cared to notice, after a student went on a shooting spree at Virginia Tech. Cho Seung-Hui, who killed thirty-two people on that campus in April 2007, had been diagnosed with mental illness while still in middle school and had been treated while at college. The creepy videotapes he left behind demonstrated a long-standing grievance. And he had firearms: a 9mm Glock and a .22-caliber Walther.

American society, unlike many others around the globe, has no effective means for removing the one factor in that deadly triad that outside forces can control—a fact that barely got mentioned in the extensive news coverage following the shootings. In a cover story, *Newsweek* magazine puzzled instead over Cho's background. "A Cho who grew up in, say, Japan, would almost certainly not have acted on his hatred and fury: biology and psychology set the stage for homicidal violence, but the larger culture would likely have prevented its execution." That in the "larger culture" of Japan it is extremely difficult to buy a handgun somehow eluded the writer and her editors.[42]

True to form after gun disasters, *Newsweek*, along with other media outlets, politicians, and pundits, engaged in lots of head-scratching over criminal minds, negligent parents, powerless teachers, and ineffective mental health workers. Access to guns was treated as just one of many factors contributing to violence on campus, when in truth, as Alfred Blumstein of Carnegie Mellon University succinctly put it, "Guns transform what is widespread teenage behavior into disasters."[43]

The same can be said of disputes between adults that need not be deadly. Pick any one-month period, search news and police sources, and you're almost guaranteed to find dozens of instances of jealous lovers or ex-lovers, disgruntled employees or ex-employees, shooting and killing one another and, often, unlucky bystanders as well. With close to 30,000 Americans dying and more than twice that number wounded by firearms annually, the carnage is not only tragic, it is expensive. The leading cause of uninsured hospital stays, gunshot injuries cost the nation's hospitals about $800 million a year. Yet regardless how familiar or surprising the event—be it everyday gunfire by estranged partners or shooting rampages at a nursing home, immigration center, health club, or church (all occurred in 2009)—little will be heard from political leaders or media analysts about the unique and preventable role that firearms played.[44]

When reporters bother to look beyond the propaganda that "gun rights" advocacy groups shower upon them, they discover that much can be done to reduce those numbers. Indeed, they learn that some measures that could save thousands of lives do not even raise the ire of any but the most ultra-radical pro-gun forces. Gary Fields, a *Wall Street Journal* reporter, was a case in point with an article he authored in 2008 about a ten-year-old program in Richmond, Virginia. Supported by everyone from the NRA to the Brady Campaign to Prevent Gun Violence, "Project Exile" does not attempt to control gun sales or ownership. Instead, it metes out harsh punishment to anyone who commits a gun crime, no matter how minor, including illegal possession of a firearm. By means of television, radio, and outdoor advertising, the program doggedly reminds local residents that, as a forty-foot sign on city buses says, "An Illegal Gun Gets You 5 Years in Federal Prison."

With bail unlikely and parole nonexistent, the number of guns on the street dropped 31 percent in the first year, Fields reported.[45]

9/11 All the Time

There was another powerful group, in addition to the gun lobby, who diverted legislators, journalists, and the broader public from addressing firearm violence: the Bush administration. Risks to innocent Americans from gun violence were among a long list of imminent, avertable dangers that the Bush administration chose to ignore during its eight years in Washington from 2000 to 2008, for reasons of political expediency and ideology. (The collapse of the banking and housing sectors toward the end of the Bush years comes immediately to mind as another example where sensible regulation could have prevented a great deal of human suffering.)

How did the Bush administration and its allies dispense with social issues and Democratic rivals the White House found bothersome? They developed an effective machinery for drumming into every citizen unease over a danger the administration insisted loomed larger than all others.

Through a variety of channels, they repeated time and again the eerie incantation: *9/11 can happen again.*

Before I discuss how the Bush administration kept that incantation foremost in Americans' minds and public policy for a full seven years, let me be clear about the gravity of the attacks that occurred on September 11, 2001. Without question, they were singular in their horror. When nineteen men hijacked four passenger jets and used them to strike the United States, the tragedy tapped one of our most enduring fears—the random, catastrophic plane crash—and multiplied it exponentially. I find it hard to imagine a more nightmarish vision than United Flight 175 plunging into one of the World Trade Center's Twin Towers while the other tower blazed beside it, debris spiraling 100 stories downward. Terrified office workers fled as the towers collapsed; dazed, ash-covered firefighters wandered through the wreckage; citizens sobbed and clutched one another; a huge chunk of the Pentagon lay in ruins from an assault by another plane; still another was a gray gash in the earth; and all of it was replayed on television ceaselessly over the coming weeks.

In the years that followed, America's culture of fear evolved in a number of ways. First, as I mentioned at the top of this chapter, the basic fear narrative shifted from "there are monsters among us" to "foreign terrorists want to destroy us." In the first weeks after 9/11, the homegrown scares of the previous three decades about crime, teenagers, drugs, metaphorical illnesses, and the like seemed trivial, obsolete, beside the point. The nation's collective fear sensibly coalesced against a hard target: Osama bin Laden and his organization, al Qaeda.

The administration of President George W. Bush quickly redirected that fear, however, to what they dubbed the "worldwide war on terror," a war and associated enemies similar in their vagueness to those denoted in previous decades by the "war on drugs" and the "war on crime." From those earlier wars, American journalists and their audiences had been conditioned to treat more seriously than they ought shocking statistics that were not fully explained or verified; dire warnings that flared and faded, often without any actual effect on our daily lives; and testimony from self-appointed experts with vested interests in whipping up anxieties. Following 9/11 and throughout the subsequent wars in Afghanistan and Iraq, the same patterns ensued, only this time the statistics, warnings, and expert testimony came almost entirely from the administration. A study found, for example, that more than 90 percent of news stories about Iraq on NBC, ABC, and CBS during a five-month period in 2002–03 came from the White House, Pentagon, or State Department.[46]

Following the attacks of 9/11, journalists dared not question the White House's interpretation of events. "It starts with a feeling of patriotism within oneself," explained CBS anchorman Dan Rather, speaking with a British journalist in May 2002. "It carries through with a certain knowledge that the country as a whole—and for all the right reasons—felt and continues to feel this surge of patriotism within themselves. And one finds oneself saying, 'I know the right question, but you know what? This is not exactly the right time to ask it.'"[47]

Wearing flag label pins and crying on camera, journalists suspended even the pretense of objectivity as they affirmed the administration's claim that the attacks of 9/11 constituted a fundamental turning point in human history. "*The world is different,*" a phrase repeated endlessly in late 2001 and 2002, became a kind of password that opened the door for an extraordinary degree of fear mongering on the part of the administration, as would its successor adage, "*9/11 can happen again.*"[48]

This wasn't the first time a White House had been behind a massive and expensive fear campaign. As we saw earlier in this book, other such efforts—the war on drugs, in particular—dragged on for years, consuming many millions of dollars. But it is difficult to find an earlier example where an administration amassed so much machinery to the cause.

Before we review that machinery, let us consider the premise upon which it was based. *Was* the world so different after 9/11? Certainly the average citizen and even the average journalist could be forgiven for feeling frightened and disoriented after September 11. At first, the estimated loss of life at the Twin Towers was reported to be as high as 50,000 (the actual death toll was 2,752). No one knew if other cities would be hit within days. Throughout the fall of 2001, anthrax-laced letters threatening the United States were mailed to various news organizations and political offices. Though the letters were later traced to a U.S. military laboratory and ascribed to an American biodefense researcher, at the time they were understandably assumed to be the work of foreign terrorists.[49]

But by the end of 2001, no attacks other than the anthrax letters had occurred in the United States. According to figures published by the U.S. State Department, the total number of deaths from terrorist attacks worldwide in 2001 was 3,547, more than three-quarters of which were on 9/11. About the same number of Americans died that year from drowning. Nearly three times as many died from gun-related homicides, and five times as many in alcohol-related motor vehicle accidents. In *Overblown,* a book on America's response to 9/11, John Mueller, a professor of political science at Ohio State University, notes that over the last four decades, lightning has killed as many Americans as have terrorists.[50]

Even if terrorist acts in the United States had increased significantly, the risk to an average citizen of serious harm or death would have been less than from everyday dangers such as accidents and hypertension. In a worst-case scenario, if a terrorist group were to somehow detonate a nuclear bomb in a major U.S. city, the highest casualty rate is predicted to be around 250,000. As gruesome as that would be, the nation has borne worse. The influenza epidemic of 1918 killed 600,000.[51]

Post-9/11 and throughout the first decade of the twenty-first century, although terrorists continued to attack various targets around the world, no major events took place in the United States. Those that occurred elsewhere, while deplorable, were nowhere near the magnitude of 9/11. Wars, genocide, famines, and economic crises unfolded with depressing regularity, but little changed as a result of September 11 apart from what the Bush administration and its allies generated through a tireless campaign that kept large numbers of Americans alarmed, confused, and vulnerable to manipulation, and parts of the world under attack by U.S. forces.

The Bush Administration's Fear Machine

From the beginning, the language of the administration was apocalyptic. "Americans should not expect one battle, but a lengthy campaign unlike any other we have ever seen," President Bush proclaimed in late September 2001. The following January, in his State of the Union Address, he announced that our enemies were not only bin Laden and al Qaeda, but an "axis of evil" consisting of Iraq, Iran, and Korea, as well as any nation that harbored terrorists. At home, Americans should brace themselves for attacks by members of al Qaeda sleeper cells who lived among us, as the 9/11 terrorists had, and could strike at any moment.[52]

The administration began warning of a far more distant danger as well. Throughout 2002, they claimed that Iraq had aided bin Laden and was building weapons of mass destruction (WMD). Those claims have since proved false, but the administration used them to garner broad support from Congress, pundits, and the public for its 2003 invasion and occupation of Iraq. And over the next five years, as casualties mounted and the financial costs of Bush's self-described "crusade" soared to several trillion billion dollars, it was crucial to the administration that Americans remain frightened about possible terrorist attacks on U.S. soil so that they would continue to support the Iraq war and broader "war on terror."

As time passed and such attacks did not occur, skeptics began to ask the obvious questions: Why hadn't terrorists blown up freeways and bridges? Poisoned the water supply? Gassed the subways? Grabbed an automatic weapon and shot up a mall? The most reasonable conclusion was that sleeper cells full of impassioned, highly trained terrorists did not exist. How, then, to keep the fears alive?

In large measure, the Bush administration relied on an entity of its own founding, whose very existence suggested both imminent and never-ending dangers. Formed in 2002, the Department of Homeland Security (DHS) placed a number of federal agencies under one umbrella organization created "to secure our country against those who would disrupt the American way of life." The mission of the DHS was to prevent and respond to terrorist attacks in the United States, because "today's terrorists can strike at any place, at any time and with virtually any weapon."[53]

One of the DHS's first creations was a color-coded terror alert chart that reflected what the department deemed the degree of risk at any given time. An ingenious mechanism for fear mongering, the color chart reminded the populace, graphically and continually, that they were in danger. Sometimes the risk was greater, sometimes lesser, but always there was danger.

Between its inception in March 2002 and June 2003, government officials repeatedly issued terror alerts, citing "code orange"—a "high" risk—eight times. In each instance, a public official such as the attorney general or the director of Homeland Security appeared before the press, promised that the alert was based on "credible" or "reliable" sources, and offered no further information. No attacks occurred, but the Bush administration benefited from the scares. A study published in 2004 in the journal *Current Research in Social Psychology* found that when the terror warnings increased, so did Bush's approval rating—an effect that was not lost on the administration. In a memoir published after Bush left office, Tom Ridge, the first director of the Department of Homeland Security, reported that senior members of the administration had pressured him to raise the terrorism threat level at key moments during Bush's re-election campaign of 2004.[54]

When it comes to sustaining fear, one scare supports another. The administration and Homeland Security rolled out alerts, warnings, and predictions of various types of attacks steadily throughout the decade. Some were laughable from the start, as when the government advised citizens in late 2001 to stockpile duct tape and rolls of plastic in order to seal their homes against chemical weapon attacks—despite the fact that experts knew these measures were probably pointless (when chemical agents are released outdoors, they are almost immediately diluted by the wind). Since the risk of dying in a chemical weapon attack is far less than a million to one, a person is more likely to die in a car accident en route to purchase the duct tape, as one clear-eyed journalist noted in the *New York Times.* Paradoxically, when fearful people buy guns, drive instead of fly, or isolate themselves in their homes, their risk from these more prosaic dangers increases.[55]

The DHS hyped as well the threat of bioterrorism, warning of the intentional release of anthrax or smallpox, though the only actual incident, the anthrax attack mentioned earlier, killed only five people. The danger of a smallpox epidemic was even more remote, as the disease is rarely fatal and must be spread from person to person. Any release of smallpox into a population would probably be limited in scope and quickly isolated by public health authorities. But armed with eerie images and chilling scenarios of poxed populations from the past, the administration's mouthpieces got plenty of attention in the print and electronic media.[56]

Then there was the ominously named "dirty bomb," a conventional explosive spiked with radioactive isotopes that got depicted as a rogue-style nuclear weapon. The real damage by such a bomb would be in the explosion, not the radioactivity, some media eventually noted, albeit too late to prevent bad dreams by Americans who heard Attorney General John Ashcroft's announcement on June 8, 2002, of "an unfolding terrorist plot to attack the United States by exploding a radioactive 'dirty bomb.'" His remarks set off a fresh run on duct tape and plastic, and a number of federal agencies began stockpiling potassium iodide pills, which can protect against radiation. (The terrorist plot, it turned out, was no more than "some fairly loose talk," Assistant Secretary of Defense Paul Wolfowitz subsequently admitted.)[57]

By the time George Bush's re-election campaign got under way in 2004, there was little doubt he'd make terrorism the focal point of all of his speeches and press conferences. His surrogates went farther still, overtly portraying a vote for his Democratic rival, Senator John Kerry, as an invitation to annihilation. "If we make the wrong choice," Vice President Dick Cheney warned a Des Moines audience, "the danger is that we'll get hit again—that we'll be hit in a way that will be devastating from the standpoint of the United States." In May, just prior to the Democratic Convention, Attorney General John Ashcroft announced that al Qaeda's preparations for an attack were 90 percent complete; immediately after the convention, the Department of Homeland Security issued yet another terrorist alert, which diverted America's attention away from Kerry and back to the "wartime" president, George Bush.

The strategy worked. Bush won re-election in November 2004, and in the four years that followed the administration followed the lead of music groups who survive year after year by performing extended versions of their only hit song. The Bush administration kept droning on about 9/11, clear to their final days in Washington.

Among their latter-day ploys, used multiple times, was the purportedly leaked report. In 2005, for instance, the DHS issued a report, "National Planning Scenarios," that they said was never intended for public view—thereby making it seem particularly portentous. Somehow it got posted on a Hawaii state government website and picked up by the *New York Times*. Among the plan's twelve possible terror scenarios were attacks using plague, blister agent, dirty bombs, food contamination, nerve agents, toxic chemicals, and a chlorine tank explosion. Not surprisingly, the report's disclaimer—in a small paragraph on page iv—got considerably less play than the horrifying *what ifs*: "Neither the Intelligence Community nor the law enforcement community is aware of any credible specific intelligence that indicates that such an attack is planned, or that the agents or devices in question are in possession of any known terrorist group."[58]

As Josef Joffe, editor of the German newspaper *Die Zeit,* noted in an op-ed in the *Washington Post,* "The demand for security is like an obsession, spreading relentlessly, for which there is no rational counterargument. DHS always asks, 'What if?'—which always trumps 'Why more?'"[59]

Americans have paid, Joffe suggests, what he dubs a "fear tax" in the form of hundreds of millions of potentially productive hours lost in security lines; freight delays at borders, ports, and airports; and lost revenues and opportunities from abroad. As an example of the latter, Joffe cited a survey of international travelers that examined factors behind the 17 percent decline in overseas visitors to the United States in the five years following 9/11. The largest factor: a perception that U.S. policies made international visitors feel unwelcome. Seventy percent of respondents said they worried about how they'd be treated by U.S. immigration officers.

The total cost of the Bush administration's reaction to the 9/11 attacks will be the subject of reflection for decades to come. Surely the heaviest toll was paid by the tens of thousands of American, Iraqi, and Afghan soldiers and civilians who were killed or seriously wounded, and by their families, and the trillions of dollars the United States spent is hardly trivial. Harder to measure are the losses in civil liberties from the USA Patriot Act. Signed into law by President Bush in October 2001, the act gave broad surveillance powers to intelligence agencies. (To those who protested the Patriot Act, John Ashcroft warned back then, "Your tactics only aid terrorists, for they erode our national unity. . . . They give ammunition to America's enemies.")[60]

Enter Barack Obama

A fear campaign can eventually become sufficiently stale and suspect that adept politicians benefit from challenging it. By the time of the presidential election of 2008, frustration with the administration, its terror scares, and its war in Iraq opened the door for a presidential candidate who had opposed the war from the start and held out promises of a brighter future. Republicans yammered on about how "the terrorists" hoped the Democrat would win, and Barack Hussein Obama's full name (emphasis on Hussein) was pointedly used at rallies for presidential candidate John McCain and his running mate, Sarah Palin, who claimed that Obama was "palling around with terrorists."[61]

During the campaign, Obama refused to take the bait. While he never opened himself to charges of being weak or reckless by downplaying the risks of terrorism—or for that matter, other overblown frights I've discussed—Obama deftly mounted a campaign of optimism whose byword was *hope*.

His election was hopeful not just on issues, but in one important regard, in its outcome as well. The election of an African American offered real hope that large numbers of Americans had put aside the long-entrenched fears of black men that I discussed in chapter 5.

It would be a mistake to presume, however, as did a range of commentators after the 2008 presidential election, that prejudice played little or no role in that contest. Obama beat his Republican challenger decisively in the general election—by a 7-point margin. But among white voters, he lost to McCain, and by a still wider margin—12 points. Nationally, 43 percent of the white electorate voted for Obama, and in some states in the Deep South, only about one in ten whites voted for him (10 percent in Alabama and 11 percent in Mississippi).[62]

Nor should anyone imagine that fears of black men will not continue to be exploited by advocacy groups in search of contributions; ratings-hungry media outlets; and local, regional, and national politicians. Contrary to Larry King's claim the day after Obama's inauguration, that "there's a lot of advantages to being black," studies that came out around that time give lie to the Panglossian view. Among the more revealing was conducted by sociologists from the University of Oregon and University of California. In a clever analysis, they looked at how interviewers classified nearly 13,000 people they surveyed every year or two from 1979 to 2002. At the end of each survey, the interviewers, the great majority of whom were white women, were asked to classify the race of the person they'd interviewed. The results show that racial stereotypes of African Americans as criminals and on the dole are so powerful, they actually influence what someone's race is assumed to be. A person the interviewers initially perceived as white was almost twice as likely to be classified as black the next time they were surveyed if they had become unemployed, impoverished, or incarcerated.[63]

Or consider another study released in the late '00s, in which sociologists from Northwestern and Princeton looked at how Americans estimate various risks. Whites give realistic assessments of risks related to work and health, the researchers found, but greatly overestimate the likelihood of being the victim of crime, especially if they live in areas with substantial numbers of African Americans. "White respondents overestimate their risk of crime victimization more than twice as much in heavily black zip codes relative to areas with few black residents," Lincoln Quillian and Devah Pager reported. Noting that the misperceptions come not from actual crime levels in these areas, they suggest the main cause is exaggerated emphases in the media on crimes committed by African Americans, and the sociologists point out how these biases are costly and self-perpetuating.

"African-American neighborhoods suffer from perceptions of high crime, beyond any actual association between race and crime. Even in the case of affluent blacks moving into white neighborhoods, white observers are likely to perceive elevated risks of crime. Likewise, in the location decisions of white households and businesses, the attribution of high crime rates to mostly black neighborhoods is likely to deprive these areas of local jobs and more affluent residents."[64]

Add to all that studies that find that black men are significantly more likely to be stopped, searched, and arrested by police than are whites, and it is little wonder that African Americans are 13 percent of the U.S. population but 55 percent of the population of federal prisons. At the time of Obama's election, one in nine black men between the ages of twenty and thirty-four was behind bars. In the late '00s, though the statistics attracted little media attention, blacks also had the highest rates of poverty in the United States—24.5 percent, about twice the rate for the nation as a whole. During the economic crisis of that period,

African American homeowners were two and a half times more likely to be in foreclosure than were whites.[65]

As well, there continue to be newsworthy, if underreported, health disparities of the sort I noted in chapter 5. Overall death rates are significantly higher for blacks than whites—1,027 per 100,000 for blacks and 786 for whites—and for some fatal diseases, things actually got worse since I wrote the earlier edition. In the mid-1900s, death rates from heart disease for blacks and whites were roughly equal. At the start of the twenty-first century, blacks had a 28 percent higher rate than whites. And even as prospects improved for AIDS patients, the gap in death rates between whites and blacks with AIDS was strikingly large. Blacks who died from HIV lost about eleven times as many years of potential life as whites.[66]

Each of these disparities resulted in no small measure from discrimination and unequal access—to decent health care, education, jobs, and unpolluted neighborhoods (whites are 79 percent less likely than African Americans to live in polluted neighborhoods)—and in the case of home ownership, outright targeting of blacks by lenders pushing subprime mortgages. Black applicants were significantly more likely than whites to receive high-cost mortgages, even where the incomes of the two groups were roughly the same.[67]

Still, none of those disturbing states of affairs cancels out the fact that an anti-fear candidate won the White House. Very early in that race, in August 2007, several months before even the Democratic primaries began, the would-be president's wife, Michelle Obama, spoke to supporters in rural Iowa about why she agreed to let her husband run. "Barack and I talked long and hard about this decision. This wasn't an easy decision for us," she explained, "because we've got two beautiful little girls and we have a wonderful life and everything was going fine, and there would have been nothing that would have been more disruptive than a decision to run for president of the United States.

"And as more people talked to us about it, the question came up again and again, what people were most concerned about. They were afraid. It was fear. Fear again, raising its ugly head in one of the most important decisions that we would make. Fear of everything. Fear that we might lose. Fear that he might get hurt. Fear that this might get ugly. Fear that it would hurt our family. Fear.

"You know the reason why I said 'Yes'? Because I am tired of being afraid. I am tired of living in a country where every decision that we have made over the last ten years wasn't for something, but it was because people told us we had to fear something. We had to fear people who looked different from us, fear people who believed in things that were different from us, fear one another right here in our own backyards. I am so tired of fear, and I don't want my girls to live in a country, in a world, based on fear."

May her words reverberate well into the future.

NOTES

Introduction to the Tenth Anniversary Edition

1. Rick Ginsberg and Leif Frederick Lyche, "The Culture of Fear and the Politics of Education," *Educational Policy*, 22, no. 1 (January 2008): 10–27; Kerri Augusto, "The (Play) Dating Game: Our Culture of Fear Means that We Can No Longer Count On Spontaneity to Bring Children Together," *Newsweek*, 8 September 2008, p. 19. Discussion of both the concept and the book has been vigorous in the blogosphere, with bloggers offering their own interpretations of discussions in the chapters that follow, and finding echoes of my argument in movies and literature. My favorite example is an entry on a film discussion website in 2009 that quoted from Frank Capra's 1938 classic, *You Can't Take It With You*. A character in the film "sounds like she's been cribbing from Barry Glassner's *The Culture of Fear*, [though] she is actually speaking to her fiancé over four decades before Glassner's book was written," the blogger remarks. He quotes a scene in which a character relays her grandfather's view that "most people these days are run by fear–fear of what they eat, fear of what they drink, fear of their jobs, their future, fear of their health." The blame, the character suggests, lies with "people who commercialize on fear. You know they scare you to death so they can sell you something you don't need." http://1morefilmblog.com/wordpress/you-cant-take-it-with-you-capra-1938/.

2. Zbigniew Brzezinski, "Terrorized by 'War on Terror,'" *Washington Post*, 25 March 2007.

3. Brzezinski, "Terrorized."

4. "Chubb Personal Insurance: Masterpiece Family Protection," http://www.chubb.com/personal/family_protection.jsp; Robert J. Flores, "National Incidence Studies of Missing, Abducted, Runaway, and Thrownaway Children," U.S. Department of Justice, Office of Justice Programs, Office of Juvenile Justice and Delinquency Prevention, October 2002, pp. 2, 11, http://www.ncjrs.gov/pdffiles1/ojjdp/196467.pdf.

5. Charles Piller and Lee Romney, "State Pays Millions for Contract Psychologists to Keep Up with Jessica's Law," *Los Angeles Times*, 10 August 2008.

6. Piller and Romney, "State Pays Millions."

7. Dennis C. Blair, "Annual Threat Assessment of the Intelligence Community for the Senate Select Committee on Intelligence" (unclassified statement for the record), 12 February 2009, http://intelligence.senate.gov/090212/blair.pdf.

8. David Ropeik, *Risk: A Practical Guide for Deciding What's Really Safe and What's Really Dangerous in the World Around You* (Boston: Mariner Books, 2002); Kids Risk Project: http://www.kidsrisk.harvard.edu; Alan Woolf, "What Should We Worry About?" *Newsweek*, 22 September 2003.

9. Elizabeth Gudrais, "Unequal America: Causes and Consequences of the Wide— and Growing—Gap Between Rich and Poor," *Harvard Magazine*, July-August 2008.

10. Daniel McGinn, "Marriage by the Numbers," *Newsweek*, 5 June 2006.

11. Mike Cooper, " 'Crack' Babies' Future Bleak," *CDC AIDS Weekly*, 21 May 1990, p. 8; Susan Okie, "The Epidemic That Wasn't," *New York Times*, 27 January 2009.

Introduction

1. Crime data here and throughout are from reports of the Bureau of Justice Statistics unless otherwise noted. Fear of crime: Esther Madriz, *Nothing Bad Happens to Good Girls* (Berkeley: University of California Press, 1997), ch. 1; Richard Morin, "As Crime Rate Falls, Fears Persist," *Washington Post* National Edition, 16 June 1997, p. 35; David Whitman, "Believing the Good News," *U.S. News & World Report*, 5 January 1998, pp. 45–46.

2. Eva Bertram, Morris Blachman et al., *Drug War Politics* (Berkeley: University of California Press, 1996), p. 10; Mike Males, *Scapegoat Generation* (Monroe, ME: Common Courage Press, 1996), ch. 6; Karen Peterson, "Survey: Teen Drug Use Declines," *USA Today*, 19 June 1998, p. A6; Robert Blendon and John Young, "The Public and the War on Illicit Drugs," *Journal of the American Medical Association* 279 (18 March 1998): 827–32. In presenting these statistics and others I am aware of a seeming paradox: I criticize the abuse of statistics by fearmongering politicians, journalists, and others but hand down precise-sounding numbers myself. Yet to eschew all estimates because some are used inappropriately or do not withstand scrutiny would be as foolhardy as ignoring all medical advice because some doctors are quacks. Readers can be assured I have interrogated the statistics presented here as factual. As notes throughout the book make clear, I have tried to rely on research that appears in peer-reviewed scholarly journals. Where this was not possible or sufficient, I traced numbers back to their sources, investigated the research methodology utilized to produce them, or conducted searches of the popular and scientific literature for critical commentaries and conflicting findings.

3. Bob Herbert, "Bogeyman Economics," *New York Times*, 4 April 1997, p. A15; Doug Henwood, "Alarming Drop in Unemployment," *Extra*, September 1994, pp. 16–17; Christopher Shea, "Low Inflation and Low Unemployment Spur Economists to Debate 'Natural Rate' Theory," *Chronicle of Higher Education*, 24 October 1997, p. A13.

4. Bob Garfield, "Maladies by the Millions," *USA Today*, 16 December 1996, p. A15.

5. Jim Windolf, "A Nation of Nuts," *Wall Street Journal*, 22 October 1997, p. A22.

6. Andrew Ferguson, "Road Rage," *Time*, 12 January 1998, pp. 64–68; Joe Sharkey, "You're Not Bad, You're Sick. It's in the Book," *New York Times*, 28 September 1997, pp. N1, 5.

7. Malcolm Dean, "Flesh-eating Bugs Scare," *Lancet* 343 (4 June 1994): 1418; "Flesh-eating Bacteria," *Science* 264 (17 June 1994): 1665; David Brown, "The Flesh-eating

Bug," *Washington Post* National Edition, 19 December 1994, p. 34; Sarah Richardson, "Tabloid Strep," *Discover* (January 1995): 71; Liz Hunt, "What's Bugging Us," *The Independent*, 28 May 1994, p. 25; Lisa Seachrist, "The Once and Future Scourge," *Science News* 148 (7 October 1995): 234–35. Quotes are from Bernard Dixon, "A Rampant Non-epidemic," *British Medical Journal* 308 (11 June 1994): 1576–77; and Michael Lemonick and Leon Jaroff, "The Killers All Around," *Time*, 12 September 1994, pp. 62–69. More recent coverage: "Strep A Involved in Baby's Death," UPI, 27 February 1998; see also, e.g., Steve Carney, "Miracle Mom," *Los Angeles Times*, 4 March 1998, p. A6; KTLA, "News at Ten," 28 March 1998.

8. Jim Naureckas, "The Jihad That Wasn't," *Extra*, July 1995, pp. 6–10, 20 (contains quotes). See also Edward Said, "A Devil Theory of Islam," *Nation*, 12 August 1996, pp. 28–32.

9. Lewis Lapham, "Seen but Not Heard," *Harper's*, July 1995, pp. 29–36 (contains Clinton quote). See also Robin Wright and Ronald Ostrow, "Illusion of Immunity Is Shattered," *Los Angeles Times*, 20 April 1995, pp. A1, 18; Jack Germond and Jules Witcover, "Making the Angry White Males Angrier," column syndicated by Tribune Media Services, May 1995; and articles by James Bennet and Michael Janofsky in the *New York Times*, May 1995.

10. Tom Morganthau, "The Lull Before the Storm?" *Newsweek*, 4 December 1995, pp. 40–42; Mike Males, "Wild in Deceit," *Extra*, March 1996, pp. 7–9; *Progressive*, July 1997, p. 9 (contains Clinton quote); Robin Templeton, "First, We Kill All the 11-Year-Olds," *Salon*, 27 May 1998.

11. Statistics from "Violence and Discipline Problems in U.S. Public Schools: 1996–97," National Center on Education Statistics, U.S. Department of Education, Washington, DC, March 1998; CNN, "Early Prime," 2 December 1997; and Tamar Lewin, "Despite Recent Carnage, School Violence Is Not on Rise," *New York Times*, 3 December 1997, p. A14. Headlines: *Time*, 15 January 1996; *U.S. News & World Report*, 25 March 1996; Margaret Carlson, "Children Without Souls," *Time*, 2 December 1996, p. 70. William J. Bennett, John J. DiIulio, and John Walters, *Body Count* (New York: Simon & Schuster, 1996).

12. CNN, "Talkback Live," 2 December 1997; CNN, "The Geraldo Rivera Show," 11 December 1997; Richard Lacayo, "Toward the Root of Evil," *Time*, 6 April 1998, pp. 38–39; NBC, "Today," 25 March 1998. See also Rick Bragg, "Forgiveness, After 3 Die in Shootings in Kentucky," *New York Times*, 3 December 1997, p. A14; Maureen Downey, "Kids and Violence," 28 March 1998, *Atlanta Journal and Constitution*, p. A12.

13. Jocelyn Stewart, "Schools Learn to Take Threats More Seriously," *Los Angeles Times*, 2 May 1998, pp. A1, 17; "Kindergarten Student Faces Gun Charges," *New York Times*, 11 May 1998, p. A11; Rick Bragg, "Jonesboro Dazed by Its Darkest Day" and "Past Victims Relive Pain as Tragedy Is Repeated," *New York Times*, 18 April 1998, p. A7, and idem, 25 May 1998, p. A8. Remaining quotes are from Tamar Lewin, "More Victims and Less Sense in Shootings," *New York Times*, 22 May 1998, p. A20; NPR, "All Things Considered," 22 May 1998; NBC, "Today," 25 March 1998. See also Mike Males, "Who's Really Killing Our Schoolkids," *Los Angeles Times*, 31 May 1998, pp. M1,

3; Michael Sniffen, "Youth Crime Fell in 1997, Reno Says," Associated Press, 20 November 1998.

14. Overestimation of breast cancer: Willam C. Black et al., "Perceptions of Breast Cancer Risk and Screening Effectiveness in Women Younger Than 50," *Journal of the National Cancer Institute* 87 (1995): 720–31; B. Smith et al., "Perception of Breast Cancer Risk Among Women in Breast and Family History of Breast Cancer," *Surgery* 120 (1996): 297–303. Fear and avoidance: Steven Berman and Abraham Wandersman, "Fear of Cancer and Knowledge of Cancer," *Social Science and Medicine* 31 (1990): 81–90; S. Benedict et al., "Breast Cancer Detection by Daughters of Women with Breast Cancer," *Cancer Practice* 5 (1997): 213–19; M. Muir et al., "Health Promotion and Early Detection of Cancer in Older Adults," *Cancer Oncology Nursing Journal* 7 (1997): 82–89. For a conflicting finding see Kevin McCaul et al., "Breast Cancer Worry and Screening," *Health Psychology* 15 (1996): 430–33.

15. Philip Jenkins, *Pedophiles and Priests* (New York: Oxford University Press, 1996), see esp. ch. 10; Debbie Nathan and Michael Snedeker, *Satan's Silence* (New York: Basic Books, 1995), see esp. ch. 6; Jeffrey Victor, "The Danger of Moral Panics," *Skeptic* 3 (1995): 44–51. See also Noelle Oxenhandler, "The Eros of Parenthood," *Family Therapy Networker* (May 1996): 17–19.

16. Mary DeYoung, "The Devil Goes to Day Care," *Journal of American Culture* 20 (1997): 19–25.

17. Dorothy Rabinowitz, "A Darkness in Massachusetts," *Wall Street Journal*, 30 January 1995, p. A20 (contains quote); "Back in Wenatchee" (unsigned editorial), *Wall Street Journal*, 20 June 1996, p. A18; Dorothy Rabinowitz, "Justice in Massachusetts," *Wall Street Journal*, 13 May 1997, p. A19. See also Nathan and Snedeker, *Satan's Silence*; James Beaver, "The Myth of Repressed Memory," *Journal of Criminal Law and Criminology* 86 (1996): 596–607; Kathryn Lyon, *Witch Hunt* (New York: Avon, 1998); Pam Belluck, "'Memory' Therapy Leads to a Lawsuit and Big Settlement," *New York Times*, 6 November 1997, pp. A1, 10.

18. Elliott Currie, *Crime and Punishment in America* (New York: Metropolitan, 1998); Tony Pate et al., *Reducing Fear of Crime in Houston and Newark* (Washington, DC: Police Foundation, 1986); Steven Donziger, *The Real War on Crime* (New York: HarperCollins, 1996); Christina Johns, *Power, Ideology and the War on Drugs* (New York: Praeger, 1992); John Irwin et al., "Fanning the Flames of Fear," *Crime and Delinquency* 44 (1998): 32–48.

19. Steven Donziger, "Fear, Crime and Punishment in the U.S.," *Tikkun* 12 (1996): 24–27, 77.

20. Peter Budetti, "Health Insurance for Children," *New England Journal of Medicine* 338 (1998): 541–42; Eileen Smith, "Drugs Top Adult Fears for Kids' Well-being," *USA Today*, 9 December 1997, p. D1. Literacy statistic: Adult Literacy Service.

21. "The State of America's Children," report by the Children's Defense Fund, Washington, DC, March 1998; "Blocks to Their Future," report by the National Law Center on Homelessness and Poverty, Washington, DC, September 1997; reports released in 1998 from the National Center for Children in Poverty, Columbia University, New York; Douglas Massey, "The Age of Extremes," *Demography* 33 (1996): 395–412; Trudy Lieberman, "Hunger in America," *Nation*, 30 March 1998, pp. 11–16; David

Lynch, "Rich Poor World," *USA Today*, 20 September 1996, p. B1; Richard Wolf, "Good Economy Hasn't Helped the Poor," *USA Today*, 10 March 1998, p. A3; Robert Reich, "Broken Faith," *Nation*, 16 February 1998, pp. 11–17.

22. Inequality and mortality studies: Bruce Kennedy et al., "Income Distribution and Mortality," *British Medical Journal* 312 (1996): 1004–7; Ichiro Kawachi and Bruce Kennedy, "The Relationship of Income Inequality to Mortality," *Social Science and Medicine* 45 (1997): 1121–27. See also Barbara Chasin, *Inequality and Violence in the United States* (Atlantic Highlands, NJ: Humanities Press, 1997). Political stability: John Sloan, "The Reagan Presidency, Growing Inequality, and the American Dream," *Policy Studies Journal* 25 (1997): 371–86 (contains Reich quotes and "will haves" phrase). On both topics see also Philippe Bourgois, *In Search of Respect: Selling Crack in El Barrio* (Cambridge: Cambridge University Press, 1996); William J. Wilson, *When Work Disappears* (New York, Knopf, 1996); Richard Gelles, "Family Violence," *Annual Review of Sociology* 11 (1985): 347–67; Sheldon Danziger and Peter Gottschalk, *America Unequal* (Cambridge, MA: Harvard University Press, 1995); Claude Fischer et al., *Inequality by Design* (Princeton, NJ: Princeton University Press, 1996).

23. Mike Tharp and William Holstein, "Mainstreaming the Militia," *U.S. News & World Report*, 21 April 1997, pp. 24–37.

24. Burger King: "Notebooks," *New Republic*, 29 April 1996, p. 8. Statistics from the FBI's Uniform Crime Reports, Centers for Disease Control reports, and Timothy Egan, "Oregon Freeman Goes to Court," *New York Times*, 23 May 1998, pp. A1, 8.

25. Bill Thompson, "It's Not Guns, It's Killer Kids," *Fort Worth Star-Telegram*, 31 March 1998, p. 14; "Guns Aren't the Problem," *New York Post* 30 March 1998 (from *Post* Web site); "Arkansas Gov. Assails 'Culture of Violence,'" Reuters, 25 March 1998; Bo Emerson, "Violence Feeds 'Redneck,' Gun-Toting Image," *Atlanta Journal and Constitution*, 29 March 1998, p. A8; Nadya Labi, "The Hunter and the Choir Boy," *Time*, 6 April 1998, pp. 28–37; Lacayo, "Toward the Root of Evil."

26. Alan Kerckhoff and Kurt Back, *The June Bug* (New York: Appleton-Century-Crofts, 1968), see esp. pp. 160–61.

27. Stephen Jay Gould, *Questioning the Millennium* (New York: Crown, 1997); Todd Gitlin, "Millennial Mumbo Jumbo," *Los Angeles Times Book Review*, 27 April 1997, p. 8.

28. Karen Frost, Erica Frank et al., "Relative Risk in the News Media," *American Journal of Public Health* 87 (1997): 842–45. Media-effects theory: Nancy Signorielli and Michael Morgan, eds., *Cultivation Analysis* (Newbury Park, CA: Sage, 1990); Jennings Bryant and Dolf Zillman, eds., *Media Effects* (Hillsdale, NJ: Erlbaum, 1994); Ronald Jacobs, "Producing the News, Producing the Crisis," *Media, Culture and Society* 18 (1996): 373–97.

29. Madriz, *Nothing Bad Happens to Good Girls*, see esp. pp. 111–14; David Whitman and Margaret Loftus, "Things Are Getting Better? Who Knew," *U.S. News & World Report*, 16 December 1996, pp. 30–32.

30. Blendon and Young, "War on Illicit Drugs." See also Ted Chiricos et al., "Crime, News and Fear of Crime," *Social Problems* 44 (1997): 342–57.

31. Steven Stark, "Local News: The Biggest Scandal on TV," *Washington Monthly* (June 1997): 38–41; Barbara Bliss Osborn, "If It Bleeds, It Leads," *Extra*, September–October 1994, p. 15; Jenkins, *Pedophiles and Priests*, pp. 68–71; "It's Murder," *USA Today*, 20 April

1998, p. D2; Lawrence Grossman, "Does Local TV News Need a National Nanny?" *Columbia Journalism Review* (May 1998): 33.

32. Regarding fearmongering by newsmagazines, see also Elizabeth Jensen et al., "Consumer Alert," *Brill's Content* (October 1998): 130–47.

33. ABC, "20/20," 16 March 1998.

34. Thomas Maugh, "Killer Bacteria a Rarity," *Los Angeles Times*, 3 December 1994, p. A29; Ed Siegel, "Roll Over, Ed Murrow," *Boston Globe*, 21 August 1994, p. 14. Crier quote from ABC's "20/20," 24 June 1994.

35. Sheryl Stolberg, "'Killer Bug' Perfect for Prime Time," *Los Angeles Times*, 15 June 1994, pp. A1, 30–31. Quotes from Brown, "Flesh-eating Bug"; and Michael Lemonick and Leon Jaroff, "The Killers All Around," *Time*, 12 September 1994, pp. 62–69.

36. Lewin, "More Victims and Less Sense"; Tamar Lewin, "Study Finds No Big Rise in Public-School Crimes," *New York Times*, 25 March 1998, p. A18.

37. "Licensing Can Protect," *USA Today*, 7 April 1998, p. A11; Jonathan Kellerman, "Few Surprises When It Comes to Violence," *USA Today*, 27 March 1998, p. A13; Gary Fields, "Juvenile Homicide Arrrest Rate on Rise in Rural USA," *USA Today*, 26 March 1998, p. A11; Karen Peterson and Glenn O'Neal, "Society More Violent, So Are Its Children," *USA Today*, 25 March 1998, p. A3; Scott Bowles, "Armed, Alienated and Adolescent," *USA Today*, 26 March 1998, p. A9. Similar suggestions about guns appear in Jonathan Alter, "Harnessing the Hysteria," *Newsweek*, 6 April 1998, p. 27.

38. Sharon Walsh, "Gun Sellers Look to Future–Children," *Washington Post*, 28 March 1998, pp. A1, 2.

39. John Schwartz, "An Outbreak of Medical Myths," *Washington Post* National Edition, 22 May 1995, p. 38.

40. Richard Preston, *The Hot Zone* (New York: Random House, 1994); Malcolm Gladwell, "The Plague Year," *New Republic*, 17 July 1995, p. 40.

41. Erik Larson, "A False Crisis: How Workplace Violence Became a Hot Issue," *Wall Street Journal*, 13 October 1994, pp. A1, 8; Cynthia Crossen, "Fright By the Numbers," *Wall Street Journal*, 11 April 1996, pp. B1, 8. See also G. Pascal Zachary, "Junk History," *Wall Street Journal*, 19 September 1997, pp. A1, 6.

42. On variable definitions of obesity see also Werner Cahnman, "The Stigma of Obesity," *Sociological Quarterly* 9 (1968): 283–99; Susan Bordo, *Unbearable Weight* (Berkeley: University of California Press, 1993); Joan Chrisler, "Politics and Women's Weight," *Feminism and Psychology* 6 (1996): 181–84.

43. Mary Douglas and Aaron Wildavsky, *Risk and Culture* (Berkeley: University of California Press, 1982), see esp. pp. 6–9; Mary Douglas, *Risk and Blame* (London: Routledge, 1992). See also Mary Douglas, *Purity and Danger* (New York: Praeger, 1966). Asbestos and schools: Peter Cary, "The Asbestos Panic Attack," *U.S. News & World Report*, 20 February 1995, pp. 61–64; Children's Defense Fund, "State of America's Children."

44. See Marina Warner, "Peroxide Mug-shot," *London Review of Books*, 1 January 1998, pp. 10–11.

45. Nathan and Snedeker, *Satan's Silence* (quote from p. 240). See also David Bromley, "Satanism: The New Cult Scare," in James Richardson et al., eds., *The Satanism Scare* (Hawthorne, NY: Aldine de Gruyter, 1991), pp. 49–71.

46. Of girls ages fifteen to seventeen who gave birth, fewer than one in ten were unmarried and had been made pregnant by men at least five years older. See Steven Holmes, "It's Awful, It's Terrible, It's . . . Never Mind," *New York Times*, 6 July 1997, p. E3.

47. CNN, "Crossfire," 27 August 1995 (contains Huffington quote); Ruth Conniff, "Warning: Feminism Is Hazardous to Your Health," *Progressive*, April 1997, pp. 33–36 (contains Sommers quote). See also Susan Faludi, *Backlash* (New York: Crown, 1991); Deborah Rhode, "Media Images, Feminist Issues," *Signs* 20 (1995): 685–710; Paula Span, "Did Feminists Forget the Most Crucial Issues?" *Los Angeles Times*, 28 November 1996, p. E8.

48. See Katha Pollitt, "Subject to Debate," *Nation*, 26 December 1994, p. 788, and idem, 20 November 1995, p. 600.

49. Henry Nelson Coleridge, ed., *Specimens of the Table Talk of the Late Samuel Taylor Coleridge* (London: J. Murray, 1935), entry for 5 October 1830. Nixon quote cited in William Safire, *Before the Fall* (New York: Doubleday, 1975), Prologue.

Chapter One

1. Hitchcock quoted in Leslie Halliwell, *Halliwell's Film Companion* (New York: HarperCollins, 1995). ABC, "20/20," 5 July 1996.

2. "Oprah," 5 September 1997; Jerry Adler et al., "Road Rage," *Newsweek*, 2 June 1997. See also CBS, "This Morning," 4 June 1998.

3. Andrew Ferguson, "Road Rage," *Time*, 12 January 1997, pp. 64–68; Kim Murphy, "Driven to Extremes in the Northwest," *Los Angeles Times*, 11 January 1998, pp. A1, 14; Maria Puente, "Students Get Lesson in 'Road Rage'," *USA Today*, 16 October 1997, p. A3; Murphy, "Driven to Extremes."

4. Kathy Free, "Make Their Day," *People Weekly*, 1 September 1997, pp. 59–60. Additional details on the AAA numbers: Jason Vest et al., "Road Rage," *U.S. News & World Report*, 2 June 1997, pp. 24–30. Quote from Murphy, "Driven to Extremes."

5. Patrick O'Driscoll, "In Hot Pursuit of Road Rage," *USA Today*, 9 December 1997, p. A3. On the amount of coverage see also Jane Hall, "Newsmagazines Spread Across TV's Table," *Los Angeles Times*, 30 September 1997, p. F5.

6. David Levy, *Tools of Critical Thinking* (Boston: Allyn & Bacon, 1997), ch. 22.

7. Incident: KTLA "News at 10," 14 January 1998; Solomon Moore and Scott Glover, "'Road Rage'-type Crash Kills 2," *Los Angeles Times*, 15 January 1998, pp. B1, 5.

8. Robert Ourlain, "Freeway Chase Ends in Slaying," *Los Angeles Times*, 19 January 1998, p. A1; Scott Glover and Geoff Boucher, "Corrections' Officer's Husband Gives Account of Slaying," *Los Angeles Times*, 20 January 1998, pp. A3, 10; KTLA, "News at 10," 27 January 1998; Scott Glover and Bonnie Hayes, "Slain Guard's Spouse Decries Police Actions," *Los Angeles Times*, 28 January 1998, p. B1.

9. ABC, "20/20," 5 July 1996.

10. NPR, "Morning Edition," 24 July 1997.

11. O'Driscoll, "In Hot Pursuit of Road Rage."

12. For an example of calls for more police see Tustin Amole, "Aurora Police Crack Down on Road Rage," *Rocky Mountain News*, 27 January 1998 (Internet edition). General information on Nerenberg from O'Driscoll, "In Hot Pursuit of Road Rage," his Web site, and Joe Sharkey, "You're Not Bad, You're Sick. It's in the Book," *New York Times*, 28 September 1997, pp. N1, 5. Quotes from Free, "Make Their Day"; ABC "World News Tonight," 17 July 1997; Puente, "Students Get Lesson in 'Road Rage'"; Adler et al., "Road Rage."

13. Quote from Free, "Make Their Day."

14. "Oprah," 5 September 1997.

15. CNN, "CNN Today," 28 August 1997; Vest et al., "Road Rage."

16. Ralph Hingson, "Prevention of Drinking and Driving," *Alcohol Health and Research World* 20 (1996): 219–26; Matthew Wald, "A Fading Drumbeat Against Drunken Driving," *New York Times*, 15 December 1996, p. D5; Jay Winsten, "Promoting Designated Drivers," *American Journal of Preventive Medicine* 10 (May 1994): 11–14. On my selection and use of statistics see note 2 in the Introduction.

17. Statistics: Hingson, "Prevention of Drinking and Driving"; Matthew Wald, "Safety Group Reports Rise in Fatalities on Highways," *New York Times*, 10 October 1996, p. A17. Survey: Vest et al., "Road Rage." Quote: Don Russell, "Get Out of the Way, Jerk," *Philadelphia Daily News* (online edition), 7 August 1997. See also Sally Steenland, "Road Rage," *Philadelphia Inquirer* (online edition), 7 August 1997.

18. Quote from O'Driscoll, "In Hot Pursuit of Road Rage."

19. Dan McGraw, "A Texas Town Heals Its Wounds," *U.S. News & World Report*, 26 October 1998, pp. 24–25; Steve Lopez, "To Be Young and Gay in Wyoming," *Time*, 26 October 1998, pp. 38–40.

20. Quotes from John Wilson, *The Myth of Political Correctness* (Durham, NC: Duke University Press, 1995), pp. 7, 23; Brian Siano, "The Great Political Correctness Conspiracy Hoax," *Skeptic* 4, no. 3 (1996): 52–61.

21. "Excerpts from President's Speech to University of Michigan Graduates," *New York Times*, 5 May 1991, p. 32. On incivility in a diverse society see Rebecca Alpert, "Coming Out of the Closet as Politically Correct," *Tikkun* (March 1996): 61–63.

22. See Phil Ryan, "On Political Correctness," *Rationality and Society* 8 (1996): 353–57.

23. Siano, "Conspiracy Hoax," p. 54; Wilson, *Myth of Political Correctness*, pp. 20–21.

24. Alice Jardine, "Illiberal Reporting," in C. Newfield and R. Strickland, eds., *After Political Correctness* (Boulder, CO: Westview Press, 1995), pp. 128–37.

25. Siano, "Conspiracy Hoax," p. 54; Wilson, *Myth of Political Correctness*, pp. 20–21; Jardine, "Illiberal Reporting."

26. Paul Craig Roberts, "Decline and Fall of the White Male," *San Francisco Examiner*, 9 January 1996, p. A13.

27. Studies: "The Chilly Classroom Climate," report by the National Association for Women in Education, 22 February 1996; Siano, "Conspiracy Hoax"; Jack Levin and Jack McDevitt, "The Research Needed to Understand Hate Crime," *Chronicle of Higher Education* 4 August 1995, p. B1; Wilson, *Myth of Political Correctness*, esp. pp. 43–49 and

ch. 6; Verta Taylor and Nicole Raeburn, "Identity Politics as High-Risk Activism," *Social Problems* 42 (1995): 252–73. See also Michael Warner, ed., *Fear of a Queer Planet* (Minneapolis: University of Minnesota Press, 1993); John Davidson, "The Tenure Trap," *Working Woman* (June 1997): 36–37.

28. Linda Chavez, "'Dynamic' Newest Banned Word," *USA Today*, 10 January 1996, p. A11. Information about the incident: Courtney Leatherman, "Cal State Advertisement Spurs Debate over 'Dynamic' Professors," *Chronicle of Higher Education*, 5 January 1996, p. A17; letter to the editor from Zaida Giraldo (Director of Affirmative Action at California State), *Chronicle of Higher Education*, 16 February 1996, p. B4.

29. Debra Saunders, "Dynamic Profs Need Not Apply," *San Francisco Chronicle*, 10 January 1996, p. A19; Roberts, "Decline and Fall."

30. George Will, "Sensitivity Cops on the Trail of the 'D' Word," *Washington Post*, 11 January 1996, p. A23; John Leo, "PC Crimes and Misdemeanors," *U.S. News & World Report*, 12 February 1996, p. 18.

31. Statistics from Nexis searches conducted by the author.

32. Ellen Messer-Davidow, "Manufacturing the Attack on Liberalized Higher Education," in Newfield and Strickland, eds., *After Political Correctness*, pp. 38–78; Wilson, *Myth of Political Correctness*, pp. 26–30; Siano, "Conspiracy Hoax"; Paul Pekin, "Schoolhouse Crock," *Extra*, January 1998, pp. 9–10.

33. Siano, "Conspiracy Hoax."

34. Letter from Dean Robert Lawton, *USA Today*, 21 March 1996, p. A10. "Dumbing down" appears in Rick Telander, "College Sports Grow in Stature as Shakespeare Takes a Hike," *Chicago Sun-Times*, 22 March 1996, p. 131.

35. John Wilson, "Come Not to Bury Shakespeare," *Chronicle of Higher Education*, 14 February 1997, p. B6. See also Maureen Dowd, "A Winter's Tale," *New York Times*, 28 December 1995, p. A21.

36. Censorship in the schools: Annie Gowen, "Maryland Schools Remove Two Black-Authored Books," *Los Angeles Times*, 11 January 1998, p. A6; see also Pekin, "Schoolhouse Crock"; Katha Pollitt, "Sweet Swan of Avon," *Nation*, 4 March 1996, p. 9.

37. "Pro-Lifers Use Breast Cancer as a Cheap Scare" (reprinted from *The Economist*), *Chicago Tribune*, 7 March 1996, p. 27; Susan Estrich, "Right Plays Politics with Breast Cancer," *Los Angeles Times*, 1 February 1996, p. A11; Tina Rosenberg, "The Stealth War Against Abortion," *Rolling Stone*, 27 June 1996, pp. 47–50.

38. Judith Koehler, "Abortion–Breast Cancer Link," *Chicago Tribune*, 1 December 1995, p. 27; NPR, "All Things Considered," 23 January 1996; J. R. Darling et al., "Risk of Breast Cancer Among Young Women: Relationship to Induced Abortion," *Journal of the National Cancer Institute* 86 (1994): 1584–92.

39. See Christine Gorman, "Do Abortions Raise the Risk of Breast Cancer?" *Time*, 7 November 1994, p. 61; Thomas Maugh, "Study Adds to Discourse on Cancer, Abortion," *Los Angeles Times*, 12 October 1996, p. A17.

40. Alison Bass, "Link Between Abortion and Breast Cancer Is Downplayed," *Boston Globe*, 24 January 1996, p. 4; NPR, "All Things Considered," 23 January 1996.

41. CNN, "Worldview," 11 October 1996; Richard Knox, "Bias in Abortion Study Is Charged," *Boston Globe*, 12 October 1996, p. A1.

42. See "Abortion and Gulf War Studies," *New York Times*, 10 January 1997, p. A32; Jane Brody, "Big Study Finds No Link in Abortion and Cancer," *New York Times*, 9 January 1997, p. A12.

43. Rick Weiss, "Study Disputes Breast Cancer, Abortion Link," *Washington Post*, 9 January 1997, p. A1.

Chapter Two

1. Don Phillips, "Death in Detroit," *Washington Post*, 20 March 1991, p. A1.

2. Amy Harmon, "Soldier Uninjured in War Is Killed in Detroit," 19 March 1991, *Los Angeles Times*, p. A8; "Widow Found Guilty in Slaying of Gulf War Veteran," Associated Press, 9 June 1994, p. A19.

3. Joe Treen et al., "The Murder of Gulf War Veteran Tony Riggs Was a Mystery— Then Detroit Police Arrested His Widow," *People*, 8 April 1991, p. 111; "Wife Freed in Killing of GI Just Back from Gulf," *Chicago Tribune*, 30 April 1991, p. A5.

4. Rhonda Gibson and Dolf Zillmann, "Exaggerated Versus Representative Exemplification in News Reports," *Communication Research* 21 (1994): 603–24; Todd Burke and Charles O'Rear, "Armed Carjacking," *Police Chief* 60 (1993): 18–23; Michael Rand, *Carjacking, National Crime Victimization Survey* (Washington, DC: Bureau of Labor Statistics, 1994).

5. Coffey quote: David Shaw, "A Negative Spin on the News," *Los Angeles Times*, 17 April 1996, p. A10.

6. John R. MacArthur, *Lapdogs for the Pentagon Second Front: Censorship and Propaganda in the Gulf War* (New York: Hill and Wang, 1992); Jack Anderson and Dale Van Atta, *Stormin' Norman: An American Hero* (New York: Zebra Books, 1991); Eliot Cohen, "The Mystique of U.S. Air Power," *Foreign Affairs* 73 (1994): 11–29; Edward Herman, "The Media's Role in U.S. Foreign Policy," *Journal of International Affairs* 47 (1993): 23–45; Daniel Hallin, "TV's Clean Little War," *Bulletin of the Atomic Scientists* 47 (1991): 16–20. See also Jean Baudrillard, *The Gulf War Did Not Take Place* (Bloomington: Indiana University Press, 1996).

7. Anastasia Toufexis, "Workers Who Fight Firing with Fire," *Time*, 25 April 1994, pp. 35–37.

8. Lara Wozniak, "Violence Growing as a Job Hazard," *St. Petersburg Times*, 28 August 1994, p. H1. See also Tom Dunkel, "Newest Danger Zone: Your Office," *Working Woman* 19 (1994): 38–45.

9. Erik Larson, "A False Crisis: How Workplace Violence Became a Hot Issue," *Wall Street Journal*, 13 October 1994, pp. A1, 8. See also "Taxi Driving Termed Riskiest Job in U.S.," *New York Times*, 9 July 1996, p. A9; Marlene Cimons, "Coping with Working Under the Gun, Literally," *Los Angeles Times*, 11 June 1998, p. A5; Greg Warchol, *Workplace Violence, 1992–96* (Washington, DC: Bureau of Justice Statistics, July 1998).

10. Donna Rosato, "New Industry Helps Managers Fight Violence," *USA Today*, 5 August 1995.

11. "Violence in the Workplace Becoming More of a Problem," Associated Press, 10 September 1995; Kirstin Downey Grimsley, "Risk of Homicide Is Higher in Retail Jobs," *Washington Post,* 13 July 1997, p. A14; Larson, "False Crisis."

12. See also Janice Lewis, "Workplace Violence," *RQ,* 22 March 1995, p. 287.

13. See Mary Ellen Schoonmaker, "Is There Life After Layoff?" *Columbia Journalism Review* (May 1996): 48–52; Seth Mydans, "Los Angeles Times Announces Plans for 450 Layoffs," *New York Times,* 19 July 1995, p. A9; James Barron, "For News Employees, Thin Envelope Is Knife," *New York Times,* 8 January 1993, p. B2; Sydney Schanberg, "The Murder of New York Newsday," *Washington Monthly* (March 1996): 29–34.

14. Louis Uchitelle and N. R. Kleinfield, "On the Battlefields of Business, Millions of Casualties," *New York Times,* 3 March 1996, pp. A1, 14–17. On limitations in the *Times* series see Janine Jackson, "We Feel Your Pain," *Extra,* May 1996, pp. 11–12. Crime statistics derived from Bureau of Justice Statistics reports. Specific victimization estimates based on Uchitelle and Kleinfield, "Battlefields of Business," and Ray Surette, "Predator Criminals as Media Icons," in Gregg Barak, ed., *Media, Process, and the Social Construction of Crime* (New York: Garland, 1994), pp. 131–58.

15. Downsizing effects: Barry Glassner, *Career Crash* (New York: Simon and Schuster, 1994); Uchitelle and Kleinfield, "Battlefields of Business"; David Gordon, *Fat and Mean* (New York: Free Press, 1996); Paul Krugman, "Superiority Complex," *New Republic,* 1 November 1997, pp. 20–21. Continuation of the trend: Robert Reich, "Broken Faith," *Nation,* 16 February 1998, pp. 11–17; Aaron Bernstein, "Who Says Job Anxiety Is Easing?" *Business Week,* 7 April 1997, p. 38. Amount of coverage: Barbara Bliss Osborn, "If It Bleeds, It Leads," Extra, September 1994, p. 15; Larry Platt, "Prime Suspects," *Philadelphia Magazine,* November 1994, pp. 90–93, 119; Roy Edward Lotz, *Crime and the American Press* (New York: Praeger, 1991), pp. 2–3; Mark Fitzgerald, "Newspapers and Violence Coverage," *Editor and Publisher,* 18 June 1994, pp. 14, 40; Max Frankel, "The Murder Broadcasting System," *New York Times Magazine,* 17 December 1995, pp. 46–47; Franklin Gilliam, Shanto Iyengar et al., "Crime in Black and White," working paper, Center for American Politics and Public Policy, UCLA, September 1995; Stephen Budiansky et al., "Local TV: Mayhem Central," *U.S. News & World Report,* 4 March 1996, p. 63; Steven Stark, "Local News: The Biggest Scandal on TV," *Washington Monthly* (June 1997): 38–41. Some evidence suggests that the amount of coverage declined in the late 1990s: Alan Finder, "Something New in News: Drop in Crime Reporting Follows the Drop in the Crime Rate," *New York Times,* 6 September 1998, p. A23.

16. Judy Klemesrud, "Those Treats May Be Tricks," *New York Times,* 28 October 1970, p. 56.

17. "The Goblins Will Getcha," *Newsweek,* 3 November 1975, p. 28.

18. Abby, quoted in Jan Harold Brunvand, "The Halloween Saboteurs," column syndicated by United Feature Syndicate, October 1991. Polls cited in Joel Best, *Threatened Children* (Chicago: University of Chicago Press, 1990), p. 132.

19. Brunvand, "Halloween Saboteurs."

20. Best, *Threatened Children;* Joel Best and Gerald Horiuchi, "The Blade in the Apple," *Social Problems* 32 (June 1985): 488–99; and private correspondence with Best.

21. Bill Ellis, "New Halloween Traditions in Response to Sadism Legends," in Jack Santino, ed., *Halloween and Other Festivals of Death and Life* (Knoxville: University of Tennessee Press, 1994), pp. 24–44 (quote on p. 27). Ellis and Best interpret the Halloween sadism stories as an "urban legend." While I do not disagree with that categorization, my concern here is with the specific fears that the news stories promoted and dodged.

22. Klemesrud, "Those Treats May Be Tricks."

23. See, e.g., Ted Thackrey, "Trick or Treat Subdued Amid Poisoning Scares," *Los Angeles Times*, 1 November 1982, pp. 1, 28; James Barron, "Poison Worries Lead to Precautions for Halloween," *New York Times*, 28 October 1982, pp. B1, 4.

24. Best, *Threatened Children* (NBC quote on p. 98); Debbie Nathan and Michael Snedeker, *Satan's Silence* (New York: Basic Books, 1995), pp. 39–44 (Goodman quote on p. 42); Lawrence Stanley, "The Child Porn Myth," *Cardozo Law Journal* 7 (1989): 313–15. For historical accounts of panics over child molesters see Joel Best, *Images of Issues* (New York: Aldine, 1989); Henry Jenkins, *Moral Panic: Changing Concepts of the Child Molester in Modern America* (New Haven: Yale University Press, 1998).

25. Hiroshi Fukurai et al., "Sociologists in Action: The McMartin Sexual Abuse Case, Litigation, Justice, and Mass Hysteria," *American Sociologist* 25 (1994): 44–71; Nathan and Snedeker, *Satan's Silence*, p. 88 (quotes from, respectively, those two sources); David Shaw, "Reporter's Early Exclusives Triggered a Media Frenzy," *Los Angeles Times*, 20 January 1990, p. A1.

26. Nathan and Snedeker, *Satan's Silence*; survey cited in Fukurai et al., "Sociologists in Action."

27. Lizette Alvarez, "House Passes Bill to Confront Pedophiles Who Use Internet," *New York Times*, 12 June 1998, p. A17.

28. Ibid.; Mark Clayton, "'Off-Line' Hazards Lie in Web's Links, Lures," *Christian Science Monitor*, 8 August 1996, p. 10; ABC, "20/20," 31 October 1997. See also Wendy Cole, "The Marquis de Cyberspace," *Time*, 3 July 1995, p. 43; NBC, "Dateline," 16 June 1995; NBC, "Today," 17 September 1998.

29. John Rather, "A Look at Perils the Internet Poses to Children," *New York Times* (Long Island Edition), 12 October 1997, sec. 14, p. 1; Rajiv Chandrasekaran, "Undercover on the Dark Side of Cyberspace," *Washington Post*, 2 January 1996, p. D1; William Rashbaum and Helen Kennedy, "Talkin' Dirty," *New York Daily News*, 15 September 1995, p. 6; Jon Jeter, "FBI Agents Posed as Teenagers . . . ," *Washington Post*, 15 September 1995, p. A3. See also "Why Pedophiles Go On-line," *Redbook*, April 1997, p. 102.

30. Clayton, "'Off-Line' Hazards"; Rather, "Perils the Internet Poses"; ABC, "20/20," 31 October 1997; Cori Anne Natoli, "FBI Knew of Manzie's Cry for Help," *Asbury Park Press*, 5 April 1998, p. A1. See also Joan Feldman, "Computer Detectives Uncover Smoking Guns," *Computerworld*, 9 June 1997, pp. 1, 26.

31. Quote from Chandrasekaran, "Dark Side of Cyberspace."

32. Steven Levy, "Did the Net Kill Eddie?" *Newsweek*, 13 October 1997 (contains quotes). See also Terri Somers, "Manzie's Alleged Abuser Faults Police for Slaying," *Asbury Park Press*, 1 July 1998, p. A1; Jim Curran, "Insanity Defense Planned for Teen in Boy's Killing," *Bergen Record*, 28 April 1998, p. A3.

33. Kim Murphy, "Youngsters Falling Prey to Seducers in Computer Web Crime," *Los Angeles Times*, 11 June 1995, p. A1. See also National Public Radio, "All Things Considered," 31 August, 1993.

34. National Center on Child Abuse and Neglect, *Study Findings: National Study of the Incidence and Severity of Child Abuse and Neglect* (Washington, D.C.: U.S. Dept. of Health and Human Services, 1988); Lisa A. Fontes, ed., *Sexual Abuse in Nine North American Cultures* (Thousand Oaks, CA: Sage, 1995); Carole Jenny et al., "Are Children at Risk for Sexual Abuse by Homosexuals?" *Pediatrics* 94 (1994): 41–44; Leslie Margolin, "Child Sexual Abuse by Uncles," *Child Abuse and Neglect* 18 (1994): 215–24; Murray A. Straus and Richard Gelles, *Physical Violence in American Families* (New Brunswick, NJ: Transaction, 1990).

35. John Dreese, "The Other Victims of Priest Pedophilia," *Commonweal* 121 (22 April 1994): 11–15.

36. Andrew M. Greeley, *Fall from Grace* (New York: Putnam, 1993); idem, "Priestly Silence on Pedophilia," *New York Times*, 13 March 1992, p. A31; idem, "How Serious Is the Problem of Sexual Abuse by Clergy?" *America* 168 (20 March 1993): 6–11.

37. James L. Franklin, "Priest Puts Number of Abused at 100,000," *Boston Globe*, 19 March 1993, p. 14; Philip Murnion et al., "Regarding A. Greeley's Data on Sexual Abuse by Priests," *America* 168 (17 April 1993): 21–22. On methodology issues see also Dennis Howitt, *Pedophiles and Sexual Offenses Against Children* (New York: Wiley, 1995); Richard Parker and John Gagnon, *Conceiving Sexuality* (New York: Routledge, 1995); Edward O. Laumann et al., *The Social Organization of Sexuality* (Chicago: University of Chicago Press, 1994); Rick Zimmerman and Lilly Langer, "Improving Estimates of Prevalence of Sensitive Behaviors," *Journal of Sex Research* 32 (1995): 107–17. For a more detailed analysis of these issues see Philip Jenkins, *Pedophiles and Priests* (New York: Oxford University Press, 1996).

38. Christopher B. Daly, "Sexual Abuse Cases Take Their Toll on Catholic Dioceses," *Washington Post*, 1 November 1994, p. A3; Jenkins, *Pedophiles and Priests*.

39. Walter Russell Mead, "A Crisis of Faith Bedevils Roman Catholic Church," *Los Angeles Times*, 12 December 1993, p. M1.

40. Daniel Pedersen, "Death in Dunblane," *Newsweek*, 25 March 1996, pp. 25–29 (quote on p. 25); Hugo Young, "The Myth That America Is Unique," *Newsweek*, 25 March 1996, p. 29.

41. One reason Catholic clergy (rather than, say, Baptist or Methodist clergy) are targets for accusations about pedophilia is, paradoxically, their unmarried status. See Jenkins, *Pedophiles and Priests*, pp. 9, 50–51. Reuters quote from Maggie Fox, "Dunblane 'Pervert' Who Struck Back at Whispers," Reuters, 17 March 1996.

42. Fox, "Dunblane 'Pervert'." For an example of the coverage see Louis J. Salome, "Killer of 17 Liked Boys, Guns," *Austin American–Statesman*, 15 March 1996, p. A1. On myths and realities about molesters: Jenny et al., "Are Children at Risk"; Best, *Threatened Children*; National Center on Child Abuse and Neglect, *Study Findings*; Pauline Bart and Eileen Moran, eds., *Violence Against Women* (Newbury Park, CA: Sage, 1993).

43. Bill Hewitt et al., "Innocents Lost," *People*, 1 April 1996, pp. 42–49 (quotes from pp. 48, 49). Hamilton's letter is quoted in several news accounts cited.

44. Pedersen, "Death in Dunblane" (quote in sidebar).

45. Philip Jenkins, *Using Murder* (New York: Aldine de Gruyter, 1994), pp. 183–87.

46. Jenny et al., "Are Children at Risk"; Bettina Boxall, "Statistics and Science Can Be Twisted to Suit Debate," *Los Angeles Times,* 12 November 1993, p. A18; Nicholas Groth, *Men Who Rape* (New York: Plenum, 1979). The pedophile–homosexual connection is made in coverage of pedophile priests as well: see Jenkins, *Pedophiles and Priests,* ch. 6. Sheldon quote from "C.C. Watch," Electronic News Service, April 1996.

47. Lance Morrow, "The Unconscious Hums, 'Destroy!'" *Time,* 25 March 1996, p. 78.

48. Hewitt et al., "Innocents Lost"; Associated Press, "Scottish Killer Ran Boys' Groups . . . ," *Chicago Tribune,* 15 March 1996, p. 6.

49. *Newsweek* quote from Pedersen, "Death in Dunblane," p. 25; *People* quote from Hewitt et al., "Innocents Lost."

50. "What Is Sporting About Such Guns?" *Daily Mail,* 18 March 1996, p. 8.

51. On the news media's irresponsibility regarding guns see Thomas Winship, "Step Up the War Against Guns," *Editor and Publisher,* 24 April 1993, p. 24. Quote from Young, "Myth That America Is Unique," p. 29.

52. Daniel Schorr, "TV Violence," *Christian Science Monitor,* 7 September 1993, p. 19. That media violence is often cited as a cause for serial murder see Jenkins, *Using Murder,* p. 125.

53. Patrick Cooke, "TV Causes Violence?" *New York Times,* 14 August 1993, p. 11 (contains quote).

54. The UCLA study, released in report form in September 1995, was directed by Jeffrey Cole, Center for Communication Policy, UCLA. On the advantages of painful portrayals of violence see also Robert Scheer, "Violence Is Us," *Nation,* 15 November 1993, p. 555.

55. Cooke, "TV Causes Violence?"

56. Among the more cogent critiques: Brian Siano, "Frankenstein Must Be Destroyed," *The Humanist* 54 (January–February 1994): 19–25. On non-U.S. studies see Oene Wiegman et al., "A Longitudinal Study of the Effects of Television Viewing on Aggressive and Prosocial Behavior," *British Journal of Social Psychology* 31 (1992): 147–64. An overview and elaboration of the complexities of causal analysis in this body of research: Cecilia von Feilitzen, "Media Violence," in C. Hamelink and O. Linne, eds., *Mass Communication Research* (Norwood, NJ: Ablex, 1994), pp. 147–70.

57. Brandon Centerwall, "Our Cultural Perplexities," *Public Interest,* no. 111 (Spring 1993): 56–72; David Horowitz, "V Is for Vacuous Censorship," *Los Angeles Times,* 8 February 1996, p. B9.

58. David McDowall, "Firearm Availability and Homicide Rates in Detroit," *Social Forces* 69 (1991): 1085–1101; Daniel Webster et al., "Gun Violence Among Youth . . . ," *Pediatrics* 94 (1994): 617–22; Arthur Kellerman et al., "Gun Ownership as a Risk Factor for Homicide in the Home," *New England Journal of Medicine* 329 (1993): 1084–92; Howard Schubiner et al., "Exposure to Violence Among Inner-City Youth," *Journal of Adolescent Health* 14 (1993): 214–19; Joseph Sheley et al., "Gun-related Violence in and Around Inner-City Schools," *American Journal of Diseases of Children* 146 (1992): 677–82;

Colin Loftin et al., "Effects of Restrictive Licensing of Handguns on Homicide . . . ," *New England Journal of Medicine* 325 (1991): 1615–20; D. Weatherburn, "Gun Control and Homicide," *Australian and New Zealand Journal of Criminology* 28 (1995): 116–20; Patrick O'Carroll et al., "Preventing Homicide," *American Journal of Public Health* 81 (1991): 576–81; William Bratton, "Mr. Heston, the Police Are Not the Enemy," *New York Times*, 20 June 1998, p. A20; Richard Alba and Steven Messner, "Point-blank Against Itself," *Journal of Quantitative Criminology* 11 (1995): 391–410; David Lester and Antoon Leenaars, "Gun Control and Rates of Firearms Violence in Canada and the United States," *Canadian Journal of Criminology* 36 (1994): 463–64. Dunblane upshot: "Heaven's Door," *Time*, 6 January 1997, p. 133.

59. Scheer, "Violence Is Us" (contains Bochco remark); Charles Anderson, "Violence in Television Commercials During Nonviolent Programming," *Journal of the American Medical Association* 278 (1 October 1997): 1045–46.

60. George Gerbner, "Violence and Terror in and by the Media," in M. Raboy and B. Dagenais, eds., *Media, Crisis and Democracy* (Newbury Park, CA: Sage, 1992), pp. 94–107. See also Nancy Signorielli, "Television's Mean and Dangerous World," in N. Signorielli and M. Morgan, eds., *Cultivation Analysis* (Newbury Park, CA: Sage, 1990), pp. 85–106; Marilyn Elias, "Watching TV News Can Shake Up Kids," *USA Today*, 18 August 1998, p. D1. Evidence that people's feelings about crime follow from what they see in the media: Jeffrey Alderman, "Leading the Public," *Public Perspective* 5 (1994): 26–27; Cheryl Russell, "True Crime," *American Demographics* (August 1995): 22–32. George Gerbner, "Television Violence," in G. Dines and J. Humez, eds., *Gender, Race and Class in Media* (Thousand Oaks, CA: Sage, 1995), pp. 547–57 (quote on p. 553).

61. George Gerbner, "The Politics of Media Violence," in Hamelink and Linne, *Mass Communication Research*, pp. 133–45. For another example of the reception to his ideas see *TV Guide*, "Violence on Television," symposium sponsored by *TV Guide* in 1992, subsequently published in pamphlet form.

62. Mark Warr, "Fear of Victimization," *Public Perspective* 5 (1993): 25–28; Joan Barthel, "How Crime Has Victimized Us Over–50s," *New Choices for Retirement Living* 34 (1994): 18–25; "Older Women's Fear," segment on Cable News Network, 6 September 1994; Mohsen Bazargan, "The Effects of Health, Environmental, and Socio-Psychological Variables on Fear of Crime . . . ," *International Journal of Aging and Human Development* 38 (1994): 99–115; Arthur Patterson, "Fear of Crime . . . ," *Journal of Architectural and Planning Research* 2 (1985): 277–88; Glen Allen, "A Dark Season of Fear," *Maclean's* 102 (6 November 1989): 18–19; Neal Krause, "Stress and Isolation from Close Ties in Later Life," *Journal of Gerontology* 46 (1991): 183–95; "Behind the Numbers," *Modern Maturity* 38 (May–June 1995): 93–94. See also Alderman, "Leading the Public."

63. Judith Gaines, "Crimes Against Elderly Put Them in a Prison of Fears," *Boston Globe*, 22 June 1994, p. 1; John Hurst, "Crime and the Elderly of L.A.," *Los Angeles Times*, 24 October 1994, p. B1. On earlier overreporting of crimes against the elderly see Mark Fishman, "Crime Waves as Ideology," *Social Problems* 25 (1978): 531–43.

64. Statistic from Bureau of Justice Statistics, "Elderly Crime Victims," Washington, DC, March 1994. Quotes from "Rosa Parks's Mugging," *Washington Post*, 4 September

1994, p. C6. For other portrayals of the elderly as particularly vulnerable see Jon Jeter, "Slaying Heightens Anxiety Among Elderly," *Washington Post*, 24 November 1994, p. A1; Bill McClellan, "Vulnerable Victim Can Set Stage for Perfect Crime," *St. Louis Post–Dispatch*, 26 February 1995, p. C1.

65. Parks's and neighbors' cautions: James Bennet, "Sadness and Anger After a Legend Is Mugged," *New York Times*, 1 September 1994, p. A16. Other quotes from Donna Britt, "Parks Once Again Becomes a Symbol," *Washington Post*, 2 September 1994, p. C1.

66. John Ritter, "For Some Elderly, Fear Darkens Golden Years," *USA Today*, 17 November 1994, p. A7.

67. Timothy Egan, "Old, Ailing and Finally a Burden Abandoned," *New York Times*, 26 March 1992, p. A1; "Granny Dumping by the Thousands," *New York Times*, 29 March 1992, p. E16. Another example of the coverage: J. Madeleine Nash, "When Love Is Exhausted," *Time*, 6 April 1992, p. 24.

68. Leslie Bennetts, "Apparent Dumping," *Columbia Journalism Review* (September–October 1992): 15–17; Associated Press, "Woman convicted in father dumping," *New York Times*, 4 December 1992, p. A24.

69. ABC, "20/20," 20 January 1995.

70. "Malnutrition Hits Many Elderly," *New York Times*, 3 July 1995, p. 28.

Chapter Three

1. Ira Berkow, "An Athlete Dies Young, but by His Own Hand," *New York Times*, 1 October 1995, pp. 20, 24.

2. Rajiv Chandrasekaran, "Prescription Error Claims Dad's 'Angel'," *Washington Post*, 31 October 1994, pp. A1, 11.

3. Ibid., p. 14; Berkow, "Athlete Dies Young."

4. Hunger statistics based on reports from the Institute for Food and Development Policy, Oakland, CA, and the Urban Institute, Washington, DC.

5. On the estimation and relative significance of adolescent suicide see Kirk Astroth, "Beyond Ephebiphobia: Problem Adults or Problem Youths?" *Phi Delta Kappan* 75 (January 1994): 411–14; Mike Males and Kim Smith, "Teen Suicide and Changing Cause of Death Certification," *Suicide and Life Threatening Behavior* 21 (1991): 245–59; John McIntosh, "Older Americans: The Next Suicide Epidemic?" *Suicide and Life Threatening Behavior* 22 (1992): 322–32.

6. Statistics: David Shaffer, "Advances in Youth Suicide Research Update," article distributed by the American Suicide Foundation, 1995; Kim Painter, "Suicide Among Young Teens Increases 120%," *USA Today*, 21 April 1995, p. 2D. Local upturns: Brian MacQuarrie, "Best Friends in Life, Mysteries in Death," *Boston Globe*, 5 April 1998, p. B1; ABC, "Good Morning America" (story on suicides in Michigan), 22 October 1997. L.A.: Mike Males, "State's Teenage Suicide Rate Declines," *Los Angeles Times*, 14 December 1997, p. M1; Elizabeth Gleick, "Suicide's Shadow," *Time*, 22 July 1996, pp. 39–42.

7. *Firearm Suicide in the U.S.*, report by the Educational Fund to End Handgun Violence, Washington, DC, May 1995, pp. 14–15.

8. Shaffer, "Advances in Youth Suicide"; Christina Del Valle, "The Specter of Teen Suicide," *Newsday*, 8 November 1997, p. B1; "Youth with Runaway, Throwaway and Homeless Experiences," report by the Dept. of Health and Human Services, Washington, DC, 1995; Janice Arenofsky, "Teen Suicide," *Current Health* 24 (1997): 16–18. See also Jan Neeleman, Simon Wessely, and Michael Wadsworth, "Predictors of Suicide, Accidental Death, and Premature Natural Death in a General-Population Birth Cohort," *Lancet* 351 (1998): 93–97.

9. Berkow, "Athlete Dies Young."

10. *USA Today*, "Special Report," 15 April 1995, pp. A1–3, 8; Doug Sword, "Many Indiana Teens Are Gambling," *Indianapolis Star*, 11 July 1998, p. C1; Art Levine, "Playing the Adolescent Odds," *U.S. News & World Report*, 18 June 1990, p. 51; ABC News, "World News Sunday," 12 March 1995. See also Ricardo Chavira, "The Rise of Teenage Gambling," *Time*, 25 February 1991, p. 78.

11. David Holmstrom, "Teenage Gambling Addiction Grows," *Christian Science Monitor*, 8 December 1992, p. 1; Howard Shaffer, Richard LaBrie, et al., "Pathological Gambling Among Adolescents," *Journal of Gambling Studies* 10 (1995): 339–62; Ken Winters, Randy Stinchfield, and Jayne Fulkerson, "Patterns and Characteristics of Adolescent Gambling," *Journal of Gambling Studies* 9 (1993): 371–86; Eric Griffen, Kenneth Sandler, and Cynthia Lees, "Multiple Addictions Among Dually Diagnosed Adolescents," *Journal of Adolescent Chemical Dependency* 2 (1992): 35–44; Mark Griffiths, "Factors in Problem Adolescent Fruit Machine Gambling," *Journal of Gambling Studies* 9 (1993): 31–45; Howard Shaffer et al., eds., *Compulsive Gambling* (Lexington, MA: Lexington Books, 1989); Douglas Carroll and Justine Huxley, "Cognitive, Dispositional, and Psychophysiological Correlates of Dependent Slot Machine Gambling in Young People," *Journal of Applied Social Psychology* 24 (1994): 1070–83.

12. Sue Fisher, "The Pull of the Fruit Machine," *Sociological Review* 41 (1993): 446–74.

13. Jim Nesbitt, "Teens Vulnerable to Betting Addiction," *Seattle Times*, 29 March 1998, p. A1; Brett Pulley, "Those Seductive Snake Eyes," *New York Times*, 16 June 1998, pp. A1, 23.

14. Chavira, "Rise of Teenage Gambling"; Susan Howlett, "Risky Business," *Los Angeles Times*, 14 September 1993, pp. E1–2; Holmstrom, "Teenage Gambling Addiction Grows."

15. Howard Shaffer and Matthew Hall, "Estimating the Prevalence of Adolescent Gambling Disorders," *Journal of Gambling Studies* 12 (1996): 193–214; Constance Holden, "Gambling on the Increase," *Science* 279 (23 January 1998): 485; Howard Shaffer, "Youthful Addiction and Gambling," talk delivered 27 October 1995 and distributed through the National Center for Responsible Gaming; Pulley, "Seductive Snake Eyes." On maturing out see also Barry Glassner and Julia Loughlin, *Drugs and Crime in Adolescent Worlds* (New York: St. Martin's Press, 1987).

16. Pulley, "Seductive Snake Eyes."

17. Ray Robinson, "Is Rimm's Porn Study 'Cyberfraud'?" *The Press of Atlantic City Online*, 11 July 1995; Philip Elmer-Dewitt, "On a Screen Near You: Cyberporn," *Time*, 3 July 1995, pp. 38–45.

18. Robinson, "Is Rimm's Porn Study 'Cyberfraud'?"; Philip Elmer-Dewitt, "Fire Storm on the Computer Nets," *Time*, 24 July 1995, p. 57.

19. Donna Hoffman and Thomas Novak, "A Detailed Critique of the Time Article," posted in July 1995 at http://www.vanderbilt.edu/Owen/HomePage.html; Brock N. Meeks, "CyberWire Dispatch on Time and the Rimm Study," posted in July 1995 at http://www.cyberwerks.com:70/1/cyberwire.

20. Elmer-Dewitt, "On a Screen Near You."

21. Hoffman and Novak, "A Detailed Critique"; Meeks, "CyberWire Dispatch."

22. The technological generation gap: Laura Miller, "Fear of net.sex," *Wired*, November 1995, p. 138. The act: Floyd Abrams, "Clinton vs. the First Amendment," *New York Times*, 30 March 1997, p. F42 (contains Frankfurter quote); Joshua Quittner, "Free Speech for the Net," *Time*, 24 June 1996, pp. 56–57; Steven Levy, "U.S. v. the Internet," *Newsweek*, 31 March 1997, pp. 77–79. On blocking software and other resources available to parents see also Michael Banks, "Filtering the Net in Libraries," *Computers in Libraries* 18 (March 1998): 50–54; Donna Rice Hughes, *Kids Online: Protecting Your Children in Cyberspace* (Grand Rapids, MI: Revell, 1998).

23. *Time*'s follow-up piece: Elmer-Dewitt, "Fire Storm," p. 57. On the rarity of a news medium admitting it got a story wrong: Conrad Smith, *Media and Apocalypse* (Westport, CT: Greenwood Press, 1992), pp. 24–25, 187–88.

24. Abductions: Gunnar Stickler et al., "Parents' Worries About Children Compared to Actual Risks," *Clinical Pediatrics* 30 (1991): 522–28; press releases in 1995 from SafeCard Services reporting surveys by Audits and Surveys; David Finkelhor, Gerald Hotaling, and Andrea Sedlak, "The Abduction of Children by Strangers and Nonfamily Members," *Journal of Interpersonal Violence* 7 (1992): 226–43; information from the National Center for Missing and Exploited Children. On the history of panics over missing children see Paula Fass, *Kidnapped* (New York: Oxford University Press, 1998).

25. See Kim Pittaway, "Sex Offenders: What You Need to Know," *Chatelaine* 68 (March 1995): 57; Kenneth Wooden, *Child Lures* (Arlington, TX: Summit, 1995).

26. Joel Best, *Threatened Children* (Chicago: University of Chicago Press, 1990), ch. 2; Jay Grelen, "Sorting Out Myth, Mystery of '81 Slaying," *Rocky Mountain News*, 15 May 1995, p. A22 (contains Walsh quote).

27. Best, *Threatened Children*, and "Dark Figures and Child Victims," in J. Best, ed., *Images of Issues* (New York: Aldine de Gruyter, 1989), pp. 21–38 (contains Young quote).

28. Barbara Vobejda, "Abduction Publicity Could Scare Children," *Washington Post*, 25 November 1985, pp. A1, 6. Another example: "Teaching Fear," *Newsweek*, 10 March 1986, pp. 62–63. On concerns in Britain about frightening children see Sally Weale, "Watch Out with Mother," *The Guardian* 26 July 1993, p. 10.

29. NBC, "Today Show," 15 June 1995. Regarding "America's Most Wanted": Gray Cavender and Lisa Bond-Maupin, "Fear and Loathing on Reality Television," *Sociological Inquiry* 63 (1993): 305–17. Examples of other coverage around Missing Children's Day: Rob Haeseler, "Many Questions Whether Databases Help or Hurt," *San Francisco*

Chronicle, 25 May 1995, p. A1; "American Agenda" segment, "ABC World News Tonight," 25 May 1995. For another example of more recent coverage see Tom Gorman, "A Parent's Worst Fear Come True," *Los Angeles Times,* 26 April 1997, pp. A1, 16, 17.

30. Dale Russakoff, "The Power of Grief," *Washington Post* National Edition, 22 June 1998, p. 27.

31. Louise Continelli, "A Father Fights Back," *Buffalo News,* 5 July 1998, p. M16. For skeptical reporting about the Walsh murder see Grelen, "Sorting Out Myth"; Kent Andrade, "Crimes of the Hearth," *LA Village View,* 2 June 1995, pp. 7, 9.

32. "Geraldo," 13 January 1997 and 4 December 1997.

33. Ernie Allen, "Missing Children," *USA Today Magazine,* July 1994, pp. 46–48.

34. Paula Statman, *On the Safe Side* (New York: HarperCollins, 1995), p. 119.

35. Wooden, *Child Lures,* CBS, "48 Hours," 7 December 1995. On "The Mark Warberg Show" (18 December 1995) and ABC's "Primetime Live" (6 April 1997) Wooden staged mock abductions from playgrounds. Wooden's activities in previous decades: Philip Jenkins, *Using Murder* (New York: Aldine de Gruyter, 1994), pp. 127, 198–99.

36. Angela Mickalide, "Creating Safer Environments for Children," *Childhood Education* 70 (1994): 263–67; Best, *Threatened Children,* p. 125.

37. Marilyn Ivy, "Have You Seen Me? Recovering the Inner Child in Late Twentieth-Century America," in S. Stephens, ed., *Children and the Politics of Culture* (Princeton, NJ: Princeton University Press, 1995).

38. Ibid.; Bettijane Levine, "For Sale: A Sense of Security," *Los Angeles Times,* 31 May 1995, pp. E1–2.

39. Levine, "For Sale."

40. Except as otherwise specified, information on Ideon and the Network from Rob Haeseler, "Credit Card Protection Firm Turns to Missing Kids," *San Francisco Chronicle,* 5 May 1995, p. A1; Sam Stanton, "Critics Find Fault in Missing Kids Service," *Sacramento Bee,* 25 May 1995, p. A1; Haeseler, "Many Questions"; Levine, "For Sale"; and information provided by the company and contained in their advertisements.

41. Barbara Kantrowitz, "Stalking the Children," *Newsweek,* 20 December 1993, pp. 28–29; Haeseler, "Many Questions" (contains Swartz quotes).

42. Rob Haeseler, "Missing Child Service Being Sued," *San Francisco Chronicle,* 11 May 1995, p. A9.

43. Peter Annin, "'Superpredators' Arrive," *Newsweek,* 22 January 1996, p. 57; Barbara Kantrowitz and Connie Leslie, "Wild in the Streets," *Newsweek,* 2 August 1993, pp. 40–47; Michele Ingrassia, "Life Means Nothing," *Newsweek,* 19 July 1993, pp. 16–17; Bettijane Levine, "A New Wave of Mayhem," *Los Angeles Times,* 6 September 1995, pp. E1, 4 (contains quote).

44. Statistic from Steven Holmes, "It's Awful, It's Terrible," *New York Times,* 6 July 1997, p. E3; quote from Kenneth Noble, "Mistaken Killing of Three Teen-Agers Erodes a California City's Confidence," *New York Times,* 2 December 1994, p. A11.

45. Noble, "Mistaken Killing." Additional information is from my own observations in Pasadena and reports in Pasadena community publications and other local media.

46. Dale Kunkel, "How the News Media 'See' Kids," *Media Studies Journal* 8 (Fall 1994): 74–84.

47. Lori Dorfman et al., "Youth and Violence on Local Television News in California," *American Journal of Public Health* 87 (1997): 1311–16.

48. Isabel Wilkerson, "2 Boys, a Debt, a Gun, a Victim: The Face of Violence," *New York Times*, 16 May 1994, pp. A1, C10–11. See also Levine, "New Wave of Mayhem"; Dean Wright, "Alarming Rise in Kids Who Kill," *Los Angeles Times*, 16 August 1992, pp. A1, 18; Celia Dugger, "A Boy in Search of Respect Discovers How to Kill," *New York Times*, 15 May 1994, pp. A1, 36.

49. Debbie Howlett, "Chicago Tot's Young Killers Test System," *USA Today*, 28 November 1995, p. 3A; FBI Uniform Crime reports, 1985–1995, Washington, DC; Robin Templeton, "First, We Kill All the 11-Year-Olds," *Salon*, 27 May 1998; Annette Fuentes, "The Crackdown on Kids," *Nation*, 15 June 1998, pp. 20–22 (contains Justice quote).

50. Wilkerson, "2 Boys, a Debt."

51. Margaret Tinsley, "You and Your Family," *Daily Telegraph*, 26 February 1993, p. 3.

52. Ibid.

53. Bob Dole, "Clinton's Boast on Crime Misses Real Story," *USA Today*, 7 November 1995, p. 13A; Ron Harris, "A Nation's Children in Lockup," *Los Angeles Times*, 22 August 1993, pp. A1, 20–21; Ira Schwartz, Shenyang Guo, and John Kerbs, "The Impact of Demographic Variables on Public Opinion Regarding Juvenile Justice," *Crime and Delinquency* 39 (1993): 5–28; Bruce Shapiro, "The Adolescent Lockup," *Nation*, 7 July 1997, pp. 6–7; Fox Butterfield, "Profits at Juvenile Prisons Earned at Chilling Cost," *New York Times*, 15 July 1998, pp. A1, 14.

54. Steven Donziger, "Fear, Crime, and Punishments in the U.S.," *Tikkun* 12, no. 6 (1997): 24–27, 77; idem, "The Hard Cell," *New York*, 9 June 1997, pp. 26–28; Bruce Shapiro, "Portfolio Prisons," *Nation*, 20 October 1997, pp. 4–5; Eric Bates, "Private Prisons" and "Private Prisons, Cont.," *Nation*, 5 January 1998, pp. 11–18, and 4 May 1998, p. 5.

55. ABC, "World News Tonight," 22 February 1995.

56. Mike Males and Faye Docuyanan, "Crackdown on Kids," *Progressive*, February 1996, pp. 24–26; Robin Templeton, "Superscapegoating," *Extra*, January 1998, pp. 13–14; Maria Puente, "Law Getting Tougher on Children," *USA Today*, 1 April 1998, p. A3; David Moore, "Majority Advocate Death Penalty for Teenage Killers," *Gallup Poll Monthly*, September 1994, pp. 2–7.

57. David Anderson, "When Should Kids Go to Jail?" *American Prospect* (May 1998): 72–78; Barry Glassner et al., "A Note on the Deterrent Effect of Juvenile vs. Adult Jurisdiction," *Social Problems* 31 (1983): 219–21; David Savage, "Florida's Tough Teen Crime Stance May Be Wrong Cure," *Los Angeles Times*, 11 July 1996, pp. A1, 14; Russell Eisenman, "Characteristics of Adolescent Felons in a Prison Treatment Program," *Adolescence* 28 (1993): 695–99; Lawrence Sherman, "Defiance, Deterrence, and Irrelevance," *Journal of Research in Crime and Delinquency* 30 (1993): 445–73; Jerome Miller, "Juvenile Justice: Facts vs. Anger," *New York Times*, 15 August 1998, p. A23; Carl Keane et al., "Deterrence and Amplification of Juvenile Delinquency by Police Contact," *British Journal of Criminology* 29 (1989): 336–52; Harris, "Nation's Children in Lockup."

58. Jan Fisher, "Prison Boot Camps Offer No Quick Fix," *New York Times*, 10 April 1994, p. 11; Joe Davidson, "Boot Camps for Young Criminals Lose Favor," *Wall Street*

Journal, 18 April 1997, p. A20; "The Bust in Boot Camps," *Newsweek,* 21 February 1994, p. 26; Doris MacKenzie and Alex Piquero, "The Impact of Shock Incarceration Programs on Prison Crowding," *Crime and Delinquency* 40 (1994): 222–49; Merry Morash and Lila Rucker, "A Critical Look at the Idea of Boot Camp as a Correctional Reform," *Crime and Delinquency* 36 (1990): 204–22.

59. Later that year another page-one story in the *Times,* this time about youth violence in a housing project in New Orleans, began, "Once, before the children had guns, she could see them running from her stoop as if her voice were thunder and her accusing finger were lightning . . ." Rick Bragg, "Where a Child on the Stoop Can Strike Fear," *New York Times,* 2 December 1994, pp. A1, 10.

60. Truman quoted in William Hillman, *Mr. President* (New York: Farrar, Straus and Young, 1952). Violence against Chinese: David Zucchino, "Today's Violent Crime Is Old Story with a Twist," *Philadelphia Inquirer,* 30 October 1994, p. 1. Other historical items: Ruskin Teeter, "Coming of Age on the City Streets in 19th Century America," *Adolescence* 23 (1988): 909–12. See also Cheng-Tsu Wu, *"Chink!"* (New York: Meridian, 1972); Thomas Bernard, *The Cycle of Juvenile Justice* (New York: Oxford University Press, 1992), ch. 3; Gerald Moran and Maris Vinovskis, "Troubled Youth," in R. Ketterlinus and M. Lamb, eds., *Adolescent Problem Behaviors* (Mahwah, NJ: Lawrence Erlbaum, 1994), pp. 1–16.

61. Howlett, "Chicago Tot's."

62. Barry O'Neill, "The History of a Hoax," *New York Times Magazine,* 6 March 1994, p. 46.

63. O'Neill, "History of a Hoax"; Tamara Henry, "Textbooks Too Few, Too Old, Say Teachers," *USA Today,* 29 February 1996, p. A1; "In His Own Words" (excepts from a speech by Ross Perot), *New York Times,* 14 September 1996, p. 8.

64. "Schools Are Relatively Safe, U.S. Study Says," *New York Times,* 19 November 1995, p. 20; Mike Males, "Who's Really Killing Our Schoolkids?" *Los Angeles Times,* 31 May 1998, pp. M1, 3.

65. Peter Applebome, "For the Ultimate Safe School, Official Eyes Turn to Dallas," *New York Times,* 20 September 1995, pp. A1, B8; "Townview Troubles" (editorial), *Dallas Morning News,* 14 November 1995, p. A16. See also Terrence Stutz, "Security Expenses Surge in Urban Texas Schools," *Dallas Morning News,* 30 September 1997, p. A1. For an example of another high-security school see CBS, "Sunday Morning," 3 May 1998.

66. Natalie Angier, "The Debilitating Malady Called Boyhood," *New York Times,* 24 July 1994, p. E1 (contains Konner quote). Statistics and contemporary approach: Susan Okie, "Hyperactivity Drugs Given to Very Young," *Washington Post,* 2 July 1998, p. Z7; Thomas Armstrong, "ADD: Does It Really Exist?" *Phi Delta Kappan* 77 (1996): 424–28; Charles Hurt, "Ritalin Prescription: For Teachers or Kids?" *Denver Post,* 23 April 1998, p. A19; Leslie Sowers, "The Mental Health of Children, Part II," *Houston Chronicle,* 28 June 1998, p. 6. On medicalization see Peter Conrad and Joseph Schneider, *Deviance and Medicalization* (St. Louis: Mosby, 1980). Research supporting medicalization: Alan J. Zametkin, "Attention-Deficit Disorder: Born to Be Hyperactive? *Journal of the American Medical Asssociation* 273 (1995): 1871–75; J. M. Swanson et al., "Attention-Deficit Hyperactivity Disorder and Hyperkinetic Disorder," *Lancet* 351 (7 February 1998):

429–33. Examples of media accounts positive toward medicalized interpretation: Claudia Wallis, "Life in Overdrive," *Time*, 18 July 1994; Larry Letich, "Attention! A.D.D. Not Just for Kids Anymore," *Utne Reader* (September–October 1994): 46–49; Merrell Noden, "Dan O'Brien," *Sports Illustrated*, 27 June 1994, pp. 64–65.

67. Kenneth Gergen, "Psycho- versus Bio-Medical Therapy," *Society* 35 (November 1997): 24–27. See also PBS, "The Merrow Report: A.D.D.: A Dubious Diagnosis?" November 1995.

68. Lawrence Diller, "The Run on Ritalin," *Hastings Center Report* 26 (March 1996): 12–18.

69. Lois Weithorn, "Mental Hospitalization of Troublesome Youth," *Stanford Law Review* 40 (1988): 773–838; Sandra Boodman, "Advertising for Psychiatric Hospitals," *Washington Post*, 5 May 1992, p. A17; Lynette Lamb, "Kids in the Cuckoo's Nest," *Utne Reader* 50 (March–April 1992): 38, 40; Mary Keegan Eamon, "Institutionalizing Children and Adolescents in Private Psychiatric Hospitals," *Social Work* 39 (1994): 588–94.

70. Joe Sharkey, *Bedlam* (New York: St. Martin's Press, 1994), p. 114.

71. Lamb, "Kids in the Cuckoo's Nest"; Peter Breggin and Ginger Breggin, *The War Against Children* (New York: St. Martin's Press, 1994).

72. Weithorn, "Mental Hospitalization," p. 786.

73. Sue Greer and Paul Greenbaum, "Fear-Based Advertising and the Increase in Psychiatric Hospitalization of Adolescents," *Hospital and Community Psychiatry* 43 (1992): 1038–39.

74. Sharkey, *Bedlam*, chs. 5–6; Weithorn, "Mental Hospitalization," pp. 796–97; Lamb, "Kids in the Cuckoo's Nest." See also Robert Friedman et al., "Psychiatric Hospitalization of Children and Adolescents," testimony before the Florida State Senate, Tallahassee, 6 February 1990.

75. Greer and Greenbaum, "Fear-Based Advertising"; Mary Jane England, president of the American Psychiatric Association, interview with author, 31 May 1995.

76. Robert Friedman, "Admission of Minors to Psychiatric Hospitals and Residential Treatment Centers," duplicated paper, Florida Mental Health Institute, Tampa, University of South Florida, September 1991; Eamon, "Institutionalizing Children."

77. Sandra Blakeslee, "Child-Rearing Is Stormy When Drugs Cloud Birth," *New York Times*, 19 May 1990, pp. A1, 9; Michele Norris, "And the Children Shall Need," *Washington Post*, 1 July 1991, pp. A1, 8; "Crack Babies: The Numbers Mount," *Los Angeles Times*, 13 March 1990, p. B6.

78. Michael Dorris, "A Desperate Crack Legacy," *Newsweek*, 25 June 1990, p. 8; and see also Charles Krauthammer, "Children of Cocaine," *Washington Post*, 30 July 1989, p. C7. Foster mother quoted in W. Russell Neuman et al., *Common Knowledge* (Chicago: University of Chicago Press, 1992), p. 73.

79. Anastasia Toufexis, "Innocent Victims," *Time*, 13 May 1991; and Norris, "And the Children Shall Need."

80. Norris, "And the Children Shall Need"; Toufexis, "Innocent Victims."

81. Barry Zuckerman, "'Crack Kids': Not Broken," *Pediatrics* 89 (1992): 337–39; Drew Humphries, "Crack Mothers, Drug Wars, and the Politics of Resentment," in K. Tunnell, ed., *Political Crime in Contemporary America* (New York: Garland, 1993), pp.

31–48; John Morgan and Lynn Zimmer, "The Social Pharmacology of Smokable Cocaine," in C. Reinarman and H. Levine, eds., *Crack in America* (Berkeley: University of California Press, 1997), pp. 131–70; Gretchen Vogel, "Cocaine Wreaks Subtle Damage on Developing Brains," *Science* 278 (3 October 1997): 38–39.

82. Associated Press story: Dana Kennedy, "Children Born Addicted to Crack Defy Experts," *Los Angeles Times*, 27 December 1992, p. A16. Joseph Treaster, "For Children of Cocaine, Fresh Reasons for Hope," *New York Times*, 16 February 1993, pp. A1, B4; Stephanie Mencimer, "Nursing a Miracle: A D.C. Story," *Washington Post*, 6 February 1994, pp. C1, 4. See also Bernard Gavzer, "Can They Beat the Odds?" *Parade Magazine*, 27 July 1997, pp. 4–5. The *Post* eventually published a more neutral report: Susan FitzGerald, "'Crack Baby' Fears May Have Been Overstated," *Washington Post*, 16 September 1997, p. Z10.

83. Sheila Simmons, "Greater Cleveland's First Crack Babies Are Now in School," *Cleveland Plain Dealer*, 11 December 1994, p. 8. Another example of a corrective story: Annmarie Sarsfield, "Struggles of a Mother and Son," *Tampa Tribune*, 9 April 1995, p. 1.

84. Humphries, "Crack Mothers"; Katharine Greider, "Crackpot Ideas," *Mother Jones*, July–August 1995, pp. 50–56; and see letters to the editor in the subsequent issue. Chasnoff quotes: Kennedy, "Children Born" ("us-versus-them") and Vogel, "Cocaine Wreaks Subtle Damage" ("poverty"). Government statistics: Richard Kusserow, *Crack Babies*, (Washington, DC: Dept. of Health and Human Services, 1990).

85. Toufexis, "Innocent Victims."

86. ABC, "20/20," 12 January 1996.

87. CBS, "CBS This Morning," 19 January 1996.

88. Ibid.

Chapter Four

1. Julia Prodis, "Odyssey Ends for Pregnant 10-Year-Old, 22-Year-Old Boyfriend," Associated Press story in *Chicago Tribune*, 25 January 1996, p. C2.

2. John Hiscock, "Fears Rise for Pregnant 10-Year-Old," *Daily Telegraph*, 25 January 1996, p. 3.

3. Jeff Franks, "Pregnant Runaway Older Than Thought, U.S. Officials Say," Reuters, 25 January 1996; Tony Clark, CNN, 25 January 1996; Prodis, "Odyssey Ends."

4. Michael Graczyk, "Pregnant Runaway Older Than 10, Officials Say," *Austin American–Statesman*, 26 January 1996, p. 3; Sandra Sanchez, "In Texas, Worlds Collide," *USA Today*, 29 January p. D1; Franks, "Pregnant Runaway."

5. "Ricki Lake," 3 January 1996.

6. Ibid.

7. NPR, "Morning Edition," 11 September 1995. Whenever journalists focus on unusually young mothers without pointing out their novelty, they substantiate the misimpression. Another example was a *New York Times* article subtitled "Should a Pregnant Girl, 13, Wed Her Boyfriend, 20?" See B. Drummond Ayres, "Marriage Advised in Some Youth Pregnancies," *New York Times*, 9 September 1996, p. A10.

8. Diane Scott-Jones, "Adolescent Childbearing," *Phi Beta Kappan* 75 (November 1993): 1.

9. Sally Macintyre and Sarah Cunningham-Burley, "Teenage Pregnancy as a Social Problem," in A. Lawson and D. Rhode, eds., *The Politics of Pregnancy* (New Haven: Yale University Press, 1993), pp. 59–73.

10. "Doomed," *Newsday*, 26 February 1995, p. A33; Claudia Morain, "A Freedom Fighter Packs for Washington," *Los Angeles Times*, 8 March 1993, p. E1; James Goldsborough, "The Unwed Birthrate," *San Diego Union–Tribune*, 28 July 1994, p. B11; Jean Bethke Elshtain, "The Lost Children," *New Republic*, 21 October 1996, pp. 30–36; Stephen Caldas, "Teen Pregnancy," *Phi Beta Kappan* 75 (January 1994): 402.

11. Alan Guttmacher Institute, *Sex and America's Teenagers* (New York: Guttmacher Institute, 1994). See also Kristin Luker, *Dubious Conceptions* (Cambridge, MA: Harvard University Press, 1996). On my selection and use of statistics see note 2 in the Introduction.

12. Elizabeth Gleick et al., "Special Report: The Baby Trap," *People*, 24 October 1994, pp. 38–55; Joan Moore, *Going Down to the Barrio* (Philadelphia: Temple University Press, 1991), p. 114; Deborah Rhode, "Adolescent Pregnancy and Public Policy," in Lawson and Rhode, eds., *Politics of Pregnancy*, pp. 301–26; Arline Geronimus, "Mothers of Invention," *Nation*, 12 August 1996, pp. 6–7; Arline Geronimus and Sanders Korenman, "The Socioeconomic Costs of Teenage Childbearing," *Demography* 30 (May 1993): 281–91; Diane Scott-Jones and Sherry Turner, "The Impact of Adolescent Childbearing on Education Attainment and Income of Black Females," *Youth and Society* 22 (1990): 35–53; Frank Furstenberg et al., *Adolescent Mothers in Later Life* (New York: Cambridge University Press, 1987); Ann Phoenix, *Young Mothers* (Cambridge, MA: Blackwell, 1991); Constance W. Williams, *Black Teenage Mothers* (Lexington, MA: Heath, 1991); Dawn Upchurch and James McCarthy, "The Timing of a First Birth and High School Completion," *American Sociological Review* 25 (1990): 224–34; Mike Males, *Scapegoat Generation* (Monroe, ME: Common Courage Press, 1996); Emory Thomas, "Is Pregnancy a Rational Choice for Poor Teenagers?" *Wall Street Journal*, 18 January 1996, pp. B1, 12.

13. Ethan Bronner, "Lawsuit on Sex Bias by 2 Mothers, 17," *New York Times*, 6 August 1998, p. A14.

14. Sally Macintyre and Sarah Cunningham-Burley, "Teenage Pregnancy as a Social Problem," in Lawson and Rhode, eds., *Politics of Pregnancy*, pp. 59–73; Arline Geronimus, "Clashes of Common Sense: On the Previous Child Care Experience of Teenage Mothers-to-Be," *Human Organization* 51 (1992): 318–29; Congressional Budget Office, *Sources of Support for Adolescent Mothers*, Washington, DC, 1990. See also Judy Jones, "Babies of Teenagers Fare Well in Early Years," *The Independent*, 12 May 1992, p. 4; Shawn Hubler, "Some Teens Measure Success by Motherhood," *Los Angeles Times*, 12 November 1995, pp. E1, 2.

15. Diane E. Eyer, *Mother-Infant Bonding* (New Haven: Yale University Press, 1992), ch. 3.

16. Geronimus, "Mothers of Invention"; Luker, *Dubious Conceptions*; Males, *Scapegoat Generation*.

17. Statistics: Luker, *Dubious Conceptions*; Pat Wingert, "The Battle over Falling Birthrates," *Newsweek*, 11 May 1998, p. 40.

18. Elshtain, "Lost Children."

19. Unsigned editorial, "Legislating Chastity," *Nation*, 20 March 1995, p. 365 (on "illegitimacy ratio"); William Eaton, "Shalala Revives 'Murphy Brown' Pregnancy Issue," *Los Angeles Times*, 15 July 1994, p. A1 (contains Shalala quote); Richard Wolf, "States Zero in on Out-of-Wedlock Births," *USA Today*, 21 November 1997, p. A4.

20. Joe Klein, "The Out-of-Wedlock Question," *Newsweek*, 13 December 1993, p. 37; David Broder, "Illegitimacy: An Unprecedented National Catastrophe," *Washington Post*, 22 June 1994, p. A21; Richard Cohen, "Dealing with Illegitimacy," *Washington Post*, 23 November 1993, p. A21. Another example: Charles Krauthammer, "Subsidized Illegitimacy," *Washington Post*, 19 November 1993, p. A29.

21. Timothy Biblarz and Adrian Raftery, "Family-Structure and Social-Mobility," *Social Forces* 75 (1997): 1319–41; Stephanie Coontz, "The American Family and the Nostalgia Trap," *Phi Delta Kappan* 76 (1995): K1–20; Constance Ahrons, *The Good Divorce* (New York: HarperCollins, 1995); Susan Golombok et al., "Children Raised in Fatherless Families from Infancy," *Journal of Child Psychology & Psychiatry & Allied Disciplines* 38 (1997): 783–91; Arlene Skolnick, "Family Feud–Response," *American Prospect*, July 1997, p. 16. See also Melissa Ludtke, *On Our Own* (New York: Random House, 1997); Diane Eyer, *Motherguilt* (New York: Times Books, 1996); Nancy Dowd, *In Defense of Single Mothers* (New York: New York University Press, 1997).

22. Research cited in Coontz, "American Family."

23. Unsigned editorial, "Denying Honor-Society Status to Teen Moms Discriminatory," *Ft. Lauderdale Sun–Sentinel*, 9 August 1998, p. G4; Haya El Nasser, "Unmarried Dads a Surging Social Phenomenon," *USA Today*, 12 June 1997, p. A7.

24. Clinton's speech was delivered 15 November 1995. CBS "Evening News" broadcast was 9 March 1995. See David Blankenhorn, *Fatherless America* (New York: Basic Books, 1995); and for another example of the genre, David Popenoe, *Life Without Father* (New York: Free Press, 1996).

25. Tamar Lewin, "Creating Fathers out of Men with Children," *New York Times*, 18 June 1995, p. 1.

26. Laura Flanders, "Life Without Father," *Extra*, September 1997, pp. 6–8 (contains Horn quote); CBS "Evening News," 9 March 1995. See also Sara McLanahan and Gary Sandefur, *Growing Up with a Single Parent* (Cambridge, MA: Harvard University Press, 1994).

27. Lesbian parents: Charlotte Patterson, "Children of Lesbian and Gay Parents," *Child Development* 63 (1992): 1025–42, and "Lesbian and Gay Families," *Current Directions in Psychological Studies* 3 (1994): 62–64; Judith Stacey, *In the Name of the Family* (Boston: Beacon Press, 1996), ch. 5 (contains Blankenhorn quote); Deb Price, "Three New Studies Confirm Lesbian Parents Are Fit for the Job and Raise Well-Adjusted Kids," *Detroit News*, 25 April 1997 (online edition); Golombok et al., "Children Raised in Fatherless Families"; Nanette Gartrell et al., "The National Lesbian Family Study," *American Journal of Orthopsychiatry* 66 (1996): 272–81.

28. Eyer, *Motherguilt*, pp. 132, 152. See also Judith Stacey, "Virtual Truth with a Vengeance," *Contemporary Sociology* (in press); Ahrons, *Good Divorce*; Biblarz and Raftery, "Family Structure and Social Mobility"; Marsha Kline et al., "The Long Shadow of Marital Conflict," *Journal of Marriage and the Family* 53 (1991): 297–310; Cynthia Harper and Sara McLanahan, "Father Absence and Youth Incarceration," paper presented at meetings of the American Sociological Association, San Francisco, August 1998.

29. Stacey, *Name of the Family*, pp. 139–40. See also Lillian Rubin, *The Transcendent Child* (New York:, Basic Books, 1996).

30. Vicky Phares, "Where's Poppa?" *American Psychologist* 47 (1992): 656–64; Demie Kurz, *For Richer, for Poorer: Mothers Confront Divorce* (New York: Routledge, 1995); Males, *Scapegoat Generation*; Arlie Hochschild, *The Second Shift* (New York: Viking Penguin, 1989); Deborah Rhode, "To Fault or Not To Fault," *National Law Journal* (13 May 1996): A19.

31. Margaret L. Usdansky, "Single Motherhood: Stereotypes vs. Statistics," *New York Times*, 11 February 1996, p. D4.

32. Except as otherwise cited, media portrayals of Lopez are from Richard Goldstein, "Monster Mom," *Village Voice*, 19 December 1995, p. 21.

33. David Van Biema, "Abandoned to Her Fate," *Time*, 11 December 1995, pp. 32–36.

34. Ibid.

35. Katha Pollitt, "The Violence of Ordinary Life," *Nation*, 1 January 1996, p. 9; Bruno Bettelheim, *The Uses of Enchantment* (New York: Knopf, 1976), p. 69.

36. Quotes from, respectively, Biema, "Abandoned to Her Fate"; Goldstein, "Monster Mom"; Michael deCourcy Hinds, "The Instincts of Parenthood Become Part of Crack's Toll," *New York Times*, 17 March 1990, p. A8. For examples of media depictions of crack moms see also Douglas Besharov, "Crack Babies: The Worst Threat Is Mom Herself," *Washington Post*, 6 August 1989, p. B1; "Crack Comes to the Nursery," *Time*, 19 September 1988, p. 85; "Call to Remove Addicts' Children," *New York Times*, 28 April 1990, p. A8; Jan Hoffman, "Pregnant, Addicted–and Guilty?" *New York Times Magazine*, 19 August 1990, pp. 34–57. On the maltreatment of these women see Lisa Maher, "Punishment and Welfare: Crack Cocaine and the Regulation of Mothering," in C. Feinman, ed., *The Criminalization of a Woman's Body* (London: Harrington Park Press, 1992), pp. 157–92.

37. See Lee Daniels, "The American Way: Blame a Black Man," *Emerge*, February 1995, pp. 60–66; Joe Feagin and Hernán Vera, *White Racism* (New York: Routledge, 1995), ch. 4; Caryl Rivers, *Slick Spins and Fractured Facts* (New York: Columbia University Press, 1996), ch. 12; Regina Brett, "Urban Myth of Race Attacks Lives on After Stories Die," *Houston Chronicle*, 28 November 1995, p. 2.

38. John McCormick, "Why Parents Kill," *Newsweek*, 14 November 1994, pp. 27–34; Rick Bragg, "Smith Defense Portrays a Life of 'Chaos'," *New York Times*, 27 July 1995, p. A14. See also David Smith, with Carol Calef, *Beyond All Reason* (New York: Kensington, 1995).

39. Jennifer Gonnerman, "Omissions of Guilt," *In These Times*, 21 August 1995, pp. 9–10; Robert Scheer, "The River of Hypocrisy Runs Wide and Deep," *Los Angeles*

Times, 1 August 1995, p. B9. See also George Rekers, *Susan Smith: Victim or Murderer?* (Lakewood, CO: Glenbridge, 1995).

40. Margaret Kearney, Sheigla Murphy, and Marsha Rosenbaum, "Mothering on Crack Cocaine," *Social Science and Medicine* 38 (1994): 351–61; Marsha Rosenbaum, Sheigla Murphy et al., "Women and Crack," in A. Treback and K. Zeese, eds., *Drug Prohibition and the Conscience of Nations* (Washington, DC: Drug Policy Foundation, 1990), pp. 69–72. See also Loren Siegel, "The Pregnancy Police Fight the War on Drugs," in C. Reinarman and H. Levine, eds., *Crack in America* (Berkeley: University of California Press, 1997), pp. 229–48; Margaret Kearney, Sheigla Murphy, and Marsha Rosenbaum, "Learning by Losing," *Qualitative Health Research* 4 (1994): 142–62; Stephen Kandall, *Substance and Shadow* (Cambridge, MA: Harvard University Press, 1996); Drew Humphries, "Crack Mothers at 6," *Violence Against Women* 4 (1998): 45–61.

41. For an alternate but compatible interpretation of contemporary stories about homicidal mothers see Annalee Newitz, "Murdering Mothers," in M. Ladd-Taylor and L. Umansky, eds., *"Bad" Mothers* (New York: New York University Press, 1998), pp. 334–55.

42. Michael Shapiro, "The Lives We Would Like to Set Right," *Columbia Journalism Review* (November 1996): 45–48.

43. Unsigned editorial, "Courting Fairness for Voters," *New York Daily News*, 15 June 1996, p. 16; Jorge Fitz-Gibbon, "Ex-Foster Mom's Tears at Death Photos" and "Mom Blames Hubby in Girl's Slay," *New York Daily News*, 3 May and 4 May 1996, pp. 11 and 5, respectively; Douglas Martin, "Children Testify in Murder Trial of Mother," *New York Times*, 30 April 1996, p. B5. The other murders: Chuck Sudetic, "Mother Charged in Assault of Girl Found with Burns," *New York Times*, 3 January 1996, p. B2; Randy Kennedy, "Mother Kills Children and Herself After Family Dispute," *New York Times*, 21 January, 1996, p. A26.

44. Kennedy, "Mother Kills Children."

45. U.S. Department of Health and Human Services news release, 18 September 1996.

46. Steve Calvin, "First Came Legal Abortions, Then Rise in Child Abuse," *Minneapolis Star–Tribune*, 2 October 1996, p. A15.

47. NCPCA figures from Douglas Besharov, with Jacob Dembosky, "Child Abuse: Threat or Menace?" *Slate*, 3 October 1996 (online).

48. U.S. Department of Health and Human Services news release, 18 September 1996; Barbara Vobejda, "HHS Study Finds Sharp Rise in Child Abuse," *Washington Post*, 19 September 1996, p. A8; "Child Abuse Has Become a Human Rights Dilemma in U.S.," *Dallas Morning News*, 20 September 1996, p. A24. Critique of Shalala study: Besharov, "Child Abuse: Threat or Menace?" and see a follow-up exchange, "Fact Abuse," posted in *Slate*, 23 October 1996.

49. Armin Brott, "When Women Abuse Men: It's Far More Widespread Than People Think," *Washington Post*, 28 December 1993, p. C5; "Husbands Are Battered as Often as Wives," *USA Today*, 23 June 1994, p. D8; Wendy McElroy, "The Unfair Sex?" *National Review*, 1 May 1995, p. 74; John Leo, "Things That Go Bump in the Home,"

U.S. News & World Report, 13 May 1996, p. 25; Dennis Byrne, "Men Taking Their Lumps," *Chicago Sun-Times,* 21 May 1998, p. 33.

50. Other examples of misuse of Gelles's research: Katherine Dunn, "Truth Abuse," *New Republic,* 1 August 1994, pp. 16–18; Judith Sherven and James Sniechowsky, "Women Are Responsible, Too," *Los Angeles Times,* 21 June 1994, p. B7; Warren Farrell, "Spouse Abuse: A Two-Way Street," *USA Today,* 29 June 1994, p. A15; John Leo, "Monday Night Political Football," *U.S. News & World Report,* 8 January 1996, p. 21.

51. Richard Gelles, "Violence Toward Men: Fact or Fiction?" paper prepared for the American Medical Association Council on Scientific Affairs, September 1994; James Ledbetter, "Press Clips," *Village Voice,* 21 May 1996, p. 25. Quotes from Richard Gelles, "Domestic Battering," *The Tennessean,* 1 November 1994. For further evidence see Russell Dobash et al., "The Myth of Sexual Symmetry in Marital Violence," *Social Problems* 39 (1992): 71–91; Jack Straton, "The Myth of the 'Battered Husband Syndrome'," *Masculinities* 2 (1994): 79–82; Pam Belluck, "A Woman's Killer Is Likely to Be Her Partner, a Study Finds," *New York Times,* 31 March 1997, p. A12; Karen Peterson, "Partners Unequal in Abuse," *USA Today,* 8 November 1997, p. D1.

52. Larry Elder at KABC radio in Los Angeles was among the talk show hosts who reiterated the claims late in the 1990s.

Chapter Five

1. Glenn Loury, "Unequalized," *New Republic,* 6 April 1998, pp. 10–11; Janet Hook, "Clinton Offers Plan to Close Health Gap," *Los Angeles Times,* 22 February 1998, p. A20; Pam Belluck, "Black Youths' Rate of Suicide Rising Sharply," *New York Times,* 20 March 1998, p. A1. See also David Shaffer et al., "Worsening Suicide Rate in Black Teenagers," *American Journal of Psychiatry* 151 (1994): 1810–12. On my selection and use of statistics see note 2 in the Introduction.

2. Caryl Rivers, *Slick Spins and Fractured Facts* (New York: Columbia University Press, 1996), p. 161; David Krajicek, *Scooped* (New York: Columbia University Press, 1998); Robert Elias, "Official Stories," *Humanist* 54 (1994): 3–8; Bill Kovach, "Opportunity in the Racial Divide," *Nieman Reports* 49 (1995): 2; Franklin Gilliam, Shanto Iyengar et al., "Crime in Black and White," Working Paper, Center for American Politics and Public Policy, UCLA, September 1995; Mark Fitzgerald, "Covering Crime in Black and White," *Editor and Publisher,* 10 September 1994, pp. 12–13; Carey Quan Gelernter, "A Victim's Worth," *Seattle Times,* 28 June 1994, p. E1; Suzan Revah, "Paying More Attention to White Crime Victims," *American Journalism Review* (1995): 10–11; Bruce Shapiro, "One Violent Crime," *Nation,* 3 April 1995, pp. 437, 445–52; Bruce Shapiro, "Unkindest Cut," *New Statesman* 8 (14 April 1995): 23; Gregory Freeman, "Media Bias?" *St. Louis Post-Dispatch,* 14 November 1993, p. B4; Debra Saunders, "Heeding the Ghost of Ophelia," *San Francisco Chronicle,* 4 September, 1995, p. A19.

3. Arnold Barnett, "How Numbers Can Trick You," *Technology Review* 97 (1994): 38–44; Karen Smith, "Tourism Industry Tries to Reduce Visitors' Fears," *Ann Arbor News,* 16 January 1994, p. D5. See also Kim Cobb, "Media May Be Fanning a New

Deadly Crime," *Houston Chronicle*, 18 September 1993, p. A1; Bill Kaczor, "Crimes Against Tourists Worry Florida Officials," *Ann Arbor News*, 24 February 1993, p. A7; James Bernstein, "Violence Threatens to Kill Florida's Winter Vacation Business," 2 November 1993, p. A1.

4. Henry Brownstein, "The Media and the Construction of Random Drug Violence," *Social Justice* 18 (1993): 85–103; and my own analysis of Dennis Hevesi, "Drug Wars Don't Pause to Spare the Innocent," *New York Times*, 22 January 1989, p. A1.

5. Brownstein, "The Media and the Construction." See also Maggie Mulvihill and Joseph Mallia, "Boston Police 'Sorry' for Fatal Mistake," *Boston Herald*, 27 March 1994, p. 1; Joe Hallinan, "Misfires in War on Drugs," *The Plain Dealer*, 26 September 1993, p. A17; Andrew Schneider, "Botched Drug Raid Leaves Deep Distrust," *Arizona Republic*, 14 September 1995, p. A1.

6. Robert Davis and Sam Meddis, "Random Killings Hit a High," *USA Today*, 5 December 1994, p. A1; Richard Moran, "Morning Edition," 18 April 1996. The FBI report was the Uniform Crime Report for 1993.

7. Jill Smolowe, "Danger in the Safety Zone," *Time*, 23 August 1993, pp. 28–33 (quote from issue's cover).

8. Ray Surette, "Predator Criminals As Media Icons," in G. Barak, ed., *Media, Process, and the Social Construction of Crime* (New York: Garland, 1994), pp. 131–58; Philip Jenkins, *Using Murder* (New York: Aldine de Gruyter, 1994), p. 156; Bureau of Justice Statistics, "Highlights from 20 Years of Surveying Crime Victims" (NCJ-144525), Washington, DC, 1993; National Center for Health Statistics, *Vital Statistics of the United States* (reports during early and mid-1990s), Washington, DC; Dave Shiflett, "Crime in the South," *The Oxford American* (Spring 1996): 136–41.

9. Krajicek, *Scooped*, p. 102. On how the news media perpetuates negative images of African Americans see also Mikal Muharrar, "Media Blackface," *Extra*, September 1998, pp. 6–8; Dennis Rome, "Stereotyping by the Media," in C. R. Mann and M. Zatz, eds., *Images of Color, Images of Crime* (Los Angeles: Roxbury, 1998), pp. 85–96.

10. Ted Rohrlich and Frederic Tulsky, "Not All L.A. Murders Are Equal," *Los Angeles Times*, 3 December 1996, pp. A1, 14–15; Gelernter, "Victim's Worth"; Shapiro, "One Violent Crime"; Gilliam, et al., "Crime in Black and White"; Jerome Skolnick, "Police Accountability and the Media," *American Bar Foundation Research Journal* (1984): 521–57; Renée Kasinsky, "Patrolling the Facts," in Barak, ed., *Media, Process, and the Social Construction of Crime*, pp. 203–34; Zhongdang Pan and Gerald Kosicki, "Assessing News Media Influences on Whites' Race Policy Preferences," *Communication Research* 23 (1996): 147–79. See also Van Jones, "Lessons from a Killing," *Extra*, May 1998, pp. 23–24.

11. Helen Benedict, *Virgin or Vamp: How the Press Covers Sex Crimes* (New York: Oxford University Press, 1992); Esther Madriz, *Nothing Bad Happens to Good Girls* (Berkeley: University of California Press, 1997), p. 155.

12. Scott Harris, "The Color of News," *Los Angeles Times*, 31 December 1995, p. B1. See also David Pritchard, "Race, Homicide and Newspapers," *Journalism Quarterly* 62 (1985): 500–507.

13. See Gilliam, et al., "Crime in Black and White."

14. Shaw made the comments during conversations in 1998. See also his "Minorites and the Press," *Los Angeles Times*, 11 December 1990.

15. Richard Goldstein, "What's Race Got to Do With It?" *Village Voice*, 9 April 1996, pp. 18–19.

16. Ibid. My depiction of the reporting relies on Goldstein's analysis of the *New York Post* and other outlets, coupled with my own review of articles on the shooting and trial published in the *New York Times*, *Newsday*, and *New York Daily News*.

17. See also Rebecca Alpert, "Coming Out of the Closet as Politically Correct," *Tikkun* 11 (March 1996): 61–63.

18. Joe Feagin and Hernán Vera, *White Racism* (New York: Routledge, 1995), p. 79.

19. Quoted in Christopher J. Farley, "Enforcing Correctness," *Time*, 7 February 1994, p. 37.

20. Ibid.; A. M. Rosenthal, "Bigots and Journalists," *New York Times*, 4 February 1994, p. A23. See also James R. Gaines, "To Our Readers," *Time*, 28 February 1994, in which the magazine's managing editor defends the original piece and argues against another set of critics: those who claim that the media devote too much space to black–Jewish conflicts. In Gaines's view, "there could be no more significant conflict than the one between Jewish and black people" (p. 11).

21. Steven Holmes, "Howard University Is Stung by Portrayal as Anti-Semitic," *New York Times*, 21 April 1994, p. A1; Otesa Middleton and Larry Brown, "Howard University Is No Bastion of Anti-Semitism," *Los Angeles Times*, 29 May 1994, p. M3; Christopher Shea, "Howard University Condemns Bigotry and Attacks on Its Reputation," *Chronicle of Higher Education*, 27 April 1994, p. A32. For a description of Muhammad's visit see also Michael Kelly, "Howard's End," *New Republic*, 21 March 1994, pp. 11–12. On other of Howard's woes at the time: Joye Mercer and Julie Nicklin, "Howard University Lays Off 400," *Chronicle of Higher Education*, 16 November 1994, p. A28.

22. Abby Goodnough, "Organizers Press on with Plan for Million Youth March," *New York Times*, 8 August 1998, p. A19; Bob Herbert, "The Hate Virus," *New York Times*, 10 August 1998, p. A19 (contains anti-Semitic quotes); Nat Hentoff, "The Return of Khalid Muhammad," *Village Voice*, 26 November 1996, p. 10 (other quotes).

23. Hentoff, "Return of Khalid Muhammad" (contains Edwards quote); Letty Cottin Pogrebin, "Five Questions for My African-American Friends," *Common Quest* 1 (Spring 1996): 32–34; Jonathan Kaufman, "Not an Anti-Semitic March," *Common Quest* 1 (Spring 1996): 35–36.

24. *Newsweek*, 2 September 1996 (Farrakhan quote), p. 19; Susan Douglas, "The Framing of Race," *Progressive*, December 1995, p. 19 (Barnes quote). Information on Terry and Wildmon from Skipp Porteous, *Anti-Semitism: Its Prevalence Within the Christian Right* (Great Barrington, MA: Institute for First Amendment Studies, 1994). On Buchanan's anti-Semitism see David Frum, *What's Right* (New York: Basic Books, 1996); Michael Lind, *Up from Conservatism* (New York: Free Press, 1996).

25. James Baldwin, "Negroes Are Anti-Semitic Because They're Anti-White" (reprinted essay from 1967), in *The Price of the Ticket: Collected Nonfiction* (New York: St. Martin's Press, 1985), pp. 425–33; Hubert G. Locke, *The Black Anti-Semitism Controversy* (Selinsgrove, PA: Susquehanna University Press, 1994). See also Doris Wilkinson,

"Anti-Semitism and African Americans," *Society* (September, 1994): 47–50; Paul Berman, "The Other and the Almost the Same," *Society* (September 1994): 4–16; Jonathan Rieder, "Beyond Frenzy and Accusation," *Common Quest* 1 (Spring 1996): 2–6.

26. Associated Press, "Report Finds Rise in Campus Anti-Semitism," *New York Times*, 3 February 1993, p. A13.

27. Ibid.

28. Clyde Haberman, "Campus Newspaper's Excursion into a Bitter Free-Speech Debate," *New York Times*, 1 November 1995, p. B3.

29. "Slurs in Student Newspaper Prompt Protests in Wisconsin," *Chronicle of Higher Education*, 24 November 1995, p. A6. See also "North Carolina Fraternity Council Elects Author of Lewd Memo," *Chronicle of Higher Education*, 8 December 1995, p. A33. For an example of strong reaction to the column at Columbia see Nat Hentoff, "College Degrees in Anti-Semitism?" *Village Voice*, 5 December 1995, p. 12, and Nat Hentoff, "Hentoff v. Wilkins," *Washington Post*, 18 May 1996, p. A19. Hentoff posits that prestigious universities are awarding "advanced degrees in anti-Semitism."

30. "Thousands Protest at Penn State over Racist Graffiti," *Chronicle of Higher Education*, 24 November 1995, p. A7; "Students Rally Against Racism at Dartmouth College," *Chronicle of Higher Education*, 16 February 1996, p. A4.

31. Jack Levin and Jack McDevitt, "The Research Needed to Understand Hate Crime," *Chronicle of Higher Education*, 4 August 1995, p. B1.

32. Marna Walthall, "Jonesboro Teacher Says Rap Music, School Killings May Be Linked," *Dallas Morning News*, 17 June 1998, p. A5; Timothy Egan, "From Adolescent Angst to Shooting Up Schools," *New York Times*, 14 June 1998, pp. A1, 20; ABC, "World News Tonight," 16 June 1998.

33. Steve Hochman, "Rap Artist Is Jailed over Anti-Police Lyrics," *Los Angeles Times*, 4 March 1998, p. A3; Benjamin Adair, "Jailhouse Rap," *L.A. Weekly*, 13 March 1998, p. 18 (contains lyrics); Steve Hochman, "A Rapper's Risky Challenge," *Los Angeles Times*, 21 February 1998, pp. F1, 20.

34. Investment boycotts: Eric Boehlert, "Culture Skirmishes," *Rolling Stone*, 21 August 1997, pp. 29, 32; David Hinckley, "Rap Takes the Rap for Our Real Problems," *New York Daily News*, 4 June 1996, p. 33 ("civilization" quote). Tucker and Bennett: Judith Weinraub, "Delores Tucker, Gangsta Buster," *Washington Post*, 29 November 1995, C1 (contains Tucker quote); William Bennett, "Reflections on the Moynihan Report," *American Enterprise*, January 1995, pp. 28–32; Frank Rich, "Hypocrite Hit Parade," *New York Times*, 13 December 1995, p. A23; Peter Range, "MM Interview: William J. Bennett," *Modern Maturity* (March 1995): 26–30.

35. Nelson George, *Buppies, B-Boys, Baps, and Bohos: Notes on Post-Soul Black Culture* (New York: HarperCollins, 1992), p. 156; Kevin Chappell, "What's Wrong (and Right) About Black Music," *Ebony*, September 1995, p. 25. For an example of the collaboration that was used for fundraising see William Bennett, Joe Lierberman, and C. DeLores Tucker, "Rap Rubbish," *USA Today*, 6 June 1996, p. A13, which ends with a toll-free telephone number. Those of us who dialed it got a recording that invited us to press 1 for information about the dangers of rap music, 2 for literature on a flat-rate tax proposal, or 3 to contribute money to Empower America. On political alliances against

rap see Leola Johnson, "Silencing Gangsta Rap," *Temple Political & Civil Rights Law Review* (October, 1993): no pages listed.

36. George F. Will, "America's Slide into the Sewer," *Newsweek,* 30 July 1990, p. 64; Henry Louis Gates, Jr., "2 Live Crew, Decoded," *New York Times,* 19 June 1990, p. A23. "Laughing" quote in Kimberlé Williams Crenshaw, "Beyond Racism and Misogyny," in M. Matusda et al., *Words That Wound* (Boulder, CO: Westview Press, 1993), pp. 111–32. See also James Jones, "Gangsta Rap Reflects an Urban Jungle," *USA Today,* 2 January 1991, p. D13; Hinckley, "Rap Takes the Rap," p. 33; Nelson George, *Hip Hop America* (New York: Viking, 1998).

37. Crenshaw, "Beyond Racism." On the extent of sexism in rap and internal dialogues among rappers about the matter see Tricia Rose, *Black Noise* (Hanover, NH: Weslyan University Press, 1994), and Tricia Rose's review of *A Sister Without Sisters* by Sister Souljah, *Women's Review of Books,* June 1995, pp. 21–22. On overt homophobia and covert homoeroticism in rap see Touré, "Hiphop's Closet," *Village Voice,* 27 August 1996, pp. 59, 66. On the racist subtext in attacks on rap see Amy Binder, "Constructing racial rhetoric," *American Sociological Review* 58 (1993): 753–67; Tricia Rose, "Rap Music and the Demonization of Young Black Males," *USA Today Magazine,* May 1994, pp. 35–36; Jon Pareles, "On Rap Symbolism and Fear," *New York Times,* 2 February 1992, p. B1; Todd Boyd, "Woodstock Was Whitestock," *Chicago Tribune,* 28 August 1994, p. 36.

38. On Dole's remarks see Linda Stasi's column, *New York Daily News,* 5 June 1995, p. 3; "Dole Blasts 'Depravity' in Film, Music," *Facts on File World News Digest,* 8 June 1995.

39. Edward G. Armstrong, "The Rhetoric of Violence in Rap and Country Music," *Sociological Inquiry* 63 (1993): 64–83; John Hamerlinck, "Killing Women: A Pop-Music Tradition," *Humanist* 55 (1995): 23.

40. Milwaukee and Texas incidents: Rogers Worthington, "Gangsta Rap Blamed for Cop's Killing," *Chicago Tribune,* 10 September 1994, p. 4; Elizabeth Sanger, "Change of Venue for Gangsta Rap Debate," *Newsday,* 28 June 1995, p. 31; Chuck Philips, "Texas Death Renews Debate over Violent Rap Lyrics," *Los Angeles Times,* 17 September 1992, p. A1; Jon Pareles, "Tupac Shakur, 25, Rap Performer Who Personified Violence, Dies," *New York Times,* 14 September 1996, pp. A1, 34. Other headline: David Van Biema, "'What Goes 'Round . . .' ," *Time,* 23 September 1996, p. 40. Tucker continued to take on Shakur after his death: Johnnie Roberts, "Grabbing at a Dead Star," *Newsweek,* 1 September 1997, p. 48.

41. Ford and Cash songs quoted in Armstrong, "Rhetoric of Violence."

42. Quoted in "Obituary: Tupac Shakur," *The Economist,* 21 September 1996.

43. Songs quoted in Christopher Farley, "From the Driver's Side," *Time,* 30 September 1996, p. 70; Donnell Alexander, "Do Thug Niggaz Go to Heaven?" *Village Voice,* 20 September 1996, p. 51.

44. Worthington, "Gangsta Rap"; Natasha Stovall, "Death Row," *Village Voice,* 24 September 1996, pp. 29–30 (contains definition of "THUG LIFE"); Chuck Philips, "Q & A with Tupac Shakur," *Los Angeles Times,* 25 October 1995, p. F1. Songs quoted in Armstrong, "Rhetoric of Violence." Pereles quote from "Tupac Shakur." On rap being

blamed see also Jon Pareles, "On Rap, Symbolism and Fear," *New York Times*, 2 February 1992, p. B1.

45. Kenneth Carroll, "A Rap Artist's Squandered Gift," *Washington Post* National Edition, 30 September 1996, p. 25; Ernest Hardy, "Do Thug Niggaz Go to Heaven," *L.A. Weekly*, 20 September 1996, p. 51. On the content and purposes of gangsta rap see also Eric Watts, "Gangsta Rap as Cultural Commodity," *Communication Studies* 48 (1997): 42–58.

46. "All Eyes on Him," *Vibe*, February 1996.

47. Ralph Ellison, *Invisible Man* (New York: Random House, 1952), p. 1.

Chapter Six

1. On the importance and persistence of combined fearmongering by presidents and the media about drugs see William Elwood, *Rhetoric in the War on Drugs* (Westport, CT: Praeger, 1994), and Eva Bertram et al., *Drug War Politics* (Berkeley: University of California Press, 1996).

2. Bertram et al., *Drug War Politics*, p. 107; Glenn Frankel, "The Longest War," *Washington Post* National Edition, 7 July 1997, pp. 6–8; Mack Reed, "Teenage Addiction Escalates," *Los Angeles Times*, 22 September 1996, p. B1; Christopher Wren, "At Drug Summit, Clinton Asks Nations to Set Aside Blame," *New York Times*, 9 June 1998, p. A6.

3. Drug problem statistic: Daniel Greenfield, *Prescription Drug Abuse and Dependence* (Springfield, IL: Charles Thomas, 1994); physician statistic: Dan Weikel, "Prescription Fraud," *Los Angeles Times*, 18 August 1996, p. A1; DEA: ABC, "Primetime Live," 27 May 1993; budget statistic: "When It Comes to Drugs, Legal Doesn't Mean Safe," *Los Angeles Times*, 25 August 1996, p. M4. See also Christopher Wren, "Many Women 60 and Older Abuse Alcohol and Prescribed Drugs," *New York Times*, 5 June 1998, p. A10.

4. Edward Jay Epstein, *Agency of Fear* (London and New York: Verso, 1990), pp. 61, 165–72.

5. Elwood, *Rhetoric in the War on Drugs*, chs. 2 and 3 (Reagan quote on p. 45); Bertram et al., *Drug War Politics*, pp. 110–16; William Gonzenbach, "A Time-Series Analysis of the Drug Issue," *International Journal of Public Opinion Research* 4 (1992): 126–47.

6. David Fan, "News Media Framing Sets Public Opinion That Drugs Is the Country's Most Important Problem," *Substance Use and Misuse* 31 (1996): 1413–21.

7. Availability heuristic: Russell Eisenman, "Belief That Drug Usage in the U.S. Is Increasing When It Is Really Decreasing," *Bulletin of the Psychonomic Society* 31 (1993): 249–52; Karen Frost, Erica Frank et al., "Relative Risk in the News Media," *American Journal of Public Health* 87 (1997): 842–45. Disjuncture between drug-abuse patterns and coverage: Craig Reinarman and Harry Levine, "The Crack Attack," in C. Reinarman and H. Levine, eds., *Crack in America* (Berkeley: University of California Press, 1997), pp. 18–51; Jimmie Reeves and Richard Campbell, *Cracked Coverage* (Durham, NC:

Duke University Press, 1994), see esp. ch. 9; James Orcutt and J. B. Turner, "Shocking Numbers and Graphic Accounts," *Social Problems* 40 (1993): 190–206. Bush quote: Elwood, *Rhetoric in the War on Drugs,* p. 41.

8. Elwood, *Rhetoric in the War on Drugs,* pp. 40–42, 71–72 (contains Dowd quote); Reinarman and Levine, "Crack Attack."

9. Reinarman and Levine, "Crack Attack"; Elliott Currie, *Reckoning: Drugs, the Cities, and the American Future* (New York: Hill & Wang, 1993); Jeff Leen, "A Shot in the Dark on Drug Use?" *Washington Post* National Edition, 12 January 1998, pp. 32–33; Elwood, *Rhetoric in the War on Drugs,* p. 39 (contains addiction statistics).

10. Peter Kwong, *The New Chinatown* (New York: Hill & Wang, 1996); Ed Knipe, *Culture, Society and Drugs* (Prospect Heights, IL: Waveland Press, 1995), chs. 6 and 10; H. Wayne Morgan, *Drugs in America* (Syracuse, NY: Syracuse University Press, 1981), ch. 4; Thomas Szasz, *Ceremonial Chemistry* (New York: Anchor, 1974) (contains Gompers quote).

11. Diana Gordon, *The Return of the Dangerous Classes* (New York: Norton, 1994), p. 25.

12. Reeves and Campbell, *Cracked Coverage*; Reinarman and Levine, "Crack Attack," pp. 21–22.

13. Michael Tonry, *Malign Neglect* (New York: Oxford University Press, 1995); Reinarman and Levine, eds., *Crack in America,* chs. 11 and 13; Natalie Hopkinson, "Crack Case Puts Fairness on Trial," *Atlanta Journal and Constitution,* 27 February 1996, p. 1; Michael Massing, "Crime and Drugs: The New Myths," *New York Review of Books,* 1 February 1996, pp. 16–20; Carl Rowan, "Racism in Drug Sentencing Laws Puts Black America Behind Bars," *Chicago Sun–Times,* 10 November 1995; Maxine Waters, "Confronting the Realities of Public Policy Gone Wrong," *Tikkun* 12 (September 1997): 31–32.

14. National Public Radio, "Morning Edition," 19 September 1996; Walter Shapiro, "The Drug Issue," *USA Today,* 18 September 1996, p. A2; D. James Romero, "Election '96: The Young and the Restless," *Los Angeles Times,* 24 October 1996, p. E1. See also David Savage, "Clinton Not to Blame for Rise in Teen Drug Use, Experts Say," *Los Angeles Times,* 18 September 1996, p. A5.

15. Kristina Sauerwein and Aisha Sultan, "Baby Boomers Tolerate Teen Drug Use," *St. Louis Post–Dispatch,* 15 September 1996, p. D1.

16. Jane Daugherty, "Boomers Come Face-to-Face with Kids' Drug Abuse," *Detroit News,* 27 February 1996. CBS report cited in Reeves and Campbell, *Cracked Coverage,* p. 150. See also Joseph A. Califano, "Dangerous Indifference to Drugs," *Washington Post,* 23 September 1996, p. A19.

17. ABC, "20/20," 14 March 1997.

18. Statistics about parents: Christopher Wren, "Marijuana Use by Youths Continues to Rise," *New York Times,* 20 February 1996, p. A11; ABC News Special, "Straight Talk About Drugs," 12 March 1997.

19. "Drug Use by Teen-Agers," *New York Times,* 23 August 1996, p. A26.

20. ABC, "Good Morning America," 5 March 1997.

21. See Leslie Savan, "ABC Fries," *Village Voice,* 18 March 1997, pp. 34–35. Clinton quote from ABC, "Good Morning America," 31 March 1997.

22. Examples of the stories on mothers: ABC, "Good Morning America," 3 March and 7 March 1997; ABC, "World News Tonight," 3 March and 25 March 1997. "Grace Under Fire" episode aired 14 March 1997.

23. Critics: Jennifer Nix, "Worse-Than-Useless Anti-Drug Propaganda?" *Salon*, 12 March 1997 (online); Jacob Weisberg, "This Is Your Network on Drugs," *Slate*, 15 March 1997; Savan, "ABC Fries"; Robert Scheer, "Fighting Abuse Only When It Doesn't Pay," *Los Angeles Times*, 11 March 1997. "Popsicle" quote from ABC, "Good Morning America," 3 March 1997; ABC, "Turning Point," 6 March 1997 (contains "allure" quote). See also stories on ABC, "Good Morning America," 4 March 1997, and ABC, "World News Tonight," 17 March 1997.

24. Criticism of ABC: Weisberg, "This Is Your Network"; Savan, "ABC Fries." Headlines cited in Jack Shafer, "Smack Happy," *Slate*, 19 July 1996. ABC's "Turning Point" aired 6 March 1997. "Stemming the Flow on the Heroin Trail," *The Age* (Melbourne, Australia), 2 August 1997 (contains statistic).

25. Shafer, "Smack Happy" (contains *Newsweek* citation); Brent Staples, "Closing in on Death," *New York Times*, 26 May 1997, p. A22; Ike Flores, "Heroin Has Its Deadly Hooks in Teens Across the Nation," *USA Today*, 9 October 1996, p. A4. Other quotes from Mike Miles, "Another Anti-Teen Fix," *Extra*, November–December 1996, pp. 15–17.

26. ABC News, "Turning Point," 6 March 1997; ABC, "World News Tonight," 17 June 1996.

27. Bruce Johnson, Andrew Golub, and Jeffrey Fagan, "Careers in Crack, Drug Use, Drug Distribution, and Nondrug Criminality," *Crime and Delinquency* 41 (July 1995): 275–95; Mike Males and Faye Docuyanan, "The Return of Reefer Madness," *Progressive*, May 1996, pp. 26–29; Mike Males, "Another Anti-Teen Fix," *Extra*, November–December 1996, pp. 15–17; Michael Massing, "Heroin and Red Herrings," *New York Times*, 6 December 1997, p. A21.

28. Massing, "Crime and Drugs."

29. Christopher Wren, "Drugged Look in Fashion Ads Angers Clinton," *New York Times*, 22 May 1997, p. A12. Comparison statistics: Males, "Another Anti-Teen Fix."

30. CNN, "Prime News," 13 August 1997; Dina Bass, "Poll Finds Sharp Rise in Drug Use Among Youngsters," *Los Angeles Times*, 14 August 1997, p. A4; NBC, "Nightly News," 13 August 1997. See also ABC "This Week," 17 August 1997.

31. Household survey: Eric Lekus, "Use of Illegal Drugs Declined for Adolescents in 1996," *Baltimore Sun*, 7 August 1997, p. A1; CNN, "Prime News," 13 August 1997. See also Christopher Wren, "Survey Suggests Leveling Off in Use of Drugs by Students," *New York Times*, 21 December 1997, p. A12.

32. Christopher Wren, "Drugs Common in Schools, Survey Says," *New York Times*, 9 September 1997, p. A12.

33. On fluctuations and trends see Barry Glassner and Julia Loughlin, *Drugs and Crime in Adolescent Worlds* (New York: St. Martin's Press, 1987); Michael Massing, "Reefer Madness Strikes Again," *New York Times*, 27 August 1996, p. A17; Walter Shapiro, "The Drug Issue," *USA Today*, 18 September 1996, p. A2; Wren, "Survey Suggests Leveling Off"; Karen Peterson, "Survey: Teen Drug Use Declines," *USA Today*, 19 June 1998, p. A6. Specific statistics are culled from annual summaries of the National

Household Survey on Drug Abuse and the National College Health Risk Behavior Survey (conducted by the Centers for Disease Control).

34. Longitudinal study: Jerald Bachman, Katherine Wadsworth et al., *Drug Use in Young Adulthood* (Mahwah, NJ: Lawrence Erlbaum, 1997). See also Oscar Bukstein, *Adolescent Substance Abuse* (New York: Wiley, 1995), pp. 69–71.

35. Information about Koontz (here and following section) from "A Crack in the All-American Dream," *Pittsburgh Post-Gazette*, 1 December 1996, p. E1; "Man Goes on Trial in Slaying of Homecoming Queen," Associated Press, 31 March 1996; Peter Wilkinson, "Who Killed the Homecoming Queen?" *Rolling Stone*, 23 January 1997, pp. 54–62.

36. Shafer, "Smack Happy" ("resurgence" quote). Cobain overdose: see Arthur Santana and Charles Hall, "Banned 'Date Rape' Drug Is Linked to Six Assaults," *Washington Post*, 14 June 1996, p. B1; Laura Evenson and Sam Whiting, "Heroin's in Fashion and Death Statistics Prove It," *San Francisco Chronicle*, 30 July 1996, p. A1 ("couldn't kick" claim).

37. ER statistics: Mike Males, *The Scapegoat Generation* (Monroe, ME: Common Courage Press, 1996), ch. 6. See also Pete Stark, "Increased Regulations of Prescription Drugs Is Necessary," in D. Bender and B. Leone, eds., *Drug Abuse: Opposing Viewpoints* (San Diego: Greenhaven Press, 1994), pp. 142–49.

38. Gary Logan, "Stress and Access Make Doctors Vulnerable," *Washington Post*, 3 September 1996, p. Z11; National Public Radio, "Morning Edition," 28 January 1997.

39. Cynthia Cotts, "The Pushers in the Suites," *Nation*, 31 August 1992, pp. 208–11; Tracy Weber, "Tarnishing the Golden Years with Addiction," *Los Angeles Times*, 20 December 1996, p. A1; 2.8 million statistic: Wren, "Many Women"; Robert McCarthy, "It Takes More Than a Phone Call to Manage Demand," *Business and Health* 15 (May 1997): 36–40.

40. See Celia Moore, "Prozac Fact Sheet," *Ms.*, July 1997, p. 65; Elizabeth Ettorre and Elianne Riska, *Gendered Moods* (New York: Routledge, 1995).

41. PAC figure from the Federal Election Commission; other information from Cotts, "Pushers in the Suites."

42. Helen Thorpe, "A New Low," *Texas Monthly*, September 1995, p. 88; Mireya Navarro, "In South, Drug Abusers Turn to a Smuggled Sedative," *New York Times*, 9 December 1995, p. A6; Tom Masland, "Bootlegged Drugs Hit Africa Hard," *Chicago Tribune*, 31 July 1988, p. 21.

43. Julie Hirschfeld, "Rape Is Only Thing That This Drug Is For," *St. Louis Post-Dispatch*, 17 July 1996, p. B5 (contains Biden quote); Vicky Edwards, "Wake Up," *Chicago Tribune*, 22 October 1996, p. 3; David Kidwell and Connie Piloto, "Parents, Officials Are Alarmed over Sedative's Use," *Dallas Morning News*, 18 February 1996, p. A12 (contains "mightiest" quote). For another Mickey Finn reference see Carol M. Miller, "Forget Me Pill," *St. Petersburg Times*, 17 June 1996, p. B1.

44. Julio Laboy, "Police Suspect Illegal Sedative Used in Date Rapes," *Dallas Morning News*, 17 December 1995, p. A40 ("lots of" quote); Tim Friend, "Date-Rape Drug," *USA Today*, 20 June 1996, p. A1. For a story that included a correction see CNN, 15 June 1996.

45. Karla Haworth, "The Growing Popularity of a New Drug Alarms Health Educators," *Chronicle of Higher Education*, 10 July 1998, pp. A31–32; additional information provided by Hoffmann-LaRoche. (Testing was done by El Sohly Laboratories, a forensic toxicology facility certified by the National Institute of Drug Abuse.)

46. Dan Weikel, "Prescription for an Epidemic," *Los Angeles Times*, 19 August 1996, p. A10. Statistics are from Hoffmann-LaRoche; Kathleen Day, "Countering Ill Effects of an Abused Drug," *Washington Post*, 2 November 1996, p. H1; Tamara Henry and Carrie Hedges, "Date-Rape Drug Target of New Law," *USA Today*, 14 October 1996, p. A1.

47. Ann Scales, "Dole Trumpets Antidrug Slogan," *Boston Globe*, 19 September 1996, p. A26; Lance Morrow, "Kids and Pot," *Time*, 9 December 1996, p. 26; "Clinton OKs Penalties for 'Date-Rape' Drug," *Baltimore Sun*, 14 October 1996, p. A3; "Date-Rape Pill Law Signed," Associated Press, 14 October 1996.

48. Studies: Mary Koss and S. L. Cook, "Finding the Facts," in R. J. Gelles, ed., *Current Controversies on Family Violence* (Newbury Park, CA: Sage, 1993), pp. 104–19; Diana Russell, *Sexual Exploitation* (Beverly Hills, CA: Sage, 1984); Marshall Clinard and Robert Meier, *Deviant Behavior* (Ft. Worth, TX: Harcourt Brace, 1995), pp. 167–68; Caryl Rivers, *Slick Spins, Fractured Facts* (New York: Columbia University Press, 1996), pp. 130–31. Critics: Neil Gilbert, "The Phantom Epidemic of Sexual Assault," *The Public Interest* 103 (1991): 54–65; Katie Roiphe, *The Morning After: Sex, Fear, and Feminism on Campus* (Boston: Little, Brown, 1993).

49. Anita Manning, "Clemson Case Shows Prosecution Difficulties," *USA Today*, 29 October 1996, p. D2; Nicole Peradotto, "A Little Pill That Brings Devastating Consequences," *Buffalo News*, 14 August 1996, p. C1.

50. Ilsa Lottes and Martin Weinberg, "Sexual Coercion Among University Students," *Journal of Sex Research* 34 (1997): 67–76; Koss and Cook, "Finding the Facts." Commonplace date rape was not entirely ignored by the media. See, e.g., a segment on ABC, "Good Morning America," 14 November 1997.

51. John Carpenter, "Warning on Date-Rape Drugs," *Chicago Sun-Times*, 14 August 1997, p. 1; ABC, "Good Morning America," 12 September 1996. For other examples see Cindy Horswell, "Among Claims for 'Date-Rape Drug' Is a New One," *Houston Chronicle*, 15 September 1996, p. 1; CNN, "Impact," 22 June 1997.

Chapter Seven

1. Susan Sontag, *AIDS and Its Metaphors* (New York: Farrar, Straus & Giroux, 1989), p. 14.

2. I do not use the term *metaphoric* to refer to the agonizing symptoms that sufferers endure, but rather to how the illnesses that those symptoms are said to constitute are put to use in political and social discourse. Nor do I intend to suggest, by virtue of my assessment of published studies, that future research will not support what currently appear to be unlikely theories about these ailments.

3. See Arthur Kleinman, *Social Origins of Distress and Disease* (New Haven: Yale University Press, 1986); Norma Ware and Arthur Kleinman, "Culture and Somatic Experience," *Psychosomatic Medicine* 54 (1992): 546–60; Abba Terr, "Clinical Ecology," *Journal*

of Allergy and Clinical Immunology 79 (1987): 423–26,; Tom Lutz, *American Nervousness* (Ithaca, NY: Cornell University Press, 1991); Simon Wessely, "The History of Chronic Fatigue Syndrome," in S. Straus, ed., *Chronic Fatigue Syndrome* (New York: Marcel Dekker, 1994), pp. 3–44; and Susan Abbey and Paul Garfinkel, "Neurasthenia and Chronic Fatigue Syndrome," *American Journal of Psychiatry* 148 (1991): 1638–46.

4. Jean Baudrillard, *The Gulf War Did Not Take Place* (Bloomington: Indiana University Press, 1995), pp. 62, 68; John R. MacArthur, *Lapdogs for the Pentagon Second Front: Censorship and Propaganda in the Gulf War* (New York: Hill & Wang, 1992); George Gerbner, "Persian Gulf War, the Movie," in H. Mowlana et al., eds., *Triumph of the Image* (Boulder, CO: Westview Press, 1992), pp. 243–65; PBS, "Frontline: The War We Left Behind," 29 October 1991; Eliot Cohen, "The Mystique of U.S. Air Power," *Foreign Affairs* 73 (1994): 11–29.

5. Lauren Rabinovitz and Susan Jeffords, "Introduction," in L. Rabinovitz and S. Jeffords, eds., *Seeing Through the Media* (New Brunswick, NJ: Rutgers University Press, 1994), pp. 1–17; Alicia Munday, Arthur E. Rowse, and Ana Arana, "Is the Press Any Match for Powerhouse P.R.?" *Columbia Journalism Review* 31 (1992): 27–34; Tara Parker-Pope, "Hill and Knowlton Polishes Its Own Image," *Wall Street Journal*, 19 February 1997, pp. B1, 8.

6. Arthur E. Rowse, "Lapdogs for the Pentagon," *Progressive* 56 (1 July 1992): 38; PBS, "Frontline: The Gulf War," January 1996.

7. PBS, "Frontline: The Gulf War," January 1996; Sandra Moriarty and David Shaw, "An Antiseptic War," *News Photographer* 50 (April 1995): 4–9; Elaine Showalter, *Hystories: Hysterical Epidemics and Modern Media* (New York: Columbia University Press, 1997), ch. 9 ("bleak" quote on p. 140).

8. Philip Shenon, "Two Studies Seem to Back Veterans Who Trace Illnesses to Gulf War," *New York Times*, 26 November 1996, pp. A1, 10; Robert Haley et al., "Is There a Gulf-War Syndome?" and "Self-Reported Exposure to Neurotoxic Chemical-Combinations in the Gulf War," *Journal of the American Medical Association* 277 (1997): 215–22 and 231–37; Seymour Hersh, *Against All Enemies* (New York: Ballantine, 1998).

9. William Lowther, "Mystery Illness and the Gulf War," *Maclean's*, 23 August 1993, pp. 32–33; Gregory Jaynes, "Walking Wounded," *Esquire*, May 1994, pp. 70–76; Michael Fumento, "Gulf War Syndrome and the Press," *Wall Street Journal*, 4 March 1997, p. A18.

10. J. R. Moehringer, "Legacy of Worry," *Los Angeles Times*, 22 November 1995, pp. A3, 27. For another article about babies with GWS see Kenneth Miller, "The Tiny Victims of Desert Storm," *Life*, November 1995, pp. 46–62.

11. Moehringer, "Legacy of Worry." For another example see Christopher Cook and Nancy Ann Jeffrey, "Gulf War Veterans Can't Escape Strange Diseases, Nightmares," *Knight-Ridder Newspapers*, 16 December 1993.

12. David Cowan et al., "The Risk of Birth Defects Among Children of Persian Gulf War Veterans," *New England Journal of Medicine* 336 (1997): 1650–56; Terence Monmaney, "Study Finds No Gulf War Link to Birth Defect Risk," *Los Angeles Times*, 5 June 1997, pp. A1, 27; J. R. Moehringer, "Gulf War Syndrome Feared to Be Contagious," 9 March 1997, pp. A1, 24, 25.

13. Moehringer, "Gulf War Syndrome."

14. CNN, "Defense Chief: 'No Evidence' Gulf War Illness Is Contagious," 10 March 1997; "Medical Professionals Say Gulf War Illness Contagious," Associated Press, 10 March 1997; "Gulf War Ills May Be Contagious," *Roanoke Times*, 10 March 1997, pp. A1, 2. On the transmissibility of GWS see also Showalter, *Hystories*; PBS, "Frontline: Last Battle of the Gulf War," 20 January 1998.

15. See also L. A. McKeown, "A 'Disease' with No Conclusive Evidence," MSNBC, 1997 (Web posted).

16. MacArthur, *Lapdogs for the Pentagon* (contains Rather quotes); Michelle Kendrick, "Kicking the Vietnam Syndrome," in Rabinovitz and Jeffords, eds., *Seeing Through the Media*, pp. 59–76. For an example of an article highly suspicious and critical of the Pentagon see Dennis Bernstein and Thea Kelley, "The Gulf War Comes Home," *Progressive*, March 1995, pp. 30–34.

17. Showalter, *Hystories*, p. 142.

18. For examples in the *New York Times* see Eric Schmitt, "No Proof Is Found Of Chemical Cause For Gulf Illness," 8 January 1997, pp. A1 and C23; Philip Shenon, "Oversight Suggested for Study of Gulf War Ills," 14 November 1996, p. A10; Gina Kolata, "No Rise Found in Death Rates After Gulf War," 14 November 1996, pp. A1, 10 ("leading critics" quotes); Philip Hilts, "Panel Doubts Gulf War 'Syndrome' Is New," 1 January 1996. See also John Ritter, "Report: Military Knew Risks of Gulf War Drugs," *USA Today*, 8 December 1994, p. A3 (includes gas chamber example); and Bernstein and Kelley, "Gulf War Comes Home."

19. See John Kennedy, "The Last Campaign," *George*, April 1997, pp. 108–11; Haley et al., "Is There a Gulf-War Syndrome?" and "Self-Reported Exposure." For a summary of the refutations, see PBS, "Frontline: Last Battle."

20. Kate McKenna, "Missed Story Syndrome," *American Journalism Review* (May 1997): 22–30; Dana Priest, "The Gulf War's Credibility Fallout," *Washington Post* National Edition, 24 November 1996, pp. 8–10; Philip Shenon, "Powell Says He Had No Evidence of Toxic Chemicals in Gulf War," *New York Times*, 3 December 1996, p. A1.

21. Kolata, "No Rise Found"; Joyce Lashof and Joseph Cassells, "Illness Among Gulf War Veterans," *Journal of the American Medical Association* 280 (1998): 1010–11.

22. David Brown, "The Gulf Between 'Syndrome' and Poison Gas," *Washington Post*, 2 January 1997, p. A1.

23. Hersh, *Against All Enemies*; Philip Shenon, "Study Links Memory Loss to Nerve Gas, as in Gulf," *New York Times*, 14 May 1997, p. A12; idem, "On Gulf-Illness Panel, Outlook Begins to Shift," *New York Times*, 19 August 1997, p. A11; idem, "Investigators Find Excerpts of Gulf War Chemical Logs," *New York Times*, 24 October 1997, p. A12; idem, "Bombing Gas Sites May Pose Risk of Gulf War Syndrome," *New York Times*, 11, February 1998, p. A6. "Thanks of a Grateful Nation" first aired 31 May 1998 on Showtime; John Sacret Young, "This Is the 'Thanks' They Get," *Los Angeles Times* television section, 31 May 1998, p. 3; Philip Shenon, "Another Televised Strike Against the Pentagon," *New York Times*, 31 May 1998, p. 34.

24. Gina Kolata, "Stress Study May Hold Clues to Gulf War Illness, Scientists Say," *New York Times*, 28 May 1998, p. A25; PBS, "Frontline: Last Battle." See also Lashof and Cassells, "Illness Among Gulf War Veterans."

25. Michael Haederle, "He Fights So Your Next Breath Won't Make You Sick," *Los Angeles Times*, 5 May 1996, p. E3. Stories connecting Gulf War Syndrome and MCS: Ed Timms and Steve McGonigle, "Gulf War Vets' Ailments Still Stymie Experts," *Dallas Morning News*, 12 December 1993, p. A1; Bernstein and Kelley, "Gulf War Comes Home"; Associated Press, "Medical Professionals"; Jerome Marmorstein, "Getting at the Real Cause of Vets' Ills," op-ed on MSNBC, 1997 (Web posted).

26. "Common Chemicals Sicken Some," Associated Press, 10 February 1995.

27. Michael Castleman, "This Place Makes Me Sick," *Sierra* 78 (1993): 106–19.

28. Terr, "Clinical Ecology," and idem, "Multiple Chemical Sensitivities," *Journal of Allergy and Clinical Immunology* 94 (1994): 362–66; American College of Physicians, "Clinical Ecology," *Annals of Internal Medicine* 111 (1989): 168–78; Donald Black et al., "Environmental Illness," *Journal of the American Medical Association* 264 (1990): 3166–71; A. Kay and M. Lessoff, "Allergy: Conventional and Alternative Concepts," *Clinical and Experimental Allergy* 22, Suppl. 3 (1992): 1–44; Council on Scientific Affairs, "Clinical Ecology," *Journal of the American Medical Association* 268 (1992): 3465–67; John Salvaggio, "Psychological Aspects of 'Environmental Illness'," *Journal of Allergy and Clinical Immunology* 94 (1994): 366–70. Minnesota story: William Souder, "A Fragrant Violation," *Washington Post*, 11 December 1994, pp. F1, 4.

29. Environmental illness: Steve Kroll-Smith and Anthony Ladd, "Environmental Illness and Biomedicine," *Sociological Spectrum* 13 (1993): 7–33; Associated Press, "Common Chemicals."

30. Linda and Bill Bonvie, "Gulf War's Toxic Truth," *Cleveland Plain Dealer*, 27 November 1994.

31. Showalter, *Hystories*, p. 6. See also John Selner et al., "Double-Blind Provocation Chamber Challenges in 20 Patients Presenting with 'MCS'," *Regulatory Toxicology and Pharmacology* 18 (1993): 44–53.

32. Pamela Reed Gibson, "Multiple Chemical Sensitivity, Culture and Delegitimization," *Feminism and Psychology* 7 (1997): 475–93; Steve Kroll-Smith and H. Hugh Floyd, *Bodies in Protest* (New York: New York University Press, 1997), p. 5.

33. Kroll-Smith and Ladd, "Environmental Illness." Research evidence: see, e.g., Terr, "Clinical Ecology"; Black et al., "Environmental Illness"; Ronald Gots, "Multiple Chemical Sensitivities," *Journal of Toxicology: Clinical Toxicology* 33 (1995): 111–14.

34. "Oprah," October 1995.

35. Among the more influential broadcasts prior to the FDA ban was CBS, "Face to Face with Connie Chung," 10 March 1990. See Marcia Angell, *Science on Trial* (New York: W. W. Norton, 1996), pp. 45–57.

36. FAA actions and criticism thereof: Shari Roan, "Journal Criticizes FDA for Breast Implant Restrictions," *Los Angeles Times*, 18 June 1992, p. A40; Philip Hilts, "AMA Urges Full Availability of Breast Implants," *New York Times*, 1 December 1993, p. A20. Question as unresolved: Sheryl Fragin, "Flawed Science at the *Times*," *Brill's Content*, October 1998, pp. 104–15. Epidemiological comparisons: Angell, *Science on Trial*, ch. 5; C. H. Hennekens et al., "Self-Reported Breast Implants and Connective-Tissue Diseases . . ." *Journal of the American Medical Association* 275 (28 February 1996): 616–21. Quotes from NPR, "All Things Considered," 27 February 1996.

37. ABC News, "Nightline," 17 August 1995; Susan Zimmermann, *Silicone Survivors: Women's Experiences with Breast Implants* (Philadelphia: Temple University Press, 1998); idem, "The Medicalization of Female Breasts," paper presented at the meetings of the Eastern Sociological Society, March 1995 (contains quote).

38. Jennifer Washburn, "Reality Check: Can 400,000 Women Be Wrong?" *Ms.*, March 1996, pp. 51–57. For statements from other feminists see, e.g., Naomi Wolf, *The Beauty Myth* (New York: Morrow, 1991); Leslie Laurence and Beth Weinhouse, *Outrageous Practices* (New York: Fawcett, 1994); Sharon Lieberman, "Business as Usual," *Women's Review of Books* 13 (February 1996): 8–9.

39. PBS, "Frontline," 27 February 1996.

40. Marcia Angell, "Breast Implants," *New England Journal of Medicine* 326 (1992): 1695–96; Angela Bonavoglia, "Freedom of Choice," *Ms.*, March 1996, pp. 60–63; Shari Roan, "Data May Renew Debate over Silicone Implants," *Los Angeles Times*, 26 June 1997, pp. E1, 4.

41. Elinor Brecher, telephone interview with author, 1 December 1994. Among her articles see esp. "No Reason to Panic, Doctors Tell Implant Patients," *Miami Herald*, 21 March 1992, p. E1; "Critics of Implants on Hot Seat," *Miami Herald*, 22 June 1992.

42. Elinor Brecher and Linda Monroe, "Call for Moratorium Divides Patients, Activists, Surgeons," *Miami Herald*, 7 January 1992; Angell, *Science on Trial*, pp. 84–86.

43. Claire Spiegel, "Self-Surgery on Breast Implants Stirs Warning," *Los Angeles Times*, 18 April 1992, p. A18; Jeanne A. Heaton and Nona L. Wilson, *Tuning in Trouble* (San Francisco: Jossey-Bass, 1995), pp. 177–82; "Talked to Death," Home Box Office documentary, April 1997.

44. Heaton and Wilson, *Tuning in Trouble*.

45. Implant settlements: Barry Meier, "What Accord Would Mean for Women with Implants," *New York Times*, 24 March 1994, p. B10; "Court Upholds Implant Award," *USA Today*, 12 December 1994.

46. "Dow Corning Reaches Deal on Breast Implant Claims," Reuters, 9 November 1998; Louise Brinton and S. L. Brown, "Breast Implants and Cancer," *Journal of the National Cancer Institute* 89 (1997): 1341–49; Olof Nyren et al., "Risk of Connective Tissue Disease and Related Disorders Among Women with Breast Implants," *British Medical Journal* 316 (1998): 417–22; Cyrus Cooper, "Do Silicone Breast Implants Cause Connective Tissue Disease?" *British Medical Journal* 316 (1998): 403–4; Linda Cook et al., "Characteristics of Women with and without Breast Augmentation," *Journal of the American Medical Association* 277 (1997): 1612–17.

47. Marcia Angell, "Do Breast Implants Cause Systemic Disease?" *New England Journal of Medicine* 330 (1994): 1748–49; ABC News, "Junk Science," 7 January 1997. See also Marcia Angell, "Trial by Science," *New York Times*, 9 December 1998, p. A31.

48. Joseph Nocera, "Fatal Litigation" (Parts I and II), *Fortune*, 16 October and 30 October 1995; PBS, "Frontline: Breast Implants"; Alan Abrahamson, "Payments Raise Questions over Lawyers' Fees," *Los Angeles Times*, 22 October 1995, pp. B1, 3.

49. Gina Kolata and Barry Meier, "Implant Lawsuits Create a Medical Rush to Cash In," *New York Times*, 18 September 1995, pp. A1, 8. See also Jack Fisher, "Stop Scaring Women," *USA Today*, 17 May 1995, p. A12.

50. Gina Kolata, "Legal System and Science Come to Differing Conclusions on Silicone," *New York Times*, 16 May 1995, p. C6.

51. Laura Flanders, "Beware: P.R. Implants in News Coverage," *Extra*, January 1996, pp. 8–11. For other rebukes of Kolata see Fragin, "Flawed Science at the *Times*"; Mark Dowie, "What's Wrong with the *New York Times*'s Science Reporting?" *Nation*, 6 July 1998, pp. 13–19.

52. Many perceptive critiques by Laura Flanders are collected in her book *Real Majority, Media Minority* (Monroe, ME: Common Courage, 1997). But see a critique of Flanders's coverage of Gulf War Syndrome in Showalter, *Hystories*, pp. 138–39.

53. See Angell, *Science on Trial*, ch. 10; Carl Hempel, *Philosophy of Natural Science* (Englewood Cliffs, NJ: Prentice-Hall, 1966).

54. Lawrence Altman, "Drug Firm, Relenting, Allows Unflattering Study to Appear," *New York Times*, 16 April 1997, pp. A1, 12; and idem, "Experts See Bias in Drug Data," *New York Times*, 29 April 1997, pp. B1, 12.

55. Daniel Zalewski, "Ties That Bind," *Lingua Franca*, June 1997, pp. 51–59.

56. Gina Kolata, "Safeguards Urged for Researchers," *New York Times*, 17 April 1997, p. A13; Richard Deyo et al., "The Messenger Under Attack: Intimidation of Researchers by Special-Interest Groups," *New England Journal of Medicine* 336 (1997): 1176–81.

57. In a twelve-page critique of Kolata, Sheryl Fragin ("Flawed Science at the *Times*") paints a picture of a journalist who deserves the criticisms that have been leveled at her. Yet the only implant study Fragin reproaches Kolata for failing to report is one showing a high rupture and complication rate–a well-known fact, and one that does not establish a link between implants and the diseases they are said to cause. One of Fragin's bottom lines praises Kolata with faint damnation: "If Kolata can be accused of any allegiance at all, it is to a narrow and traditional view of scientific evidence, where nothing is real until documented by large epidemiological studies or lab experiments" (p. 107).

58. Bob Dole, "Ignore the Lawyers, Help the People," *Los Angeles Times*, 27 April 1995, p. B7 (contains quote).

59. Paul Ruiz, "Media Deform the 'Legal Reform' Debate," *Extra*, May 1995, pp. 10–11; Jim Naureckas, "Defusing the 'Litigation Explosion'," *Extra*, May 1995, p. 10; Aric Press, "Are Lawyers Burning America?" *Newsweek*, 20 March 1995, pp. 32–35; Richard Schmitt, "Truth Is First Casualty of Tort-Reform Debate," *Wall Street Journal*, 7 March 1995, pp. B1, 4.

60. Statistics from Ruiz, "Media Deform." "Contract" quoted in Naureckas, "Defusing." *Ms.* article is Washburn, "Reality Check." See also Martha Middleton, "A Changing Landscape," *ABA Journal* 81 (1 August 1995): 56.

61. John Broder, "Warning: A Batman Cape Won't Help You Fly," *New York Times*, 5 March 1997, pp. C1, 2.

62. Ann Wood, "Pertussis Vaccine Scare Report Rebuffed by AAP," *Pediatric News*, May 1982, p. 1. General background about the vaccine and controversies surrounding it: interviews with Dr. Cheston Berlin, former chair of the American Academy of Pediatrics' Committee on Drugs, and Dr. Edward Mortimer of Case Western University.

63. "Comments on DTP Issues Raised on the WRC/NBC TV Program," photocopied report from the National Center for Drugs and Biologics, U.S. Food and Drug Administration, Washington, DC, 1982. Statistics and general information about whooping cough: American Academy of Pediatrics "Red Book," 1994; Lawrence Altman, "A New Focus on Whooping Cough Vaccine," *New York Times*, 8 June 1982, p. 20. On safety of the vaccines see also L. Cowan et al., "Acute Encephalopathy and Chronic Neurological Damage After Pertussis Vaccine," *Vaccine* 11 (1993): 1371–79.

64. For an example of the media commentary see "Two Ounces of Prevention," *New York Times*, 18 May 1982, p. A22. Fisher quote is from a membership solicitation letter from her organization.

65. Japanese and British epidemics: interview with Dr. Stephen Chartrand of Creighton University, an expert on childhood vaccines, 13 December 1994; Julie Marquis, "A Vocal Attack on Vaccines," *Los Angeles Times*, 12 March 1997, pp. A1, 14; E. J. Gangarosa et al., "Impact of Anti-Vaccine Movements on Pertussis Control," *Lancet* 351 (1998): 356–61. On my selection and use of statistics see note 2 in the Introduction.

66. Louise Palmer, "Government Can't Meet Vaccine Injury Claims," *New York Times*, 25 April 1993, p. 6; Sarah Glazer, "No-Fault Federal Program Compensates for Injuries," *Washington Post*, 29 January 1991, p. Z9; Catherine Clabby, "Danger of Vaccines Discounted," *Raleigh News and Observer*, 18 December 1996, p. A3.

67. M. R. Griffin et al., "Risk of Seizures and Encephalopathy After Immunization with DTP Vaccine," *Journal of the American Medical Association* 263 (1990): 1641–45; James D. Cherry, "Pertussis Vaccine Encephalopathy: It Is Time to Recognize It as the Myth That It Is," *Journal of the American Medical Association* 263 (1990): 1679–80; Lawrence Altman, "Study Backs Safety of Whooping Cough Vaccine," *New York Times*, 11 January 1994, p. C7; "Study Groups Make Vaccine Recommendations," *Journal of the American Medical Association* 272 (1994): 1088.

68. Emily Martin, *Flexible Bodies* (Boston: Beacon Press, 1994), p. 194.

69. Marquis, "A Vocal Attack"; issues of "DPT News" and "NVIC News," 1983 through 1995 (statistic from NVIC News, November 1994).

70. Alan Patureau, "Alabamian Overcomes Deafness to Compete with a Select Few in the Miss America Pageant," *Atlanta Journal and Constitution*, 16 September 1994, p. A3.

71. Gary Freed et al., "Safety of Vaccinations: Miss America, the Media, and Public Health," *Journal of the American Medical Association* 276 (18 December 1996): 1869–72; Lewis Cope, "Vaccine Did Not Cause Winner's Deafness," *Star Tribune*, 2 October 1994, p. E2; Sandra Evans, "How Safe Are Mandatory Immunizations?" *Washington Post*, 27 September 1994, p. Z9.

72. Andrea Rock, "The Lethal Dangers of the Billion-Dollar Vaccine Business," *Money*, December 1996, pp. 148–64; Marquis, "A Vocal Attack" (contains "doggedness" quote); John Schwartz, "FDA Approves New Vaccine with Fewer Risks to Control Whooping Cough," *Washington Post*, 1 August 1996, p. A24 (contains "culmination" quote); Arthur Allen, "Injection Rejection," *New Republic*, 23 March 1998, pp. 20–23.

73. Interviews with vaccine authorities Dr. Edward Mortimer of Case Western University, 12 December 1994, and Dr. Stephen Chartrand, Creighton University, 13

December 1994; "New Vaccine May Be Used For Pertussis," Associated Press, 25 November 1994; Thomas Maugh, "New Whooping Cough Vaccine Safer," *Los Angeles Times*, 24 November 1994; "Pertussis Vaccine Controversy Continues," Reuters, 2 February 1998.

Chapter Eight

1. Figures from David Hinson, Administrator of the Federal Aviation Administration, in speeches and interviews: see, e.g., "Larry King Live," CNN, 14 May 1996. See also Julie Schmit and Del Jones, "Some Drive, but Most Will Keep Flying," *USA Today*, 17 November 1994, p. A1; Paul Aldo, "Regulating Safety," paper presented at the Eastern Sociological Society meetings, March 1996.

2. "Public Deserves Faster Action on Safety Measures," *USA Today*, 15 December 1994, p. A8; Adam Bryant, "Why No Airline Brags, 'We're the Safest'," *New York Times*, 9 June 1996, pp. D1, 3.

3. Laura Parker, "Airline Accident Rate Is Highest in 13 Years," *Washington Post*, 13 January 1988, p. A8; Victor Cohn, "Probable Fact and Probable Junk," paper posted in 1996 on the Internet by the Foundation for American Communications (FACS); Melinda Beck, "How Safe Is This Flight?" *Newsweek*, 24 April 1995, p. 18.

4. Stephen J. Hedges et al., "What's Wrong with the FAA," *U.S. News & World Report*, 26 June 1995, pp. 28–34. Fatality statistics from the National Transportation Safety Board.

5. Chistopher Farley, "Air Safety–Under a Cloud," *Time*, 26 December, 1994, p. 114; "High Anxiety in the Skies," *USA Today*, 17 November 1994, p. A1.

6. "Fifth Crash in as Many Years": see, e.g., John Daly, "The Fear of Flying," *Maclean's*, 26 September 1994, pp. 26–27; Adam Bryant, "Outsted FAA Man," *New York Times*, 21 June 1996, p. A10. See also George Church, "Ripped from the Sky," *Time*, 19 September 1994, pp. 38–39.

7. Douglas Frantz, "Committed to Safety and Telling the World," *New York Times*, 27 November 1994, p. N2; Carl Quintanilla, "USAir Appoints Retired General to Oversee Safety," *Wall Street Journal*, 21 November 1994, p. B7. Gina Kolata, "When Is Coincidence Too Bad to Be True?" *New York Times*, 11 September 1994, p. D4; Arnold Barnett, "How Numbers Can Trick You," *Technology Review* 97 (1994): 38–46.

8. Barnett, "How Numbers Can Trick You." A quarter century earlier Barnett had also shown consistency in safety records among airlines: Arnold Barnett et al., "Airline Safety," *Management Science* 23 (1979): 1045–56. On rankings by safety records see also Jonathan Dahl and Lisa Miller, "Which Is the Safest Airline? It All Depends," *Wall Street Journal*, 24 July 1996, p. B1.

9. Del Jones, "Avoid Small Planes, Warns Group," *USA Today*, 15 November 1994, p. A1.

10. Farley, "Under a Cloud," p. 114. The commuter scare and the FAA's statistics: Annetta Miller, "We'll Adjust Our Schedules," *Newsweek*, 28 November 1994, p. 46; Don Phillips, "If God Had Wanted Man to Fly," *Washington Post* National Edition, 26 December 1994, p. 12; James Hirsch, "Small Planes Are Not as Safe as Big Jetliners,"

Wall Street Journal, 15 December 1994, p. B1. For more on the IAPA see Robert Moorman, "A Swarm of Experts," *Air Transport World* 32 (March 1995): 26–33.

11. Richard Newman, "How Safe Are Small Planes?" *U.S. News & World Report*, 14 November 1994, pp. 68–76. Newsmagazine statistic from Phillips, "If God."

12. Stephen Chapman, "Commuter Airline Safety," *Chicago Tribune*, 18 December 1994, p. D3.

13. Douglas Frantz, "F.A.A.'s 'Tombstone Mentality'," *New York Times*, 15 December 1994, p. A16; Adam Bryant, "Poor Training at FAA Linked to 6 Crashes," *New York Times*, 15 October 1995, p. A1; Beck, "How Safe"; Hedges, "What's Wrong." See also Owen Ullmann, "Wanted: A New Flight Plan for the FAA," *Business Week*, 1 July 1996, p. 39.

14. Jeff Brazil, "FAA's Response Record Under Fire," *Los Angeles Times*, 12 December 1994, p. A1.

15. CBS, "Evening News," 7 April 1995.

16. See Beck, "How Safe"; "The FAA: Too Slow to Act on Airline Safety?" *Consumer Reports*, June 1995, p. 385; Mark Honig, "Child Safety Sophists at CBS," *MediaNomics*, May 1995, p. 4; Cornelia Dean, "Assessing Regulation in an Era of Regulatory 'Reform'," article posted on the Internet by the Foundation for American Communications (FACS), 1996. Criticism of the FAA continued in subsequent years. See, e.g., Eric Malnic, "FAA Failure Cited in Valujet Crash Report," *Los Angeles Times*, 20 August 1997, pp. A1, 10; Mary Schiavo, *Flying Blind, Flying Safe* (New York: Avon, 1997); "Ground Unethical Trips," *USA Today*, 14 August 1998, p. A14; "Troubling New Safety Report Shows FAA's Shortcomings," *USA Today*, 1 April 1998, p. A10; Scott McCartney, "FAA Data Deficiencies Hamper Effort to Spot Airline Safety Hazards," *Wall Street Journal*, 27 July 1998, pp. A1, 7; "Problem-Prone Airline Wiring Fails to Spark FAA Urgency," *USA Today*, 10 November 1998, p. A14.

17. Don Phillips, "Personal Feud, or Professional Problem?" *Washington Post*, 16 July 1995, p. H1; Matthew Wald, "Counterfeit Airliner Parts Are Said to Be Often Used," *New York Times*, 25 May 1995, p. 18; Hedges, "What's Wrong"; Willy Stern, "Warning!" *Business Week*, 10 June 1996, pp. 84–92 (Schiavo quote and photo on p. 87). For another example of spare parts coverage see CBS, "Evening News," 24 May 1995.

18. Don Phillips, "Bogus Aircraft Parts Threat Debated," *Washington Post*, 25 May 1995, p. B12. On NTSB criticisms see, e.g.: Hedges, "What's Wrong"; ABC, "Primetime," 18 November 1994.

19. ABC, "Primetime," 18 November 1994. For more of Schiavo's fear mongering about bogus parts, see Shiavo, *Flying Blind, Flying Safe*, ch. 5.

20. Stern, "Warning!" For other coverage in 1996 see Gary Stoller, "Counterfeit," *Conde Nast Traveler*, March 1996, pp. 37–40.

21. Lance Bylow and Ian Savage, "The Effect of Airline Deregulation on Automobile Fatalities," *Accident Analysis and Prevention* 23 (1991): 443–52. Erik Larson, "Death in the Everglades," *Time*, 20 May 1996, p. 20.

22. Other articles include: "Death in the 'Glades," *Newsweek*, 20 May 1996, p. 31; "Fliers May Rethink Low Fares After Crash," *USA Today*, 14 May 1996, p. B10. FAA

study and coverage thereof: Matthew Wald, "F.A.A. Cites Problems at Valujet," *New York Times*, 18 May 1996, p. A6; ABC News "Nightline," 16 May 1996. See also "Hinson on Safety of Low-Cost Airlines," *USA Today*, 25 June 1996, p. A13.

23. Art Pine, "Budget Airlines' Repairs Endorsed," *Los Angeles Times*, 14 May 1996, p. 12; "Polls Show Confidence Gap," CNN (online), 18 May 1996; Scott McCartney, "Start-Ups Still Suffer from Valujet Crash and FAA's Missteps," *Wall Street Journal*, 9 December 1996, pp. A1, 10.

24. Mary Fackler Schiavo, "'I Don't Like to Fly," *Newsweek*, 20 May 1996, p. 32.

25. Tom Squitieri, "Outspoken Inspector Angers FAA, Others," *USA Today*, 15 May 1996, p. A3; Cindy Skrzycki, "DOT Inspector General Keeps Flying in the Face of Caution," *Washington Post*, 17 May 1996, p. F1; Adam Bryant, "Outspoken FAA Critic Quits," *New York Times*, 9 July 1996, p. A9; Asra Nomani, "Even in Leaving, DOT's Schiavo Draws Criticism," *Wall Street Journal*, 9 July 1996, pp. B1, 4; Shiavo, *Flying Blind*, p. 199.

26. Graham Boynton, "Plastique Bombs vs. Slack Security," *New York Observer*, 29 July 1996, pp. 1, 7; Pam Belluck and John Sullivan, "Despite Warnings, Most Air Cargo Is Unscreened," *New York Times*, 26 July 1996, pp. A1, 12. Other quotes from Sam Husseini, "Media Bomb on TWA Crash," *Extra*, January 1997, pp. 20–22; "Jumping the Gun," *Extra*, September 1996, p. 5 (contains Haberman quote). For a correcting piece see Matthew Purdy, "Why One Flight 800 Theory Fit All," *New York Times*, 24 November 1996, pp. E1, 4. On reporters jumping prematurely to incorrect conclusions about the causes of crashes, see William Boot, "The Accidental Journalist," *Columbia Journalist Review* (January 1990): 17–21.

27. Robert Davey, "A Missile Destroyed TWA Flight 800," *Village Voice*, 21 July 1998, pp. 34–38. See also Robert Davey, "Flight 800: The Missing Evidence," *Village Voice*, 21 April 1998, pp. 35–39.

28. Mark Hosenball, "New Static on TWA 800," *Newsweek*, 23 December 1996, p. 26.

29. See, e.g., Julie Schmit, "Some Drive, But Most Will Keep Flying," *USA Today*, 17 November 1994, pp. A1, 2; "Flyers May Rethink"; Andrea Stone, "Crashes Giving Many Fliers the Jitters," *USA Today*, 15 December 1994, p. A3; Susan Carry and Jonathan Dahl, "Flying Scared," *Wall Street Journal*, 22 July 1996, pp. B1, 8.

30. Farley, "Under a Cloud."

31. On the power of personalization see Hans-Bernd Brosius and Anke Bathelt, "The Utility of Exemplars in Persuasive Communications," *Communication Research* 21 (1994): 48–78; Conrad Smith, *Media and Apocalyse* (Westport, CT: Greenwood Press, 1992); Joel Best, *Images of Issues* (Hawthorne, NY: Aldine de Gruyter, 1995), esp. chs. 1, 2, 6, and 7. Examples of coverage of the McNitts: Doug Payne, "A Loving Family," *Atlanta Constitution*, 13 May 1996, p. A9; Gary Fields, "They Never Made It for Mother's Day," *USA Today*, 13 May 1996, p. A4; "Educator Students Admired Died in Crash," *New York Times*, 14 May 1996, p. C20.

32. B. Drummond Ayers, "At the helm, a Pilot Who Lived to Fly," *New York Times*, 14 May 1996, p. C20; "Pilot and Husband Discussed Possibility of Dying in Air Crash," *USA Today*, 14 May 1996, p. A3.

33. Hedges, "What's Wrong"; Gareth Cook, "Uncle Sam's Not-So-Friendly Skies," *Washington Monthly*, January 1996, pp. 9–16. See also "Warning: Pilot Error," a three-part series in *USA Today*, September 26–28, 1995.

34. See statements to the press by FAA administrator David Hinson on June 17 and 18, 1996; Matthew Wald, "Aviations Agency Plans to Shift Its Mission, Focusing on Safety," *New York Times*, 19 June 1996, pp. A1 and C22.

35. "Serious": see, e.g., Ralph Vartabedian, "34 Violations Found in Probe Before Shutdown," *Los Angeles Times*, 20 June 1996, p. D1; Michael Fumento, "Flight from Reality," 7 October 1996, pp. 20–22. Aviation experts' views: John Ritter, "Valujet's Infractions Are Examined," *USA Today*, 20 June 1996, p. A3. On the accidents see also comments of Lewis Jordan and Valujet pilots on ABC's "Nightline," 21 June 1996.

36. ABC, "Nightline," 16 May 1996.

37. Asra Nomani, "ValuJet Shutdown Exposes Flaws of the FAA," *Wall Street Journal*, 19 June 1996, pp. B1, 8; "The FAA Took Too Long to 'Get' the Lesson of the Valujet Crash," *San Francisco Examiner*, 20 June 1996, p. A18. Other examples: "FAA Damage Control," *San Diego Union–Tribune*, 20 June 1996, p. B12; "Time to Fix the FAA," *St. Louis Post–Dispatch*, 20 June 1996, p. B6; "FAA Took Too Long to See the Obvious," *Hartford Courant*, 19 June 1996, p. A10; ABC, "Nightline," 17 June 1996. On legal limitations on grounding an airline see also Don Phillips, "Can Safety and Rapid Growth Share the Same Plane?" *Washington Post* National Edition, 17 June 1996, pp. 20–21.

38. ABC, "Nightline," 17 June 1996.

39. See Ralph Vartabedian and Jesus Sanchez, "Carrier's Success Story Was Built on Big Savings," *Los Angeles Times*, 20 June 1996, pp. D1, 10.

40. Bureau of Labor Statistics, National Institute of Occupational Safety and Health (NIOSH); speech by Joseph A. Dear at American Industrial Hygiene Conference, Washington, DC, 22 May 1996; Peter Dorman, *Markets and Mortality* (Cambridge: Cambridge University Press, 1996), quoted on p. 191. On my selection and use of statistics see note 2 in the Introduction.

41. Dorman, *Markets and Mortality*, p. 196; Michael Weisskopf and David Maraniss, "Ruling out OSHA" and "Industry's Thumbprint on New OSHA Legislation," *Washington Post* National Edition, 4 September 1995, pp. 6–9.

42. Frank Swoboda, "The Growing Problem of Workplace Safety," *Nieman Reports* 48 (1994): 11–12; Weisskopf and Maraniss, "Ruling Out"; Dorman, *Markets and Mortality*, chs. 1 and 6.

43. ABC was among the few major media that debunked the overregulation myth. See ABC, "World News Tonight," 3 April 1995.

44. See Dear, speech at American Industrial Hygiene Conference. An article that did cover silicosis: Yvonne Daley, "Deadly Occupational Hazard Under Scrutiny," *Boston Globe*, 9 August 1998, p. D14.

45. Swoboda, *Nieman Reports*.

46. Cook, "Uncle Sam's."

47. Beck, "How Safe."

48. Church, "Ripped."

49. K. C. Cole, "What's the Price of Life?" *Los Angeles Times*, 3 April 1997, p. B2.

Chapter Nine

1. Hadley Cantril, *The Invasion from Mars* (New York: Harper & Row, 1966), p. 3.

2. Michele Ingrassia, "Life Means Nothing," *Newsweek,* 19 July 1993, pp. 16–17; *Progressive,* July 1997, p. 9 (Clinton quote); Richard Cohen, "Dealing with Illegitimacy," *Washington Post,* 23 November 1993, p. A21; Charles Krauthammer, "Children of Cocaine," *Washington Post,* 30 July 1989, p. C7("superpredators"). See also my discussions in chs. 4–6.

3. Ed Masley, "More Users Showing Signs of Compulsive Computer Behavior," *Pittsburgh Post-Gazette,* 27 February 1996, p. A1 ("smoker" quote); Amy Harmon, "Virtual Sex, Lies and Cyberspace," *Los Angeles Times,* 10 April 1997, p. A1; Carol Potera, "Trapped in the Web," *Psychology Today,* March 1998, pp. 66–72; Gregory Crouch, "Cyber Junkies," *Los Angeles Times,* 11 May 1998, pp. E1, 4; Bill Hendrick, "Internet Addiction Is Serious," *Atlanta Journal and Constitution,* 17 August 1997, p. A1; Marilyn Elias, "Modem Matchmaking," *USA Today,* 14 August 1997, p. D1; Vincent Kiernan, "Some Scholars Question Research Methods of Expert on Internet Addiction," *Chronicle of Higher Education,* 29 May 1998, pp. 25–27.

4. Cantril, *Invasion from Mars,* p. 73; ABC, "20/20," 30 June 1995; NBC, "Now," 31 August 1994.

5. Cantril, *Invasion from Mars,* p. 68.

6. On American isolationism see David S. Wyman, *The Abandonment of the Jews: America and the Holocaust* (New York: Pantheon, 1984); Bruce Russett, *No Clear and Present Danger: A Skeptical View of the United States Entry into World War II* (Boulder, CO: Westview Press, 1997); "Memories of War," *Economist,* 6 May 1995, pp. 21–23. Quotes: Cantril, *Invasion from Mars,* pp. 100, 160.

7. Cantril, *Invasion from Mars,* pp. 161–62.

8. I expect that some readers would prefer that this book end with a precise prescription for the steps we must take to rid our society of fear. But if the culture of fear operates anything like the way I suggest, a twelve-step program is not what is needed. Rather, on a persistent and widespread basis, we must resist the methods that fear mongers employ and spend our collective wealth on the abatement of genuine rather than fanciful dangers.

Chapter Ten

1. Katherine Kaufer Christoffel and Xavier Bosch, "Firearm-Related Homicides Among Teenagers and Young Adults," *Journal of the American Medical Association* 281 (1999): 323–324.

2. Marilyn Manson, "Columbine: Whose Fault Is It?" *Rolling Stone,* 24 June 1999.

3. Maureen Dowd, "All that Glitters," *New York Times,* 3 October 2001.

4. Matthew Wald and Trymaine Lee, "50 Killed as Plane Hits House Near Buffalo," *New York Times,* 13 February 2009. Print coverage was in the February 14 issue.

5. Alan Levin, "In Buffalo, a Reminder of Lingering Air Safety Issues," *USA Today,* 16 February 2009.

6. This estimate is based on an analysis of Lexis-Nexis databases of a randomized sampling of ten months during the period 2000 through 2009. On the flexibility of fears and how they are defined and manipulated, see Zygmunt Bauman, *Liquid Fear* (Cambridge, England: Polity Press, 2006).

7. CBS, "Morning News," 7 June 2006.

8. Keith Naughton et al., "The Long and Grinding Road," *Newsweek*, 1 May 2006; CBS, "Morning News," 7 June 2006; Dr. James Wright, "Coping with Modern Road Rage Crisis," *Gold Coast Bulletin*, 12 March 2008, p. 28.

9. OECD, "Society at a Glance, OECD Social Indicators," Organisation for Economic and Cooperative Development, 2006; Catherine Saillant, "Testing the Bounds of MySpace," *Los Angeles Times*, 8 April 2006.

10. U.S. Department of Health and Human Services, Administration for Children and Families, Child Maltreatment 2006, http://www.acf.hhs.gov/programs/cb/pubs/cm06/chapter3.htm#perp; Mike Males, "Two More Reasons To Believe Nothing about Teens on News at 6," 20 November 2007, posted at YouthFacts.org.

11. Janis Wolak, David Finkelhor et al., "Online 'Predators' and Their Victims," *American Psychologist*, 63 (2008): 111–128.

12. Janis Wolak, Kimberly Mitchell, and David Finkelhor, "Online Victimization," National Center for Missing & Exploited Children, Alexandria, VA, 2006. And see Nancy Willard, "Stop internet fear-mongering," posted at www.connectsafely.org.

13. Wolak, Finkelhor, "Online 'Predators'"; "Enhancing Child Safety and Online Technologies," Berkman Center for Internet and Society, Harvard University, 2009, available at http://cyber.law.harvard.edu/.

14. Brad Stone, "Report Finds Online Threats to Children Overblown," *New York Times*, 13 January 2009.

15. Mizuko Ito, Heather Horst et al., "Living and Learning with New Media," MacArthur Foundation Report, November 2008.

16. See also, "Using YouTube as a Study Aid," Associated Press, 15 December 2008.

17. Barry Glassner, "Forever Amber," *Wall Street Journal*, 27 August 2002, p. D.8; " National Incidence Studies of Missing, Abducted, Runaway, and Thrownaway Children, *NISMART Bulletin*, October 2002; "Juvenile Offenders and Victims: 2006 National Report," OJJDP, p. 44.

18. James Rainey, "Taking Comfort in Nancy Grace's World," *Los Angeles Times*, 28 January 2009.

19. See http://www.cnn.com/CNN/Programs/nancy.grace/. Accessed 10 November 2008.

20. Timothy Griffin, Monica Miller et al., "A Preliminary Examination of Amber Alert's Effects," *Criminal Justice Policy Review* 18 (2007): 378–394.

21. James Allan Fox, "Amber Alert's Dangers," *New York Times*, 17 August 2002. For another example, see "Revisit Jessica's Law," *Los Angeles Times*, 19 January 2009.

22. "An Overview of Child Well-Being in Rich Countries," UNICEF, 2007.

23. NBC, "Today," "A Katie Couric Special: The 411: Teens and Sex," 27 January 2005.

24. Mike Males, "'Tween Sex, Dating Violence Survey Finds Hardly Any," 24 February 2008, YouthFacts.org. Accessed 12 July 2008.

25. See *Entertainment Magazine*, "New Survey of American Teens Reveals Shocking Levels of Teen Dating Abuse and Violence," 25 April 2006, http://emol.org/emclub/?q=teendatingviolence.

26. For this and numerous other heartening indicators about contemporary American youths (e.g., cigarette and other drug use and violent crime), see the annual reports throughout the decade published by the Federal Interagency Forum on Child and Family Statistics and titled "America's Children In Brief," available at www.childstats.gov.

27. Kathleen Kingsbury, "Pregnancy Boom at Gloucester High," *Time*, 18 June 2008.

28. Mike Males, "The Real Mistake in Teen Pregnancy," *Los Angeles Times*, 13 July 2008. On another latter-day teen sex scare, "sexting," see Carl Bialik, "Which Is Epidemic—Sexting or Worrying About It?," *Wall Street Journal*, 8 April 2009.

29. Veronica Cassidy, "Media's 'Girls Gone Wild' Fantasies," *Extra Magazine*, October 2008.

30. Saad Bin Omer, K.S. Enger et al., "Geographical Clustering of Nonmedical Exemptions to School Immunization Requirements and its Associations with Geographical Clustering of Pertussis Cases," *American Journal of Epidemiology* 168 (2008): 1389–96; Daniel Feikin, Dennis Lezotte et al., "Individual and Community Risks of Measles and Pertussis Associated With Personal Exemptions to Immunization," *Journal of the American Medical Association* 284 (2000): 3145–50; Saad Bin Omer, William Pan et al., "Nonmedical Exemptions to School Immunization Requirements: Secular Trends and Association of State Policies With Pertussis Incidence," *JAMA* 296 (2006): 1757–63.

31. See for example, Susan King, "Vaccination Policies: Individual Rights *v* Community Health," *British Medical Journal* 319 (1999): 1448–49; Robert J. Leggiadro, "Vaccine Refusal, Mandatory Immunization, and the Risk of Vaccine-Preventable Diseases," *The Pediatric Infectious Disease Journal* 28 (2009): 613; Anita Manning, "Hib Infection in Children Makes A Deadly Return," *USA Today*, 16 February 2009; Jill Adams, "One Disease's Encore," *Los Angeles Times*, 23 February 2009; Liz Szabo, "Whooping Cough Returns in Children," *USA Today*, 26 May 2009.

32. See for example, Anders Hviid, Michael Stellfeld et al., "Association Between Thimerosal-Containing Vaccine and Autism," *Journal of the American Medical Association* 290 (2003): 1763–66; Robert Schechter and Judith Grether, "Continuing Increases in Autism Reported to California's Developmental Services System: Mercury in Retrograde," *Archives of General Psychiatry* 65 (2008): 19–24. Greg Berlanti and Marc Guggenheim, "Eli Stone Pilot," original airdate, 31 January 2008, 10:00 p.m. (ABC). Transcript provided by "Twiz Tv.Com-Free Tv Scripts Database." Originally transcribed for www.Eli-Stone.org.

33. "Speaking Out on the Autism 'Epidemic,'" *Miller-McClune*, June-July 2008.

34. Donald McNeil, "Book Rallies Resistance to the Antivaccine Crusade," *New York Times*, 13 January 2009; Jenny McCarthy and Jim Carrey, "My Son's Recovery From Autism," CNN.com, posted April 4, 2008; Weston Kosova and Pat Wingert, "Crazy Talk," *Newsweek*, 8 June 2009. See also full-page advertisements in national

publications from Carrey and McCarthy's advocacy group, Generation Rescue (e.g., *USA Today*, 25 February 2009).

35. Sharon Begley, "Anatomy of a Scare," *Newsweek*, 2 March 2009. See also, Matthew Normand and Jesse Dallery, "Mercury Rising," *Skeptic Magazine* 13, no. 3 (2007).

36. See, for example, "Gulf War Syndrome Is Real, Panel Concludes," *Washington Post*, 18 November 2008; Mary Engel and Thomas Maugh, "Report to Congress: Gulf War Syndrome Is Real," *Los Angeles Times*, 18 November 2008. See also, Harriet Hall, "Gulf War Syndrome or Gulf Lore Mythology," *Skeptic Magazine* 14 (2009): 26–29.

37. Daniel Heimpel, "The Toxic Mold Rush: California Mom Helps Fuel an Obsession," *LA Weekly*, 23 July 2008.

38. Centers for Disease Control and Prevention, "Facts About Stachybotrys Chartarum and Other Molds," http://www.cdc.gov/mold/stachy.htm#Q1. Accessed 18 November 2008.

39. "Damp Indoor Spaces and Health," National Academies Press, 2004 (quote is from the press release from the Academies.) See also, Linda Thomas-Mobley, "U.S. Evidence Laws and Their Influence on Mold Litigation Outcomes," *Journal of Professional Issues in Engineering Education and Practice* 133 (2007): 352–57; David Edmondson, Mark Nordness et al., "Allergy and 'Toxic Mold Syndrome,'" *Annals of Allergy, Asthma and Immunology* 94 (2005): 234–39; Jay Portnoy, Kristina Kwak et al., "Health Effects of Indoor Fungi," *Annals of Allergy, Asthma and Immunology* 94 (2005): 313–20; Daniel Fisher, "Dr. Mold," *Forbes*, 11 April 2005; Richard Wilson, "Ensuring Sound Science in the Courts," *Technology in Society*, 26 (2004): 501–22.

40. Danilo Yanich, "Crime Creep: Urban and Suburban Crime on Local TV News," *Journal of Urban Affairs* 26 (2004): 535–63.

41. Sheryl Gay Stolberg, "Science Looks at Littleton, and Shrugs," *New York Times*, 9 May 1999.

42. Sharon Begley, "The Anatomy of Violence," *Newsweek*, 30 April 2007. Pages away, in a separate feature devoted to "Guns: The Global Death Toll," the magazine reported that in Japan, "handguns are prohibited. Shotguns are very strictly regulated and rifle permits can be obtained only after owning a shotgun for ten years."

43. Stolberg, "Science Looks at Littleton, and Shrugs."

44. Philip Cook, Bruce Lawrence et al., "The Medical Costs of Gunshot Injuries in the United States," *Journal of the American Medical Association* 282 (1999): 447–54; Jeffrey Coben and Claudia Steiner, "Hospitalizations for Firearm-Related Injuries in the United States," *American Journal of Preventive Medicine* 24 (2003): 1–8; Naomi Duke, Michael Resnick et al., "Adolescent Firearm Violence," *Journal of Adolescent Health* 37 (2005): 171–74.

45. Gary Fields, "Going After Crimes–and Guns," *Wall Street Journal*, 5 August 2008. See also, Timothy Egan, "The Guns of Spring," *New York Times*, 8 April 2009.

46. Brent Cunningham, "Re-thinking Objectivity," *Columbia Journalism Review*, July-August 2003; David Altheide, "Terrorism and the Politics of Fear," *Cultural Studies–Criminal Methodologies* 6 (2006): 431–432.

47. M. Engel, "War On Afghanistan: American Media Cowed By Patriotic Fever, Says Network News Veteran," *Guardian*, 17 May 2002.

48. David L. Altheide, "Consuming Terrorism," *Symbolic Interaction* 27 (2004): 289–308.

49. Nancy Snow, "Media Terrorism and the Politics of Fear," The World Association for Christian Communication website. Available at: http://www.waccglobal.org/lang-en/publications/media-development/46-2007-3/465-Media-terrorism-and-the-politics-of-fear.html.

50. John Mueller, *Overblown* (New York: Free Press, 2006), p. 13 (and see numerous other comparisons throughout Mueller's book).

51. Luke Mitchell et al., "At Issue in the 2004 Election," *Harper's Magazine*, 1 March 2004.

52. George Bush, White House Press Conference, 14 September 2001; address to Congress, 20 September 2001; "State of the Union Address," 29 January 2002. See also, Mark S. Hamm, "The USA Patriot Act and the Politics of Fear," in *Cultural Criminology Unleashed* (Portland, OR: Cavendish Publishing, 2004).

53. Department of Homeland Security, Strategic Plan. Available at: http://www.dhs.gov/xabout/strategicplan/; George Bush, *The Department of Homeland Security*, June 2002. Available at: http://www.dhs.gov./xlibrary/assets/book.pdf.

54. Phillip Zimbardo, "Phantom Menace: Is Washington Terrorizing Us More Than Al Qaeda?" *Psychology Today*, May/June 2003; Robb Willer, "The Effects of Government-Issued Terror Warnings on Presidential Approval," *Current Research in Social Psychology* 10 (2004): 1–12; Tom Ridge, *The Test of Our Times* (New York: Thomas Dunne Books, 2009).

55. Gregg Easterbrook, "The Smart Way to Be Scared," *New York Times*, 16 February 2003; Matt Palmquist, "Bioterror in Context," *Miller-McClune*, June-July 2008, pp. 72–76.

56. Palmquist, "Bioterror in Context," p. 74.

57. Tony Karon, "The Dirty Bomb Scenario," *Time*, 10 June 2002. John Ashcroft, transcript of Moscow announcement on June 8, 2002, available at: http://archives.cnn.com/2002/US/06/10/ashcroft.announcement; Public Health Security and Bioterrorism Preparedness and Response Act of 2002, available at: http://www.nationalacademies.org/ocga/Laws/PL107_188.asp; Council on Foreign Relations, "Dirty Bombs," updated 19 October 2006, available at: http://www.Cfr.org/publications/9548/#5. Mark Hamm, "The USA Patriot Act and the Politics of Fear," in *Cultural Criminology Unleashed* (Portland, OR: Cavendish Publishing, 2004), p. 2296.

58. "National Planning Scenarios: Executive Summaries," April 2005, available at: http://cees.tamiu.edu/covertheborder/TOOLS/NationalPlanningSen.pdf.

59. Josef Joffe, "Here's How America Looks to the World," *Washington Post*, 4 May 2008.

60. Hamm, "The USA Patriot Act," pp. 288, 292.

61. "The Politics of Fear" (editorial), *New York Times*, 18 July 2007; Frank Rich, "The Terrorist Barack Hussein Obama," *New York Times*, 12 October 2008.

62. Timothy Noah, "What We Didn't Overcome" (parts 1 and 2), *Slate*, November 10 and 12, 2008.

63. CNN, "Larry King Live," 21 January 2009; Andrew Penner and Aliya Saperstein, "How Social Status Shapes Race," *Proceedings of the National Academy of Sciences* 105 (2008): 1962–1963.

64. Lincoln Quillian and Devah Pager, "Estimating Risk: Biased Social Perception and the Likelihood of Criminal Victimization" (unpublished manuscript), Northwestern University, 2009.

65. Regarding racial profiling, see, e.g., Ian Ayers, "The LAPD and Racial Profiling," *Los Angeles Times*, 23 October 2008; prison statistics published by the Bureau of Justice Statistics, available at http://www.ojp.usdoj.gov/bjs/prisons.html; poverty data are from the Census Bureau, Current Population Reports.

66. Bruce Link, "Epidemiological Sociology and the Social Shaping of Population Health," *Journal of Health and Social Behavior* 49 (2008): 367–84; Centers for Disease Control, "Health, United States, 2004," table 30, posted at http://www.cdc.gov/nchs/data/hus/hus04trend.pdf#03. See also, Kai Wright, "America's AIDS Apartheid," *American Prospect*, July 2008.

67. Adam Serwer, "Justice Polluted," *American Prospect*, March 2009; Kai Wright, "The Subprime Swindle," *The Nation*, 26 June 2008; Amelia Tyagi, "Amid Hope, Black Homeowners Struggle," *Marketplace*, Minnesota Public Radio, 20 January 2009; E. Scott Reckard, "NAACP Suits Claim Mortgage Bias," *Los Angeles Times*, 14 March 2009.

READER
DISCUSSION
GUIDE

About the Author

Professor of Sociology at the University of Southern California, Barry Glassner is the author of seven books on contemporary social issues, including *The Gospel of Food* and *Bodies*. He was previously chairman of the sociological departments at Syracuse University and the University of Connecticut. His articles and reviews have appeared in newspapers and journals throughout the United States and abroad, including the *New York Times*, the *Los Angeles Times*, the *Wall Street Journal*, the *Chicago Tribune*, and the *London Review of Books*. He has also published research studies in the *American Sociological Review*, *American Journal of Psychiatry*, and other leading social-science journals. In addition to being extensively quoted and profiled in dozens of newspapers and magazines, he has appeared on *The Oprah Winfrey Show*, *The Today Show*, *Good Morning America*, *Nightline*, and other television programs, as well as programs on CNN, CNBC, and MSNBC, and National Public Radio.

Professor Glassner's honors include an Outstanding Book of the Year award from *Choice* magazine and a visiting fellowship at Oxford University. *The Culture of Fear* was named a Best Book of the Year by the *Los Angeles Times Book Review* and Knight–Ridder newspapers and has been hailed by reviewers everywhere. The book and Glassner himself are featured in Michael Moore's film, *Bowling for Columbine*.

About the Book

When first published in 1999, *The Culture of Fear* was greeted with admiration and outspoken appreciation—admiration for Professor Glassner's extensive and deep research and appreciation for his calling attention to the false fears that sap the time, energy, and money of all Americans and to the *real* problems and dangers that face us all. Numerous awards, author appearances, quotations, and references later, the book has taken on renewed significance with its being featured, along with its author, in Michael Moore's prize-winning film, *Bowling for Columbine*. With each passing year since its publication, the book's central theme has become more salient and more relevant to our lives.

Glassner's eye-opening examination of the pathology of fear that affects all segments of our society reveals why Americans are overburdened with overblown fears and why those fears continue to be publicized by special-interest individuals and groups. He exposes the people and organizations that manipulate our anxieties and our views of and responses to life as it really isn't, and who benefit from that manipulation. Politicians win elections by exaggerating concerns about crime and drug use when, in fact, both are in decline. Advocacy groups raise money by inflating the prevalence of specific—and phantom—diseases. Newspapers and television news programs monger new scares on a regular basis in order to gain ratings or increase sales.

"Why," Glassner inquires, "are so many fears in the air, and so many of them unfounded?" The simple answer is the immense power and money that "await those who tap into our moral insecurities and supply us with symbolic substitutes." By identifying the actual fear mongers among us, their methods, and their motivations, Glassner aims to shift our attention to the realities that do endanger us, individually and communally, and to ways of dealing with those realities. "We waste tens of billions of dollars and person-hours every year on largely mythical hazards," Glassner asserts; and those dollars and hours could be easily redirected to effective programs rather than enervating scares.

There has never been a time in modern American history when so many people have feared so much. Glassner demonstrates, chapter after chapter, that it is our manipulated *perception* of danger that has increased, not actual dangers themselves. This vast market in trepidation can and should be replaced by programs and measures focused on correcting the true, if unpopular and unpleasant, causes of our problems. "We need to learn how to identify exaggerated or false fears from legitimate ones," Glassner has insisted. "We need to be able to distinguish between isolated events and rumors, on the one hand, and real problems and dangers on the other hand." *The Culture of Fear* goes a long way in helping us to make the correct distinctions and to identify the true dangers.

For Discussion

1. Glassner begins his book with the double question, "Why are so many fears in the air, and so many of them unfounded?" (xix) How does he answer those questions? What specific fears does he cite as unfounded or exaggerated,

and what explanations does he put forward? What fears strike you as particularly pervasive and without factual basis? How would you explain them?

2. Why do specific fears, and fear in general, seem to play such a critical role in contemporary life? What purposes—social, political, psychological, and other—might be served by the promulgation of and belief in specific fears and threats, however unfounded, misreported, or overstated they may be?

3. What potential dangers, hardships, and costs does Glassner associate with the inflated, exaggerated, unfounded, false, and overdrawn fears that he identifies? What can be done to allay or prevent those dangers, hardships, and costs? Which of Glassner's pseudodangers and scare campaigns do you consider the most important or the most threatening to the well-being, stability, and improvement of individuals, communities, and American society overall, including your own well-being? Why?

4. In Glassner's view, what organizations, groups, and individuals "promote and profit from scares" (xxxi), and in what ways do they profit? What are some of the ways by which these fear profiteers create and spread unfounded and exaggerated fears? How might they be dissuaded from doing so?

5. In what ways does what Glassner calls "psychoblather" (7) contribute to the continuation of unreasonable and unfounded public fears, and to an inaccurate view of the actions of individuals and groups and of the consequences of those actions? What might replace psychoblather in relation to the analysis of public scares?

6. In what ways do reports of contrived or questionable dangers divert us from what actually puts us at risk, enable us to avoid dealing directly with the actual dangers and social and economic ills that they mask, and—at the same time—enable us to think and talk about the *results* of those dangers and ills? What actual danger or disorder does each false scare cover up? Why don't journalists, politicians, advocacy groups, and others pay more attention to these dangers and threats? What can we do to increase attention to and concern for actual dangers?

7. In what ways do intentionally propagated false scares give their advocates the offensive advantage and defensive weapons for use in other disputes? (17)

8. What does the account of Erik Larson's *Wall Street Journal* exposé reveal about journalists' reporting concerning workplace violence, specifically, and their approach to the reporting of crime in general? Why is Larson's style of journalism so important, and why are there not more journalists—print and electronic—like him?

9. In what ways might Glassner's treatment of such issues as pedophile Catholic priests, youth violence, and other issues recently prominent in the news lead you to view those issues in a new light? In what ways have they confirmed your understanding of the importance of those issues? Might there be

explanations other than Glassner's for the misrepresentations and distortions that seem to characterize the great percentage of related news reports?

10. Which of the issues that Glassner raises are featured in Michael Moore's Academy Award-winning movie, *Bowling for Columbine*? To what degree are Moore's emphasis on and perspective toward these issues similar to or different from Glassner's? To what degree is Moore's purpose similar to or different from Glassner's?

11. To what extent is Glassner correct in his explanation of the means by which adults "justify both our fear of children and our maltreatment of them"? (74) To what extent are his remedies feasible? In addition to reports about "crack babies," what other instances of the demonization of children and other groups can you cite? What might these instances reveal about our attitudes toward children in general and toward the underprivileged?

12. What instances does Glassner identify of poor and lower-income individuals and families suffering "when middle- and upper-income Americans purchase escape hatches from their anxieties. . . "? (80) What instances do you observe in America today? How might the situation be corrected?

13. Why might people be so concerned about unwed mothers and so unconcerned about unwed fathers? What are the differences between attitudes toward unwed mothers and attitudes toward absent, unwed fathers, and what do those differences reveal about social attitudes and values in America?

14. How would you characterize anti-Semitism in the United States today? In what sources do most anti-Semitic remarks and activities originate? How do media coverage and politicians' responses perpetuate a distorted view of Jew-bashing in America and, consequently, perpetuate anti-Semitism itself? To what extent are the patterns of anti-Semitism reflected by the incidence of other bigotries?

15. What are some of the ironies brought into relief by fear mongers' projection of fearsome power and influence onto American black men? For what transgressions have black males been singled out for vilification and prosecution? Why, and by whom? What information does Glassner present that indicates circumstances other than those implied or claimed?

16. In what ways and to what degree is the promotion of fears of drug abuse, by politicians and the media, particularly representative of the nature and purposes of the culture of fear? In what ways have sensationalism and misinformation guided the national discussion of drug abuse? What other social and personal problems involving substance abuse and other addictions have been neglected as a result? In what ways has the displacement, by means of drug scares, "of brutalized citizens from the nation's moral conscience" been, in Glassner's words, an American tradition? (135) What other scares have served to free the nation's moral conscience of any accountability of ac-

tual social and other problems?

17. How might the *availability heuristic* (133) apply to the various concerns, fears, and panics that Glassner examines? To what extent are we all influenced, often unaware, by the information we receive regarding any given issue and the ways in which that information is presented to us by the media and our politicians? How might we ensure that we receive accurate and objective information on important issues?

18. How do you react to the following statement and statements like it throughout Glassner's book? "Similarly, in the 1980s as poverty, homelessness, and associated urban ills increased noticeably, Presidents Reagan and Bush, along with much of the electorate, sidestepped the suffering of millions of their fellow citizens who had been harmed by policies favoring the wealthy. Rather than face up to their own culpability, they blamed a drug." (135–36) In what ways have our political leaders, of both parties, sidestepped or whitewashed real problems and their own failures by shifting the public focus to false or misleading issues?

19. In what ways and to what degree do "metaphoric illnesses" "help us come to terms with features of our society that we are unprepared to confront directly"? (153) How do metaphoric ailments and other unfounded fears and dangers serve as "critiques of major social institutions"? (163) What metaphoric illnesses does Glassner identify and what fears, prejudices, or political ideologies do these metaphoric illnesses justify?

20. Glassner writes of "a fundamental if regrettable reality" about "the persistence of fear in American society. A scare can continue long after its rightful expiration date so long as it has two things going for it: it has to tap into current cultural anxieties, and it has to have media-savvy advocates behind it." (177) How have those two factors ensured the persistence of some of the major public fears and anxieties that Glassner discusses? What additional or other factors can you identify as contributing to the continuation of specific public panics?

21. In what ways do the media, despite an overall record of accurate reporting, continue to promote illogical fears, such as fears of flying? What explanations might be given for "this extraordinary feat of illogic" on the part of "journalists and the people they quote"? (184)

22. "In news coverage of aviation hazards," Glassner writes, "as of other dangers the media blow out of proportion, a self-justifying, perpetual-motion machinery operates." (201) How far does the author go in explaining the nature and causes of this "self-justifying, perpetual motion machinery"? "How do the news media minimize the excellent safety record of America's airlines?" (195) How might we add to or fill out Glassner's explanation?

23. To what extent might "the interests and experiences of those who oversee news organizations determine the content of the media"? (202) To what ex-

tent might this also be true of politicians, special-interest advocates, and other fear mongers? What other needs and interests are neglected when the public's attention and public moneys are directed by these special interests and experiences?

24. What are some of the underlying social or cultural anxieties to which specific public fears give expression and which are, at least momentarily, alleviated by those fears? To what extent are these fears "oblique expressions of concern about problems that Americans know to be pernicious but have not taken decisive action to quash. . . "? (209) What are some of those serious problems, and why don't we deal decisively with them rather than expending time, energy, and—in many instances—huge amounts of money on the alleviation of phantom fears?

25. Where, and to what degree, do Glassner's presentation and arguments challenge positions advanced by conservatives? Where, and to what degree, do they challenge positions advanced by liberals?

26. In what ways might Glassner's arguments and insights enable us to appropriately address issues and topics that prompt exaggerated or unfounded fears *today*—for example: weapons of mass destruction, childhood autism, job losses, and terror alerts? What fears are paramount today? In what ways—and why—are the various media, including advertising, misrepresenting or exploiting these issues and fears?

27. To what extent does Glassner enable us to distinguish unfounded and exaggerated fears and concerns from the genuine? To what extent does he enable us to recognize and effectively deal with both kinds of fears and threats?

Written by Hal Hager, Hal Hager & Associates, Somerville, New Jersey

INDEX